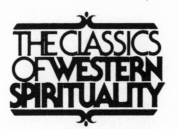

THE CLASSICS
OF WESTERN
SPIRITUALITY

THE CLASSICS OF WESTERN SPIRITUALITY
A Library of the Great Spiritual Masters

Meister Eckhart

THE ESSENTIAL SERMONS, COMMENTARIES, TREATISES, AND DEFENSE

TRANSLATION AND INTRODUCTION
BY
EDMUND COLLEDGE, O.S.A. AND BERNARD McGINN

PREFACE
BY
HUSTON SMITH

PAULIST PRESS
NEW YORK • RAMSEY • TORONTO

Covert Art:
The artist, LOUISE MURPHY, is from Long Island. Her work ranges from fashion illustrations for a major department store to "house portraits" for individual clients. She studied at the High School of Music and Art in New York City, the State University of New York at Farmingdale, and Parson's School of Design. She specializes in watercolor, the medium used for the cover of this volume.

Design: Barbini, Pesce & Noble, Inc.

Library of Congress
Catalog Card Number: 81-82206

ISBN: 0-8091-0322-2 (Cloth)
       0-8091-2370-3 (Paper)

Published by Paulist Press
545 Island Road, Ramsey, N.J. 07446

Printed and bound in the
United States of America

CONTENTS

CONTENTS

PART TWO: GERMAN WORKS

The Editors of this Volume

EDMUND COLLEDGE, O.S.A., has specialized in the study of the devotional literature, Latin and vernacular, of England, the Low Countries, and the Rhineland in the later Middle Ages. He is the author of studies and modern English translations of Ruysbroek, Tauler, and Suso. He published in 1957, in collaboration with Joyce Bazire, a critical edition of *The Chastising of God's Children*, and in 1961 an anthology, *The Medieval Mystics of England*. Father Colledge taught English Language and Philology at Liverpool University from 1937 until 1963 when he resigned his Readership there, and entered the English Novitiate of the Augustinian Friars Hermit. He taught at the Pontifical Institute of Mediaeval Studies in Toronto until his recent retirement. He continues to direct students and to do international research on spiritual texts.

BERNARD McGINN is professor of Historical Theology and of the History of Christianity at the Divinity School of the University of Chicago. He also serves as a member of the Department of New Testament and Early Christian Literature and the Chairman of the Committee on Medieval Studies in the university's Division of the Humanities. Born in Yonkers, New York, in 1937, Mr. McGinn received a Licentiate in Sacred Theology from the Pontifical Gregorian University in 1963 and a Ph.D. in History of Ideas from Brandeis University in 1970. He has also done advanced work at Columbia University and the University of Munich. His books include *The Golden Chain, Three Treatises on Man, Visions of the End,* and the volume entitled *Apocalyptic Spirituality* in this series. He has also written numerous articles on aspects of late patristic and medieval theology and spirituality.

Author of Preface

Born and raised in China of missionary parents, HUSTON SMITH taught at Washington Unversity (St. Louis) and for fifteen years was Professor of Philosophy at the Massachusetts Institute of Technology before he assumed his present position as Thomas J. Watson Professor of Religion and Adjunct Professor of Philosophy at Syracuse University.

Author of five books and over fifty articles in professional journals, he discovered the capacity of certain Tibetan lamas to sing multiple tones simultaneously (solo chords) and has produced prize-winning films on Hinduism, Tibetan Buddhism, and Islamic mysticism. His *Religions of Man* has sold over two million copies. His latest book, *Forgotten Truth: The Primordial Tradition*, was published by Harper and Row in 1976.

PREFACE

To Professors Colledge's and McGinn's masterful presentation of Meister Eckhart in these pages I have been asked to add a few lines to point out why the book is important today. I shall speak first to the importance it shares with other volumes in this series and then proceed to its unique place within the series itself.

A half-century ago a master comparativist, A. K. Coomaraswamy, wrote that Eckhart resumed and concentrated "in one consistent demonstration the spiritual being of Europe at its highest tension."[1] This tension has since slacked. Alexander Solzhenitsyn may go too far in seeing the contemporary West as "spiritually exhausted," but few seem to doubt a certain anemia. The world we face seems in many ways to be decomposing before our eyes.

If civilizations are like organisms, decline is inevitable, but with the single important exception of Oswald Spengler the West has not thought so—not since its Hebraic infusion. So it is in character for us to ask if there is a cause for our current decline, one that might be corrected. The leading candidate, it seems clear to me, is, I shall not say science, but rather the position it has come to assume in our lives.

Science in the form we have come to know it entered the seventeenth-century West as a new way of knowing, one that promised to augment our power and proceeded to deliver on that promise dramatically. The power it delivered has proved to be over nature only; it has not increased our power over ourselves (to become better people), or over our superiors (angels or God, let us say). How could it have? Power in an inclusive sense can be wielded only over one's inferiors or at most one's equals.

At the time, though—I use this phrase to cover the last three centuries—we did not see this clearly. We did not see that the scientific method has limitations built into it: It is restricted *in principle* to telling us about a part of reality only, that part (to repeat) that is beneath us in freedom and awareness. Instead, we thought we had discovered an improved way of knowing what was applicable across the board—a searchlight which in time might reach into every corner of the universe. This failure to notice that limitations are built into the very structure of the scientific method—that its power derives from its narrowness in the way the effectiveness of a dental drill derives from the smallness of its point—continues. I have spoken of it in the past tense because it can now be shown conclusively (I would say) that the scientific method is inherently limited, but the contrary view remains very much with us; in our culture as a whole it is probably still the reigning orthodoxy. On the very day that I write these lines, for example, I come upon Lévi-Strauss saying that "only through science . . . can . . . we . . . increase . . . the number and quality of the answers we are able to give."[2]

The spiritual decline of the last three hundred years—the eclipse of God sloping into the death of God with the correlative decline in our sense of transcendence and the sacred—is a direct consequence of this mistake. We made the mistake because we did not see the connection between the scientific method and power. Or rather, we saw only half of that connection. It was obvious that science *issues* in power, that our power expands by virtue of it. What we did not see is that it also *proceeds* from power; specifically, from our power to devise controlled experiments. This holds for pure science as much as for applied. That the former seeks knowledge for its own sake is irrelevant. The fact remains: Scientific knowledge, pure or applied, emerges only in regions where scientists can control—that is, have power over—the materials they work with.

The upshot of the mistake I have cited is this: In mistaking a restricted means of knowing for one we assume to be not only unrestricted but the most reliable we have, we have come to place our trust in—take for "the real world"—what appears through this restricted viewfinder. And as only aspects of reality that are inferior to us can register in this viewfinder, these being (to repeat) the aspects that we can control, the West has lowered the ceiling on its worldview, forcing us to live in a cramped, inferior world: Michael Horner calls it dis-spirited, Lewis Mumford, dis-qualified. With a single sweep of the methodological pen, one devised to write our own ticket and get our own way, our world has been stripped of the very possibility of housing things worthier than ourselves, things that exceed us in freedom, intelligence, and purpose. The consequences are severe. Causation is upward only, from the less to the more. Value proceeds in the face of enormous odds, for evolution—the only creative agency science allows—is prodigal. Our self-image is reduced, from slightly lower than angels to naked apes. And in the end time conquers all.

Remarks like the foregoing have their place, but left to themselves they have little impact. There is no effective way to argue against a system from within that system, and every statement from outside it will be translated into its own premises in a way that explains by explaining away. What helps is not arguments but vision—a new way of seeing the world. On one occasion while Elijah Mohammad was schooling Malcolm X in the teachings of the Black Muslims there was a glass of dirty water on the kitchen counter. Mr. Muhammad placed a glass of clean water beside it. "Don't condemn if you see a person has a dirty glass of water," he said. "Just show them the clean glass."[3]

Enter this series, *The Classics of Western Spirituality*, in present instance through the writings of Meister Eckhart. Eckhart doesn't argue against a science-restricted mind set, which of course had not yet emerged. He shows us an alternative. And in doing so—I am thinking especially of the way he returns repeatedly to his theme of the God-intoxicated man—we sense that he knows so vividly what he is talking about that we experience through his words an inrush of the Real. Like prisoners, we had been straining at our bars, hoping for a sliver of light. He spins us around and shows us that the door behind us is wide open. This service Eckhart shares with all the writers in this series. I turn now to his special place within the series itself.

A devout Dominican whose order took pride in its orthodoxy, Eckhart found his writings condemned. There is a paradox here not found in other volumes of this set, and there is no quicker and surer entrée to the heart of Eckhart's thought than by way of it.

Professor Colledge tells us on page 13 of this book that "the opinion seems to be growing ... that the [condemnation] was at least in part unsound," but to write it off as simply a mistake would be too simple. The paradox is tough and resilient. Colledge shows that Eckhart could have quoted the Church Fathers in his defense; yet on his deathbed he "revoked and also deplored the twenty-six articles which he admitted that he had preached." To assume that he did so for the sake of expediency or Church harmony would run counter to the whole character of the man. Colledge gives us the key to the paradox when he points out that Eckhart's retraction contained no admission that what he had taught was untrue; it pertained only to such elements in his teachings as "could generate in the minds of the faithful an heretical opinion, or one erroneous and hostile to the true faith" (p. 15).

This pinpoints the task for the remaining paragraphs of this Preface. If we can identify the features of Eckhart's thought which, though true, can give offense, this should help us not only to understand his thought but to see why it is important for our times.

The elements in question all revolve around the God/self relationship. From the human standpoint the two are separated by a categorical gulf; God appears of necessity as radically Other. But the Neoplatonic tradition in which Eckhart stands teaches that it is quite otherwise from God's vantage point. For God knows that he alone is completely real; real in every sense—all else is only partially so. And that which *is* fully real in what is other-than-God is God's presence in it. Thus from the divine perspective a sublime continuity reigns. Everything that is, to the degree that it is, is God him/her/itself—our pronouns do not fit. Thanks to the "eye of the heart" (Eph. 1:18), which Eckhart calls the Intellect and which he claims is uncreated (p. 42) and therefore divine inasmuch as only God is uncreated, we can catch glimpses of this continuity, but for the most part it is the discontinuity that obtrudes. To try to live wholly within the divine vision would be like trying with our ordinary eyes to seize the sight of the sun: It would blind us and leave us in the obscurity of our closed eyes—an experience which forces us, so to speak, to seek 'the sun' only within us, by means of the "eye of the heart."

So we are divided creatures. A part of ourselves, rarely evident, is continuous with God, while the balance remains categorically different from him. With which part do we identify?

Mystics are persons who, like Eckhart, identify with the God element in themselves emphatically. It was from this identification that Eckhart told his congregation, "Truly you are the hidden God" (*Sermon* 15, 192). If the stance seems presumptuous, we overlook its cost; it requires that we dissociate from everything in us that is profane. As this latter constitutes the bulk of our being as far as most of us can make out, the disengagement that is required is radical. Everything we encountered would have to be affirmed as God's will, or more precisely, God himself; any sentiment that resisted this glad welcome would have to be discounted as arising from our private, intrusive, and in the end only seeming selves.

What we need to catch here is the way truths in the divine, continuous perspective become false when transferred to our normal human perspective in which the discontinuity between man and God is glaringly evident and so, on pain of hypocrisy, must be emphatically affirmed. As the latter context distorts what were truths in the former context, these distortions *need* to be condemned and retracted. Eckhart's teaching that, as God wills evil, we should not will not to have sinned is a case in point; actually all the points on which he was condemned are such, but this one will suffice for illustration. If we hear that we should "not will not to have sinned" (p. 44) while we are tempted to sin—clear indication that we are identifying with the finite, willful part of ourselves—the assertion will seem to counsel sinning forthwith. The God-component in us would accent the statement differently. In its reading sin would lose none of its enormity from the human perspective; its wages for our finite selves continue to be, necessarily, death. Concurrently, however, sin's place in the divine economy taken as a whole would be discerned and therewith affirmed. Without gradations of worth from which sin and evil ultimately derive, God alone would exist and we would not even *be*. For us to exist, then, God must in some way will the separation in which sin and evil are implicated.

Spirit is free, but the letter kills—this truth can be applied at a number of levels. Eckhart speaks audaciously, from a freedom so extravagant that from a lower angle of vision it looks like caprice. A parallel case in another tradition can help us to see what is at stake. We are told that Allah once addressed the Sufi Abu 'l-Hasan al-Kharraqani saying, "Shall I tell the people of thy spiritual drunkenness [a degree of spiritual realization which involved relinquishing outward forms] so that, being scandalized, they will stone thee?" So established was the Sufi in his advanced state that he answered instantly: "Shall I tell the people of Thine infinite Mercy [which, being infinite, will redeem everyone eventually] so that they will never again bow down to Thee in prayer?"

Therein lies the key to "the Eckhartian enigma," if I may call it such; the condemnation of this devout and devoted Christian mystic—as well as to the high octaves of his thought approached simply for themselves. We are told by those who see clearly that truth is of dazzling simplicity, but the ways in which it may be perceived are vastly complex. This fact need not be daunting, since it corresponds to the variety of spiritual personality types, among which the mystic's is one. How many men and women today feel themselves driven to atheism

PREFACE

because the only version of theism they have encountered is too anthropomorphic, too person- (and therefore in the end too self-) centered, too moralistic-because-dualistic to fit the shape the God-vacuum assumes in their mystically inclined souls? As the theism they see seems childish and sentimental, some in this camp accept materialism as the only way to live without lying, while others gravitate to Zen or Vedanta or Sufism where their drive for total self-transcendence (*anatta, fana*) is recognized and welcomed at the door. No task is more important for the Church than to let such persons know that behind its outer doors that are always open stands another that is closed—closed though accessible to those who knock. When it opens, only to close again immediately for this inner door never remains ajar, Meister Eckhart will be among those waiting to welcome those who enter.

—Huston Smith

FOREWORD

Meister Eckhart's reputation as one of the key figures in the history of Western mysticism can scarcely be questioned. Since the revival of interest in his writings in the early nineteenth century, a broad stream of editions, studies, and interpretations has contributed to his growing fame. But as in his own day, so too in ours, Eckhart remains a difficult and controversial writer. Propositions from the works of this master of theology and high official in the Dominican order were posthumously condemned on March 27, 1329, by Pope John XXII, though this apparently did little to hinder the considerable influence that he continued to have on the piety of the fourteenth and fifteenth centuries. The modern revival of Eckhart has presented even more contradictory evaluations. The daring aspects of the Meister's thought, especially as revealed in his vernacular works, have provided considerable excuse for those who have stressed his radicalism. At different times Eckhart has been viewed as a pantheist, a forerunner of the Reformation, a prophet of German national religion, a Zen master in disguise, and a proto-Marxist. While serious scholars reject such extreme interpretations, these exaggerated views do serve to indicate that Meister Eckhart was and is a daring and difficult thinker, a man who escapes any easy categorization, and frequently a scandal to the timid and conventional. From the end of the last century, other scholars, relying chiefly on the Latin works, have stressed the more traditional aspects of the Meister's thought, especially its deep roots in medieval scholastic theology. These roots, as well as Eckhart's unwavering loyalty to the Church, must never be forgotten, but they should not lead us into seeing Eckhart as just another conventional scholastic thinker.

The present volume is designed to provide a general introduction to the integral Eckhart. Unlike earlier English translations, it gives equal representation to selections from both the technical Latin works

FOREWORD

and the more popular vernacular sermons and treatises to show the inner unity and coherence of the thought of one of the greatest masters of Western spirituality.

Edmund Colledge is grateful to Professor Kurt Ruh for giving him access to his Germanistisches Seminar, and for much assistance; and to Father Adolar Zumkeller, O.S.A., and the Augustinus-Institut at Würzburg for their hospitality and help. More recently, Father Eelcko Ypma, O.S.A., Mr. J. van Sint Feijth, and Mr. A. van Gorp have guided him through the invaluable resources of the Thesaurus linguae Augustinianae at Eindhoven, where the community at Marienhagen were his kind hosts.

Bernard McGinn expresses gratitude especially to Professor Frank Tobin of the University of Nevada for invaluable assistance without which this volume would have been much the poorer.

The editors of this volume and the editors of the Classics of Western Spirituality series also wish to take this opportunity to express their sincere gratitude to the directors of the Eckhart edition sponsored by the Deutsche Forschungsgemeinschaft for their permission to make use of that critical text as the basis for this translation.

Introduction

KEY TO ABBREVIATIONS

I. The abbreviations used for the books of the Bible follow the practice of the Jerusalem Bible. The translations of scriptural texts, however, have been made directly from Eckhart's Latin and German, which is usually close to the Vulgate text.

II. Frequently cited works will be abbreviated as follows:

A. **Eckhart's Works.** Unless otherwise noted, all Eckhart's works will be cited according to the edition of the Deutsche Forschungsgemeinschaft under the general editorship of J. Quint for the German works and J. Koch for the Latin works. This is *Meister Eckhart. Die deutschen und lateinischen Werke* (Stuttgart and Berlin: W. Kohlhammer, 1936–). Hereafter abbreviated as DW and LW, followed by volume number. The letters n. and nn. will refer to numbered section(s) of the Latin edition.

Individual works will appear as follows:

LW. *Book of the Parables of Genesis (Par. Gen.)*
     Commentary on Exodus (Comm. Ex.)
     Commentary on Genesis (Comm. Gen.)
     Commentary on John (Comm. Jn.)
     Commentary on Wisdom (Comm. Wis.)
     Parisian Questions (Par. Quest.)
     Sermons, Latin (Sermon with Latin number)

DW. *Book "Benedictus" 1 and 2 (Bened.)*
     Counsels on Discernment (Couns.)
     On Detachment (Detach.)
     Sermons, German (Sermon with Arabic number)

3

KEY TO ABBREVIATIONS

B. Other Authors
1. Aristotle:
   Categories (Cat.)
   Metaphysics (Met.)
   On the Soul (Soul)
   Physics (Phys.)
   Posterior Analytics (Post. Anal.)
   Topics (Top.)

2. Augustine:
   Confessions (Conf.)
   Literal Commentary on Genesis (Lit. Comm. Gen.)
   On Christian Doctrine (Christ. Doct.)
   On the Trinity (Trin.)

3. Moses Maimonides:
   Guide to the Perplexed (Guide)

4. Thomas Aquinas:
   Commentary on the Sentences (In Sent.)
   Summa against the Gentiles (SCG)
   Summa of Theology (STh)

III. The abbreviation MHG = Middle High German.

1. HISTORICAL DATA

A. LIFE

Eckhart's baptismal or religious name seems to have been John, but it would be pedantic to give him any appellation other than the "Meister" by which he was known to his own order and to the public, in his lifetime and thereafter. He earned this title of honor in the first instance through the teaching appointment that he gained in the University of Paris, where he attracted notice by the contentious role he played in current theological controversies, which, some of his sermons show,[1] were still fresh in his mind years afterward. He was born about the year 1260. In the Middle Ages, unless a birth were to be that of, say, some future king, there is seldom any exact contemporary record of its date and place; in Eckhart's case, we can only deduce the approximate year from later events in his life that can be dated. He is said to have been born in a village in Thuringia called Hochheim, either that near Erfurt or another of the same name near Gotha. The first is his more probable birthplace, since it was in Erfurt that he was admitted as a novice into the convent of the Dominican friars.[2] The story, still commonly accepted and repeated, that he was of noble or knightly birth is a fiction that originated in a misinterpretation of archives of the period.[3] In his first years he would have received the usual rudimentary education in Latin grammar and in the liberal arts; thereafter he seems to have been sent for higher studies to the Dominicans' institute in their monastery at Cologne, where he may have known Albert the Great, who ended his career by living and perhaps by teaching there until his death in 1280. If so, this could have been Eckhart's first contact with anyone who had known Thomas Aquinas except by repute. Albert had taught Thomas too, and shortly before his death, when the University of Paris organized an attack on Thomas's

5

philosophical and theological method, Albert had attempted, not wholly successfully, to defend his old pupil's name. This story is on the authority of Bartholomew of Capua, who gave evidence in Thomas's canonization process; and he stated that he knew of it only from what Hugo Borgognoni of Lucca, one-time prior provincial of the Roman province, had told him, so that it can be accepted only with reserve.[4] Soon, Eckhart was to follow Albert and Thomas to Paris, then the center of the Western intellectual world.

For young friars of the mendicant orders to be sent there to take part—at first as assistants—in the university's teaching program was a privilege of which other teachers, from the ranks of the secular clergy and the older religious orders, were always jealous, and which the Dominicans and the other friars had to guard with care. They took pains in the selection of candidates who would represent them worthily; and for Eckhart to be so chosen was a clear indication that his teachers in Germany saw in him much promise.

Josef Koch analyzed three of his pronouncements for what light they throw on his early years as a student.[5] In an Easter sermon that he preached in 1294 he remarked: "Albert often used to say: 'I know this in the way we know; but we all know very little,'" a saying, otherwise unrecorded, the quotation of which in this form added probability, Koch considered, to the conjecture that Eckhart had been Albert's pupil in Cologne. In his *Commentary on Genesis*, n. 10, he has a similar reminiscence: "One of the world's pretentious people used to say that only one thing can be produced in immediate fashion from one, that is, one idea,"[6] which alludes to Siger of Brabant, and seemed to Koch to show that Eckhart had attended his classes in Paris in arts and philosophy. This could not have been later than March 1277, when Stephen Tempier, the bishop of Paris, issued his notorious condemnation of the "219 Propositions," which included some of Siger's Averroist doctrines, after which Siger fled to Orvieto to find refuge at the papal curia. The third such statement is in Eckhart's "Vindicatory Document," or Defense, issued in 1326 to defend his own teachings against his Cologne inquisitors; and Koch makes a strong case for interpreting this as showing that he was present in Paris while the preliminary investigations were being carried out, on Tempier's orders, by the university's theologians, which led to the condemnation of Siger and of Thomas Aquinas. Eckhart suggests—he seems to be the only witness to this—that another target for attack at this time had been "my lord, Friar Albert." By 1326 this was "long ago, but in my own lifetime," and Thomas had become St. Thomas of Aquinas.[7] Before Thomas's canonization in 1323 a successor of Tempier had revoked his condemnation, and the burden of Eckhart's observations seems to be that better theologians than those then prosecuting him in Cologne had been forced to eat their words.

Koch considers that these sayings point to a sequence by which Eckhart had studied arts in Paris about 1277, had begun theology in Cologne before 1280, had returned to Paris in the period 1293–1294 to begin to conduct the obligatory classes on Peter Lombard's *Sentences*, to take part in formal disputations, and to begin his own studies for the master's degree. His recall to Germany must soon have followed, as was regular and normal. At that time the Dominicans had at their disposal no more than two chairs, the Augustinians only one; and when a man had fulfilled his first duties, he had to return to his province to make room for others whom their orders wished to promote as masters. It was only when someone was considered to be of quite outstanding merit, and had proved himself acceptable to the whole university, that he could hope for yet further promotion. This had been so with the German Augustinian, the elder Henry of Friemar.[8] He seems to have come to Paris as a young master little before Eckhart, but by 1307 he had succeeded to his order's chair and four years later he was active as an expert consultant at the Council of Vienne. Though Eckhart did not enjoy Henry's success, he seems nonetheless to have been viewed with sufficient favor for him to return to Paris, after an interval during which he had been entrusted by his province with administrative office; and he was again teaching there while the council was sitting.

It is of the greatest significance that the first theological writings by which Henry of Friemar can have become known reflected the troubled climate in which he and Eckhart were living and working, and offer considerations that, later at all events, were to have clear applicability to Eckhart's situation. These writings are *A Treatise on "An Angel was Sent," A Treatise on the Advent of the Lord* (also called *A Treatise on Conceiving in the Mind*), and *A Treatise on the Incarnation of the Word*. In them, Henry deals with what was to become the dominant central theme of Eckhart's teaching, the birth of the Word in the soul; but he sounds notes of caution. This birth is an operation of grace in the soul, to which it is God's free gift, and for which dispositions to receive the grace and the gift are necessary. In the third, *On the Incarnation of the Word*, he deplores dangerous exaggerations, which he finds non-Christian, of the notion of human perfectibility, and the teachings of "certain people" that those who are "perfect and established in a liberty of the spirit" are not obliged to obey ecclesiastical superiors and the ordinances of the Church, but may do everything to which they feel themselves drawn by an "inner prompting of the Spirit." Henry contrasts such belief, which he emphatically calls "error," with the example of Christ, the "teacher of perfection," who obeyed not only his parents but also the civil authorities, and who can be seen to have condemned such notions.

Adolar Zumkeller is the first to have given these writings serious examination, and to perceive their wider implications. All three are preserved together in Ms. Heidelberg Pal. lat. 454, in the sequence in which they are described here. A text of the first, *A Treatise on "An Angel was Sent,"* is also found in Ms. Erlangen University Library 277, which has unique readings showing that it was copied from Henry's autograph; this is dated A.D. 1309. Zumkeller does not think that they were published in Paris, because none of these surviving witnesses calls the author "Henry of Germany," as do manuscripts of other works that he manifestly wrote and issued as a teacher of the university.

Thus, these present treatises seem to have been early compositions, written in the period when Paris was the scene of the trial as a relapsed heretic of the high priestess of "liberty of the spirit," Margaret Porette, which led to her second condemnation and her death by fire at the stake, there in 1310, for her persistence in publishing her book *The Mirror of Simple Souls,* which a bishop had already pronounced heretical.[9] Henry and Eckhart must both have known theologians who had served as representatives of the University of Paris, either as scrutineers of the articles extracted from the *Mirror* or as members of the court that pronounced the adverse sentence to which Henry gives a wider application in *On the Incarnation of the Word.* One such Churchman was Berengar of Landorra, O.P., who subscribed to Margaret Porette's condemnation, was a representative of the University of Paris at Vienne, and was elected the Dominicans' master general.[10]

In his detestation of "liberty of the spirit," Henry is voicing the opinion of all orthodox Christians of his day.[11] But he implies—it is no more than implication—that the doctrine of "the birth of the Word in the soul" can be perverted to teach that the soul is able to give birth to the Son of God just as Mary did. It may be difficult for us today to suppose anyone capable of believing such nonsense; but some of the more extravagant devotional writings that in the next generations were being passed from hand to hand among devotees, especially in the Rhineland and the Low Countries, do contain teachings of this sort; and very often in such pious anthologies these aphorisms are prefaced with "Meister Eckhart said...." Some attributions like these will be found to be spurious, but they show that the fears of those who were to become his adversaries for the influence he was exercising on the imprudent and gullible among his hearers had some foundation. It is a sign of remarkable prescience that Henry of Friemar foresaw so early that any reckless propagandist of the birth of the Word—as Eckhart's surviving genuine works show him to have been—could acquire so unhappy a reputation.

But liberty of the spirit was not the only controversy then being ventilated in international centers of learning. Critics were not wanting who would attribute the generally growing spread of heresy and the bitter strife within the Church over papal supremacy to the new enlightenment, fed from Greek, Arabic, and Hebrew sources, that was increasingly influencing the arts, sciences, and theology in the universities, as it was manifested in the academic philosophy that came to be known as Scholasticism, and especially as it was promoted by Albert the Great and Thomas Aquinas.[12] Some treated Scholasticism as paganism in disguise. Others saw it as less objectionable, but wished for a return to Augustine's appeals to subjective experience. There were yet others who questioned the entire basis of this new philosophy and theology: "Your speculations are certainly very edifying, but may not everything, under God's absolute power, be quite different?"[13] Koch has observed that Eckhart belonged to none of these schools, and in his sermons we shall find many passing remarks to show his impatience with what he regarded as the mechanical professionalism of the "great masters" and its irrelevance to the birth of the Word in the soul. Yet we can see in him, as in Peter John Olivi, Durandus of Saint-Pourçain and William of Ockham (three others who also came under heavy attack as suspected heretics), a deprecation of scholastic realism, which sought (or so they believed) to naturalize the supernatural, because of which they too wished to return to Augustine's more personal approach. These approximations, real or imagined, between the thinking of the four men were, as we shall see, to do Eckhart no good.

In the interval after his first stay in Paris, Eckhart was active as prior of Erfurt and "vicar" of Thuringia, that is, local representative of the German prior provincial, Dietrich of Freiburg. To this period of Erfurt belong his *Counsels on Discernment,* a record of his informal discourses to his community. In 1303 he was nominated to undertake the direction of the newly created subdivision of the German Dominican province, that of Saxony; and in 1307 he was given the additional office of general vicar of the Bohemian province. In 1310 his German confreres indicated once again that he had proved himself as a skilled administrator; the Teutonia provincial chapter at Speyer elected him as their prior provincial. In the next year, however, the general chapter at Naples did not confirm this election, but instead sent him again to Paris. From this second sojourn seems to have come the *Parisian Questions,*[14] first discovered in 1927, one of which, "Whether in God existence and understanding can be the same," provides us with a careful academic exposition, offered not to a popular audience but to his rightly critical peers, of the early development of his philosophical thinking. And in Paris, in the academic years 1311–1312 and 1312–1313, he was developing a most ambitious project. This was to have been the *Opus Tripartitum,* the *Three-Part Work.* How great the scope of this work was to have been is plain, but what was achieved and has survived is a mere torso. When in 1313 he returned from Paris to Germany for good, little had been written; and thereafter the whole of his attention seems to have been occupied by the audiences that he drew for his public sermons, and then by his need to defend his teachings, in yet further sermons, and by documents intended for circulation.

In 1314 we find him in Strassburg. What specific office he held there is not certain. He seems chiefly to have been concerned with spiritual direction and with preaching in convents of Dominican nuns. In 1323, at the earliest, he was in Cologne, where, though the evidence is not strong, he seems to have acted as master of the more advanced students. But his role as a popular preacher did not diminish; and it was this that was to make Cologne the scene of his downfall.

The first clear sign that trouble was developing was when the Dominican papal visitor for the Teutonia province, Nicholas of Strassburg, probably so as to accommodate the archbishop of Cologne, Henry of Virneburg, conducted an investigation of Eckhart's orthodoxy and pronounced his teachings free of heresy. Despite this assurance, the archbishop ordered an inquisitorial process.

It would be wearisome to follow step by step the course of events in the next years, and to describe the complexities of the surviving documents. We owe it to the scholarly researches of Théry,[15] Pelster,[16] and Laurent,[17] and to Koch's masterly continuation of Denifle's analyses, that we have even so clear a picture as we possess of what happened. Throughout, it is plain, Eckhart maintained that he was not guilty of the charges brought against him, because heresy is a matter of the will, and it was his intention to remain and to die a faithful son of the Church. But the archbishop's inquisitors had prepared a dossier, which seems to have been vast, of propositions that had been extracted from Eckhart's published writings and from what he was alleged to have said in his sermons, upon which he was interrogated; and in the end they pronounced against him. On 13 February 1327, before this sentence was promulgated, Eckhart had made in the Dominican church at Cologne a public protestation of his innocence. This he seems to have handled badly, and several times Koch had scathing things to say about his ineptitude. He does not seem to have admitted the possibility that the verdict could go against him; and one has the impression that in these proceedings, as in some of his later preaching, his powers were waning. But he was still capable of vigorous reaction. He issued a "Vindicatory Document," providing chapter and verse for what he had taught and what of it had been challenged; he denied competence and authority to the inquisitors and the archbishop; and he appealed to the Holy See against the verdict. He then set off for Avignon—accompanied, be it noted, by some of his Dominican superiors, who did not desert him—to wait his turn among the others, including William of Ockham, who had come there on similar charges. Doubtless the same conditions were imposed on him as on the English Franciscan: He would not be living in confinement, but would not be at liberty to leave the papal court before a verdict had been reached.

Pope John XXII set up a more august tribunal to inquire into his case, but the same procedure was followed as at Cologne, one that had been established almost two centuries before in the case of Peter Abelard.[18] The commissioners were not required to read suspect authors' complete works. Instead, they were first examined by subordinates, who drew up lists, *rotuli*, of propositions, *articuli*, that seemed to them suspect, and that were presented for examination to the commissioners. One of the most eminent concerned in Eckhart's case, and in a number of others, Cardinal James Fournier, left a remarkable document recording how unsatisfactory he considered this method to be.[19] When he was pressed to pronounce on the case, far more delicate than Eckhart's, of Durandus of Saint-Pourçain, he protested that he could not with justice do so until he had seen the contexts from which the propositions had been taken. Fournier succeeded John XXII as Benedict XII, and he had an account prepared of all such proceedings in which he had participated. Unfortunately, this has now disappeared; but there are quotations from it in the Augustinian John of Basel's *Commentary on the Sentences* and his *Ten Responses*[20] sufficient to show with what care Benedict XII's dossier was prepared. We do not know what misgivings he may have had in finding against Eckhart; all we do know is that before the papal commission could confirm (albeit in a modified form) the adverse Cologne verdict, Eckhart was dead; when and where is unknown, although the one report we have, in the papal Bull "In the Lord's field," "In agro dominico," drafted and promulgated in Avignon, suggests that it may have been there, and shows that it was before 27 March 1329, the date of promulgation.[21]

B. THE CONDEMNATION

We owe it to Koch's subtle examinations of the documents that we know that although the Avignon commissioners decided to ratify the Cologne findings, this was done with important and significant modifications.[22]

"In agro dominico" is presented in three sections. The first sets out the facts of the case, but there is a lack of precision. The Bull states that Eckhart "presented many things as dogma . . . which he put forth . . . in his sermons and also admitted into his writings," but this does not, as it seems to do, distinguish, as critics today commonly do, between his learned treatises and his popular vernacular sermons. In the second section there is a list of propositions, all of which, except two, it is stated, Eckhart admitted having "preached," but Koch points out that this is "objectively untrue," since most of the propositions were taken not from German sermons but from Latin treatises. The third section addresses the juridical question: Are these propositions heretical? The answer is formulated with an essential distinction. The first fifteen propositions, acknowledged as his by Eckhart, are heretical and are condemned, as are the last two, which he denies having taught, but which are nonetheless rehearsed. With regard to the remaining eleven, it is conceded that although they have an offensive ring (*male sonare*), are rash, and smack of heresy (*multum esse temerarios de haeresique suspectos*), they could, "with many explanations and additions," be given or already have a Catholic sense.[23] So far as concerns the two appended articles that Eckhart repudiated because he had never taught

them, the first, at least, is taken not from a Latin work but from a vernacular sermon: "That there is something in the soul which is uncreated and not capable of creation. . . ." As the footnotes to *Sermon* 48
show, he seems to have forgotten what he had said, there and elsewhere, on this topic, about which his adversaries evidently were un-
able to challenge him.

But this subdivision, into those articles that are acknowledged and
condemned as heretical, those deplored for their tone and wording but
not condemned, and those condemned but not acknowledged as his
own by Eckhart, does not seem to have been the original intention of
the commission. There is no mention of it either in their minutes or
in Cardinal Fournier's account of their proceedings.[24] Rightly, Koch
says that the afterthought cannot be attributed to the pope. John XXII
was a canon lawyer, and notoriously no theologian. Koch conjectures
that it may have been Eckhart's old Paris pupil, John Petri of Godino,
who was responsible; but for this he found no supporting evidence.
One's own guess is that it was, far more probably, James Fournier himself, whose lack of confidence in such arbitrary inquisitorial procedure
Koch was able to establish.

The opinion seems to be growing among responsible modern his-
torians of medieval spirituality that the judgment of "In agro dominico" was at least in part unsound, and that, in particular, if the
commissioners had had a better knowledge of the fathers of the
Church, both Eastern and Western, they would have perceived that
they too had taught some of what Eckhart was now being condemned
for teaching. The greatest impetus to this opinion was given by Hugo
Rahner, when he produced his detailed exposition of where, in the
writings of the fathers, Eckhart's doctrine of the birth of the Word in
the soul is to be found.[25] It is at this doctrine, as taught by Eckhart,
that the condemnation of propositions 10, 11, 12, and 13 of "In agro dominico" was aimed.

We may now add one particular detail to this. Eckhart was condemned in proposition 14 for having taught that "A good man ought
so to conform his will to the divine will that he should will whatever
God wills. Since God in some way wills for me to have sinned, I should
not will that I had not committed sins; and this is true penitence."[26]
M.-H. Laurent identifies the source of this in the *Book "Benedictus"*;[27]
but if those responsible for drawing up the first lists of propositions
had been better informed, they would have found the same teaching
in the *Counsels on Discernment*, and there in a form that might have giv-

en the assessors pause; for Eckhart supports what he writes by quoting Paul—"All things work together for good," and continues: "And, as St. Augustine says, 'Yes, even sins.' "[28] And it can be seen that this is indeed what Augustine does say in *Of the Free Will* (which Quint correctly identified as the source): "Even our sins are necessary to the universal perfection which God established." Augustine scholars will undoubtedly think that "with many necessary explanations and additions [this] might take on or possess a Catholic meaning," but this must also be true of what Eckhart wrote; and the proper place for proposition 14 is not in the condemned first section, but among the "deplored" propositions of section two.

One of the editors has already elsewhere touched on the problem of why Eckhart himself did not put up a better defense.[29] We cannot know the answers, since we were not present, either in Cologne or Avignon, to hear what was said. Perhaps Eckhart did appeal to Augustine's authority, and this was set aside; although, in general, the recollections of what Augustine had written that he produced in his German treatises and sermons are vague and at times confused. His heyday had been his teaching years in Paris, when the *Questions* show him as a brilliant young man of promise, disputing, lucidly and forcefully, among his equals. His changes of office, his administrative cares, and the demands made on him as a preacher and a spiritual director must have curtailed if not terminated his own studies. The years that followed of paradox-spinning for the scandalized delight of larger but less critical and instructed audiences do not seem to have sharpened his wits. It is evident that he had been wounded by the hostile criticism he had encountered; and we can perhaps detect signs of the apathetic fatigue experienced by an aging man, aware that he has not fulfilled his early promise and has exhausted his powers in his efforts to woo popular acclaim. But however clumsy his self-defense may have been, we can read in its Cologne records the sturdy assurance of one who knows himself free from reproach.

The Bull ends with the pope informing the archbishop, to whom it is addressed, of Eckhart's recantation on his deathbed. Undoubtedly this information was for the benefit of the laity. Koch calls it "an absolute revocation," but this is too strong. What the document says is that "the aforesaid Eckhart . . . at the end of his life . . . revoked and also deplored the twenty-six articles which he admitted that he had preached, and also any others, written and taught by him . . . insofar as they could generate in the minds of the faithful a heretical opinion, or one erroneous and hostile to the true faith."[30] The qualifying phrase, *quantum ad illum sensum,* is all-important, and it is much to the credit of whoever produced the condemnation's final form that it is there. Eckhart revoked and deplored the articles because the sense in which they were understood could engender heretical beliefs in the minds of the faithful, and he admits that these are taken from his preaching and writings; but he does not say—nor does the document make him say—that he accepts the Church's judgment that the propositions are heretical. The commissioners said that they were, but they do not say that he accepted this. We may guess that if the Avignon process had run its full course, Eckhart might have been constrained to do so or to accept the direst consequences, and that he was spared this by his death. But the papal Bull, if read aright, shows him meeting death, one will not say unrepentant but unyielding. Koch justly describes the formulation of this as exact, and he regrets that no notary's record of this deathbed profession has survived; but the precision and skill with which it avoids any admission of heretical intentions must surely be attributed to Eckhart himself, to one of his Dominican counselors, or, it may be, to the curial official responsible for the document's final form. It may not be too fanciful to suspect that in it we can see a dissenting minority opinion at work.

C. Eckhart's Posthumous Reputation

The terms of "In agro dominico," the Holy See's severe warnings, addressed through the archbishop of Cologne to the faithful in the Rhineland that they may not consider themselves good Christians or obedient children of the Church if in any way they continue to countenance or to maintain Eckhart's false teachings, carefully cataloged, should have meant that he would be consigned to complete oblivion; but what happened was very different. Our first evidence of this was recorded by his two pupils and disciples, John Tauler and Henry Suso, who had lived and suffered through these tragic events, and who, in their different ways, testified that they still revered his memory and dissented from the judgment of the Holy See.

Tauler, in one of his sermons seemingly directed, as most of his preaching appears to have been, to Dominican nuns, addressing them as those who had also been witnesses to what had happened and im-

15

plying that they must accept their share of the blame, says of unitive prayer and the contemplative effort:

> Those who have grown in natural wisdom, who have been trained in mortal activities, who have lived in their senses, cannot come here; no, they cannot come so far. Moreover, one dear teacher taught you and spoke on this subject, and you did not understand him. He spoke from the point of view of eternity, and you understood him from the point of view of time. My dear children, if I have said too much to you, it is certainly not too much for God; but nonetheless I beg you to forgive me, and if there is need I am willing to correct my words![31]

"One dear teacher taught you ... and you did not understand him." Tauler makes it plain that his auditors know well the circumstances to which he is alluding, that they were themselves involved, and that the involvement was in part one of the emotions. He seems by implication to be saying that it was his hearers' adulation that helped to accomplish Eckhart's ruin, because it was their misunderstanding of his transcendental message that encouraged his adversaries to regard and treat him as a false prophet. Tauler says, as plainly as he dares, that they were wrong in condemning him; but, warned no doubt by his example, he professes himself ready to retract "if there is need."

Henry Suso's approach is different. As Koch observed,[32] his method was to synthesize what appeared to him as true and incontrovertible in his dead master's teaching, and to contrast this with the ways in which it had been perverted by foolish devotees who "understood him from the point of view of time." This he does in his German *Little Book of Truth* by composing, in the sixth chapter, a Boethian dialogue between the "Disciple," who is Suso himself, serving as spokesman for right judgment and sound theology, and the "nameless Wild One."[33] In the "Wild One," Suso has drawn a vivid and skilled portrait of the anonymous masses who had gone astray, listening too readily to "liberty of the spirit" and such other perversions of the Christian faith, identifying Eckhart too easily with the other heresiarchs whom they had followed.[34]

That the Wild One says: "I have heard that there was a great teacher ..." shows that this chapter was written after Eckhart's death. He says that this great teacher had said many beautiful things about man formed in Christ, and that such a man can do all that Christ did.

This tenet of Eckhart's is the subject of the condemned article 13 of "In agro dominico": "That whatever is proper to the divine nature, all that is proper to the just and divine man; because of that, this man performs whatever God performs."[35] The disciple answers the Wild One: "In one place the same master says this: 'The just man performs everything which justice performs'; and he says that it is true that the just man is born of justice, as it is written: 'He who is born of flesh is flesh, and he who is born of the Spirit is spirit' (Jn. 3:6). And he says that this is true of Christ alone and of no other man, for he has no being except the being of the Father."[36] This reproduces almost word for word Eckhart's defense of article 13 at Avignon.[37] When the Wild One adds: "The master is supposed to have said that all that Christ was given is also given to me," which is condemned in article 11: "Whatever God the Father gave to his Only-Begotten Son in human nature, he gave all this to me," we can best consult *Sermon* 5a, *In hoc apparuit caritas dei in nobis,* where Eckhart remarks: "One authority says: 'When I think of that, that our nature has been exalted above created things, and sits in heaven above the angels, and is adored by them, then I must always rejoice in my heart, because Jesus Christ, my dear Lord, has made everything which is his possession my own."[38] (Here Eckhart is employing a favorite rhetorical device, and quoting himself as an "authority" whom he does not name.) During the Cologne process, the proposition, its context in this sermon exactly stated, was attacked as Eckhart's own, and as such defended by him. The Disciple replies: "The 'all' which was given to Christ is the perfect possession of essential blessedness, as he said: 'The Father has given all things to me' (Jn. 3:35), and he has given the same to us all, but not in equal fashion. And [Eckhart] says in many places that [Christ] has all that through the Incarnation, and we through union with God when we are formed like him; and therefore Christ possesses it so much more nobly, as he was able so much more nobly to receive [the Father]."[39] The beginning of this answer seems to offer Suso's own thoughts, but "and he says in many places" refers to Eckhart's *Commentary on John.* Koch's observations, shrewd as always, on this detailed defense of Eckhart's teachings are that so far from "In agro dominico" serving as a repellent warning, certain "free spirits" made use of the document's condemnations in order to represent Eckhart as one of their own, and that the chapter well displays Suso's exact knowledge of his master's writings, including the scriptural commentaries (and, we may add, of the defenses Eckhart had offered to his accusers).

Before we leave Suso, and the esteem, which we have already shown as evident, in which he held Eckhart, there is one other minor point that requires mention.

It is commonly asserted that in the German *Vita* Suso recorded that he had received a vision of the dead Eckhart, glorified and enjoying the beatific sight of God. This is a trap into which Bihlmeyer himself fell,[40] and, following him, most critics during this century, until Thomas Kaeppeli published his catalog of medieval Dominican writers, which is marked by the impeccable accuracy scholars have learned to expect of him.[41]

We may ignore the controversies about the precise share Suso himself had in the writing of the *Vita.* For our purposes it is enough that toward the end of his life he was concerned to leave a "true exemplar," an authorized, corrected copy of his four chief German treatises, and that these include the *Little Book of Truth* and the *Vita.*[42] Thus, he gave his own certificate of authenticity to this biography. In its sixth chapter, it is related that at one period of his life he was often granted visions of what was yet to come, and what was hidden from other men's eyes, and that many departed souls appeared to him to tell him of their fate,

> among others, the blessed[43] Master Eckhart.... By the Master he was told that he lived in surpassing glory, in which his soul was purely divinized[44] in God. Then the Servant[45] desired to know two things from him: One was how those men fare with God who with true self-abandonment, without any deceit, strive to attain to the highest truth. Then it was shown to him that no one can put into words how such men are received into the formless abyss. But then he went on to ask what was the best exercise for a man who longed to attain to this? Then [Eckhart] said: "He ought with profound self-abandonment to sink away from his own self, to accept everything from God and nothing from his creatures, and stand out in silent patience against all wolfish men."[46]

We may think that in these counsels there is no great originality or perception; but, nonetheless, for one religious to recount that another, who had died condemned for heresy, had appeared to him to describe the divine blessedness he now enjoyed would be an act of open contempt toward a decree that a pope had ratified. But those who have

so interpreted this passage in the *Vita* have overlooked two circumstances: There were in Suso's lifetime two German Dominicans
known as "Meister Eckhart," and it was the tradition of their order
that it was not the friar condemned for heresy who had appeared to
Suso in this vision, but the other of the same name. That there were
two such men is beyond any doubt. Among the acts of the general
chapter at Clermont in 1339 we read: "We make it known to the brethren that Friar Eckhart, diffinitor at the general chapter held [in 1337]
at Valenciennes, of the Saxony province, died returning from the chapter."[47] The editor of these acts refers to the great catalog of Dominican
writers by Quétif and Echard, where this man is called "Eckhart the
younger, a Saxon"; and they quote the work of the Tuscan Dominican
Leander Alberti (1479–1552), *Of the illustrious men of the Order of Preachers:*[48] "Eckhart the Teuton, doctor of sacred theology, outstanding for
his godly learning, famed for his holiness and celebrated for Christian
doctrine, appeared after his death to Henry, the Disciple of Everlasting
Wisdom."[49] Kaeppeli attributes to "Eckhart the younger" two Latin
sermons, a Latin epistle, and seven German extracts that seem to have
circulated as works of "Eckhart the elder." Thus, Suso has been shown
to have defended his teacher's good name; but he did not beatify him.

There is one further piece of evidence, recently found, to confirm
what we may deduce from Suso's works and Tauler's: That Eckha
writings, far from being suppressed or forgotten by his fellow
icans, continued to be copied and read. This was presen
what Josef Koch called Thomas Kaeppeli's "sensationa
1960, that Ms. Basel University Library B. VI. 16, cont
hundred excerpts from Eckhart, evidently derives f
made in the Cologne Dominican convent after the pro
agro dominico," notations from which are incorpor
do not know under what circumstances the Cologne
their copy. That which was brought to light by
owned by a Westphalian pastor, who recorded th
in the vicinity of Cologne Cathedral. Thereafter the
by the Basel Carthusians,[51] whose order has bee Cusa
active in the dissemination of another condemne ritings in
ette's *Mirror of Simple Souls.*[52] addressed,

It may be that, as Koch suggested,[53] t
Carthusians and, in the fifteenth century, the
found their justification for owning and stud
the circumstance that John XXII's Bull

through the archbishop of Cologne, to his "simple faithful," so that they considered that the learned were not so inhibited. Nicholas made great efforts to assemble for his use a collection of the Latin works, which, happily, survives in the library he formed and endowed at Kues in the Moselle valley, and is one of the most important sources for editors of these works. Nicholas caused the articles (though not the accompanying text) from "In agro dominico" to be transcribed, with his own note, "Beware," in this manuscript; but other annotations show the close and careful study he spent on it. His qualified approbation of Eckhart involved him in written controversy with John Wenck of Herrenberg, author of an anti-Eckhart pamphlet, *Of Unknown Letters*. In his reply, *An Apology for Learned Ignorance,* Nicholas wrote:

> I [the fictional disciple] did not wish to leave undiscussed what the adversary [Wenck] had alleged against Meister Eckhart, and I asked the teacher [Nicholas] if he had heard anything of him. He replied that he had seen in libraries many of his commentaries on most of the books of the Bible, numerous sermons and disputed questions, and also a number of articles extracted from his *Commentary on John,* annotated and refuted by others, and also, at Master John Guldenschaf's in Mainz, a short writing of his in which he replies to those who sought to reprehend him, explaining himself and demonstrating what his adversaries had not understood. But the teacher said that he had never read that he considered the creature to be identical with the Creator. He praised his gifts and his zeal, but he would have preferred his books to be removed from public places, because the people are not able to understand these matters, with which he often dealt differently from other teachers, even though intelligent men will find in them many subtle and profitable things.[54]

n this we can see that Nicholas had read assiduously, and that ʒ had included "In agro dominico" and the Defense. Wenck's which Nicholas denies, that Eckhart had taught an identity re with the Creator may indicate that Wenck had seen ny "Eckhart" extracts containing spurious attributions s held and preached by overtly heretical teachers. And, ʒh, Nicholas's cautions may show that there were hat were available for general consultation, where and under what circumstances we cannot know. Yet we may think that by the time that Nicholas was writing, in the 1440s, "In agro dominico" was something of a dead letter.

We have so far confined this examination of Eckhart's influence after his death to the German territories, but much still remains to be done to determine how his thinking penetrated the Low Countries. One of the present editors intends soon to make a separate study of Eckhart criticism in the house of Augustinian canons regular at Groenendael near Brussels, as it is preserved for us in the writings of John Ruysbroek and his confrere John van Leeuw. It is also much to be hoped that someone will undertake a rigorous examination of the many manuscripts, still largely unedited, that contain what purport to be extracts from his writings or quotations from his sermons. One of Stephanus Axters's last publications was his catalog of Netherlands manuscripts containing Dominican works,[55] in which he lists many "Eckhart" excerpts, divided by him into the categories "genuine," "dubious," and "spurious," but a closer examination is needed, side by side with the Koch-Quint collected edition, before one can be sure that Axters's judgments were in every instance sound.

As a final example of how Eckhart's works continued to be read and pondered in the religious houses that had survived the holocausts of the sixteenth century, in the Rhineland and in the Catholic Dutch-speaking areas adjacent that remained open to the influences of German piety and contemplation, we may cite the *Temple of our Souls*,[56] the treatise on unitive prayer by the same anonymous woman religious who wrote the *Evangelical Pearl*, first published in 1535 with a preface by the Cologne Carthusian Derk Loer. Soon after this, in 1543, a printed edition of the *Temple* followed, from the Antwerp press of Simon Cock. The *Pearl* has been shown to have been widely influential in the Counter-Reformation circles that we associate with Père Joseph, Benet Canfield, and Barbe Acarie; but it was not until Albert Ampe published his learned and perceptive edition of the *Temple* that students of the epoch came to see what a monument that work is to Eckhart's abiding and, it may justly be said, beneficent effects on sound contemplative thinking.

Ampe in his findings limited himself to the Eckhart sermons that Pfeiffer in 1857 admitted as genuine. Since then, standards have become more rigorous, though it will only be when Quint's fine edition of the German works has been completed by his successors that the validity of his criteria for excluding sermons admitted by Pfeiffer on the grounds of a medieval attribution will become fully apparent. Then those that he accepted and Quint rejected must be examined again for their doctrinal content, their language, and their style. Provisionally, one would say that Quint's rules for accepting such attributions—correspondence of their teachings with articles from "In agro dominico," allusion to them in the Defense, and so forth—are well devised, but that one would have wished for some exposition of Quint's reasons for deciding that others should be treated as spurious.

But, in the *Temple*, there is one outstanding passage where Quint's possible objections to a sermon adduced by Ampe as an Eckhart parallel would be overridden by its close correspondence with another, *Sermon 52, Beati pauperes spiritu*, admitted by Quint and all other critics to be genuine.

In chapter 11 of the *Temple*, its author writes:

> So when all things keep an inner silence in the soul, which has run its full course in the heavens, then there is that inward encounter in the soul, in which the holy Trinity has formed itself and made a heaven and united itself. In this heaven there cannot be rest, nor can there be any ascent, because the soul has once again been united in its beginning and its source, which is the divine essence, and within its chamber it rejoices in the holy Trinity; and since that power of the soul which is then called *memoria* is united and established with the heavenly Father, he then gives it true joy and a secure repose. And the second power, which is then called "understanding," is also one with the Son, who so illumines it that the soul attains a clarity in which it does not seek its source, for it finds that source in him; and the third power, which is then called "will," is one with the Holy Spirit, and with him is set free and united in a silenced love, and is free of all things which could perturb its dwelling-place; and the soul is free of itself and offers God no resistance, so that it may say: "I am no-one's 'soul', and no-one is my 'God'."[57]

Many characteristics of this passage are so evident as to need no comment: The Augustinian conception of the soul and its powers as a "created Trinity," and his teaching, which he learned from others, on *regyratio*, the soul's turning back out of its "land of unlikeness" to the place from which it had strayed and where it was first placed, like to its God. But what is salient appears in the conclusion: "I am no-one's 'soul' and no-one is my 'God'." The allusion in this and its justification are found in Eckhart's *Sermon* 52: "If he finds a man so poor as this, then God performs his own work, and the man is in this way suffering God to work, and God is his own place to work in, and so God is his own worker in himself. Thus in this poverty man pursues that everlasting being which he was and which he is now and which he will evermore remain."[58] In this, the author shows that she knows how to accept what is essential in Eckhart's teaching, that in prayer the contemplating soul can be one with God, as the Son and his Father are one, beyond perception of difference, but still that she knows how to avoid the extremes, of highly dubious ancestry, of his demonstrations, in *Sermon* 52 and elsewhere, of what is "poverty of the will,"[59] how to rest safely in simple affirmation, shorn of his extravagances and his frequent self-contradictions.

If the author of the *Temple* and the *Pearl* understood that Eckhart's teachings had been condemned, she seems not to have troubled herself on that score. Medieval heresy hunters loved to use the parable of Matthew 13, of the weed-strewing enemy and the fire that should destroy his handiwork; but she seems rather to have taken as her counsel the words of Jeremias: "What has the wheat to do with the chaff?"—and in this we might all well follow her.

—Edmund Colledge

2. THEOLOGICAL SUMMARY

A. Principles of Interpretation

Perhaps the only real consensus among students of Eckhart is that he is not an easy author to read. The widely divergent, frequently erroneous uses to which he has been put spring almost as much from the manner of his presentation as they do from the profundity of what he has to say. Not all of this can be blamed on the Meister himself. The condition of the text of his surviving works is partly at fault. The Latin works exist in only a few manuscripts and comprise a fragment of what Eckhart intended to write. The German treatises and sermons come down to us in over two hundred manuscripts, but with texts so faulty and problems of authenticity so serious that over a century of scholarship has still not solved all the issues. Nevertheless, the excellent critical edition of the Deutsche Forschungsgemeinschaft, now well past its fortieth year, provides a solid starting point both for the translations found here and for penetration of Eckhart's meaning.

Meister Eckhart was not only a highly trained philosopher and theologian, but also a preacher, a poet, and a punster who deliberately cultivated rhetorical effects, bold paradoxes, and unusual metaphors, neologisms, and wordplay to stir his readers and hearers from their intellectual and moral slumber. If even the technical Latin of his scholastic works at times displays these characteristics, how much more true this is for the vernacular texts. Generations of scholars have admired the Meister as one of the crucial figures in the development of German, especially with regard to its speculative vocabulary, and have praised him as a master of German prose.[1] While Eckhart's creative handling of language is one of the major attractions of his style, it often does not make the task of understanding him any easier. Nevertheless, the Meister's style is both attractive and difficult primarily because of

24

the depth and quality of his message. This part of the Introduction will attempt to provide an entrance for the beginner into what Eckhart has to say.

In his survey of the major themes of Eckhart's thought, Josef Quint, the editor of the Meister's vernacular works, admitted the insurmountable difficulties confronting any attempt at a brief introduction to so complex and controversial an author, and expressed the hope that the completion of the critical edition would help overcome this problem.[2] A quarter century later, with the edition far closer to completion, the difficulties seem at least as great, largely because of the variety of interpretations from which Eckhart's thought has been viewed in recent years.[3] The lesson to be drawn from this is evident. One mark of Meister Eckhart's stature as a major thinker in the history of Western theology and spirituality is that there can never be any "final" interpretation of Eckhart. No more than with Augustine, Anselm, Aquinas, or Bonaventure can we hope to attain an ultimate interpretation. He measures us more than we measure him. Hence the function of any introduction to his thought, short or long, is to serve as a set of preliminary guidelines for the real task at issue, the reading of the Meister.

While the systematic foundation of Eckhart's thought found in the *Work of Propositions* of the *Three-Part Work* survives only in fragmentary fashion,[4] the major themes of his system are evident throughout his Latin and German works, even at times repetitiously so. It is not so much a question of what these themes are—they have been studied in a host of works—as rather what interpretive principles must be established in order to clarify the relationship among them that is the task of an introduction.

The first principle on which this presentation and the selections translated in this volume have been based is that Eckhart cannot be understood without paying equal attention to both the Latin and the German works. Approaches that would favor the subtle scholastic theologian over the extravagant vernacular preacher, or reverse this by championing the originality of the German works over the more arid style of the Latin treatises and sermons, can never give us the full Eckhart. We must grasp the interaction between the *Lesemeister* (master of the Schools) and *Lebemeister* (master of preaching and living) if we wish to try to understand Eckhart whole.

As a loyal son of Saint Dominic from his early years, Eckhart's life was centered on preaching. For any Dominican the goal of the theology of the Schools was not speculation for its own sake, but for the sake of preaching. Eckhart's adherence to this fundamental concern of the Dominican life is evident not least of all in the special character of his scriptural commentaries, as Josef Koch, the editor of the Latin works, has shown.[5] In comparison with those of Thomas Aquinas, for example, the Meister's expositions demonstrate a desire to provide the preacher with apt interpretations of key texts rather than a concern for a total systematic exposition of a book of the Bible. Both the form and the content of the commentaries that are the largest part of the Meister's surviving Latin production show how central preaching was for him.

The importance of taking the Latin and the German works together as two sides of the same coin cannot be overstressed, especially if we reflect on the differences that obtain between the formulation of theology and its communication to the Church at large.[6] Though it is true that certain themes receive more explicit treatment in Eckhart's vernacular preaching than in his academic writings,[7] it is evident that these themes are based on and only comprehensible within a total theological picture that cannot be grasped apart from the technical scholastic works. Even though some essential principles of the Meister's thought analyzed at length in the Latin works appear only infrequently in explicit fashion in the vernacular ones,[8] Eckhart's preaching would be incomprehensible without them.

The second principle that has guided the formation of this volume is the necessity of viewing the total Eckhart from a theological perspective. Like so many medieval Schoolmen, the Meister has usually been treated within the context of the history of philosophy. It would be foolish to deny that Eckhart has a profound and subtle metaphysic of his own, but it would be even more misleading not to realize that this philosophy has its existence within a system that is primarily theological in intention. The point is important enough to call for some development.

B. THE NATURE OF THEOLOGY
AND THE ROLE OF SCRIPTURE

On the basis of his clear distinction between the realms of nature and grace, Thomas Aquinas had argued for the existence of a science above and beyond the "theology," or teaching about God, that was the highest part of Aristotle's speculative philosophy. This science, which Thomas preferred to call *sacra doctrina* (sacred teaching), conveyed both truths about God, such as his existence, that were accessible (though with difficulty) to human reason and the truths necessary for salvation that utterly surpassed the human intellect, such as the Trinity and the mystery of the God-man.[9] This clarity appears lost when we turn to Eckhart. The Meister seems to give away too much to reason, as when he effortlessly intermingles natural and revealed truths in the commentary on John's Prologue translated here.[10] Perhaps the only place where the Meister explicitly asserts that a truth of faith is inaccessible to reason is in a discussion of the manner of Christ's presence in the Eucharist.[11] All this seems grist for the mill of those who would see Eckhart primarily as a philosopher or metaphysician.[12]

Judged by Thomistic standards this may well be so, but the Meister's own position on the relation of faith and reason is closer to the theological traditions of Christian Platonism than to the new precisions of Thomas Aquinas. What is fundamental to Eckhart is the striking agreement between what is revealed in scripture and the truths that natural reason can uncover.[13] As he says in commenting on how the Incarnation forms a mid-point between the emanations in God and the production of creatures:

> Thus holy scripture can be interpreted according to this in a very fitting way, so that what the philosophers have written about the natures and properties of things agree with it, especially since everything that is true, whether in being or knowing, in scripture or in nature, proceeds from one source and one root of truth.... Therefore, Moses, Christ and the Philosopher teach the same thing, differing only in the way they teach, namely as worthy of belief, as probable or likely, and as truth.[14]

Thomas Aquinas would have agreed that there could be no real contradiction between the truths of revelation and what could be known by reason, but he would not have been so sanguine about the ability of philosophy to penetrate divine mysteries properly speaking. Eckhart, however, is uncompromising in his conviction that reason can find proofs for the truths revealed in scripture, even going beyond Augustine in relation to natural proofs for key passages in John's Prologue.[15] It is important to note, however, that for Eckhart natural and revealed truths are virtually coextensive only in content, not in the mode of their apprehension. What the philosophers teach as merely probable or likely, Christ, the Truth, teaches as absolutely true.[16] What the heathen philosophers see only by the light of reason, the saints see securely by a higher light in the Holy Spirit.[17] In adherence to the tradition of "faith seeking understanding," the believer would be a lazy coward not to seek out natural reasons and likenesses for what he believes.[18] Thus the Meister presents the purpose of his theological masterpiece, the *Commentary on John,* as "to explain what the holy Christian faith and the two Testaments maintain through the help of the natural arguments of the philosophers."[19] But these "arguments" do not form the basis for the believer's certainty and security. True philosophy—what we would call theology—is based on the study of the scriptures and has as its goal the work of the preacher, however much it may strive to make use of natural reasons and examples. This is the perspective from which Eckhart wrote and preached.

This position on the relation of faith and reason shows that in order to understand Eckhart's thought it is also necessary to grasp his theory of the interpretation of scripture. The majority of his surviving Latin works are exegetical in character,[20] and his numerous Latin and German sermons are also based on biblical texts. A glance at his theory of exegesis is essential, for, as the Meister once put it, scripture is a deep sea in which paradoxically lambs may walk, cows swim, and elephants sink.[21]

The Meister's major theoretical reflection on the interpretation of scripture is found in the prologue to the *Book of the Parables of Genesis.*[22] From this it is clear that Eckhart's approach to the Bible was based on a twofold division of senses, the "more evident sense" treated in the first Genesis commentary, and the sense hidden "under the shell of the letter" exemplified in the second work. All classical Christian exegesis is based on such a division, but Eckhart's understanding of it has special accents. First of all, it is significant to note how strongly he was influenced by the great Jewish religious thinker Maimonides in the theoretical aspects of his exposition of the hidden meaning.[23] He does not make use of the traditional fourfold scheme of senses (the literal and the three divisions of the hidden, spiritual meaning: allegorical, moral or tropological, and anagogical), nor does he favor the term "allegory" to describe the hidden sense, as many medieval authors did.

Rather he makes use of "mystical meaning," "figure," and especially "parable" and "in a parabolical manner" (*parabolice*—a term he learned from Maimonides) as a way of describing the inner meaning of scripture.[24] The Meister specifies the content of the inner meaning as divided into theological, natural, and moral truths,[25] a position found first in Jerome and one naturally appealing to his own view of the relation of what is found in scripture to what has been discovered by the philosophers.[26] As a succinct text in the *Commentary on Exodus* puts it: "Sacred scripture frequently tells a story in such a way that it also contains and suggests mysteries, teaches the natures of things, furnishes and sets in order moral actions."[27]

On the question of how one argues from scripture, Eckhart's position is somewhat ambiguous. He cites Thomas Aquinas's famous text (*STh* Ia.1.10) that defends the unity of the literal sense, that is, that the words of scripture can mean only one thing; but it is clear from the context that he really sides with Augustine who, especially in the twelfth book of the *Confessions*, argued that since God who knows all things is the proper author of scripture, every true sense of a passage may be called a literal sense.[28] Eckhart does agree with Thomas on two important issues, but in each case in his own way. From Thomas he learned that the literal sense of a passage may be metaphorical (e.g., to speak of God's "arm" is really a metaphor for his power), but with characteristic boldness he extends this to cover the whole third chapter of Genesis, a position for which he was attacked at Cologne.[29] Also, the Meister sides with Thomas (*STh* Ia.1.10. ad 1) to the extent that he does not claim to *prove* divine, natural, and ethical truths through parabolical arguments, but only uses them to show the agreement of what is intimated through parables and what has been demonstrated elsewhere in the *Work of Questions* and the *Work of Commentaries*.[30] In practice, however, the mode of argumentation in the *Book of Parables* is not appreciably different from his procedure in the other scriptural commentaries. Indeed, it is not always easy to see where literal reading ceases and spiritual interpretation begins, because his admission of the multiplicity of the literal sense allows him to adopt a deeply speculative approach in almost all his exegetical work. Like Augustine, whose *Literal Commentary on Genesis* was one of Eckhart's favorite works, the Meister's exegesis, even in its professedly literal moments, seeks to penetrate to the deepest level of what God has revealed.

INTRODUCTION

C. THE STRUCTURE OF REALITY
AND THE DIVINE NATURE

Guided by the above principles, we may now turn to the presentation of the main themes and inner coherence of Eckhart's theology. There are, of course, many ways to approach the thought of Eckhart. In one of the sermons translated here, the Meister provides a succinct description of the four major themes of his preaching—detachment, being formed again into God, the nobility of the soul, and the purity of the divine nature.[31] These themes present one avenue by which Eckhart's system might be presented, but perhaps a text from another of the sermons given here may afford a better starting point from which to grasp the dynamic inner unity of the major components of his teaching. Toward the end of the noted *Sermon 52* we read, "A great authority says that his breaking through (*durchbrechen*) is nobler than his flowing out (*ûzvliezen*); and that is true."[32] The same theme is present in *Sermon 15*, where it is used to interpret Luke's parable of the "noble man" who went out into a foreign land and came back richer than he went out,[33] and in *Sermon 22*, where it is expressed in the language of love drawn from the Song of Songs: "When he [the Bridegroom] went out (*ûzgienc*) from the highest place of all, he wanted to go in again (*wider îngân*) with his bride to the purest place of all. . . ."[34] It is also ascribed to God in *Sermon 53*, where we read, "God's going out is his going in," and "They [created things] are all called to return into whence they have flowed out."[35] Something quite similar appears also in the Latin works. In *Sermon XXV.1* we find it expressed in terms of the theology of grace: "Yet first grace consists in a flowing out (*effluxus*) or going out from God; second grace in a flowing back (*refluxus*) or return into God himself."[36] In another place it describes the saving works of the Trinity: "Hence it is necessary that all things be bathed in the blood of Christ and led back into the Father through the Son's mediation, just as the Father does all things through the Son; and so the flowing back will correspond to the flowing out."[37] These texts are cited not so much for any unique importance of their own as for the suggestion they afford that Eckhart's thought, like that of most other Christian Platonists before him, can be viewed as a dynamic system whose basic law is the flowing out (*exitus, effluxus, ûzvliezen*) of all things from God and the corresponding flowing back or return of all to this ineffable source (*reditus, refluxus, durchbrechen, îngânc*).

Although the pattern of emanation and return shows us what Eck-

30

hart has in common with a long and honored theological tradition, it is more important to specify the way in which the Meister made this general scheme his own. While systematization always results in some artificiality, it is nonetheless in conformity with Eckhart's thought to present the flowing out of all things from the divine ground in two broad stages: first, the inner emanation of the Trinitarian Persons, or *bullitio* as he calls it; and second, the creation of all things, or *ebullitio*, that is modeled on it.[38] Similarly, the return of all things to God can also be said to take place in the two broad stages that describe the *reditus* of the soul to its divine ground: The birth of the Word in the soul, and the "breaking-through," or penetration of the soul into the divine ground that is the God beyond God.

The divine depth, abyss, or ground (MHG: *grunt*) is the hidden source from which all things proceed and to which they return. Although the tradition of negative theology is long and rich, it has had few spokesmen to equal Eckhart. Like Saint Augustine and many others before him,[39] the Meister was fully conscious of the paradox involved in attempting to speak about what by definition could not be spoken about. This paradox by no means reduced him to silence, any more than it did his predecessors and successors in the tradition of negative or apophatic theology. But the absolute centrality of apophaticism in the Meister's thought, so splendidly expressed especially in the German sermons,[40] prompts two important observations. The first is that the task of theology for Eckhart was not so much to reveal a set of truths about God as it was to frame the appropriate paradoxes that would serve to highlight the inherent limitations of our minds and to mark off in some way the boundaries of the unknown territory where God dwells. Here too theology is ordered to preaching and through preaching to life. Only when we have come to realize what it is that we cannot realize can we begin to live out of the unknowable divine ground of our being. Second, the absolute ineffability of God provides the motive for the at times confusing variety of ways in which the Meister speaks about the divine nature. Eckhart used a number of verbal strategies or approaches to fit different circumstances and audiences. None of these strategies, taken in itself, is final; all of them taken together exhibit an inner coherence and unity of purpose as ways to explore those "limit-situations" in which God becomes present to us in a more conscious way. These strategies at times led the Meister to insist with force that it is impossible to apply any predicate of ours to God. One such passage denying the appropriateness of the language of

31

goodness to God appears among the appended articles to the Bull "In agro dominico."[41] But Eckhart also did ascribe a wide variety of terms and predicates to God, and this variation has introduced two serious problems in the interpretation of his thought that we must examine before we turn our attention to the flowing out and the breaking through of all things.

The first of these problems concerns which of the transcendental predicates of existence, unity, truth, and goodness (*esse, unum, verum, bonum*) is most appropriate to the divine nature. It is well known that in the only surviving part of the *Work of Propositions*, its prologue, Eckhart begins his systematic *summa* with an analysis of the proposition *Esse Deus est*, "Existence is God,"[42] while in the *Parisian Questions*, especially the first, he affirms that God is properly described as *intelligere*, the act of understanding that is above *esse*.[43] A similar variation is found throughout the Latin and German works, where a multitude of references to God as undifferentiated existence, or *esse simpliciter* or *indistinctum*, is qualified by frequent appearances of texts asserting that God is in some way beyond *esse*.[44] Intermittent passages, both early and late, continue to assert a priority to God conceived of as pure intellect or understanding.[45]

The best way to cut through this complicated issue and to present the coherence of the ways the Meister speaks of the divine nature is to be attentive to the way in which his theories of predication and analogy call for an understanding of God best expressed in a dialectical grasp of the transcendental predicate of *unum*, or Absolute Unity.[46] The Meister's doctrine of predication (that is, how terms are affirmed of the subject of a proposition) and his understanding of analogy (that is, how to use terms that are partly the same and partly different in meaning) are both Thomistic in outer appearance, but essentially different from Thomas in inner intent. Both predication and analogy, as understood by Eckhart, stress the radical difference between God and creation. His notion of analogy rests on formal opposition rather than on proportionality or intrinsic attribution, as is made clear in a number of places in the Latin works.[47] In the *Sermons and Lectures on Ecclesiasticus* he says:

> Analogates have nothing of the form according to which they are analogically ordered rooted in positive fashion in themselves, but every created being is analogically ordered to God in existence, truth and goodness. Therefore, every created be-

32

ing radically and positively possesses existence, life and wisdom from and in God and not in itself.[48]

What this means is that if *esse* or existence is understood in its proper transcendental sense (*esse simpliciter*), it can be properly predicated of God alone and not of creatures. Two conclusions follow from this. The first is that creatures are nothing *in themselves*, that is, insofar as they are creatures, but they possess all their being radically or virtually in the divine *esse*. This was one of the doctrines for which Eckhart was condemned at Avignon.[49] The second conclusion is that from this perspective it is proper to describe God as the existence of things. As *Sermon* 6 puts it: "If my life is God's being, then God's existence (*sîn*) must be my existence, and God's is-ness (*isticheit*) is my is-ness, neither less nor more."[50] To the unwary such expressions—and they are frequent in Eckhart—may look like a species of pantheism, but such is not the case. The Meister is always anxious to maintain the totally transcendental character of the divine reality. In response to objections to such passages brought up against him during the Cologne proceedings, he invoked the distinction between the "absolute existence" (*esse absolutum*) of God and the "formally inherent existence" (*esse formaliter inhaerens*) of creatures,[51] that is, that God is the existence of all things (*esse omnium*) in an absolute sense, but not as formally inhering in them.

At this point one question naturally arises. What is the relation between formally inhering existence and absolute existence? Eckhart does not tell us in his Cologne defense, but if we look at passages on the relation of God and creatures where the Meister starts with the existence of creatures, that is, from the formally inhering existence of particular beings (what he calls *esse hoc et hoc* to distinguish it from the *esse simpliciter* of God), we find the answer given is the reverse of the first pattern of analogy seen above. In the first pattern *esse* was properly affirmed of God and therefore denied to creatures. In this second pattern it is affirmed of creatures and hence must be denied of God. "Nothing is formally in both a cause and its effect if the cause is a true cause. Now God is the cause of all existence. It follows that existence is not formally present in God."[52] In other words, if we conceive of *esse* as *esse formaliter inhaerens*, it is better to think of God's being as totally beyond *esse*.

This self-reversing character of analogy as applied to the term *esse* suggests that Eckhart's teaching about God really needed a way of speaking about the divine nature that would combine the negative (i.e., transcendent) and the positive (i.e., immanent) moments, or the simultaneous thinking of contradictory determinations, into some higher positive unity. This way of speaking forms Eckhart's dialectic, a language he learned, or perhaps better re-created, from Neoplatonism.[53]

The key to the inner coherence of the Meister's variation in predicating transcendental terms of God lies in the passages where this dialectical way of speaking becomes explicit. The most developed of these texts is found in the *Commentary on Wisdom* 7:27: "And since it [Wisdom] is one, it can do all things."[54] The predicate *unum* has special advantages from a dialectical point of view. "We must understand that the term 'one' is the same as 'indistinct' [i.e., not-to-be-distinguished],[55] for all distinct things are two or more, but all indistinct things are one."[56] Since indistinction is the distinguishing mark of *unum*, what sets it off from everything else, to conceive of God as *unum*, or Absolute Unity, is to conceive of him as simultaneously distinct and indistinct, indeed, the more distinct insofar as he is indistinct. While this may sound like mere wordplay, Eckhart's intention is totally serious. If we paraphrase the language of indistinction and distinction into the language of immanence and transcendence, we see better what the Meister was after—a way of speaking about God as simultaneously totally immanent to creatures as their real existence and *by that very fact* absolutely transcendent to them as *esse simpliciter* or *esse absolutum*.

The other advantage of the predicate *unum* is that it "sounds negative but is in reality affirmative; it is the negation of negation, which is the purest affirmation and the fullness of the term affirmed."[57] Because *unum* adds nothing to *esse*, or to any other predicate for that matter, except the negation of negation, that is, the affirmation that it is not other than itself, "it is immediately related to *esse* and signifies the purity and core and peak of *esse* itself, something which even the term *esse* does not."[58] The understanding of God as the indistinct One who is transcendentally distinct as the negation of negation appears throughout Eckhart's works,[59] although there is only one explicit discussion of the negation of negation in the vernacular sermons.[60]

If the term *unum*, or Absolute Unity, best brings out the dialectical relation of God and creatures, this does not preclude a role for other transcendental terms as well. Thus understanding (*intelligere*) can be used as a fitting attribute for the divine nature because of its special relationship with *unum*. What is it to understand other than to become one or to be one with what is understood? Hence from the time of the *Parisian Questions* through a variety of later texts,[61] *intelligere* was used as an appropriate term to ascribe to the reality of the divine nature. But the fact remains that it is *esse*, understood as Absolute Existence, that was Eckhart's most frequently employed term for God. Texts that stress the dialectical meaning of *esse* at times even seem to give it some form of priority over *unum* as the most appropriate predicate for the divine ground. Two key texts occur in the *Commentary on John*. In commenting upon John 10:30, Eckhart says that *esse* is what is absolute and undetermined in God, that is, the hidden Godhead or essence, so that *unum* is ascribed to the Father, *verum* and *bonum* to the Son and the Holy Spirit.[62] The grounds for this become clear in a subsequent reflection on the dialectical character of being:

> The idea of being (*ens*) is that it is something common and indistinct and distinguished from other things by its own indistinction. In the same way, God is distinguished by his indistinction from any other distinct thing, and this is why in the Godhead the essence or existence (*essentia sive esse*) is unbegotten and does not beget.[63]

Hence it is evident that it is not so much whether we choose to use *esse*, *unum*, or *intelligere* as the most appropriate transcendental predicate for the divine ground or essence in any particular context; it is rather that in making use of each we grasp the ineluctably dialectical character of their application to God.[64]

The two patterns of relating the divine essence to the Trinity of Persons that Eckhart uses—the one where the essence is identified with *unum*, the Persons with *ens*, *verum* and *bonum;* and the other where the essence is *esse*, and *unum*, *verum* and *bonum* are the Persons—raise the second major problem connected with the Meister's ways of speaking about God, the priority he gives to the hidden Godhead, the God beyond God.[65] It would be foolish to deny that Eckhart holds to such a priority, just as it is evident that he did not feel that this in any way conflicted with his Christian belief that the Father, Son, and Holy Spirit were each fully God in the most proper sense of the term. His Avignon judges and Pope John XXII, however, did not agree that his account of the equality of the three Persons with the divine essence was an adequate theological explanation of Christian faith, for they included two articles relating to it in the Bull of condemnation.[66]

In order to grasp the full complexity of the Meister's thought in this area we must once again advert to the priority of the apophatic way, bearing in mind that his most intricate arguments and daring assertions are no more than appropriate paradoxes to help us along the path to union with the God who is "one without unity and three without trinity."[67] The implications of Eckhart's stress on the priority of the divine ground come out in a number of ways. In the Latin works the priority of the undifferentiated ground of the Godhead is the root for two significant differences between his teaching and that of Thomas Aquinas. Unlike Thomas, for whom the plurality of divine attributes (e.g., existence, simplicity, goodness, truth, etc.) has a foundation in the inexhaustible richness of the divine essence as well as in our own mode of understanding, for Eckhart any plurality comes solely from the poverty of our way of conceiving God.[68] This also explains why Eckhart cites without disapproval the suspect view of Gilbert of Poitiers that in God the relations that constitute the Trinity do not enter into the divine substance but remain "as if they were standing on the outside."[69] In the vernacular works the distinction between the three Persons and the hidden Godhead appears in a more pastoral vein, in the invitation to the soul to penetrate beyond the Trinity, as in this passage from *Sermon* 48:

> I speak in all truth, truth that is eternal and enduring, that this same light [the spark of the soul] is not content with the simple divine essence in its repose, as it neither gives nor receives; but it wants to know the source of this essence, it wants to go into the simple ground, into the quiet desert, into which distinction never gazed, not the Father, nor the Son, nor the Holy Spirit.[70]

There can be no distinctions in the innermost ground of God.

Such texts provided the grounds for the suspicions of Eckhart's judges and many later interpreters concerning the validity of his doctrine of God from the standpoint of Christian Trinitarianism. In order to be fair to Eckhart, though, we must also advert to another series of texts. In the Meister's writings there is no lack of passages that stress the absolute identity of the three Persons with the divine essence;[71] there are also texts that seem to hint at, if not to develop fully, a dialectical relation between the indistinct divine ground and the relational distinctions of the Persons of the Father, Son, and Holy Spirit. Thus in *Sermon* 10: "Distinction comes from the Absolute Unity, that is, the distinction in the Trinity. Absolute Unity is the distinction and distinction is the Unity. The greater the distinction, the greater the Unity, for that is the distinction without distinction."[72] Eckhart seems to be asserting that the God beyond God, the hidden ground of the Trinity, is the more indistinct insofar as he is distinct, the more one insofar as he is three. In other words, the dialectical relation between oneness and threeness in God is isomorphically similar to the transcendent-immanent relation of God to creatures. Whether this is sufficient to save the Meister from the accusations of his opponents or not is a question that must be left to the judgment of the reader, though there can be no question of the orthodox intentions of the Dominican's theology.

The dynamism of Eckhart's notion of the relation of the Trinity of Persons to the divine ground finds expression in his distinctive teaching regarding the divine *bullitio* (literally "boiling").[73] A number of crucial texts discuss this:

> The One acts as a principle (*principiat*) through itself and gives existence and is an internal principle. For this reason, properly speaking, it does not produce something like itself, but what is one and the same as itself. For what is "like" entails difference and numerical diversity, but there can be no diversity in the One. This is why the formal emanation in the divine Persons is a type of *bullitio*, and thus the three Persons are simply and absolutely one.[74]

And again:

> The repetition, namely that it says "I am who am" (Ex. 3:14), indicates the purity of affirmation excluding all negation from God. It also indicates a reflexive turning back of his existence into itself and upon itself, and its dwelling and remaining fixed in itself. It further indicates a *bullitio* or giving birth to itself—glowing in itself, and melting and boiling in and into itself. . . . Therefore, chapter one of John says, "In him was life" (Jn. 1:4). "Life" bespeaks a type of pushing out by which something swells up in itself and first breaks out totally in itself, each part into each part, before it pours itself forth and boils over on the outside (*ebulliat*).[75]

In the vernacular works *bullitio* is the equivalent to what Eckhart discusses under the heading of the "break-out" (*ûzbruch*). "The first break-out and the first melting forth is where God liquifies and where he melts into his Son and where the Son melts back into the Father."[76]

These passages introduce us to one of the most essential themes of the Meister's thought, the idea of "principle." All activity, differentiation, and causality imply a principle, and all things that are the product of activity, differentiation, and causality can be understood only when they are seen in their principle. This is as true of the dynamic process in the Godhead that gives birth to the Trinity, the reflexive conversion on itself by which the One emanates what is one with it, as it is true also of the creation, or act of *ebullitio*, by which God is the principle of all created things. The two processes exhibit a like structure, so that, as the commentary on John's Prologue makes clear,[77] every natural example of the relation of principle and what is principled contains a model of the Trinity. The differences, of course, must also be kept in mind. *Bullitio*, as formal emanation, stands in the realm of formal causality and produces a perfect image, something one and the same as itself. *Ebullitio*, which is of two kinds—the production of one thing from another, which is called making (*factio*), and the production of something from nothing (*creatio*)—is in the realm of efficient and final causality and always produces something that is different in number and reality from its principle.[78]

There are two patterns describing the divine *bullitio* found in Eckhart. The first of these places the principle in the hidden Godhead itself. Following Thomas Aquinas, Eckhart affirms that "the power of generating in the Godhead directly and more principally belongs to the essence than to the relation that is the Paternity."[79] But there is a second pattern that concentrates on the Person of the Father. "The Father is a beginning of the divinity, for he understands himself, and out of this the Eternal Word proceeds and yet remains within, and the Holy Spirit flows from them both."[80] This latter is more frequent in Eckhart's writings and receives a number of formulations, such as the Father as *unum* begetting the Son as *verum*, and the two together spirating the Holy Spirit as *bonum*, a teaching based on Augustine.[81] Typically Eckhartian is the "principial" analysis of the Father as "Unbegotten Justice" and the Son as "Begotten Justice,"[82] as well as the way in which he explains the Son as the image (*imago*) of the Father.[83] The act of vision is frequently used as a natural analogue for the formal emanation by which the Father produces the Son.[84] But it is the Johannine language of the second Person as the *Logos*, or Word of God, that is central for the German Dominican. "In the beginning," or Principle, that is, the Father, "was the Word," or Son, and since the Word cannot exist without its breath or spirit, also the Holy Spirit.[85]

D. Creation (*EBULLITIO*) and the Fall

The differences between *bullitio* and *ebullitio*, between the emanation of the divine Persons and the creation of the universe, were frequently highlighted by the Meister,[86] but their inner connection was never in question. In the text of Psalm 61:12, "God has spoken once and for all, and I have heard two things," he found a parabolical message that illuminated the inner relation between the two modes of production. God's speaking once and for all is the utterance of his Only-Begotten Word, but the two things that are simultaneously heard are the emanation of the divine Persons in the Trinity and the creation of the whole universe, whose exemplary principle is the Eternal Word.[87] Of course we must remember that insofar as he is the efficient cause of the universe, God acts as one, that is, all three Persons work as one principle.[88] For this reason Eckhart makes frequent use of the standard definitions and analyses of the act of creation throughout his works. Thus he insists that creation is the production of all things from nothing, the immediate conferring of existence on all things,[89] an operation in which God, who works more as final than as efficient cause, acts from complete freedom and not from any necessity, as the Arab philosophers had suggested.[90] It is because of this strong emphasis on the Absolute Unity of God the Creator that Eckhart so often turned to the fall into duality or number as a way of explaining the relation between *bullitio* and *ebullitio*—another indication of the primacy of a dialectical understanding of *unum* in his metaphysics.[91] What is distinctive of the Meister's own teaching on creation, however, is the way in which his analysis from the principial point of view highlights the exemplary activity of the divine Word or Logos.

Eckhart had stressed that "the metaphysician, who considers the entity of things, proves nothing through exterior causes, that is, the efficient and final causes,"[92] and so it comes as no surprise how important a role he gives to the second Person of the Trinity, who is the Image, Logos, Idea, and Ideal Reason of all things. The interpretation of the *in principio* of the opening of Genesis as both "beginning" and "principle" and its identification with the Word had been current in Latin theology since the days of Ambrose,[93] but Eckhart's adaptation of this exegesis shows special accents. Both of the Genesis commentaries and the *Commentary on John* contain investigations of what it means to say that the Word is the principle of creation.[94] The exegesis of John's Prologue gives seven different interpretations of the verse "In the beginning was the Word" as a means of understanding the Word's place and role in the Trinity. Just as the Word exists as Logos, Idea, and Image in the mind of the Father who is his Principle,[95] so too that Logos serves as the exemplary cause by which God creates all that he creates.[96] The four essential attributes of any principle given in section 38 of the text neatly sum up the Meister's teaching on the role of the Logos. An essential principle must contain what it is principle of as a "cause contains its effect" and "in a prior and more eminent way" than the thing is in itself. Such a principle "is always pure intellect" in which the effect exists as "equal in duration to the principle." Eckhart concludes: "The three latter conditions are expressed through 'the Word,' that is, the Idea."[97] This is more poetically put in one of the vernacular sermons in terms of the flowing out and its corresponding return: "Therefore, the Father speaks the Son always, in unity, and pours out in him all created things. They are all called to return into whence they have flowed out. All their life and their being is a calling and a hastening back to him from whom they have issued."[98]

Eckhart's principial analysis of the relation of creation to its divine source stresses the virtual existence all things possess in their Idea, that is, in the Word of God, and for a Neoplatonic theologian like Eckhart this virtual existence is what is "really real" in any creature.[99] Since God's Word has been spoken from all eternity, indeed, is being spoken from all eternity (if God is a Father, he must always be uttering the Word that is his Son), then the virtual existence of all things, when viewed in the Principle, is always being spoken by the Father in the one and the same eternal act in which he speaks the Son. From the viewpoint of the formally inherent existence that creatures possess in themselves creation does indeed have a temporal beginning—there are assertions to this effect in the Meister's writings[100]—but it was Eckhart's claims for the eternal aspect of the "deep" reality of creation, a position he felt clearly supported by texts in Augustine,[101] that was the source for some of the most serious objections to his theology. The first three propositions that "In agro dominico" condemned as clearly heretical are expressions of the Meister's teaching on the eternity of creation.

The first and third of these condemned propositions are drawn from a passage in the *Commentary on Genesis* translated here. "In one and the same time in which he was God and in which he begat his co-eternal Son as God equal to himself in all things, he also created the world."[102] This teaching is found in both the Latin and German works.[103] It is instructive to note how Eckhart defended his position on the eternity of creation at Cologne and at Avignon. The eighth of the propositions drawn from the *Commentary on Genesis* in the first Cologne list of suspect passages was that noted above. Eckhart supported it by distinguishing between action and passion: God's activity, as identical with his being, always takes place in the simple now of eternity, but it does not follow from this that creation in itself, considered as a *passio,* is eternal.[104] Eckhart's Avignon investigators did not accept his use of this defense, noting that in Aristotelian philosophy *actio* and *passio* always coincide in one movement that is formally in the patient or thing moved.[105] The point is well taken, and we do not know what Eckhart's reply might have been. What the exchange does point up is that the Meister was really speaking a different theological language, one not so much based on the traditional Aristotelian understanding of *actio* and *passio* as one founded on a Neoplatonic notion of the relation of the created temporal image to its eternal virtual existence in the archetype, as he tried to say in one of the Latin sermons: "Only God's action is new, because the Word is always being born and the created thing is always coming to be according to that existence which in itself precedes motion, though the thing is not always being created."[106]

Many of the technical details of Eckhart's doctrine of creation and his metaphysics set forth in the passages translated here need not delay us, since his expositions are quite clear;[107] but two important aspects of *ebullitio* deserve further comment: The unity of creation, and the role of man and the soul. The Meister's response to the query how the divine One can produce a universe that is multiple without the intervention of a series of intermediate emanations was to emphasize that the intention of God in creating falls first of all on the whole, the *one* universe composed of many levels designed to work harmoniously together to reach its end, God as Absolute Unity.[108] Of the three levels (viz., existence, life, and intelligence) that together form the universe,[109] in the concrete order it is intelligent being that holds the supreme place.[110] Each level exists principially in the next highest level, so that mere being is life in living being and living being is intellect in intellectual being.[111] To extend this is to recognize that intellectual

41

being in its principle, that is, God, is divine. This was the source of some of Eckhart's most profound insights, as well as some of his most paradoxical and dangerous statements.

As the Meister put it in *Sermon* 15, "Truly you are the hidden God (Is. 45:15), in the ground of the soul, where God's ground and the soul's ground are one ground."[112] The same theme appears frequently in the German sermons translated here, especially in the discussion of the hidden power in the soul in *Sermon* 2.[113] Eckhart uses many metaphors for this hidden power, the most common being the "spark" (*vünkelîn*),[114] and the "little town, or castle" (*bürgelîn*).[115] Its identity with the divine ground is the source of the parallel ineffability of God and the soul found in a number of texts.[116] Such a "negative anthropology" echoes positions found in a number of earlier authors and is not without parallel in contemporary theology.[117] Like the God beyond God, man can thus be spoken of as at once distinct and indistinct in relation to all things: "Just as God is most indistinct in himself according to his nature, in that he is truly and properly one and completely distinct from other things, so too man in God is indistinct from everything that is in God, for 'everything is in him' (Rm. 11:36), and at the same time he is completely distinct from all things."[118]

The most dangerous formulation of this theme in Eckhart's thought was the claim that there was something in the soul that was uncreated—"Sometimes I have spoken of a light that is uncreated and not capable of creation, and which is within the soul."[119] One such passage was condemned as heretical in the Avignon Bull, though with the proviso that Eckhart denied having made such statements.[120] This denial is puzzling. Eckhart did make such statements throughout his defense,[121] but there are just too many texts scattered through the vernacular works indicating that he used such language to be convinced that his protestations were objectively justified.[122] Perhaps we can hazard the following explanation. The Meister did speak of something in the soul that was uncreated, but took his judges' citations of these texts as indications that they thought he held that part of the soul was created and another part uncreated,[123] and hence he denied the texts. What remains puzzling, though, is why he did not defend his language by explaining its true intention, that is, that he was speaking principially of the virtual existence of the ground of the soul in God.

Despite the importance of such a difficult problem as the meaning of the uncreated part of the soul, it is more important to investigate how Eckhart portrays the relation of the spiritual and the material dimensions of human nature in order to grasp the full dimensions of his theological anthropology. Several of the texts translated here, especially *Sermons* 2 and 83, and the passage from the *Book of the Parables of Genesis* exegeting the third chapter of Genesis, are crucial for the understanding of this aspect of his thought. The division between the outer and inner man, an Augustinian commonplace based on Pauline texts, was frequently invoked by the Meister;[124] but it was another Augustinian motif—the moral interpretation of Genesis, chapter three, in which the serpent indicates the sensitive faculty, the woman the lower reason directed to externals, and the man the higher reason directed to God—that provides the basis for Eckhart's most extended anthropological investigation.[125] What is most significant about this treatment is how it emphasizes the hierarchical ordering of man's powers to their divine source through the intimate conversation and union in the kiss of love, which characterizes the relation of the higher reason to God.[126]

Still, it must be admitted that the language of this Latin passage with its emphasis on the union of superior reason with God is in general less radical than the discussions found in such texts as *Sermons* 2 and 83. *Sermon* 83 contains a traditional analysis of six powers of the soul, three inferior—rational (here the discretionary power of sense experience), irascible, and appetitive—and three superior—the Augustinian triad of memory, understanding, and will; but it goes beyond tradition in arguing for the identity of the latter with the divine ground.[127] *Sermon* 2 states that we must go beyond the intellectual power that "neither time nor flesh touches," as well as the volitional power that "flows out of the spirit and remains in the spirit and is wholly spiritual" in order to reach the essential hidden ground where the soul is identical with God.[128] Without trying to minimize the difference between the more traditional Latin text and the more radical German ones, the notion of man as the image of God (*imago Dei*) provides a way of seeing the inner harmony of Eckhart's anthropology. The Word, the true *imago Dei*, is fully one with the Father in all things, the perfect expression of formal emanation.[129] Following an ambivalence present in traditional Latin theology, which sometimes spoke of the soul as the image of God and sometimes as made *to* the image of God—that is, to the Word[130]—Eckhart also found it useful to oscillate between "radical" formulations, man as the *imago Dei*, which highlight the identity of God's ground and the soul's ground,[131] and "conservative" assertions, man as *ad imaginem Dei*, which emphasize the important differences between God and the soul.[132] Both sets of expressions are truly Eckhartian; and though he gives us no explicit framework in which to relate them, it can be suggested that the dialectical model already seen may also be helpful here. Both formulae should be taken together as expressions of the soul's distinct/indistinct relation to God.[133]

Having presented the broad lines of Meister Eckhart's picture of the universe that God created in the divine act of overflowing *ebullitio*, we must turn our attention to the problem of sin and evil, the forces that have disrupted the inner harmony of that universe. The Meister's remarks on evil align with the traditional Augustinian doctrine that evil taken in itself is nothing,[134] a defect not an effect,[135] a lack of order,[136] the privation of a good rather than anything positive.[137] He is also in line with tradition in the person of Thomas Aquinas in the explanation he gives for God's permission of evil: "The existence of evil is required by the perfection of the universe, and evil itself exists in what is good and is ordered to the good of the universe, which is what creation primarily and necessarily regards."[138] Nevertheless, it must be said that like most strongly Neoplatonist theologians, Eckhart had little appreciation for the demonic power of evil, and when he extended his remarks into the area of moral evil, or sin, his Neoplatonic optimism led him to paradoxical positions that his inquisitors were to condemn as heretical. If evil can exist only in and through what is good, and if God allows it to be only for the sake of the good of the universe, Eckhart reasoned, then sin too exists only in and for the good and cannot be separated from it. Hence the startling expressions that upset his judges, such as, "In every work, even in an evil, I repeat, in one evil both according to punishment and guilt, God's glory is revealed and shines forth in equal fashion."[139] This passage forms article 4 of "In agro dominico," and articles 5 and 6 are taken from the same text. Articles 14 and 15 also deal with sin, specifically with claims that if it is God's will that we have sinned we should not wish not to have sinned.[140] Eckhart defended himself rather weakly against the first set of articles at Avignon by appealing to how God's patience and goodness are glorified in his toleration of sin and by citing texts from Augustine that the tribunal found not to the point.[141] In support of articles 14 and 15 he claimed: "A perfect man, knowing that God has willed and wills him to have sinned, in loving God's honor wills that he had sinned, but ought not will sin for the sake of anything that is beneath God. He also knows that God would not permit him to sin if it were not for his own betterment."[142] The theological commission gave three good reasons why this hyperbolical statement remained dangerous and erroneous.[143]

Despite these real problems in Eckhart's presentation of the doctrine of sin, there can be no question of his admission of the serious effects of sin on the order God had established for the universe. Adam's fall had destroyed the natural hierarchy in man of the sensitive power to the inferior and superior reason,[144] and thus disrupted the whole universe of which man was the microcosm and lord.[145] Actual sin in all men is slavery, dissolution of order, and fall from the One.[146] Divine initiative was called for to reintegrate the universe and bring the soul back to conscious realization of its divine ground.

E. REDEMPTION AND THE RETURN
OF ALL THINGS TO GOD

One-sided interpretations of Eckhart's comparative lack of interest in the events of salvation history and the sacramental life of the Church are misleading.[147] It is true that the Meister's style of theological reflection and his mode of preaching do tend to move through the historical aspects of the economy of salvation rapidly in order to arrive at the inner meaning, but this move was not meant to negate the role that the saving mysteries of the Incarnate Christ and their presence in the Church's life have for the believer, as a number of significant texts make clear.[148]

The saving mysteries themselves as well as their application to the believer are the work of grace, and Eckhart has important texts on the nature and effects of grace. Although every action of God in the creature can be called a grace, the Meister did distinguish between the "first grace" corresponding to creation and the work of nature and the "second grace" of redeeming love that restores the universe to God.[149] The Dominican is not so much interested in analyzing the divisions of grace,[150] or in exploring the relation between grace and free will,[151] as he is in discussing the effects of redeeming grace in man.[152] Grace is the highest form of illumination,[153] that which restores the order of man's faculties by its entry into the soul's essence,[154] that which conforms us to Christ and to God.[155] An important text contained in the response to the second series of articles questioned at Cologne, an extended scholastic *quaestio* on the metaphysics of the Incarnation, demonstrates the inner connection between the two kinds of grace and the person of the God-man.[156] On the basis of the premises that "the work of creation and of nature is ordered to the work of re-creation and grace," and that "in the work of nature and creation the work of re-creation and grace shines out," Eckhart concludes that "from the first intention the Word assumed human nature, that is, this nature in Christ, for the sake of the whole human race. By assuming that nature in him and through him he bestowed the grace of sonship and adoption on all men."[157] The redemptive Incarnation is thus the central work of grace,[158] and the source of our divine sonship, as the splendid texts commenting on John 1:14 and that expounding a parable of the love of the God-man in *Sermon* 22 show.[159] The complex relations between our sonship and that of the Word will be discussed below, but two distinctive traits of Eckhart's understanding of the Incarnation deserve mention here. In becoming man the Word's first intention was directed to each individual believer and to the whole of sinful mankind far more than it was directed to the individual man who is Christ.[160] The goal of the Incarnation was to save *fallen* mankind. Further, in taking up a human nature rather than a human person, the Word has provided the grounds for our obligation to love all persons equally and without distinction. We must love human nature in them, not what is distinct, that is, human personality.[161]

In comparison with his followers John Tauler and Henry Suso, Eckhart's thought can scarcely be called "Passion-centered"; he shows no interest at all in lingering on the physical details of Christ's suffering and death. Nevertheless, the theme of the imitation of Christ, especially in adherence to the law of the cross, does appear in enough places to show that the Meister did not in any way minimize the importance of the Passion. The most extended meditation on the significance of the cross as the model for the life of the Christian appears in *Sermon* XLV,[162] but it is also present in a number of other places, especially in the vernacular works.[163]

Similarly, there are brief treatments of the nature of the Church and of the sacraments.[164] The Meister's understanding of the Church as the Body of Christ is evident in a number of places, not least in the responses to objections concerning the understanding of the divinization of man.[165] Eckhart devotes some sermons to the sacrament of the Eucharist,[166] and discusses the Eucharist and the sacrament of Penance in the *Counsels of Discernment*.[167] Although the Meister insisted on the priority of the individual's appropriation of the divine presence within,[168] he nowhere condemned external religious practices in themselves. He merely reminded his audience (rather forcefully at times) that they were indifferent and insufficient in themselves.[169]

The Meister's message about the return or *reditus* of all things to God, the central theme of his vernacular sermons and treatises as well as a major component of his scholastic works, is primarily a message about how God works in the soul. Without denying the Church's role in the mediation of grace, the Dominican's insistence on the individual's realization of union with God is so insistent that it is easy to see why some writers have claimed that Eckhart's view of religion is purely interior. The two great stages under which Eckhart discusses the inner appropriation of God are the "Birth of the Son in the Soul," and the "Breaking-Through to the Divine Ground." They mirror the flowing-out from the divine Godhead, first the *bullitio*, and then its external copy, the *ebullitio*. Eckhart's bold and challenging ways of describing the union between God and man effected by these stages of return were to be the source of major difficulties for his inquisitors.

The Meister recommended one religious practice as absolutely essential for the return to God—detachment (MHG: *abegescheidenheit*). At first glance, no concept in his thought seems more simple, though on closer inspection the richness and subtlety of his understanding of detachment become gradually evident. Detachment appears everywhere in Eckhart's works, though nowhere more profoundly than in such vernacular texts as the short treatise *On Detachment* and the meditation on the three stages in becoming a poor, or detached, person found in *Sermon 52*. In the former he says:

> True detachment is nothing else than for the spirit to stand as immovable against whatever may chance to it of joy and sorrow, honor, shame and disgrace, as a mountain of lead stands before a little breath of wind. This immovable detachment brings a man into the greatest equality with God, because God has it from his immovable detachment that he is God, and it is from his detachment that he has his purity and his simplicity and his unchangeability.[170]

The same treatise puts the fundamental dynamic of detachment in lapidary fashion when it says: "You must know that to be empty of all created things is to be full of God, and to be full of created things is to be empty of God."[171] True as the Meister always was to the harmony of natural and revealed truth, the same basic principle of the Christian life is obvious in the nature of things. Over and over again he cites the metaphysical principle that a receptive power cannot receive a form unless it is empty of all substantial forms, as, for example, the eye can see color only because it possesses no color in itself.[172] Thus, the intellect can understand all things because it has no actual existence of its own, and the soul can receive God only when it has been totally emptied through detachment.[173] Since all creatures are nothing taken in themselves, "If you want to be perfect, you must be naked of what is nothing."[174]

The Meister's teaching on the nothingness of creatures was condemned in article 26 of "In agro dominico." What of the doctrine of detachment, which depends on it? There is no explicit condemnation of detachment in the Bull, but three articles attacked there may be described as conclusions drawn from it—these involve the Meister's notion that the purest form of detachment raises us above all desire and prayer for any particular reward (*hoc aut hoc*), even that of sanctity.[175] The detached soul does not wish for any reward from God, but only for God himself.

It is a bit surprising that the inquisitors did not seize on another aspect of the Meister's understanding of detachment that also led him into a series of daring expressions. In *On Detachment* and in a variety of other places he speaks of the detached man as being able to "compel" God's activity. Thus, detachment is greater than love because it compels God to love me;[176] or "the humble man has as much power over God as he has over himself";[177] or again the statements that the Father *must* beget the Son in the soul of the just and detached man.[178] Such language is a good expression of the Eckhartian understanding of the equality of the ground of the detached soul with the divine ground, but it could easily be misinterpreted.

In the treatise *On Detachment* Eckhart praises perfect detachment above humility, the traditional foundation of the virtues, and even above love, the crown of the Christian life.[179] These statements are not as extreme as they might sound at first, because at the end of the same work he reminds us, "Whoever longs to attain perfect detachment, let him struggle for perfect humility, and so he will come close to the divinity,"[180] and throughout his works he stresses the necessity for humility in such a way that it is obvious that perfect humility is a necessary, though not sufficient, component of perfect detachment.[181]

The question of the relation of detachment to love or charity is a more complex one, not least of all because of the many discussions of the role of love in the Meister's writings. Suggestions both within *On Detachment* and elsewhere in his writings seem to indicate that the love to which detachment is superior should be seen as a lower form of love, an "interested" love by which we are compelled to love God as our final good and to suffer all things for God's love. But love is also a part of the path to detachment and in a transcendental sense may even be identified with its goal. "And when this detachment ascends to the highest place, it knows nothing of knowing, it loves nothing of loving, and from light it becomes dark."[182] In the language of apophatic theology the highest form of knowing is unknowing, and so the hint is that the highest form of loving is to love nothing of loving in the inferior, interested form, but to love in some unknown transcendental way, or, as *Sermon* 83 puts it, to love God "as he is a non-God, a nonspirit, a nonperson, a nonimage, but as he is a pure, unmixed, bright 'One,' separated from all duality."[183] It is in this sense that Eckhart can speak of the soul's becoming "indistinct" through love: "Everything that loves what is indistinct and indistinction hates both what is distinct and distinction. But God is indistinct, and the soul loves to be indistinguished, that is, to be and to become one with God."[184] Although bridal imagery is relatively rare in Eckhart's writings, when he does make use of it, as in *Sermon* 22's description of the Word as the king who suffered his torments for love in order to lead his bride, the soul, back into the marriage chamber of the "silent darkness of the hidden Fatherhood,"[185] it is in perfect harmony with the distinctive traits of his mystical theology. The mutuality of love between the God who "loves for love" and invites man to love him "for the sake of loving God" is a constant theme in Eckhart.[186]

The relationship between detachment and love may also help us to understand the image of the individual as virgin and mother that appears in *Sermon* 2. The virgin, the person who is free of all alien images, is perfectly detached; but this is not the whole story, for such a person must become at the same time a wife, "the noblest word that one can apply to the soul," and become fruitful in God.[187] The paradox of the soul that is at once virginal and fruitful, totally detached and perfectly active in love, is the heart of Eckhart's message in this sermon. While these brief comments are not a full treatment on the role of love in Eckhart, they are sufficient to suggest that love cannot be left aside in a treatment of that interior stripping away of all created things which is both preparation and expression of the soul's movement toward union with God.[188]

Detachment and love may be described as both means and ends, part of the path to union and characteristics of union itself. Only the truly detached soul that has transcended interested love is capable of experiencing the birth of the Son or Word in the soul, the most frequent way that Eckhart speaks of union in his vernacular sermons.[189]

No part of Eckhart's thought was the center of more controversy than his preaching on the birth of the Son in the soul. As the witness of Henry of Friemar mentioned in the biographical section of this Introduction indicates,[190] concern about suspicious and dangerous understandings of this theme were current from about 1309 and do not appear to have been tied to Eckhart's use alone. Nevertheless, the Meister made the suspect theme central to his preaching. One reason for this may well have been his recognition that while the birth of Christ in the believer's heart may not have been a usual theme in thirteenth-century preaching and teaching, it was a very ancient expression in the history of Christian spirituality. As Hugo Rahner has shown,[191] the notion that Christ is born in the faithful heart through baptism has deep roots in the Greek fathers, and from the time of Gregory of Nyssa the birth of Christ in the believer was also used as a way to express the mystical union of the soul and the Logos.[192] Latin theologians also spoke of the birth of Christ in the soul, usually in ascetical and moral terms; but John the Scot, in line with Gregory and Maximus the Confessor, revived the mystical interpretation, and through him elements of it appear in Cistercian and Victorine authors.[193] While Eckhart's understanding of the birth of the Son in the soul is distinctively his own, it shows many points of contact with the tradition, both direct and indirect.[194]

The birth of the Son is omnipresent in the vernacular sermons,[195] and has been the subject of an extensive secondary literature.[196] It would be foolish here to try to give a complete survey of all the appearances of the theme and the problems it raises. Since one of the sermons given here, *Sermon 6, Iusti vivent in aeternum*, is among the most detailed treatments of the birth of the Son, we will proceed by an analysis of this text in order to get a broad look at this important part of Eckhart's teaching. We will then study some of the problems associated with it by a consideration of the condemned articles in the Bull "In agro dominico."

THEOLOGICAL SUMMARY

Sermon 6 begins with something well known from the Latin works, especially the *Commentary on John,* an investigation of the relation between the just man and justice (or its equivalent, the good or noble man and goodness).[197] The truly just man, the one who gives honor to God, is perfectly detached and seeks for no reward, not even holiness, from God.[198] We must remember that in this sermon, as elsewhere when he uses this language, the Meister is speaking of the just man *insofar as* he is just, that is, from the formal and abstract point of view; he is not speaking about the just man as a concrete existing subject or person in whom distinction coexists with identity.[199] Eckhart's various formulae expressing the equality of the just man and God as justice, and the daring claim that "God's existence (MHG: *sîn* = Latin: *esse*) must be my existence, and God's is-ness is my is-ness," must be read in this light.[200] These formulations of the absolute equality theme are used to lead into an extended treatment of the birth of the Son in the soul, the central message of the sermon.

Since the Father gives birth to the Son in eternity, and since there can be no temporal dimension in God, he is always giving birth to the Son; and since God's ground is one with the soul's ground, the eternal Father must always be giving birth to the Son within the ground of the soul. Yet more, "He gives me birth, me, his Son and the same Son."[201] Lest we think that such strong expressions represent a temporary aberration on the Meister's part, we have only to look among the other sermons translated here to find equally bold texts, such as the one that tells us, "As truly as the Father in his single nature gives his Son birth naturally, so truly does he give him birth in the most inward part of the spirit."[202] Far from stopping at statements like these, Eckhart carries his boldness yet further. Given the identity of the soul's ground and God's ground, the just man must take part in the inner life of the Trinity, the divine *bullitio* itself. As he puts it in this sermon: "I say more: He gives birth not only to me, his Son, but he gives birth to me as himself [i.e., as the Father] and himself as me and to me as his being and nature."[203] Or, as *Sermon* 22 says, "He everlastingly bore me, his only-born Son, into that same image of his eternal Fatherhood, that I may be Father and give birth to him of whom I am born. . . . And as he gives birth to his Only-Begotten Son into me, so I give him birth again into the Father."[204] If the soul is one with the Father in giving birth to the Son, it must also be one with the Holy Spirit, the spirit of love proceeding from Father and Son.[205] Finally, if the identity of ground between God and the soul shows how the latter partakes of the inner-Trinitarian *bullitio*, the same is true of the divine creative activity, or *ebullitio*. This is why *Sermon* 52 can speak of the soul as its own creator: "For in the same being of God where God is above being and above distinction, there I myself was, there I willed myself and committed myself to create this man [i.e., me]."[206]

Sermon 6's formulation of the birth of the Son in the soul was condemned at Avignon not as heretical, but as "suspect of heresy." The reason for this hedge may well have been that the pope recognized that despite the boldness of the assertion, the theme of the birth of the Son in the soul was quite capable of an orthodox interpretation. As Karl Kertz has pointed out, we must distinguish between passages in which Eckhart is speaking of the "eternal eidetic pre-existence of the soul in God" (what Eckhart calls its existence in the principle) and the texts concerning the Father's begetting me as his Only-Begotten Son after the soul has received separate created existence.[207] Even in the case of the latter texts, such as that from *Sermon* 6, it is to the orthodox doctrine of the identity of the Son in the Trinity and the Son who is generated in us by uncreated grace that Eckhart appealed in defending himself at this point. "It is the same Son without any distinction whom the Father has naturally begotten in the Trinity and whom he generates in us through grace, just as many parchments are marked with one seal and many images born in many mirrors from a single face."[208] This response makes it clear that we may distinguish, but cannot separate the principial existence of the soul in the divine nature from the begetting of the Son in us in time—the former is the metaphysical ground of the latter.

Eckhart's teaching about the birth of the Son was the basis for numerous passages stressing the identity of sonship between the good or just man and Christ, the Only-Begotten Son of God. Nothing seems to have annoyed his opponents more. There are five articles of this nature condemned in the Bull, and a sixth is similar, though it asserts equality between the just man and the whole divine nature.[209] Perhaps the most unusual and troublesome of these articles was taken from the end of *Sermon* 6. In this passage Eckhart speaks of our being totally transformed into Christ the way the sacramental bread becomes the Lord's Body. "I am so changed into him that he produces his being in me as one, not just similar."[210] Despite the unfortunate analogy employed (Eckhart rejected the heretical implications and qualified the analogy at the Cologne hearing),[211] a case has been made for the orthodox intention of the passage by claiming that it was the notion of moral identity that the Meister really wished to underline.[212] But tortuous rebuttals are not necessary, nor should we feel compelled to defend every way the Meister tried to express the identity of the Son and the regenerated just man—he certainly did not feel so compelled.[213] What is most important is to grasp the fundamental logic underlying the Dominican's way of speaking. In the numerous rebuttals Eckhart gave to the attacks on his teaching on the equality between God and man there is a definite similarity of pattern and grounding principles. Over and over again, he appealed to the traditional distinctions between our sonship and that of Christ that Christian theology had always invoked. According to the Avignon report, "He says that they are erroneous as they sound, but supports them by saying that it is the same Son of God who is the Only-Begotten in the Trinity and by whom all the faithful are sons of God through adoption."[214] The various ways in which the Meister expresses the distinction of sonships are present throughout his works, but especially prominent in the commentary on John's Prologue.[215] The Word is Son by nature, we are sons by adoption; he is the true image of the Father, we are made to the image; and, finally, we are the members of Christ, a theological position showing the Meister's acquaintance with the Thomistic understanding of the Church as the Body of Christ.[216] The distinction texts, then, are vitally important for conveying the fullness of Eckhart's teaching about the relation of the soul to the Word and for interpreting the condemned identity texts. At Avignon the Meister attempted to explain the essential hermeneutical principle for interpreting the identity texts to his judges. In his response to the article that became the thirteenth of the propositions condemned as heretical in the Bull, the one claiming that whatever is proper to the divine nature is proper also to the just and divine man, he returned to his insistence that he was speaking "insofar as" (in quantum), that is, in a formal, abstract, principial sense:

> He defends this article in that Christ is the head and we the members; when we speak, he speaks in us. The union of the Word with flesh in Christ was so great that it shares modes of predication so that God may be said to have suffered and man [to be] the creator of heaven. And Christ may be properly said to be a just man insofar as he is just, the term "insofar as" being a reduplication that excludes everything foreign to the term.[217]

53

This reminds us that in the introduction to the defense he delivered at Cologne Eckhart prefixed a set of three principles necessary for the proper interpretation of his works. The first of these, the one that is the source of the other two, is this vital *in quantum* principle.[218] It appears throughout his writings, nowhere more explicitly than in the *Commentary on John*,[219] where we read:

> In him [Christ] there is no other act of existence save the act of the divine supposit, and therefore there is absolutely no way in which he can sin. But since in us there is another act of existence apart from the existence that is just, there is reason why the just man, *even though he cannot sin insofar as he is just,* can still exist apart from the just man's existence and exist as one who is not just, and thus is able to sin.[220]

In the defense of what became article 21 of the Bull ("The noble man is that Only-Begotten Son of God whom the Father generates from all eternity") the gap in understanding is even more evident, because the theological commission's response to the Meister's explanation deliberately reverses what Eckhart intended. They rebutted him with the observation, "That does nothing to prove the article, namely, that the good man *insofar as he is a man* can be said to be the Only-Begotten Son of God eternally born of the Father."[221] But the *good man insofar as he is a man* is exactly what Eckhart did not intend by his use of *in quantum* language; rather, he always employed this language to speak of the *good man insofar as he is good,* not the existent subject in the world, which is a compound of identity and difference. Eckhart's formula reduplicates the formal quality to show that in its principial ground the soul is truly one with its divine source; by transferring the reduplicating formula to the concrete subject Eckhart's investigators were able to convert him into a seeming pantheist by misunderstanding his language and intentions.

Eternally being born as the only Son of the Father, eternally begetting as the Father himself, and eternally proceeding as the Holy Spirit, the relation of the soul to the divine mystery is capable of still more radical resolution. Just as the divine ground, the hidden Godhead, has priority over as well as a dialectical relation to the Trinity of Persons, so too, above and beyond that stage of the return of the soul to union with God expressed through the theme of the birth of the Son, we find a deeper stage in the soul's return in certain passages in

Eckhart's writings—the invitation for the soul to penetrate to the divine ground behind the three Persons.

The language of "breaking-through" did not figure in Eckhart's condemnation (it is doubtful that his investigators would have been able to make much of it), but it has been the subject of considerable modern interest, especially by those who stress the "non-Christian" character of Eckhart's mysticism.[222] Some of the most striking texts on this theme occur in the vernacular sermons chosen for this volume. *Sermon* 52 ends on the note that only in the breaking-through can "I receive that God and I are one," that is, that I am one with the divine ground, and not with the "God" who is the cause of things.[223] *Sermon* 83 says much the same when it states that in contemplating God as an image or a Trinity the soul lacks what it can attain in contemplating the "naked, formless being of divine unity, which is a being above being."[224] But no text in all of Eckhart is more forceful than the passage in *Sermon* 48 that tells us that the spark in the soul is not content with Father, Son, or Holy Spirit, nor even with "the simple divine essence in its repose; as it neither gives nor receives; but it wants to know the source of this essence, it wants to go into the simple ground, into the quiet desert, into which distinction never gazed, not the Father, nor the Son, nor the Holy Spirit."[225] In the breakthrough to this solitude or desert Eckhart's theology finishes where it had begun: "End and principle are the same."[226]

As the wisdom of apophatic theology ends its discourse, the foolishness of positive, or cataphatic, theology—man's garrulous necessity to keep on talking—takes over. Since even Eckhart is not immune from this exigence, we must also investigate the positive statements he makes about the final stage of union with God. Metaphorically speaking, this ultimate stage in the Meister's sketch of man's spiritual itinerary is admirably expressed by the scriptural image of the journey into the desert or wilderness.[227] "I, says our Lord through the prophet Osee, will lead the noble soul out into the desert, and there I will speak to her heart, one with one, one from one, one in one and in one, one everlastingly. Amen."[228] Naked the soul goes forth to meet the naked Godhead in a wilderness without name; but just as Israel's encounter with God in the desert was not a barren and sterile one, but rather the formation of the fruitful people of God, so too when the soul strips herself through total detachment and goes forth into the wilderness she is preparing for the meeting that will make her not only a virgin but also a mother.

The union that is achieved by the breaking-through to the divine ground is a union that is without a medium,[229] a union totally without distinction.[230] These are its essential characteristics. The soul does not seek the mere uniting of two things that remain distinct, but desires the true union in which there is nothing but Absolute Unity, the "Simple One." Eckhart frequently illustrates the lack of medium in this union by reflections on natural examples of "medium-less" union, such as the union of form and matter. In such cases, "the greater the nakedness, the greater the union";[231] and "the more naked, the more open."[232] The Meister's stress on the absolute character of the beatifying oneness led him to employ expressions that go beyond those deemed prudent by earlier medieval mystical theologians. Bernard of Clairvaux, for example, in describing the mutual love between God and the soul, was careful to remind his readers that in the highest stage of union God and the soul become "one spirit" (*unus spiritus*), but not one substance or thing (*unum*).[233] Eckhart, on the other hand, was willing to use both forms of expression—"All the saints are one thing, not one person, in God";[234] "He who is one with God, is 'one spirit' with God, *the same existence*."[235] Taken in isolation, these passages have a pantheistic ring; seen in the light of Eckhart's dialectical understanding of *unum* or the One, they preserve the difference in identity that other mystics have expressed in less daring ways.

The notion of union in the ground where God and the soul are one helps explain the passages in which the Meister reflects on the familiar scholastic debate about whether beatitude consists primarily in the satisfaction of the intellect or of the will. As a Dominican and an idiosyncratic student of Thomas Aquinas, Eckhart, of course, defended the primacy of the intellect in disputing with the Franciscan theologian Gonsalvo of Spain,[236] and numerous texts in the Latin works echo the position in emphasizing that beatitude is found essentially in the intellect's union with God in contemplation.[237] Since we have seen that understanding (*intelligere*) was one of the transcendental predicates that could be used to disclose the dialectical character of the divine essence, this position should not surprise us. But there is another way to describe beatitude in Eckhart that is closer to the main themes of his thought. This appears in *Sermon 52* where, in answer to the question whether blessedness consists in knowing or in loving, he responds:

> But I say that it does not consist in either knowing or loving, but that there is that in the soul from which knowing and lov-

ing flow; that something does not know or love as do the powers of the soul. Whoever knows this knows in what blessedness consists.[238]

True blessedness, then, is found in the soul's return to its divine ground.

F. ECKHART'S ETHICS AND MYSTICISM

The final area to be investigated is what we might describe as Eckhart's ethics. What rules of conduct and manner of life follow on the principles that the Meister advanced? How ought man to live in order that the Son may be born in him and that he may return to oneness in the divine ground? In analyzing the role of detachment and love in Eckhart's thought we have already surveyed central elements in Eckhartian ethics, but the particular modalities of the life of the "poor man," "just man," "good man," or "noble man" (all synonyms for the true Christian) need to be pursued on some important details.

The detachment to which Eckhart invites us is principally an internal one. While the Meister does not condemn the external poverty that Christ used when he was on earth ("The less we own, the more it is our own," as he said),[239] he makes it quite clear that true freedom consists in an interior detachment from things. This inner detachment extends to exterior religious exercises, for those who are "attached to their own penances and external exercises" cannot understand divine truth.[240] In the *Counsels of Discernment* he gives good practical advice regarding the equality of all pious practices and the importance of imitating Christ spiritually and not physically.[241] "Whoever is seeking God by ways is finding ways and losing God, who in ways is hidden. But whoever seeks for God without ways will find him as he is in himself."[242] The Dominican theologian recognized the redemptive value of learning to accept trials with complete detachment as expressions of God's will. He composed a number of powerful passages on the role of the cross in the life of the Christian, notably in the treatise called the *Book "Benedictus,"* or *Book of Divine Consolation;*[243] but he does not usually suggest that suffering in itself apart from its reception in the proper spirit is of particular value, nor does he urge taking on voluntary penances or ascetical practices.

The interior attitude that Eckhart strove to induce in his readers and hearers can best be put in terms of the polarities of complete detachment from creatures and total love of God. The perfect conformity to God's will that springs from the realization of the soul's indistinct union with the divine ground appears throughout the Latin and German works in Eckhart's repetition of the evangelical command that we must love God above all things for his own sake alone.[244] As we might expect, the Meister's single-minded attention to the implications of disinterested love led him to adopt at least one position that seemed problematic or erroneous to his opponents. Eckhart insisted that to love in the truest sense of the word is to love all things equally. Indeed, when we love God above all things with our whole heart and soul, only then do we come to love ourselves and all other things truly and equally.[245] If love means to become indistinct in the One, then the act of loving must also be indistinct, that is, it must not differentiate among its objects. This notion of absolute equality in loving led to an odd passage singled out in the Bull in which the Meister, commenting on the twenty-first chapter of John, reproved Peter's "greater love" for Jesus as an imperfect form of love.[246]

There were also more serious problems that the inquisitors found with aspects of Eckhart's ethical teachings. The most important of these, to judge from the number of condemned propositions it produced, was the issue of the relation of the interior and exterior aspects of the morally good act. No less than four articles, all drawn from the Latin works,[247] center on his teaching that the exterior act adds nothing to the goodness of the interior one. It is a doctrine that we would expect the Meister to advance, given the profoundly interior character of his theology; and it is one that was not unnaturally attacked in an atmosphere of fear of the heresy of the "Free Spirit" (*spiritus libertatis*) that was thought to encourage immoral forms of activity by the souls who had reached interior perfection.[248] The surprising thing is that Eckhart apparently thought that Thomas Aquinas agreed with him on the issue of the internal and external act, a rather serious misreading of the Angelic Doctor.[249] In any case, it is important to note how integral to Eckhart's entire approach it is to emphasize that it is the interior act alone that counts and that for four reasons: First, because the exterior act can be hindered; second, only the interior act is properly commanded by God; third, the inner act is never oppressive; and fourth, the interior act always praises God directly as its author.[250] Eckhart's emphasis on the interior act is repeated throughout his Latin and vernacular works,[251] and is one of the most distinctive features of Eckhartian ethics. As his response at Avignon and the twenty-third counsel of the *Counsels of Discernment* indicate,[252] Eckhart felt that the ideal situation was one in which the interior and the exterior act co-existed in one form of working, but for him God's command was always properly directed to the inner work.

A second major center of concern for the judges who grilled Eckhart at both Cologne and Avignon involved the role of prayer. The Meister's emphasis on the necessity of realizing the unity of ground between God and the soul led to statements seeming to deny the value of petitioning God for anything and thus appeared to eliminate prayer from the Christian life. The treatise *On Detachment* denies that one who is detached can pray if prayer is understood as petition, but affirms that if prayer is understood as union with God then detachment has its own form of prayer.[253] If God and the soul share the same ground, then there is a sense in which it is foolish or impossible for the soul to ask anything from God, or at least to ask for anything that is less than God.[254] Articles 7, 8, and 9 from the papal Bull, the first drawn from the *Commentary on John*[255] and the latter two from *Sermon* 6,[256] are paradoxical expressions of this ban on petition for the noble soul insofar as it is united with the divine ground. At the risk of boring the reader, we must repeat that the proper way to understand such texts, as the Meister insisted at the beginning of his Cologne defense,[257] is to realize that they are true only according to the *in quantum* principle, that is, speaking exclusively, abstractly, and formally. The same holds for the proper understanding of the many passages in which the Meister speaks of the just man as being able to perform divine works.[258]

If we ask what inner attitude or style describes the daily life of the just man, Eckhart's deepest response can be found in the passages where he speaks about "living without a why":

> If anyone went on for a thousand years asking of life: "Why are you living?" life, if it could answer, would only say, "I live so that I may live." That is because life lives out of its own ground and springs from its own source, and so it lives without asking why it is itself living.[259]

> He who lives in the goodness of his nature lives in God's love; and love has no why.[260]

> It is proper to God that he has no "why" outside or beyond himself. Therefore, every work that has a "why" as such is

not a divine work or done for God. "He works all things for his own sake" (Pr. 16:4). There will be no divine work if a person does something that is not for God's sake, because it will have a "why," something that is foreign to God and far from God. It is not God or godly.[261]

The inner oneness of ground shared by God and the soul once again provides the basis for this fundamental theme. Just as God's mode of being and acting is characterized by absolute inner self-sufficiency and spontaneity, not being and acting "for," but simple joy in the reality of supreme being and omnipotent activity, so too the soul that is one with God lives without a "why" in the sheer delight of its existence. This is the goal of human life, the height of Eckhart's mysticism.

It should be clear by now that living without a why does not involve any form of radical separation from the world, or seeking after some form of special or privileged experience, even after ecstasy or rapture. Eckhart's position on the relation between action and contemplation is paradoxically put, but this should not surprise us by now. In the eighty-sixth of the vernacular sermons the Meister commented on the story of Mary and Martha from the tenth chapter of Luke's Gospel.[262] Tradition had identified Martha, "busy about many things," with the active life, and Mary who sought the "one thing necessary" with the higher contemplative life, but Eckhart reverses this, at least in this text.[263] As long as we find ourselves in this life, Martha's way is to be preferred to Mary, who is advised to get up and "learn life." Martha is the type of the soul who in the summit of the mind or depth of ground remains unchangeably united to God, but who continues to occupy herself with good works in the world that help her neighbor and also form her total being closer and closer to the divine image.[264] Martha, then, is the soul that is both a virgin and a fruitful wife, free and detached, and yet by that very reason able to work "without a why." This teaching on the continuing necessity for the performance of good works is found in both the Latin and German writings.[265] It is paralleled by another crucial point, the insistence that God can be found everywhere and in all works: "When people think that they are acquiring more of God in inwardness, in devotion, in sweetness and in various approaches than they do by the fireside or in the stable, you are acting just as if you took God and muffled his head up in a cloak and pushed him under a bench."[266] Eckhart, of course, recognizes that "praying is a better work than spinning, and the church is a better place than the street," as a parallel passage from the *Counsels of Discernment* puts it,[267] but it is not so much what we do or where we do it as what spirit we do it in that is important for the Meister. "It is not what we do which makes us holy, but we ought to make holy what we do."[268]

Eckhart's "this-worldliness," as Reiner Schürmann has called it,[269] promotes a form of mysticism that is uninterested in special states of experience, as noted above, either those of the sensible variety (visions, locutions, feelings of light and sweetness, etc.), or even of the higher reaches of rapture. The Meister is highly suspicious of any form of sensible consolation or vision,[270] tartly condemning those who want to see God with the same eyes with which they behold a cow.[271] But a like distrust, or at least a lack of interest, marks the few references he makes to the traditional height of the mystical experience, the *raptus* on which many of his predecessors and contemporaries had lavished so much attention. Eckhart does not doubt that such experiences occur; he cites the examples of Paul and Augustine, and once paraphrases Thomas Aquinas's teaching on the subject.[272] But the Meister is not an ecstatic or a student of ecstasy in any way.[273] For him the purpose of theology and preaching was not to invite his hearers to search out the extraordinary, but to attain to true insight into the meaning of the ordinary. Echhart is pleading for us to open our eyes to see what has always been the case, that God and the soul are truly one in their deepest ground.

> I say yet more, do not be startled, for this joy is near you and is in you. There is no one of you so crude, or so small in understanding or so removed, that he cannot joyfully and intelligently find this joy within him in the truth in which it exists, even before you leave this church today or before I finish the sermon today. He can as truly find it and live it and possess it within him as God is God and I am a man.[274]

In the last analysis Eckhart's theology is both theocentric and at the same time fully anthropocentric. God is God and man is man, and yet God's ground and the soul's ground are one ground.

—Bernard McGinn

3. A NOTE ON ECKHART'S WORKS AND THE PRESENT SELECTIONS

This is scarcely the forum, given the nature of the volume, to try to do justice to the complex questions surrounding the authenticity of Eckhart's works; but it is important to give the reader some sense of the present state of the question, as well as the rationale behind the selections chosen for this book.

When interest in Meister Eckhart revived in the early nineteenth century under the influence of the Romantic movement,[1] it was to the available fragments of the vernacular works ascribed to the Meister that scholars turned their attention. The need for some form of collected edition of Eckhart's German works soon became obvious, and this need was met in 1857 by the edition of Franz Pfeiffer (1815–1868). Pfeiffer was a scholar of great energy, and Eckhart studies remain in his debt to this day. A kind of Schliemann of Eckhartiana, like his archeologist contemporary he was responsible for a multitude of discoveries, but worked quickly and uncritically by modern standards. Pfeiffer's edition contains no less than one hundred and eleven sermons and eighteen treatises, as well as a number of sayings and fragments—a number far in excess of those that most would claim as authentic today when there is greater recognition of the fact that Eckhart's fame led to many works being put under his name in later years.

The second major stage in the recovery of Eckhart's text was initiated by the Dominican scholar Heinrich Denifle (1844–1905), who first began to make the Meister's Latin works available to the public in 1886.[2] Unlike the vernacular works, today known in over two hundred manuscripts, the Latin writings are found in only a handful of witnesses (five major mss. are presently known), but Denifle argued convincingly that these Latin treatises which Eckhart carefully prepared for publication were essential to a full understanding of the

Meister and served to correct one-sided interpretations based on vernacular works alone, these frequently of doubtful authenticity. Denifle's challenge led to a series of efforts on the part of scholars of the late nineteenth and early twentieth centuries to work out canons of authenticity for the Middle High German texts ascribed to Eckhart. These were frequently based on internal criteria of style and agreement with the Latin writings.[3] One unfortunate by-product of the rediscovery of the Latin works, still present in some modern writing on Eckhart, has been the split between those who would stress the more conservative, scholastic Eckhart and those who favor the supposedly more original preacher and author of the vernacular works. As pointed out previously, the premise of this volume is that such a division forms a grave hindrance to real understanding of the integral Eckhart.

A crucial tool for the authentication of the disputed vernacular works was the Defense (*Rechtfertigungsschrift*, or "Vindicatory Document"), the record of Eckhart's responses to two of the series of propositions brought against him at Cologne. Surviving in a single manuscript, this key text was first published by A. Daniels in 1923 and again by G. Théry in 1926. Extracts from sermons and treatises found in these lists and accepted as his own by Eckhart provided sound external criteria for the authenticity of a number of the vernacular works. The task that remained, however, was still a formidable one—how to deal with the mass of material not guaranteed by presence in the Defense, and how to provide good critical editions of all the genuine Latin and German works.

A brief "war of editions" erupted in the troubled 1930s. An edition of the Latin works sponsored by the Dominicans of Santa Sabina under the editorship of R. Klibansky and G. Théry began to appear between 1932 and 1936, but in 1934 when the Deutsche Forschungsgemeinschaft took an active interest in sponsoring a complete edition of all Eckhart's works, one result was to deny access to manuscripts in Germany to the opposing project, which soon ceased publication.

The critical edition of the Deutsche Forschungsgemeinschaft, arguably among the great medieval editing projects of the century, began publication in 1936. Although such a vast task has profited from the cooperation of many hands, the success of the edition has been primarily the work of two scholars, Josef Koch, O.P. (1885–1967), who was given major responsibility for the Latin works, and Josef Quint (1898–1977), who exercised virtually sole responsibility over the edition of the German works. The coming of the Second World War delayed the progress of the edition severely due to loss of materials and the deaths of valuable contributors. Since the 1950s, the edition has moved ahead slowly but steadily, always with an eye more on critical accuracy and scholarly completeness than on haste. Today, of the planned eleven volumes, four of five of the DW are complete, and two of five of the LW (though two others are virtually done, and the other is well on the way). There will also be a volume of indices.

There is no dispute about the genuine character of the Latin works presented in the LW, and there are few difficulties in the establishment of the text, given the paucity of manuscripts.[4] The major problem regarding the Latin writings is that they represent a small portion of the systematic synthesis that Eckhart planned, and apparently only a part of what he wrote, as numerous references to lost texts indicate. The Meister tells us that he planned a vast *Three-Part Work (Opus Tripartitum)* to consist of a *Work of Propositions (Opus Propositionum)*, a *Work of Questions (Opus Quaestionum)* and a *Work of Commentaries (Opus Expositionum)*. The first part, the systematic grounding of the whole, was to consist of over a thousand propositions divided into fourteen treatises, as the General Prologue to the *Three-Part Work* informs us.[5] This type of synthesis presented through axioms or propositions organized according to opposed terms (e.g., the first treatise was to deal with "existence and being and its opposite which is nothing") is reminiscent of a number of Eckhart's Neoplatonic sources, such as Proclus's *Elements of Theology* and the Arabic *Book of Causes* that was based on it. Unfortunately, the only part that remains is the Prologue illustrating the first proposition, "Existence is God,"[6] though references in Eckhart's other works indicate that other parts were produced that do not survive.

The *Work of Questions* was to deal with a selection of disputed questions, following the order of the *STh* of Thomas Aquinas. None of this work survives, though we do have five important questions that Eckhart delivered at Paris, at least some of them directed against the Franciscan theologian Gonsalvo of Spain.[7] Whether these were to be incorporated into the *Work of Questions* or not is difficult to tell.[8] The major portion of Eckhart's Latin works that remain to us consists of extensive parts of the *Work of Commentaries* in two sections, formal commentaries (*expositiones*) on the books of the Old and New Testaments, and Latin sermons (undoubtedly delivered before ecclesiastical audiences) where the Meister expounded on selected texts. As pointed out in the theological section of this Introduction,[9] Eckhart saw the work of scriptural exegesis and preaching as inseparable.

The *Work of Commentaries* consists of a Prologue (in two versions, one of which is translated here), six commentaries, and fifty-six sermons, some found in several related versions. Despite the importance of the Prologues and the *Parisian Questions*, the lengthy commentaries must take pride of place as Eckhart's most important surviving Latin works. There are two commentaries on Genesis, the more literal *Commentary on the Book of Genesis*, and the more allegorical *Book of the Parables of Genesis*.[10] The Meister also left extensive commentaries on Exodus and Wisdom among the Old Testament books,[11] as well as a briefer text, *Sermons and Lectures on the Twenty-fourth Chapter of Ecclesiasticus* (Sirach).[12] Fragments of his *Commentary on the Song of Songs* are also now being edited.[13] From the New Testament the only exposition that survives is the lengthy *Commentary on John*.[14] It has been justly described as Eckhart's theological masterpiece, though the Exodus and Wisdom commentaries are scarcely inferior to it. Finally, the fifty-six Latin sermons found in LW IV are of widely varying quality. Some are no more than sermon notes, and many seem pedestrian in comparison with their more lively vernacular counterparts; but more than a few are equal to anything Eckhart ever wrote.[15]

Aside from a brief treatise on the Lord's Prayer that is largely an anthology culled from earlier authorities,[16] the other surviving Latin texts of Eckhart all concern the process conducted against him first at Cologne and then at Avignon from 1326 to 1329.[17] The most important of these is the Defense, or "Vindicatory Document," already noted (not yet available in the critical edition in LW V). Other documents relating to the trial are the Vatican archive materials published by M.-H. Laurent,[18] and the important "Opinion," or *votum theologicum*, of the Avignon commission edited by Franz Pelster.[19]

Selecting a representative offering from Eckhart's Latin works is not an easy task. The Latin commentaries are long and discursive, being organized to provide the preacher with apt theological material for sermons on individual texts, rather than to give an extended treatment of a single book. Nevertheless, one text does stand out as a sustained analysis that deals with a passage central to the history of Christian thought and to the Meister's own theological position. This is the lengthy comment on the Prologue of the Gospel of John (Jn. 1:1–14). Most of the key notions of the Dominican theologian's thought are present here, put forth with a power and precision equal to anything found throughout his *corpus.*

The "In the beginning (principle) was the Word" of John 1:1 for Eckhart immediately called to mind the "In the beginning (principle) God created heaven and earth" of Genesis 1:1. The exegesis of the two passages is mutually illuminating in a variety of ways, and therefore both versions of Eckhart's commentary on the first verse of the Bible have been translated here as the most fitting complement for the exposition of the Johannine Prologue. In addition, the Prologue to the *Book of the Parables of Genesis,* the Meister's most detailed treatment of his exegetical principles, is also translated here, as well as the whole of his commentary on chapter three of Genesis from the same work. This comment forms a short treatise on theological anthropology, an area of such importance to Eckhart's thought as to merit inclusion.

Meister Eckhart's views have always been controversial. Hence, the first section of the part of this volume devoted to the Latin works contains translations of two of the documents relating to the trial. The whole Defense is too long and arid for a full translation: Eckhart's responses to the various articles are often elliptical, polemical, or highly technical; but in several places he advances general principles for the correct interpretation of his works or summarizes his responses to his opponents, and a selection of these passages has been included here. In addition, there is a new translation of the whole of the Bull of condemnation, "In agro dominico."

Questions concerning the authenticity of the Middle High German texts are legion. The problems involve not only whether a particular sermon or treatise is to be judged authentic or pseudonymous, but also, given the large number of manuscripts and the fragmentary condition of many of them, whether it is even possible to establish the text for some of the pieces accepted as genuine. The Meister's sermons are "reportings" (*reportationes*), that is, versions written down by others from memory or from notes, a practice filled with possibility of error, even in an age when the memory was better trained than in our own. Eckhart himself recognized this difficulty when he noted: "I am not held to respond to the other articles taken from the sermons ascribed to me, since even learned and studious clerics take down what they hear frequently and indiscriminately in a false and abbreviated way."[20] It is noteworthy that the articles in the trial that the Meister admitted as incorrect or evil-sounding all came from the German sermons.

Dependent as this volume is on the critical edition found in DW

I–III, for our purposes it is sufficient to note Quint's principles of authenticity for the eighty-six sermons included there without entering into questions of detail. On the basis of a lifetime of critical study devoted to Eckhart's vernacular works, Quint divided the sermons into three groups. The first, comprising *Sermons* 1–16b (DW I, pp. 1–276), are proved authentic by direct citation in the trial documents. The second group, *Sermons* 17–24 (DW I, pp. 277–423), have such close textual affinities with Latin sermons recognized as genuine that their authenticity also seems well established. The third group, comprising *Sermons* 25–86 for Quint (DW II–III) are more difficult to judge. The German scholar used a number of criteria to defend the authenticity of these pieces, involving both style and content. Questions will undoubtedly continue to be raised about individual sermons, and arguments will continue to be advanced for the genuine nature of sermons excluded by Quint,[21] but it is fair to say that his detailed arguments on these questions represent the necessary foundation for all subsequent study.

The nine sermons chosen for this volume are a deliberately mixed group designed to illustrate the major theological themes of Eckhart's preaching as expounded in the Theological Summary section of this Introduction. They also represent all three of Quint's divisions of reliability, including both well-known and much-studied pieces, such as *Sermons* 2, 6, 22, and 52, and less familiar sermons, like 5b, 15, 48, and 53. In addition, *Sermon* 83, which belongs among the Meister's finest addresses but is one that has been somewhat neglected, closes the section. There are doubtless many other important sermons that might have been included here, and whose absence Eckhart scholars will regret. Fortunately, the Meister's vernacular preaching, centering on a few crucial and oft-repeated themes as it does, can be introduced through a fairly modest selection.

Modern criticism has been especially harsh on the multitude of vernacular treatises ascribed to the Meister. Following criteria similar to those used for the sermons, Quint admitted only four as authentic, and there have been doubts expressed about one of these. The longest of the genuine treatises, the *Counsels on Discernment*,[22] is probably his earliest surviving work, a set of spiritual instructions that Eckhart gave to young Dominicans in the 1290s. Consisting of twenty-three separate chapters, the counsels represent a more conventional side of Eckhart's thought—practical, ascetical, sober. While many of the Meister's favorite themes are absent, some others, including at least one condemned at Avignon,[23] are evident.

More typical of the mature Eckhart is the work known as the *Book "Benedictus,"* which really consists of two related treatises, the *Book of Divine Consolation,*[24] and the sermon entitled "Of the Nobleman."[25] The *Book of Divine Consolation* belongs to a genre well known in the Middle Ages, the message of consolation sent to someone in time of need. Later references tell us that the recipient was Queen Agnes of Hungary (c. 1280–1364); the hour of need in which it was sent may well have been 1308, when her father, Albert of Hapsburg, was murdered. Loosely divided into three sections, the work is a remarkable summary of the most difficult and speculative aspects of the Meister's teaching, and tells us much about the Queen's intelligence and spiritual maturity. Closely connected with this text in the manuscripts, and also indubitably authentic because of its appearance in the Defense, is the long sermon "Of the Nobleman," a vernacular summary of the stages of the return of the noble, good, or just person to God.

The final vernacular treatise admitted as authentic by Quint is that entitled *On Detachment,* a clear and well-organized presentation of one of the most distinctive themes of Eckhart's message.[26] Although it was not a part of the trial documents and doubts have been expressed about its authenticity by previous scholars, its profundity of tone and true Eckhartian style have convinced Quint and most modern investigators that it is one of the finest products of the Meister's pen.

Part One

Latin Works

translated by
Bernard McGinn

1. DOCUMENTS RELATING TO ECKHART'S CONDEMNATION

A. Selections from Eckhart's Defense

I. RESPONSE TO THE LIST OF FORTY-NINE ARTICLES

In the year of our Lord 1326, the 26th of September, on the day set for the response to the articles taken from the books, remarks and sermons ascribed to Meister Eckhart that seem to some erroneous, or what is worse, to smack of heresy, as they say.

A. Introduction

I, the aforesaid Brother Eckhart of the order of Preachers, respond. First, I protest before you the Commissioners, Master Reiner Friso, Doctor of Theology, and Peter of Estate, lately Custodian of the order of Friars Minor,[1] that according to the exemption and privileges of my order, I am not held to appear before you or to answer charges.[2] This is especially true since I am not accused of heresy and have never been denounced overtly, as my whole life and teaching testify, and as the esteem of the brethren of the whole order and men and women of the entire kingdom and of every nation corroborates.[3]

Second, it is evident from this that the commission given you by the venerable father and lord, the Archbishop of Cologne (may God preserve his life!), has no force inasmuch as it proceeds from a false suggestion and an evil root and stem.[4] Indeed, if I were less well known among the people and less eager for justice, I am sure that such attempts would not have been made against me by envious people. But I ought to bear them patiently, because "Blessed are they who suffer for justice' sake" (Mt. 5:10), and according to Paul, "God scourges every son he receives" (Heb. 12:6), so that I can deservedly say with the

Psalm, "I have been made ready in scourges" (Ps. 37:18). I ought to do this particularly because long ago, but in my own lifetime, the masters of theology at Paris received a command from above to examine the books of those two most distinguished men, Saint Thomas Aquinas and Brother Albert the Bishop, on the grounds that they were suspect and erroneous.[5] Many have often written, declared and even publicly preached that Saint Thomas wrote and taught errors and heresies, but with God's aid his life and teaching alike have been given approval, both at Paris and also by the Supreme Pontiff and the Roman curia.[6]

So much said, I respond to the articles brought up against me. The forty-nine articles are divided into four groups. First, there are fifteen taken from a book I wrote that begins "Blessed be God."[7] Second are six articles taken from a response of mine or from my remarks.[8] Third are twelve articles taken from my first commentary on Genesis. I am surprised that they do not bring up more objections against what is written in my different works, for it is well known that I have written a hundred things and more that their ignorance neither understands nor grasps. Fourth, there are sixteen articles taken from the sermons ascribed to me.

As far as the first three groups are concerned, I state and declare that I said and wrote these things. As my declaration will make clear, I hold that they are all true, although many are uncommon and subtle. If there is something false I do not see in them or in my other remarks and writings, I am always ready to yield to a better understanding. As Jerome said to Heliodorus, "Small talents will not support great matters, and in attempting something beyond their powers they will fail."[9] I can be in error, but I cannot be a heretic, because the first belongs to the intellect, the second to the will.

To clarify the objections brought against me, three things must be kept in mind. The first is that the words "insofar as," that is, a reduplication, exclude from the term in question everything that is other or foreign to it even according to reason. Even though existence and understanding are the same in God, still we do not say that God is evil although we can say that he understands evil.[10] Although in God the Father essence and paternity are the same, he does not generate insofar as he is essence, but insofar as he is Father, even though the essence is the root of generation. Even the absolute acts of the Godhead proceed from God according to the property of his attributes, as a theological maxim says.[11] Hence, in the fifth book of *On Consideration*

Bernard says that "God loves as charity, knows as truth, sits in judgment as justice, rules as majesty, . . . operates as strength, reveals as light, etc."[12]

The second is that the good man and goodness are one.[13] The good man insofar as he is good signifies goodness alone, just as something white signifies only the quality of whiteness. These two things, being good and goodness, are univocally one in the Father, Son and Holy Spirit. They are analogically one in God and in us considered as good.[14]

The third is that everything that begets, indeed everything that acts, insofar as it begets and acts, at that moment possesses two characteristics. The first characteristic is that by nature it does not rest or stop until it introduces its form in what it acts upon and begets. When the form as such has been introduced, bestowed and communicated, it confers existence,[15] as well as everything that belongs to it, namely operation and any type of property. That is why according to Aristotle what has not been moved is not moved and what does not touch something does not act.[16] The second characteristic is that every agent insofar as it is an agent, or everything that begets insofar as it begets, is unbegotten, neither made nor created, because it is not derived from another.[17] Rather, what begets, insofar as it begets and is an active principle, is opposed by relation to what is begotten, the offspring, the son, the created, the made, or what has existence from another. For example, the form of a work of art (think of a house in the architect's mind) is a kind of begotten and made offspring. If I may speak in this way, it is created from something outside, namely from a real house or the architect's teacher.[18] It does not beget as such; it is not a father or a principle that produces. "The Son can do nothing of himself" (Jn. 5:19). From this it clearly follows that the begetter and begotten are one in reality, but are opposed and distinct by relation, either by a real relation in the Godhead where the relation and the real being are the same thing, or by relation and reason in created things.[19] This is because acting and being acted upon are two equally primary principles, but are one motion. To move and to be moved according to the nature of their relations begin and end at one and the same time.[20]

On the basis of these points, I can clearly demonstrate the truth of everything brought up against me from my books and remarks. I can also show the ignorance and irreverence of my opponents, according to the passage from Proverbs, "My throat will meditate truth," in relation to the first task, and "My lips shall hate wickedness," in relation to the second (Pr. 8:7).

B. Summary of Response to the First Three Groups and Preparatory Remarks Regarding Responses to the Fourth Group

It is clear therefore that the truth and the ground of the truth appear in every one of the articles comprised above, that is, first, in those from the book that begins "Blessed be God," second, in the things brought up to me from the contents of my remarks and responses, and third, in the points from the contents of my first commentary on Genesis—all of which I admit I wrote and said. I say that the truth and its ground appear in each of these on the basis of the points I put down above, as well as from the confirmed malice or gross ignorance of my opponents who are trying to judge divine, subtle and incorporeal things by means of material imagination against Boethius's statement in *On the Trinity:* "In divine matters, we ought to use intellectual concepts and not be led away into imaginings."[21] I protest that in the case of these articles and of all the things I have written in different interpretations of various books of the Bible, as well as in anything and everything else, I am not held to respond to you or to anyone except the Pope and the University of Paris. The only exception would be if anything (God forbid!) were perhaps to touch the faith that I always profess.[22] From my own generosity, though with a protestation of the exemption of my order, I still wanted to write down and present these things to you so that I do not seem to be avoiding what has been falsely brought against me.

Furthermore, I am not held to respond to the other articles taken from the sermons ascribed to me, since even learned and studious clerics take down what they hear frequently and indiscriminately in a false and abbreviated way. This I will say—I do not judge, have not judged or held, and have not preached any of them to the extent that they sound and imply what is false and smack of heresy or error.[23] I still claim that truths are touched upon in some of them that can be upheld by true and sound understanding. There is no false teaching that does not have some truth mixed in with it, as Bede says in a homily.[24] I reject them and abhor them where they imply error or at least beget it in the hearers' souls. This error or errors cannot and ought not be blamed on me by the envious. . . .[25]

C. Conclusion

Finally, I want to note that even though the ignorance and stupidity of those who try to condemn them appear in considering each of the articles I preached, taught or wrote, their truth also is evident from the expositions given above. The first mistake they make is that they think that everything they do not understand is an error and that every error is a heresy, when only obstinate adherence to error makes heresy and a heretic, as the laws and the doctors hold.[26] The second error is that although they say they are inquisitors in search of heresy, they turn to my books and object to things that are purely natural truths. Third, they object to things as heretical that Saint Thomas openly uses for the solution of certain arguments and that they either have not seen or not remembered. An example is the distinction and nature of univocal, equivocal and analogous terms, and the like.[27]

Fourth, they attack as harmful places where I have merely used the words of Cicero, Seneca and Origen's gloss, such as on the divine seed in the soul.[28] "He who is born from God does not commit sin, because his seed [i.e., God's] abides in him" (1 Jn. 3:9). Fifth, they attack many things as erroneous that are the common opinion of the doctors. An example would be that the exterior act of itself has no moral goodness and consequently adds to the goodness of the internal act only accidentally.[29] Likewise, they think that God exists and creates in another now than the now of eternity,[30] although the world was created in time.[31] They do not know what Augustine says: "All tomorrows and beyond them, and all yesterdays and what is behind them, you are making today and have made today. What is it to me if someone does not understand this?"[32]

Sixth, they oppose some things as false and heretical [and thus imply] that man cannot be united with God, which is against the teaching of Christ and the Evangelist. "You, Father, are in me, and I am in you, that they also may be one in us" (Jn. 17:21). Seventh, they say that a creature or the world is not nothing in itself apart from God, which is against the Gospel text, "All things were made through him, and without him was made nothing" (Jn. 1:3). Further, to say that the world is not nothing in itself and from itself, but is some slight bit of existence is open blasphemy.[33] If that were so, God would not be the First Cause of all things and the creature would not be created by God in possessing existence from him. Eighth, they attack the idea that the godlike man can perform God's works, against the teaching of Christ and the Evangelist: "He who believes in me, the works I do he shall also do, and greater than these" (Jn. 14:12). Again, they also deny that the godlike man by means of charity receives the things made in charity that are nothing outside charity, contrary to what the Apostle says in the thirteenth chapter of First Corinthians. That is enough for now.

II. RESPONSE TO THE LIST OF FIFTY-NINE ARTICLES

A. Introduction

The articles that follow are contained in a list that was shown to me after I had responded to the articles given above. Know that these articles that follow, just like the earlier ones, are always or almost always false and erroneous in the sense in which my opponents take them, but reasonably and devoutly understood they contain excellent and useful truths of faith and moral teaching. They demonstrate the mental weakness and spite of my adversaries, and even their open blasphemy and heresy, if they obstinately defend the following points, which are against the teaching of Christ, the Evangelist, the saints and the doctors.[34]

First, when they say that man cannot be united to God. Second, when they say that the creature is not nothing by itself, but is some kind of slight existence, as we say a drop of salt water is a slight bit of the sea. Third, when they say God created the world in another now than in the now of eternity, although every action of God is his substance, which is eternal. They do not understand what Augustine in the first book of the *Confessions* says to God: "All tomorrows and beyond them, and all yesterdays and what is behind them, you are making today and have made today. What is it to me if someone does not understand this?"[35] Augustine's words in *Confessions* 11:11 say: "Their heart up to now casts about in vain between the motions of things past and to come. . . . Who shall hold it fast so that it may grasp the beauty of unchanging eternity?" Fourth, when they say that the exterior act adds something to the moral goodness of the interior act. Finally, fifth, when they think that the Holy Spirit and his grace are given to a man who is not God's son, although the Holy Spirit proceeds from the Son. "Because you are sons, God has sent his Spirit into your hearts" (Ga. 4:6). Why give more? It is just about the same with all the objections they make, such as when they wrongly think it is false to say God is existence.

B. The Bull "In agro dominico" (March 27, 1329)

John, Bishop, Servant of the Servants of God, to perpetual memory.

In the field of the Lord over which we, though unworthy, are guardians and laborers by heavenly dispensation, we ought to exercise spiritual care so watchfully and prudently that if an enemy should ever sow tares over the seeds of truth (Mt. 13:28), they may be choked at the start before they grow up as weeds of an evil growth. Thus, with the destruction of the evil seed and the uprooting of the thorns of error, the good crop of Catholic truth may take firm root. We are indeed sad to report that in these days someone by the name of Eckhart from Germany, a doctor of sacred theology (as is said) and a professor of the order of Preachers, wished to know more than he should, and not in accordance with sobriety and the measure of faith, because he turned his ear from the truth and followed fables. The man was led astray by that Father of Lies who often turns himself into an angel of light in order to replace the light of truth with a dark and gloomy cloud of the senses, and he sowed thorns and obstacles contrary to the very clear truth of faith in the field of the Church and worked to produce harmful thistles and poisonous thornbushes. He presented many things as dogma that were designed to cloud the true faith in the hearts of many, things which he put forth especially before the uneducated crowd in his sermons and that he also admitted into his writings.

From the inquiry previously made against him concerning these matters on the authority of our Venerable Brother Henry, the Archbishop of Cologne, and at last renewed on our authority in the Roman curia, we have discovered, as is evident from the same Eckhart's confession, that he preached, taught and wrote twenty-six articles having the following content.

The first article. When someone once asked him why God had not created the world earlier, he answered then, as he does now, that God could not have created the world earlier,[1] because a thing cannot act before it exists, and so as soon as God existed he created the world.[2]

The second article. Also, it can be granted that the world has existed from eternity.[3]

The third article. Also, in the one and the same time when God was, when he begot his coeternal Son as God equal to himself in all things, he also created the world.[4]

The fourth article. Also, in every work, even in an evil, I repeat, in one evil both according to punishment and guilt, God's glory is revealed and shines forth in equal fashion.[5]

The fifth article. Also, a person who disparages someone, by the disparagement itself, that is, by the sin of disparaging, praises God; and the more he disparages and the more gravely he sins, the more he praises God.

The sixth article. Also, anyone who blasphemes God himself praises God.

The seventh article. Also, that he who prays for anything particular[6] prays badly and for something that is bad, because he is praying for the negation of good and the negation of God, and he begs that God be denied to him.[7]

The eighth article. Those who are not desiring possessions, or honors, or gain, or internal devotion, or holiness, or reward or the kingdom of heaven, but who have renounced all this, even what is theirs, these people pay honor to God.[8]

The ninth article. Recently I considered whether there was anything I would take or ask from God. I shall take careful thought about this, because if I were accepting anything from God, I should be subject to him or below him as a servant or slave, and he in giving would be as a master. We shall not be so in life everlasting.[9]

The tenth article. We shall all be transformed totally into God and changed into him. In the same way, when in the sacrament bread is changed into Christ's Body, I am so changed into him that he makes me his one existence, and not just similar. By the living God it is true that there is no distinction there.[10]

The eleventh article. Whatever God the Father gave to his Only-Begotten Son in human nature, he gave all this to me. I except nothing, neither union, nor sanctity; but he gave the whole to me, just as he did to him.[11]

The twelfth article. Whatever holy scripture says of Christ, all that is also true of every good and divine man.[12]

The thirteenth article. Whatever is proper to the divine nature, all that is proper to the just and divine man. Because of that, this man performs whatever God performs, and he created heaven and earth together with God, and he is the begetter of the Eternal Word, and God would not know how to do anything without such a man.[13]

The fourteenth article. A good man ought so to conform his will to the divine will that he should will whatever God wills. Since God in some way wills for me to have sinned, I should not will that I had not committed sins; and this is true penitence.[14]

The fifteenth article. If a man had committed a thousand mortal sins, if such a man were rightly disposed he ought not to will that he had not committed them.[15]

The sixteenth article. God does not properly command an exterior act.[16]

The seventeenth article. The exterior act is not properly good or divine, and God does not produce it or give birth to it in the proper sense.

The eighteenth article. Let us bring forth the fruit not of exterior acts, which do not make us good, but of interior acts, which the Father who abides in us makes and produces.[17]

The nineteenth article. God loves souls, not the exterior work.[18]

The twentieth article. That the good man is the Only-Begotten Son of God.[19]

The twenty-first article. The noble man is that Only-Begotten Son of God whom the Father generates from all eternity.[20]

The twenty-second article. The Father gives birth to me his Son and the same Son. Everything that God performs is one; therefore he gives me, his Son, birth without any distinction.[21]

The twenty-third article. God is one in all ways and according to every respect so that he cannot find any multiplicity in himself either in intellect or in reality. Anyone who beholds the number two or who beholds distinction does not behold God, for God is one, outside and beyond number, and is not counted with anything.[22] There follows: No distinction can exist or be understood in God himself.[23]

The twenty-fourth article. Every distinction is foreign to God, both in nature and in Persons. The proof is that the nature itself is one and this one thing, and each Person is one and that same one thing that the nature is.[24]

The twenty-fifth article. When it says, "Simon, do you love me more than these men?" (Jn. 21:15sqq.), it means, that is, more than these others—and indeed well, but not perfectly. In the case of what is more and less there is an order and a degree, but there is no order and degree in the One. Therefore, whoever loves God more than his neighbor loves well, but not yet perfectly.[25]

The twenty-sixth article. All creatures are one pure nothing. I do not say that they are a little something or anything, but that they are pure nothing.[26]

In addition, an objection exists against the aforesaid Eckhart that he preached two other articles under these words.

The first article. There is something in the soul that is uncreated and not capable of creation; if the whole soul were such, it would be uncreated and not capable of creation, and this is the intellect.[27]

The second article. That God is neither good, nor better, nor best; hence I speak as incorrectly when I call God good as if I were to call white black.[28]

Now we saw to it that all the above articles were examined by many doctors of sacred theology, and we ourselves have carefully examined them along with our brethren. Finally, both from the report of the doctors and from our own examination we have found the first fifteen articles in question as well as the two final ones to contain the error or stain of heresy as much from the tenor of their words as from the sequence of their thoughts. The other eleven, the first of which begins "God does not properly command, etc.," we have found quite evil-sounding and very rash and suspect of heresy, though with many explanations and additions they might take on or possess a Catholic meaning. Lest articles of this sort and their contents further infect the hearts of the simple among whom they were preached, and lest in any way whatsoever they should gain currency among them or others, on the advice of our brethren mentioned above we condemn and expressly reprove the first fifteen of these articles and the other two at the end as heretical, the other eleven as evil-sounding, rash and suspect of heresy, and likewise any books or writings of this same Eckhart that contain the above-mentioned articles or any one of them.

If anyone should presume to defend or approve the same articles in an obstinate manner, we desire and order a process of heresy against those who would so defend or approve the fifteen articles and the two last, or any one of them, as well as a process of suspicion of heresy against those who would defend or approve the other eleven articles according to their literal sense.

Further, we wish it to be known both to those among whom these articles were preached or taught, and to any others to whose notice they have come, that the aforesaid Eckhart, as is evident from a public document drawn up for that purpose,[29] professed the Catholic faith at the end of his life and revoked and also deplored the twenty-six articles, which he admitted that he had preached, and also any others, written and taught by him, whether in the schools or in sermons, insofar as they could generate in the minds of the faithful a heretical opinion, or one erroneous and hostile to the true faith.[30] He wished them to be considered absolutely and totally revoked, just as if he had revoked the articles and other matters severally and singly by submitting both himself and everything that he had written and preached to the judgment of the Apostolic See and our own judgment.

Given at Avignon, on March 27, in the thirteenth year of our pontificate.

2. SELECTIONS FROM THE COMMENTARIES ON GENESIS[1]

A. PROLOGUE TO THE WORK OF EXPOSITIONS I[2]

"In the beginning God created heaven and earth." The third principal part of the *Three-Part Work*, namely the *Work of Commentaries*, begins here.

By way of preface it should be noted beforehand that I have gone through the Old and the New Testaments in order from beginning to end and I have written down whatever came to me then and whatever I remembered I said about the interpretation of these authoritative texts at any time. Not to be long-winded, I have taken care to abbreviate or to omit completely most of it, especially so that the better and more useful interpretations that the saints and venerable teachers, particularly Brother Thomas, have written are not neglected. On a few occasions I decided merely to note where their interpretations are to be found. Sometimes I thought that they should be briefly discussed. Let us begin with the words "In the beginning."

B. THE COMMENTARY ON THE BOOK OF GENESIS[3]

1. Augustine treats this introduction of the Book of Genesis at length, especially in his *Literal Commentary on Genesis*, his *On Genesis against the Manichaeans* and in the three final books of the *Confessions*. Ambrose and Basil do the same in their *Commentaries on the Hexaemeron*.[4] Rabbi Moses treats it especially in book two, chapter thirty-

one, of the *Guide to the Perplexed;*[5] and Thomas in the *Summa of Theology* Ia, qq. 44–47, and later qq. 65–74.

"In the beginning God created heaven and earth."

2. Four preliminary points about this text must be discussed. First, what this "beginning" is in which God is said to have created heaven and earth.[6] Second, how he is said to have created heaven in the beginning when it says in the Psalm and in Hebrews, "In the beginning, Lord, you founded the earth" (Ps. 101:26; Heb. 1:10), and Ecclesiasticus says, "He who lives forever created all things at the same time" (Si. 18:1).[7] Third, since what is born one always has the power to produce only what is one,[8] how can God, who is simply one and always possesses himself in the same way, have produced or created such different things as heaven and earth, in the beginning and all at the same time? Fourth, the conclusion from this is that everything except God possesses existence from somewhere else and from someone else, and nevertheless nothing is so intimate, so primary and so proper to anything as its own existence.[9]

3. On the first point you must recognize that the "principle" in which "God created heaven and earth" is the ideal reason.[10] This is what the first chapter in John says, "In the principle was the Word" (the Greek has "Logos," that is, "reason"), and, later, "All things were made through him, and without him nothing was made."[11] The universal principle and root of each thing whatever is its reason.[12] This is why Plato held that the ideas or the reasons of things were the principles of the existence and knowledge of everything.[13] And thus, in the third place, Averroes in his commentary on the seventh book of the *Metaphysics* says that the "what-it-is" of a sensible thing was always what the ancient philosophers wanted to know because knowing it they would know the First Cause of everything.[14] Averroes does not say that God himself is the First Cause (as many erroneously think), but he calls the "what-it-is" of things (their reason, which the definition signifies) the First Cause. This reason is the "what" of a thing, and is the "why" of all its properties.[15] Aristotle says that definition and demonstration differ only in the order of the terms.[16]

4. Further, the reason of things is a principle in such a way that it does not have or look to an exterior cause, but looks within to the essence alone. Therefore, the metaphysician who considers the entity of things proves nothing through exterior causes, that is, efficient and final causes.[17] This is the principle, namely the ideal reason, in which

God created all things without looking to anything outside himself. Boethius puts it very clearly in the third book of the *Consolation of Philosophy*:

> Creator of Heaven and earth . . .
> No external causes compelled you.
> . . . You lead all things forth from
> The Supreme Exemplar; Most Beautiful Yourself,
> You bear the beauteous world in your Mind and form it to
> be like that image.[18]

5. This is the reason why the saints commonly explain that God created heaven and earth in the "Principle," that is, in the Son who is the Image and Ideal Reason of all things.[19] So Augustine says, "He who denies the ideas denies the Son of God."[20] Hence "God created all things in the principle," that is, in reason and according to the ideal reason—man according to one reason, lion according to another, and so on with each creature. Again, he also created all things in reason because he did so reasonably and wisely—"You have made all things in wisdom" (Ps. 102:24). In the third book of *On Free Choice* Augustine says: "Whatever suggests itself to you as the better course by means of a true reason, be assured that it has been made by God as the creator of all good things."[21]

6. In the second place, note that the "principle" in which "God created heaven and earth" is the nature of the intellect. "He made the heavens in the intellect" (Ps. 135:5). Intellect is the principle of the whole of nature, as it says in the comment on the ninth proposition of the *Book of Causes* with the words "Understanding rules nature through divine power." Below it says, "Understanding grasps the things that are generated, nature and the soul that borders on nature"; thus concluding, "therefore, understanding contains all things."[22] So, "He created heaven and earth in the principle," that is, in the intellect. This is against those who say that God created and produced things from necessity of nature.[23]

7. Again, in the third place, the "beginning" in which "God created heaven and earth" is the first simple now of eternity. I say that it is the very same now in which God exists from eternity, in which also the emanation of the divine Persons eternally is, was and will be.[24] Moses said that God created heaven and earth in the very first beginning in which he himself exists, without any medium or time interval.

So when someone once asked me why God had not created the world earlier, I answered that he could not because he did not exist. He did not exist before the world did. Furthermore, how could he have created earlier when he had already created the world in the very now in which he was God?[25] It is false to picture God as if he were waiting around for some future moment in which to create the world. In the one and the same time in which he was God and in which he begot his coeternal Son as God equal to himself in all things, he also created the world.[26] "God speaks once and for all" (Jb. 22:14). He speaks in begetting the Son because the Son is the Word; he speaks in creating creatures, "He spoke and they were made, he commanded and they were created" (Ps. 32:9). This is why it says in another Psalm, "God has spoken once and for all and I have heard two things" (Ps. 61:12).[27] The "two things" are heaven and earth, or rather "these two," that is, the emanation of the Persons and the creation of the world, but "he speaks" them both "once and for all"; "he has spoken once and for all." So much for the first of the premises.

8. What the first chapter of Hebrews says in agreement with the Psalm but in reverse order ("In the beginning, Lord, you founded the earth, and the heavens are the works of your hands," Heb. 1:10) presents no difficulty. First, because sentences in which the subject and predicate are reversed still mean the same.[28] Second, just as things that we make not at one time and once and for all, such as the foundation, wall and roof of a house, can be expressed at one time by a single noun (e.g., "house"), so in reverse manner the things that God makes at the same time cannot be expressed by us at one time. This is because unlike us God's speaking is his making, and also unlike us his speaking is the cause of the entire work and of all its parts. Note that if a house's matter came completely from the architect and totally obeyed his least command, then by just thinking of really building a house he would at the same time bring the house and all its parts into existence. Our activity, like our knowledge, arises from things, and so depends on them and is changed when they are. In opposite fashion, things themselves take their origin from and depend upon God's knowledge, so that God's knowledge does not change when they do, because they are posterior. This is why the Psalmist and Paul later make the important addition in speaking of the heavens: "You will change them and they will be changed; but you are the same" (Ps. 101:27; Heb. 1:12).

9. In the third place, it should be noted that because in creatures nothing is perfect in every way, frequently the last beings in certain

ways surpass those that are first. Therefore, the *Topics* say that when one of two things is more like something that is better, it itself is not better than the other unless it is like the better thing in its superior properties.[29] Thus, in relation to stability and immobility the earth surpasses even the heavens. For this reason Averroes and his followers locate the heaven through the earth or center.[30] You will find more on this in the proper place in the *Work of Questions*.[31] So the text is appropriate, "You, Lord, founded the earth in the beginning" (Heb. 1:10), according to the Psalm passage, "You have founded the earth upon its own stability" (Ps. 103:5). This is the reason why with us motion is naturally and properly ascribed more to the right side, while being fixed is ascribed to the left. A person who begins to walk puts his right foot forward while he holds himself fixed on his left,[32] and a worker works with his right hand and holds what he is working on with his left. Concerning the passage in Ecclesiasticus, "He who lives forever created all things at the same time" (Si. 18:1), you will find sufficient exegesis in other authors.[33] So much for the second main question of the four.

10. In the third place, we have to see the way in which many distinct and different things, such as heaven and earth and the like, can immediately exist, or be produced from one simple thing, namely God. For it says, "In the beginning God created heaven and earth." A good response to this is that an agent who works from necessity of nature is different from an agent who works through will and intellect, such as God is, as Thomas says in the *Summa* Ia. 47. 1.[34] What was said above—that is, "In the principle," namely the intellect, "he created heaven and earth"—is relevant to this point. Second, Avicenna has a rather subtle answer to this in his *Metaphysics* 9.4, but in the passage cited above Thomas refutes it, and so does Maimonides in the *Guide to the Perplexed* 2. 23. One of the world's pretentious people used to say that only one thing can be produced in immediate fashion from one, that is, from one idea.[35]

11. I used to give a different and threefold response to this. First, even given that God acts from necessity of nature, then I say: God acts and produces things through his divine nature. But God's nature is intellect, and for him existence is understanding.[36] Therefore, he produces things in existence through intellect. Consequently, just as there is no contradiction between his simplicity and his understanding many things, so too there is none in the case of his producing many things immediately. Second, fire generates fire and gives warmth through its form and the property of heat. But if it possessed in equal fashion the

form of water and the property of cleansing and cooling, at the same time and equally it would generate fire and water, and would warm, cleanse and cool. But God naturally has prior possession of all forms and of the forms of all. Therefore, in his natural manner of producing he can immediately produce different things and everything.

12. Third and better, I say that it is true that only one thing always proceeds immediately from a single thing that is uniform in relation to itself. But this one thing is the whole universe itself, which proceeds from God as one whole thing, though in many parts, just as God himself the producer is one or the simple One in existence, life, understanding and activity, although he is quite diverse according to the ideal reasons. It is universally true that a nature first and necessarily looks to and intends the whole in immediate fashion.[37]

In this case you should note first that the more perfect and simpler a thing is in existence the richer it is in reasons and powers. For example, the rational soul is the most perfect among all the forms of matter, and therefore is the simplest in existence and substance, but the richest in powers, as the diversity and distinction of the human body's organs show and testify. Second, the more perfect the universe or world is, the simpler its existence and the greater the number and distinction of its parts.

13. This is the answer to the ignorant question and difficulty of those who asked whether God produced an angel or some other kind of creature before the rest. He did not immediately produce this or that part of the universe, but immediately produced the whole universe, because, as I say, he would not produce the universe, nor would it be a universe, if any essential part of it were lacking. If stone or wood or the nature of the angelic spirit were lacking, it is equally true that it would not be the universe. So much for the third principle point of the four cited above.

14. The fourth main point, namely that everything except God possesses existence from something else and from somewhere else, follows from what has been said in the following way. We said that "God created heaven and earth," that is, the highest things, the lowest things and therefore everything. Creation is the conferring of existence. This is what Proclus says in the eleventh proposition: "All beings proceed from one First Cause."[38] Augustine in the first book of the *Confessions* puts it this way: "Existence and life flow into us from no other source, Lord, than from the fact that you create us."[39] Do not imagine that existence comes to us from the outside, because God as the Highest and

Supreme is completely natural, delightful and suitable, as the treatise on "The Superior" in the *Work of Propositions* shows by argument and example.[40]

Let these points suffice for the present regarding the literal exposition of the text under discussion, "In the beginning God created heaven and earth." You will find other interpretations I have put down in the "General Prologue" to the whole *Three-part Work*.[41]

15. For the moral meaning, note that it says God created "heaven and earth," with heaven put first and earth last. This strikes out first against those who prefer earthly to heavenly things, contrary to Matthew's text, "Seek first the kingdom of God" (Mt. 6:33). They are like the dog who in snapping at the shadow of the meat lost the meat itself.[42] Second, it censures those who do good out of fear rather than love. Such people first look to the "earth," that is, the penalty, not the "heaven," or love of good. The poet says of them,

Evil men hate sinning for fear of punishment.[43]

In chapter thirty-eight of *On True Religion* Augustine says against such people that they reverse the pen to write with the blunt end and erase with the point.[44] They have their heads on the bottom and their feet on the top so that heaven is below them. "I saw men as though they were trees walking about" (Mk. 8:24). So no wonder they have great labor and suffer much pain, for they are working against nature's order, against the force of natural inclination, against the order of the God who "In the beginning created heaven." "You have set me opposite to you, and I am become burdensome to myself" (Jb. 7:20).

16. Further, it says that God created "heaven and earth in the principle," that is, rationally, as interpreted above,[45] because the godly man sets in good order both favorable and unfavorable, both good and bad, and uses them well, as Romans says: "For those who love God all things work together unto good" (Rm. 8:28). "In the principle God created heaven and earth"—"In the principle," that is, rationally.

17. Note two points from Rabbi Moses about these words. First:

There is a difference between a principle and what is first. A principle is something that is in or with that of which it is the principle even though it does not precede it temporally. Thus the heart is the principle of the life of animals ... The first is predicated of something that is older temporally even

88

though it is not the cause of that which comes after it, as if we were to say, "Peter was the first to live in that house, and after him came John." . . . The word that begins the book of Genesis in Hebrew means "principle" and is taken from "head," that which is the principle of the body of any animal whatever.[46]

18. Second, note that "God created heaven and earth" and everything in them "in their state of being and their beauty, . . . in perfect species and form and with the choice of the proper accidents" at the same time, even though they do not appear at the same time. The example given ". . . is of the farmer who sows different kinds of seeds in the earth at the same time. Some come up after one day, some after two days or three days, but all the seeds were scattered in the one hour."[47]

19. A third remark. Summarizing what "In the principle God created heaven and earth" means, we can say that "God created heaven and earth in the principle," that is, in existence, or to existence, or for the sake of existence, namely, he created them that they might be. "He created all things that they might be" (Ws. 1:14). Existence is what is first and it is the principle of all intentions and perfections, as I have remarked in detail in my commentary on the first chapter of Wisdom.[48] Second, "He created in the principle," that is, he created in such a way that things do not exist outside him. The case is different with every artificer lower than God. The architect makes the house outside himself. In the fourth book of the *Confessions* Augustine says, "He did not create and depart, but the things that are from him are in him."[49]

20. Third, "He created in the principle," that is, he created in such a way that he always creates. "My Father works even until now" (Jn. 5:17). Fourth, "In the principle," that is, in the Son. "I am the principle" (Jn. 8:25). Here note that just as no one becomes just apart from the activity of the Justice that gives birth and is as such Unbegotten, as well as through the activity of the justice that is brought forth, or Begotten Justice, so too nothing is created that is not from Unbegotten Existence and in the Begotten Existence that is the Son.[50] Fifth, "He created in the principle," that is, in reason, for reason, the Logos or Word is the principle and cause of all things.

21. Sixth, "He created heaven and earth in the principle," because inferior beings have the same primary and equal relation to and in existence that superior beings do. This accords with the text: "If I ascend

into heaven you are there, if I descend into hell you are present" (Ps. 138:8). This is against the view of Avicenna and others who say that "In the principle God created" the Intelligence and then by its means created other things.[51] All things possess existence immediately and equally from God alone. An example can be found in the powers of the soul and the organs of the body, because they all immediately and equally have existence from the soul, and in this case there is no order in relation to levels of existence, life and rationality.[52] Seventh, "He created heaven and earth," that is, good and evil. "Creating evil and making peace" (Is. 45:7). The existence of evil is required by the perfection of the universe, and evil itself exists in what is good and is ordered to the good of the universe, which is what creation primarily and necessarily regards.[53]

22. The eighth moral sense. He creates "heaven and earth in the principle," that is, in the Son, because God gives heavenly and earthly gifts to the just and perfect man, one who is God's son, as it says in John, "He gave them the power to become sons of God" (Jn. 1:12). This agrees with the texts, "He will set him [i.e., the Son] over all his goods" (Mt. 24:47), and "All power in heaven and earth is given to me" (Mt. 28:18).

23. Ninth, and still in the moral sense, God creates "heaven" and hence at the same time with time the "earth," because the godlike man does everything that he does out of love of the heavenly good. This is the natural order. Darkness can only be dispelled by light, and cold by the heat that first comes into something and inheres in it. The imperfect man, in that he is unlike God, does the reverse, first creating the earth (because he acts for the sake of the evil he fears) and later the heavenly good.

24. Tenth, "In the principle he created heaven and earth," that is, what is active and what is passive. Although what is active is prior in dignity to what is passive (just as heaven is to earth), nevertheless they exist together at the same time,[54] which is what creation means. Again, form and matter, like heaven and earth, not only exist together at the same time, but also, just as matter does not have existence without form and has the essential characteristic of being subject to form and "informed" without any mediating power, so too, though in reverse order, through its essence and without any intermediary, form receives existence in matter and in the act of informing. Informing is its very existence. Form and matter, active and passive, heaven and earth, are

produced at the same time "in the principle," that is, in the act of existence.

25. Eleventh, God created heaven and earth "in the principle," because the ideas of things in God look to a double kind of existence, namely intellectual existence in the soul, which is understood by heaven ("He made the heavens in intellect," Ps. 135:5), and also the material existence outside the soul that is signified through earth. This is why Plato held that the ideas are the principles of knowledge and of generation.[55] This is what John means, "You call me master and lord" (Jn. 13:13)—master signifies knowledge, lord external activity. And so twelfth, "heaven" is what is superior, "earth" what is inferior. What is inferior is always empty and imperfect, what is superior is never so. I have written about this in the treatise "The Nature of the Superior and the Inferior."[56]

26. Finally, it must be observed that it says "God" created "heaven and earth in the principle," two things, not more, such as three or four and so forth. It does not say that he created one thing. The reason is because by the fact that anything is or has been created it falls away from unity and simplicity. Unity and simplicity are proper to God and are his property, as I have written at length on the text "God is one" (Dt. 6:4; Gal. 3:20).[57] Again, everything that falls away from the One, the First of all things, immediately falls into two and into the other numbers by means of duality.

27. And so Ibn Gabirol says that "the question 'whether a thing is' is asked in relation to the One because it is pure existence," and it alone belongs to God alone, who is "one, exalted and holy." "Under him the questions 'whether a thing is' and 'what a thing is' in the manner of duality belong to the intelligence, which is the first thing below God. In a threefold way the questions 'whether a thing is,' 'what it is,' and 'what sort it is' belong to the soul. In a fourfold way, the questions 'whether,' 'what,' 'what sort,' and 'why' a thing is belong to nature or the realm of generation that is below the soul. The fourth question refers to the first three."[58]

28. The first equal number, namely two, is the root of all division, plurality and number, just as the unequal or the One is the root and reason of lack of division. So everything that is unequal insofar as it is unequal is indivisible. The proof of this is that the division of such a thing cannot be equivalent or equal, but is always unequal, incorrect and faulty, because it is a division into unequal parts.

MEISTER ECKHART

C. THE BOOK OF THE PARABLES OF GENESIS[59]

Prologue

1. Having set forth in the first *Commentary* what seemed worthy of note as far as the more evident sense of the Book of Genesis is concerned, our intention in this *Book of the Parables* is to run through some places both of this book and of others in the holy canon in order to bring to light the more hidden sense of some things contained in them in parabolical fashion "under the shell of the letter." I do this to arouse the more skilled readers to seek better and richer explanations of the theological, natural and moral truths hidden beneath the form and surface of the literal sense, both in the few passages I briefly treat and in the many others I omit.[60] As Rabbi Moses says, the whole Old Testament is either "natural science" or "spiritual wisdom."[61] "We know that the Law is spiritual" (Rm. 7:14). Augustine in the sixth book of the *Confessions* says:

> The authority of sacred scripture appeared so much the more venerable and more worthy of holy faith to me by just as much as it was ready at hand for all to read and still hid the dignity of its secret in a more profound understanding. . . . It offers itself to all in a most humble style of speaking and it arouses the attention of those who are not light-hearted.[62]

This is what Proverbs says, "Like golden apples on silver beds" (Pr. 25:11), which Rabbi Moses explains as follows:

> You should understand how agreeable this comparison is, for every parable has two faces. . . . The external face must be beautiful in order to attract; the interior must be more beautiful and compared to the exterior like gold to silver. Therefore, the truth of scripture is like a golden apple covered with a net of engraved silver figures. . . . When one looks at it from afar or without understanding, he thinks that it is only silver; but when a sharp-eyed man looks at it, he will see what lies hid within and will know that it is gold.[63]

Perhaps this is what Wisdom says, "The Holy Spirit of discipline will flee from what is deceitful and will withdraw itself from thoughts that are without understanding" (Ws. 1:5). When we can dig out some mystical understanding from what is read it is like bringing honey forth from the hidden depths of the honeycomb,[64] or like rubbing the ears of grain with our hands to find the hidden kernels in imitation of Christ's disciples, as Augustine says in a homily.[65]

2. The reason for this is evident. "The holy men of God spoke as they were moved by the Holy Spirit" (2 P. 1:21). The Holy Spirit teaches all truth (Jn. 16:13). Since the literal sense is that which the author of a writing intends, and God is the author of holy scripture, as has been said, then every true sense is a literal sense.[66] It is well known that every truth comes from the Truth itself; it is contained in it, derived from it and is intended by it. Augustine gives an example in the twelfth book of the *Confessions* when he speaks of a spring and the streams that are drawn or flow from it.[67] Hence in speaking to God earlier in the same book he says: "As long as anyone in reading the holy scriptures is trying to understand what their author meant to say, what harm is there if he lays hold of something that you, the light of all truthful minds, shows him to be true, even if the author he is reading did not grasp it—though the author did grasp a truth, just not this one?"[68] Right before that he says, "What harm does it do to me that different meanings can be taken from the same words as long as they are true,"[69] and true in the single truth of the Light? God, the Truth Himself, the author of scripture, comprehends, inspires and intends all truth at one time in his intellect.[70] This is the reason why Augustine says that he made scripture fruitful in such a way that everything that any intellect could draw from it has been sown in it and sealed upon it.[71] This is also the reason why the philosophers of the Academy used to hold that all the intellectual sciences, the theological and the natural, and even the virtues in relation to the ethical sciences, were created together with the soul.[72] Plato himself and all the ancient theologians and poets generally used to teach about God, nature and ethics by means of parables. The poets did not speak in an empty and fabulous way, but they intentionally and very attractively and properly taught about the natures of things divine, natural and ethical by metaphors and allegories.[73] This is quite clear to anyone who takes a good look at the poets' stories. As the poet Horace himself says in his *Art of Poetry*:

Poets want either to be useful or to entertain.

And later:

> He who mingles the useful and the entertaining wins all the applause.[74]

With us the Song of Solomon and John's Apocalypse disclose the same, as well as the very name of Solomon's Proverbs, which are entitled "Parables."[75] Thus it says there, "He shall understand a parable and its interpretation, the words of the wise and their mysterious sayings" (Pr. 1:6). Christ, the Truth himself, in parabolical fashion in the Gospels both gives moral instruction and also transmits the general roots of profound, hidden truths to those who have "ears to hear" (Mt. 13:9, etc.). "But why go further?" as Ambrose says.[76] Or in Terence's words, "Why should I linger over many things?"[77] There is almost nothing in sacred scripture that the *Glosses* of the saints do not explain in a mystical way. A good example of this is the whole of q. 102 of the *Prima Secundae* of the *Summa*.[78] As I have noted in my commentary on the sixteenth chapter of John,[79] it was not idly said that the Spirit that Christ was to send from the Father would teach the disciples all truth (Jn. 16:13).

3. We ought also to add that there is no doubt that anyone who wishes to search the scriptures in the way we have described will surely find that Christ is hidden in them. "You search the scriptures . . . and it is they that bear witness to me" (Jn. 5:39); and below, "If you believed Moses, you would also believe me, for he wrote of me" (Jn. 5:46). "I have used similitudes by the hands of the prophets" (Hos. 12:10). No one can be thought to understand the scriptures who does not know how to find its hidden marrow—Christ, the Truth. Hidden under the parables we are speaking of are very many of the properties that belong to God alone, the First Principle, and that point to his nature. Enclosed there are to be found the virtues and the principles of the sciences,[80] the keys to metaphysics, physics and ethics, as well as the universal rules. Also there we find the most sacred emanation of the divine Persons with their property of distinction under and in one essence, one act of existence, life and understanding. We find the production of creatures derived from them as their exemplar. We find how the Unbegotten Father, the Son Begotten from the Father alone, and the Holy Spirit breathed forth or proceeding from the Father and the Son as one principle, the Essential Concomitant Love and Notional

Love, shine out in every natural, ethical and artistic work.[81] This will soon be clear in this *Book of the Parables of Genesis*, even in the first chapter.

4. Three preliminary remarks must be made to this *Book of the Parables*. The first is that you must not think that from the parables we intend to prove divine, natural and ethical truths through parabolical arguments of this kind.[82] Rather, we intend to show that what the truth of holy scripture parabolically intimates in hidden fashion agrees with what we prove and declare about matters divine, ethical and natural.

5. The second is that there are two kinds of parables, as Rabbi Moses teaches in the introduction to the *Guide to the Perplexed*. The first kind or mode of parable is when "every, or almost every, word of the parable separately stands for something. The second mode is when the whole parable is the likeness and expression of the whole matter of which it is a parable."[83] Then indeed "many words" are introduced that do not directly relate to the details of the matter of the parable, "but which are used for the beauty of the comparison and parable, or for the deeper concealment of the matter of the parable according to what agrees with its surface meaning."[84] An example of the first mode is the passage in Genesis, chapter twenty-eight, where in a dream Jacob saw a ladder that stood on the earth, and so forth. An example of the second mode is what Proverbs, chapter five, says about prime matter under the parable of the adulterous woman, "Do not pay attention to a deceiving woman; the lips of a harlot are like a dripping honeycomb, etc." (Pr. 5:2–3).[85]

6. The third preliminary remark. I have passed over much in relation to these parabolical passages and have briefly set down only a few things merely in order to stimulate students to treat similar passages more fully. The proofs and extended treatments of the parabolical passages I treat here are to be sought out more fully in the *Work of Questions* and in the *Work of Commentaries*.

7. The mode of proceeding in the work is this. First, the text itself will always be literally interpreted. Second, the things that seem to be hidden in parabolical fashion under the words of each text will be treated in a summary and succinct way. Third, the nature and properties of the divine, natural or ethical truths contained under the parable or surface of the letter will be explained in a more extensive way. The end of the Prologue to the *Book of the Parables of Genesis*.

MEISTER ECKHART

Chapter One

Verse 1. In the beginning God created heaven and earth.

8. This text was interpreted in many ways in the first Genesis commentary. Now I wish to show how these words suggest first the production or emanation of the Son and the Holy Spirit from the Father in eternity, then the production or general creation of the whole universe from the one God in time, and many of the properties of both Creator and creature.[86]

9. You should know that in every natural action or production that is directed to what is outside the one who produces and which implies a passage from something that is not an existing being to something that is, the principle of such production has the nature of a cause and that which is produced has the name and nature of an external effect. The first point is clear from Aristotle, who says: "A cause is that to which or from which something follows."[87] The second point stands from the name itself. "Effect" is derived from *extra factus,* or "made outside the maker." From this it follows that what is produced in that way has the nature of something created or a creature, both because it is produced outside the producer and also because it is produced from something that is not an existing being to become some existing being, for example, a horse from what was not a horse,[88] something white from what was not white.[89] From this first conclusion regarding natural productions it is clear that in the Godhead, since every production or emanation is not directed to what is outside the producer, and is not from something that is not an existing being or from nothing, and in the third place is not directed to particular existence, what is procreated does not have the nature of something made or created and is not an effect. It is also clear that the producer does not have the nature of a creator or a cause, and that what is produced is not outside the producer and is not different from it, but is one with it. "I am in the Father, and the Father is in me" (Jn. 14:11); "The Father and I are one" (Jn. 10:30). In the Godhead the Son and the Holy Spirit are not from nothing, but are "God from God, light from light, one light, one God" with the Father.[90] "These three are one" (1 Jn. 5:7). This is why it says here, "God created heaven and earth." Creation is a production from nothing; heaven and earth are particular beings. As we said, the Son and the Holy Spirit are not particular beings, but are simple, total and full existence.[91] They are not from nothing.

10. The second point is that in nature the first thing in any genus

is always one.[92] Therefore, what is simply first in all things is perfectly one "in complete simplicity."[93] This is what the text says, "In the principle God created." "Created" is in the singular and so is "God," since it is speaking about what is simply one. As if giving the reason for the unity of God and of his activity it begins by saying "In the principle." By the fact that God is the simple principle he is God and is one, and it follows that his activity is necessarily one insofar as it is in him and from him. For what is in the One is one, just as what is in Wisdom is wise and what remains in Justice is just.[94] This is what this text signifies, "In the principle he created," that is, because he is the principle, or based on the fact that he is the principle, he is God, he is one, and his activity is one. It says "God created"—one creation and one Creator.

11. The third point is that in nature, according to the Philosopher, what is one, as long as it remains one, is always geared to make what is one, and thus what proceeds from what is one insofar as it is one is always one.[95] Again, from the same reason what proceeds outside the One necessarily falls away into plurality. The first fall or departure and lapse from the One sinks into what is two and only two. The reason for this is evident from what was said above. What remains in the One by this fact and this alone is one; therefore, what falls from the One and proceeds outside it, since it is divided and distinct from the One, is no longer one. So then, just as everything that the One produces as an effect (i.e., as made outside itself) necessarily as something produced falls outside the One and into number and division, the same is true of the reverse. Everything that the One produces that is not an effect, or something made on the outside, is necessarily one inasmuch as it remains in the One. It is not an effect, or something made on the outside, but it is before what is made,[96] prior in nature to what is made, not divided from the One, but one with the One, from the One, through the One and in the One—one, I say, in unity, entity, wisdom and in all similar immanent things. It is produced indeed, but it is not made, or something different or created. This is what is expressly said here: "He created heaven and earth," two things that are divided and numbered because they are created. Moses says, "He created heaven and earth."

12. The first point that follows from this concerning the Godhead is that a Person who proceeds and is produced, but is not brought forth on the outside, namely outside the One (I refer to the Son and the Holy Spirit who are not outside the One, but are the same as the One and

the one Unity itself), is not an effect of the Father to whom unity is attributed.[97] They are not made as effects outside the One, outside the Father; they are prior and before all making and creating.[98] Therefore, there is no division or exteriority or anything that implies any of the above in these Persons.

13. The second point that follows from this is that the Son is in the Father and the Father in the Son ("I am in the Father and the Father is in me," Jn. 14:11), and that the Son is one with the Father ("The Father and I are one," Jn. 10:30). The same is true of the Holy Spirit, who is in the Son and the Son in him. He is in the Father and the Father is in him; he is "with the Son and with the Father."[99] This is why "These three are one" (1 Jn. 5:7), both because the Son and Holy Spirit proceed from and remain in the One, "in whom there is no number," as Boethius says,[100] and also because they are prior to everything that is on the outside and to the fall into what is exterior. The same holds in the case of everything that proceeds from the One, but does not withdraw and depart from it. Hence what is in God is not created or made, but is prior to all this. The Father is not the cause of such things.[101] The same is true universally of everything that either is one, or is convertible with the One, or proceeds from and remains in the One. Such a thing is prior to what falls away from the One or implies a fall from it.

14. The third point that follows is that he who proceeds is a different Person but not a different thing from him from whom he proceeds. "Different thing" as neuter pertains to nature or essence; "different Person" is masculine and belongs to the person or supposit.[102] Since it is neither masculine nor feminine, what is neuter neither begets nor is begotten, but what is male or masculine has the property of begetting. It would not beget if there were not someone to be begotten. This is why Augustine says: "If there is a Father, he begets; if he is always a Father, he always begets."[103]

15. The fourth point that follows is that "The works of the Trinity are indivisible."[104] The one activity that belongs to the Father also belongs to the Holy Spirit and the Son. Thus the words "God created," for God is one in the Father, Son and Holy Spirit. The activity is one, for Moses says "created" in the singular. The one God and his one activity are not divided into many different things, but they unite many things and gather together what has been divided. Thus, the One or Unity is not divided into numbers, but unites numbers in itself according to Proclus's principle, "Every multitude somehow participates in

the One."[105] Every number is one number—something as true of a thousand as it is of eight. Macrobius puts it this way: "The One . . . which is called Unity is both male and female, odd and even. It is not a number, but the source . . . of all numbers. Although it is not a number or numbered, it creates from itself and contains within itself innumerable kinds of numbers. . . . It does not permit any division of its unity."[106] His message is that the One or Unity is not divided or numbered in numbers or in the things that are enumerated, but gathers and unites numbers and what is enumerated into itself. This is why we have "God" in the singular here.

16. The fourth main thing to be noted is that because nature does not make a leap,[107] but descends in an ordered process or progressive order by degrees and the smallest steps possible, therefore the first falling away and departure from the One is into two and only two. This is what the text means. "In the beginning," that is, first of all, "God created heaven and earth." "God," the One, "created heaven and earth," that is, what was twofold. This is very clearly put in the Psalm, "Once and for all God has spoken two things" (Ps. 61:12), and in Job, "God speaks once and for all and does not repeat the selfsame a second time" (Jb. 33:14). The repetition by means of which something is said "once and for all and yet a second time" does not touch the "Selfsame,"[108] that is, God insofar as he produces, but it touches the things that are produced outside him who is one and whose activity is one. Thus the Psalm text: "You will change them and they will be changed; but you are always the Selfsame" (Ps. 101:27–28). In the ninth book of the *Confessions* Augustine says to God: "You are surpassingly that Selfsame that does not change, and in you is rest . . . since there is no other besides you, . . . but you, O Lord, are unique."[109]

17. There are three points to be noted in relation to these remarks for their clarification. First, number and division always belong to imperfect things and come from imperfection. In itself number is an imperfection, because it is a falling away or lapse outside the One that is convertible with being. This is the reason why only inferior and corruptible beings are numbered and divided under a single species.[110]

18. Second, just as all things desire existence, as Avicenna says,[111] so too they detest and avoid number and imperfection inasmuch as it is a departure or fall from existence. The greater the departure from the One that is convertible with being, the more offensive a thing is to God and nature. This is why the fall from the One is first into two, because of all the numbers this is the least distant and fallen from the

One and from existence. And so it says, "In the beginning God created heaven and earth," that is, the One created two things.

19. From which follows a third, because if the question arises why ten is a larger number than eight, I would answer that the reason is because it is more and further distant from the One than eight is. For example, the reason why someone is a fool is because he falls away from prudence, and the further he falls away from it and the more distant he is, the more a fool he is. Again, the more and more varied the ways that anyone departs from the good, the worse he is or the more evil. If someone perhaps says that ten is a larger number than eight because ten has more units collected and contained in it than does eight,[112] I would not disagree, but I prefer the first explanation. If this second reason is well investigated it will be seen to have its efficacy from the first reason, as the two examples given above show. Thus, according to the first reason, two is the least distant number from the One, from existence and from perfection. It has the least degree of imperfection. Therefore, the first departure from the One, existence and perfection immediately arrives at two, and this is again signified here in saying, "In the beginning God created heaven and earth," that is, the first fall of all is from the One into two, from unity into number, from what is perfect, undivided and indistinct into imperfection, division and distinction, and from the whole into parts. Parts are always many; they are divided and distinct from one another and are subject to number.

20. The fifth observation. In nature nothing is counted in its principle; it does not form a plural number with it.[113] Again, the principle of anything is never the thing itself, but is outside and above the genus of the thing of which it is the principle. For example, a point has no quantity of magnitude and does not lengthen the line of which it is the principle.[114] Nothing that involves the genus of magnitude belongs to the point. Second, the same is true with the One that is the principle of numbers: It is not a number and is not numbered with any of the numbers of which it is the principle, but rather it changes the species of the number to which it is added. Unity acting as a principle of the number six does not make six more than itself, but makes it exactly and absolutely six. Third, the principle of a changeable and divisible thing is not changeable and is not divided when the thing of which it is the principle is. As Augustine says, the idea of the corruptible circle does not corrupt, but is eternal.[115] The idea of the circle is not enumerated along with the circle and is not subject to number, but it is and remains

one in every circle. Circles are not different in their idea, that is, their principle, but are one. As a wise man says, "Many men are one man by participation in the idea of man."[116] Outside the idea that is their principle circles are directly divided and numbered, first and necessarily into two. Therefore, a genus necessarily requires a minimum of two species; one does not suffice.[117] Again, privation and possession, two things, are the root of all oppositions. This is why it says here, "In the principle God created heaven and earth." Logos, idea and principle are the same. "In the principle was the Logos," that is, the idea, according to the Greek. So then, "In the principle," namely in the One, the one "God created heaven and earth," two things, by one activity.

21. Now for the second interpretation of "In the principle God created heaven and earth." These words point to the nature of the principles of the whole created universe, both in relation to their primary distinction and also to what characterizes them as distinct. As far as the primary distinction goes, recognize that the entire universe created by God is distinguished into two principles, the active and the passive. These two can be found in every nature, as the third book of *On the Soul* says.[118] This is what it means here: "In the principle God created heaven and earth," that is, two principles of everything that exists, the active and the passive. "Heaven" is the active, the first "unchangeable thing that changes others";[119] "earth" is the passive inasmuch as it is especially material.

22. As far as the second point goes, namely concerning what characterizes the two distinct principles that are active and passive, heaven and earth, six things must be noted. The first is that heaven and earth do not have any common matter and consequently do not belong to one genus, except in a merely logical sense.[120] As a universal rule what is active in relation to an entire species, because it is truly and simply active, naturally speaking never shares a real genus with the passive thing it acts upon. It is always outside and above the genus of what is passive.[121] Second, what is active in the way in which heaven is, is not acted upon when it acts. It is not affected, and therefore does not become weary or old, but always acts uniformly.[122]

23. Third, the effect of an active cause of the sort that is suggested here by the word "heaven" does not remain in the thing subject to the action in the absence of the active cause. For example, in contrast to heat, light does not remain in a medium in the absence of a luminous body.[123] The reason is because the effect or the impression of such an active cause on what it acts upon does not have any root in the latter

and does not adhere to or inhere in it. The thing subject to the action always constantly receives the effect of what perfects it from without, that is, from the active cause where the root of the perfection is found. This is the reason why it is always in a state of becoming and becoming is its very existence.

24. The reason is from what has been said. The root of light is heaven or heaven's form, which can never be shared with a body made up of elements. The root and foundation of heat is the form of fire, which can be received by the matter of the medium. For this reason the medium itself can be disposed for and changed into the form of fire by the heat of an illuminating or active body, and thus heat and fire send out a root into the medium that adheres to and inheres in it and becomes in a somewhat imperfect way an heir of the form of fire and the accompanying heat. It is otherwise with the form of heaven to which the medium can never be disposed in the slightest way. The reason is because nature, which does not act in vain,[124] never begins what it cannot complete. Therefore, neither heaven's form nor light, its proper quality, sends out a root in air or in any element whatever. Consequently, light never stays in a medium in the absence of a luminous body because it does not have a root there. "They possess no roots" (Lk. 8:13)—a parable that is to be understood not only morally, but also naturally in relation to the variety of formal perfections, as I will indicate about this text.[125] I have noted it in commenting on the verse, "He will cleave to his wife" (Gn. 2:24), in the second chapter.[126]

25. Thus the fourth point, what is passive always thirsts for what is active even when drinking it. "They that drink me, shall yet thirst" (Si. 24:29), as I have explained more fully in commenting on this verse.[127]

From this comes the fifth point, that what is passive is universally the praise, honor and glory of its essential active cause. "The woman is the glory of the man" (1 Co. 11:7)—the woman signifies what is passive, the man what is active. Earlier in the same chapter it says, "Christ is the man's head" (1 Co. 11:3). Paul here signifies the four orders of active and passive principles, as I have fully explained in commenting on this verse.[128] The same point is made in the verse, "Honor and glory belong to God alone" (1 Tm. 1:17), and "Bless the Lord, all you works of the Lord, etc." (Dn. 3:57). Scripture is full of such passages that everywhere teach that no one is to give praise and honor to himself, but only to God.[129] From what has been said it will be clear that in and from every perfection and good of its own the passive principle proclaims and testifies to its own need and indigence, and announces the riches and mercy of the active principle that is its superior. It naturally teaches that what it possesses it does not have from itself as something that inheres in it, but that it has begged it and received it as something that is continually on loan. It has it in passing, as a reception, and not like a received quality given by its superior active cause.[130] Thus, its act of existence is not its own, but it is from another and in another to whom is "all honor and glory" because it is his.[131] For example, an expensive coat that a servant wears when he attends his master does not give honor to the servant but to the master, because it belongs to him and not the servant.

26. The sixth point follows. The active principle of which we are speaking takes nothing at all from its passive principle and is not formally affected by anything that belongs to it or exists in it. In contrast, everything that is in the passive principle insofar as it is passive is all a complete gift that the active principle itself has poured into its passive counterpart. This is the significance of the words, "In the principle God created heaven and earth," that is, two principles of all created beings, the active and the passive. "Heaven" is the active, "earth" is the passive. Thus under a metaphor and in parabolical fashion with the words "heaven" and "earth" we have a suggestion of the nature, natural property and the number of the first principles of the whole created universe.

27. In addition you should know that the same metaphor teaches us a moral lesson, namely, who the godlike, perfect and celestial man is and what his character is, and the same for the vicious, diabolical and earthly man. "Their glory is in their shame who mind the things of earth, but our citizenship is in heaven" (Ph. 3:19–20). "There are heavenly bodies and earthly bodies. . . . The first man was of the earth, earthly, the second man is from heaven, heavenly. As was the earthly man, such also are the earthly; and as is the heavenly man, such also are the heavenly" (1 Co. 15:40, 47–48). It is evident who the celestial and terrestrial man is and what his character is from the properties of heaven and earth referred to previously. But enough of this.

28. Now for a third interpretation of "In the beginning God created heaven and earth," in which "heaven" and "earth" are parabolically understood as form and matter.[132] The first thing to recognize is that matter and form are not two beings, but are two principles of created beings. This is what the text says: "In the beginning God created heaven and earth," that is, form and matter, the two principles of

things. Second, note that form and matter are related in such a way that matter is for the sake of form, not the contrary. "Man was not created for woman, but woman for man" (1 Co. 11:9).

29. Third, recognize that despite the fact that matter exists for the sake of form, nevertheless substantial form has no more power to exist without matter than matter does without form, as Avicenna teaches in the second book of his *Metaphysics*.[133] This is why after the Apostle said that "woman was for man," he added, "Yet neither is man independent of woman, nor woman of man" (1 Co. 11:11).

30. Fourth. Matter is its own passive potency,[134] and form its own act, and thus the potency that is active and passive on respective sides is not something that is added to the substance, but the matter and the form, each in its own way, in themselves are the naked substance. What is said of man and woman in Genesis, chapter two, is a figure of this, "They were both naked, Adam and his wife" (Gn. 2:25). What follows ("They were not ashamed"), and almost everything put down there about Adam and Eve, is a very beautiful and exact figurative expression of the properties of matter and form, as will appear regarding chapter two below.[135]

31. The fifth thing to be known, following from what we said about point four, is that there is no medium or disposition between form and matter, as book two of *On the Soul* says.[136] Moses says, "They were both naked, Adam and his wife," man and woman, form and matter. From this text it is evident that there can be no doubt that every substantial form that matter initially, necessarily and essentially looks toward is united to it for the purpose of existence without any medium or disposition. The matter of such a substantial form looks toward and desires the essence, not anything outside the essence and existence of form. Thus it is a universal rule that any receptive potency, such as the soul's powers, must always be naked. For example, the power that receives color must be without any color, and the same for the others.[137] It is also a universal rule that the same body cannot receive different forms at the same time. Everything is always formed out of what is without form; this is its process of becoming. It is different in the case of actual existence, for nothing is at the same time both without form and with form or given form by two forms. Here you should note that if matter and form were united in some medium, or if they were not united through their substances, but through different powers belonging to the essence of each, it would follow that what they compose

would not be properly one, but merely united. It would not be one substantially, but accidentally. Every receptive and passive potency must be stripped of every act, and every active potency as such must be stripped of everything received, for he says, "They were both naked." For this reason "A simple form cannot be a subject" according to Boethius.[138] Therefore the Philosopher also says that the power of sight must be free from color,[139] and later (as if it followed from this) says that the power of sight and the visible object are one in act.[140] Two beings in act or two beings in potency never make a third that is truly and simply one.

32. Relevant to this nakedness is the saying of Anaxagoras that the intellect must be separated, unmixed and naked in order to understand.[141] Aristotle himself says that the intellect must be an empty or naked tablet.[142] The greater the nakedness, the greater the union. Therefore, prime matter, since among the passive and receptive powers it alone is utterly naked and pure, is worthy to receive the utterly first act, which is existence or form.

33. The sixth point is that matter and form are the two principles of things in such a way that they are still one in existence and have one act of existence and one activity. Operation follows existence. This is what the figure in chapter two declares, "They were two in one flesh" (Gn. 2:24). And so the sense faculty and the sense object, the intellect and the intelligible object, though two in potency, are one in act. The one act belongs to both. The faculty of sight is actually seeing and the visible object is actually seen in the same utterly simple act.[143]

34. There is still a fourth explanation of "In the beginning God created heaven and earth," in which "heaven" is understood as that "by-which-a-thing-is," or its act of existence, and "earth" is understood parabolically as that which a thing is, or its essence and "what-it-is." These two things are different in every created being and are the principles and properties of all created things.[144] Only in the uncreated being is that by which it is and that which it is one and the same, and this is so because it is uncreated. This is what the text means, "In the beginning God created heaven and earth," that is, he created two principles of all beings that have been created by the very fact that they have been created, namely that by which they are and that which they are. These two are two and not one in every created being and only in created being. The reason is that everything that comes from another and has been created has existence, or that by which it is, from

another. That which it is (its "what-it-is") it does not have from another, as Avicenna says.[145] That man is an animal is not something possessed from another. Whatever thing is established as really existing or not, it is still always true that man is an animal. But the fact that a man actually exists he has from another. Thus in every created being and only in created being that by which it is and that which it is are the two properties and principles of creatures. This is the meaning of "In the beginning God created heaven and earth."

35. There is a fifth way that this passage can be explained in parabolical fashion in which "heaven" is understood as the existence that created things have in their original causes (think of color in light and heat in the sun), and "earth" is taken as the formal existence things have in themselves.[146] There is still a sixth explanation of "In the beginning God created heaven and earth" where "heaven" is taken as the existence of things under the aspect of truth by which they are directed to the intellect ("He made the heavens in intellect," Ps. 135:5), and "earth" is taken as the existence of things under the aspect of goodness ("The things he made were very good," Gn. 1:31).[147] I have written more on these last two interpretations in my first commentary on Genesis.[148]

36. A seventh explanation of "In the beginning God created heaven and earth" understands "heaven" as the good and "earth" as evil. "I am the Lord . . . forming the light and creating the darkness. I make peace and create evil" (Is. 45:6–7). In my exposition of this passage I have given a full argument and proof of this.[149] These are some of the natural and divine truths that seem to be hidden and concealed in parabolical fashion under the words, "In the beginning God created heaven and earth." There is still an eighth one where "heaven" is understood as the intellectual nature and "earth" as the bodily nature, but I have spoken of this in the first commentary and below on chapter twenty-nine.[150]

37. As far as moral meaning is concerned there are ten points to note. First, that the godlike and virtuous man ought to strive for God and heavenly things first of all, and secondarily and almost by accident for temporal things. "Seek first the kingdom of God and his justice, and all these things shall be given to you besides" (Mt. 6:33). For in this text "heaven" comes first and "earth" follows after it. From this you can deduce that simony is committed both in spiritual matters and in the things that are connected to them, for Moses says "heaven and

earth." Second, we are taught to do good works from love not fear. Love is understood in "heaven" and fear in "earth." "You have not received a spirit of bondage in fear, but a spirit of adoption as God's sons" (Rm. 8:15).

38. Third, "heaven" and "earth" are slave and son. Augustine says on Psalm 32: "You are a slave, be also a son! From a good slave become a good son. Do not do evil out of fear and you will learn not to do it also out of love. The punishment that deters you has some of justice's beauty."[151] Fourth, "heaven" and "earth" are the heavenly man and the terrestrial man. "The first man was of the earth, earthly; the second man is from heaven, heavenly" (1 Co. 15:47). Immediately before that comes, "It is the sensual and not the spiritual that comes first" (1 Co. 15:46). Fifth, "heaven" and "earth" are the sensual man and the spiritual man: "The sensual man does not perceive the things that are of the Spirit of God, . . . but the spiritual man judges all things" (1 Co. 2:14–15).

39. Sixth, "heaven" and "earth" are Sarah and Hagar and their sons, as in Genesis, chapter sixteen, and Galatians, chapter four.[152] Seventh, "heaven" and "earth" are flesh and spirit.[153] "The flesh lusts against the spirit and the spirit against the flesh" (Ga. 5:17); and "He who sows in the flesh from the flesh will reap corruption, but he who sows in the spirit, from the spirit will reap life everlasting" (Ga. 6:8). "If you live according to the flesh, you will die; but if you put to death the deeds of the flesh in the spirit, you will live" (Rm. 8:13). Eighth: "heaven" and "earth" are reason and the sensitive faculty in man, as I have remarked below on the third chapter concerning the serpent and Adam and Eve.[154] Or you can also say that "heaven" and "earth" are the superior and inferior reason in one man, as Augustine treats in *On the Trinity* 12.7 and 8 and 13.1.[155]

40. Ninth. "Heaven" and "earth" are the fault that perverts order and the penalty always joined to it that punishes the fault and restores order. In the *Confessions* Augustine says, "Every disordered soul punishes itself";[156] and Seneca says in Letter 87, "The great punishment of evildoers lies in themselves; they are being punished as soon as they commit crimes."[157] Tenth, "heaven" and "earth" are charity and cupidity, the roots of the two cities of life everlasting and the pains of hell.[158] In our explanation of the order of nature we already discussed how far cupidity can be said to be from God.[159] You will find other things pertaining to the moral meaning in our first commentary. . . .[160]

Chapter Three

Verse 1. Now the serpent was more subtle than any of the beasts of the earth.

135. Note that this chapter teaches us very clearly about three things, though in parabolic fashion: First, the natures of things; second, the nature of our intellect and how it knows; and third, moral instruction regarding everyman's escape from or fall into sin, as well as the punishments that lead sinners back to virtue and virtue's Lord. For the present it is enough to remember that in the twelfth book of *On the Trinity* Augustine explains the moral meaning of the serpent as the sensitive faculty that we share with brute beasts, the woman as the rational faculty that is directed to external things, and the man as the superior rational faculty that cleaves to God.[161] In chapters eight and nine of the same book he teaches us especially about sins and their punishment. A second main point to note is that from this it is clearly evident that sacred scripture must be interpreted in a parabolic fashion.[162] The saints and doctors generally interpret what is said in this third chapter in parabolic fashion, saying that the serpent is the sensitive faculty, the woman the inferior reason, and the man the superior reason.[163]

136. This said, it seems that without prejudice to other interpretations, both historical and tropological, of the saints and doctors it is perhaps probably correct to say that the tropological sense of the serpent, the woman and the man is the same as the historical or literal.[164] This is also true of the passage in Judges: "The trees went to anoint a king over them, and they said to the olive tree, 'Reign over us'" (Jg. 9:8). And so when we say "the meadow laughs" or "water runs," the literal meaning is that the meadow is in flower and its flowering is its laughing and its laughing is its flowering.[165] If we interpret what is said here about the serpent, the woman and the man according to this principle many doubtful questions that are usually brought up vanish, such as how the serpent and the woman spoke to each other and the like. A second advantage of this approach is that this interpretation of the passage easily explains various texts in different books of both Testaments. Yet a third is that it generally makes clear what actions are good and what better, and what sins are bad and what worse or more grave.

137. Fourth, it will be evident that in the words "serpent, woman

and man" are expressed the substantial being and nature of the human creature and how it is constituted in relation to its principles and their natural properties. It will also be evident how the serpent, namely the sensitive faculty, can truly and literally speak to the woman, that is, the inferior reason, and how that inferior rational faculty speaks with its superior and how this highest faculty speaks to God, as well as how God addresses all three. It will also be clear how these three things are related to man's threefold state, that is, before sin, under sin and after sin. Each of the three things by nature belongs to the essential principles of man.

138. In order to prove this I assume that man, inasmuch as he is a rational animal and made to God's image,[166] is something higher than the sensitive faculty and is an intellectual being. In us intellect is like a naked and empty tablet, according to the Philosopher,[167] and, as the Commentator says, in the order of intellectual beings it has the same place as prime matter does in the order of corporeal beings.[168] Moreover in our case "we cannot understand without phantasms,"[169] just as we cannot "weave or build without corporeal instruments."[170] "Imagination is a movement produced by sensation."[171] All the premises from the first to the last make it necessary for the integrity of man that he have a sensitive faculty. This sensitive faculty is by nature under the intellective faculty, and like a servant it is outside the genus of what is intellective through its essence, because it serves man's intellect with the phantasm without which we cannot understand. We have an example in bodily things where change, which is concerned with accidental qualities, is at the service of generation, which dwells upon and is interested in essential things. It is the handmaid of generation, although it is outside generation's species and has its own. Again, just as in the case of generation in bodily things we find two principles under the same species, namely form and matter, the active and the passive,[172] so too our intellectual faculty is distinguished into a superior part and an inferior one, which Avicenna calls the two faces of the soul,[173] but which Augustine calls superior reason and inferior reason.[174]

139. In the second place, I assume that everything that is and that is good "has been made and ordered by God" (Rm. 13:1). It is order that makes something good, so that it is impossible for there to be good outside order and conversely for there to be evil where order exists.[175] A natural order is one in which the highest point of what is inferior touches the lowest point of its superior.[176] In us the highest point of

the soul is the intellect. This is why Rabbi Moses in the next to last chapter of his whole work says that "The intellect that is poured out upon us" ("The light of your countenance is signed upon us, O Lord," Ps. 4:7), this intellect, I say, "is what joins us to the Creator."[177] God, the Creator, "regards us in the same light and is always with us, as David said: 'In your light we will see light' " (Ps. 35:10).[178] Augustine says that the superior reason is always directed to, cleaves to, is joined to and beholds the unchangeable rules that are set above it in God, according to his version of the Psalm text, "I have poured out my soul upon me" (Ps. 41:5).[179] In *Confessions* 10.26 he says: "Where have I found you that I might know you, save in yourself above me?"[180] This order and mutual glance between God and the height of the soul is completely natural, full of truth and delight, inasmuch as it is totally appropriate and founded in the root and source of all good, namely order. It agrees with the texts: "Let your voice sound in my ears, for your voice is sweet" (Sg. 2:14); and "My soul melted when my beloved spoke" (Sg. 5:6); and "Blessed are those who hear the word of God" (Lk. 11:28). On the basis of this conversation of our highest faculty, which is the image of God with God and God with it, the whole book of the Song of Songs seems to be based and developed. This conversation is between what is holy and the Holy of Holies, between the holy and holiness, the good and goodness, the just and justice, as I have written in my exposition of this book.[181] For what could be more delightful to the just man insofar as he is just than justice itself?

140. This is just what we have said about the height of the soul, which is the superior reason ordered to what is above it, namely God whose image it is. It accords with the texts, "It is good for me to adhere to God" (Ps. 72:28), and "My soul has adhered to you" (Ps. 62:9). (The whole Sixty-second Psalm is fittingly explained in this sense.) The same holds for the inferior rational part, which is subordinated to its superior, that is, the superior rational part, and by means of the superior to God. This agrees with the passages: "Draw me after you; we will run in the odor of your ointments" (Sg. 1:3); and "Let him who hears say 'Come' " (Rv. 22:17).

141. From this it follows in the third place that the inferior rational faculty—when it is filled with the light and power of its superior and also of the divine light it drinks in, in the superior—sensing and hearing this, calls, forms, informs, leads and draws to itself its inferior, the sensitive faculty. The sensitive faculty is not essentially rational, but serves and waits upon the rational faculty, according to the text,

"He calls things that are not as though they are" (Rm. 4:17). God not only calls the things that are essentially rational, but also those that are not, for he also imparts virtues to the sense appetite. This is what Acts says in a passage taken from Joel, "The Lord says, 'In the last days I will pour out my Spirit upon all flesh,' and below, 'I will pour forth my spirit upon my servants and upon my handmaids' " (Ac. 2:17–18; Jl. 2:28–29). The powers or potencies of the sensitive faculty serve as handmaids to the essentially rational faculty, as has been said. Hence Aristotle also calls the sense appetite rational through participation.[182] This is why in speaking of the sensitive faculty here it says in parabolic fashion that "The serpent was more subtle than any of the beasts of the earth." Man's sensitive faculty is more excellent than those of all the other animals by reason of its participation in the rational faculty. Genesis 1:28 says, "Rule . . . over all living creatures."

A passage from the *Book of Causes* agrees with this transformation, mutual conformation and ordering. "The noble soul has three activities, for among its activities there is an animal one, an intellectual one and a divine one."[183] The superior reason is called the "noble soul," from which flows the "animal activity" that is proper to what is essentially rational and the "divine activity" that when it has been transformed learns and imbibes from God who is immediately above it. This agrees with the text: "With faces unveiled, reflecting the glory of the Lord, we are being transformed into the same image from glory to glory, as through the Spirit of the Lord" (2 Co. 3:18).

142. A clear example of what has been said is found first in the simple bodies,[184] where the lower spheres share in the motion from the east of the first highest sphere (the more perfectly, the more immediately they are joined with it), as well as in the motion from the west of their proper mover. The elements also receive spherical motion from the east by the mediation of the planetary spheres.[185] If it is rightly understood, this example fits perfectly, so that the *primum mobile*, or highest sphere, that receives its power and motion directly from God, the First Mover, as Thomas teaches,[186] is the superior reason, which is immediately formed by God. The planetary spheres are the inferior reason, also rational in nature, just as the lower spheres belong to the nature of the first sphere, namely the nature of the fifth essence.[187] The elements are the sensitive faculty, because just as this power is essentially outside reason, the four inferior elements are outside the fifth essence's nature.[188] Needles and a magnet provide a second example. When a magnet is touched by a needle it hands its power over to the

needle so that when this needle touches another with its point it attracts it and calls "Come" to it. The second needle adheres to the first with its head, and the same is true in the case of a third and a fourth, as far as the power handed over and absorbed from the magnet reaches.

143. "This was," and is, "man's correct condition,"[189] when the sensitive faculty obeys, looks to and is ordered to the inferior reason, and the inferior reason cleaves and adheres to the superior reason as it in turn does to God. Thus the texts, "God made man right" (Qo. 7:30); and "God created man from the earth, and made him after his own image; and he turned him into it again" (namely, into his image), "and he clothed him with strength according to himself" (Si. 17:1-2). This was and is the state of nature that was set up before sin, "the state of innocence."[190]

144. When the bond and order of the height of the soul to God was dissolved through the injury of sundering sin ("Your iniquities have divided you from your God," Is. 59:2), it followed that all the powers of the soul, inferior reason and the sensitive faculty as well, were separated from contact with the rule of the superior reason. This is evident in the example of the magnet and the needles: As long as the contact of the first needle with the magnet lasts, the other needles will also stick; but if the bond and contact of the first with the magnet is lost, the second and third will not stick to it or to each other, according to the axiom, "If the first in a series is destroyed none of the others can remain."[191] This is man's state under sin, and it is what the Psalm says, "Unless the Lord guard the city, he watches in vain that guards it" (Ps. 126:1).

145. The state of man after sin is when through grace he is redirected to God.[192] Then the more that the height of the soul adheres to God himself, the more what is beneath it, even the sensitive faculty, obeys it. In this state the fullness and perfection of grace give perfect men the ability to have the sensitive faculty obey inferior reason and inferior reason superior reason in such a way that what Isaiah writes is fulfilled: "The lion and the sheep will abide together, and a little child shall lead them" (Is. 11:6). The little child is the superior rational faculty, which cleaves to God and leads together and reconciles the lion (the sensitive faculty) and the sheep (the inferior reason). I have further comments on this in my exposition of "You shall not covet" (Ex. 20:17).[193] Because this grace concerns and is given to an individual man, to the supposit of a nature, that is, to a person and not to the nature itself, the nature remains naked and abandoned, as the kind of na-

ture that is destitute, not yet restored to the state in which it was created.[194] What we said is therefore clear. The serpent, the woman and the man describe and express the three principles of man, namely the sensitive, the rational through participation, and the essentially rational in number, nature and properties.[195]

146. In order to clarify what has been said, as well as many other points, we should also note that in the contact, meeting and union of what is essentially superior with the highest point of its inferior both sides kiss each other and embrace in a natural and essential love that is inward and very delightful. This agrees with the passage where the just man speaks to Unbegotten Justice from which, through which and in which he is begotten insofar as he is just, and in his desire to be totally perfected and transformed without any medium whatsoever says: "Let him kiss me with the kiss of his mouth" (Sg. 1:1).[196] This is the mutual touch in which the superior gazes on the inferior and vice versa. They kiss and embrace each other in this touch and encounter with a love that is natural and essential. Indeed, the shared touch by which the superior beholds the inferior and the inferior returns the superior's gaze is the voice and word, utterance and speech and name, by which the superior recognizes the inferior and unfolds, opens and manifests itself to it. I say that it manifests everything that it has. "All the things that the Father has are mine" (Jn. 16:15); "All the things I have heard from my Father I have made known to you" (Jn. 15:15). It manifests itself by itself, and this is what the doctors say about the higher angels illuminating the lower regarding everything they know in natural fashion.[197]

147. Justice with respect to the just man is a good example of what has been said.[198] Justice manifests everything that belongs to it through itself and manifests its total self in itself without any medium. It opens, unfolds, and pours all this into the just man insofar as he is just. It would be wicked to divide justice in half, for half-justice is no justice. This manifestation and opening up is an utterance, a word, a messenger. "He shows his friend that it is his possession, and that he may ascend to it" (Jb. 36:33). I say that this manifestation is the word and utterance by which the superior and inferior speak to each other and converse together "face to face," the face of the superior beholding and examining the inferior's face as it gazes back. "I have seen God face to face and my soul has been saved" (Gn. 32:30). "We see now through a mirror . . . , but then face to face" (1 Co. 13:12). Justice justifies by speaking; the just man is justified by hearing justice. The just

man is begotten and becomes a son of justice when he loses and dissolves everything in him that is not just and is transformed and conformed into justice. "My soul dissolved when he spoke" (Sg. 5:6).

148. This utterance and conversation by means of which the concrete being and the essence (the "what-it-is" of a thing) address each other,[199] kiss and are united intimately in their depths is the truest and most delightful natural utterance, as I have remarked on the text, "The heavens show forth God's glory, and the firmament declares the works of his hands.... There are no speeches nor languages" (Ps. 18:2,4).[200] Exterior discourse and speech is only a kind of trace and imperfection, some kind of analogous assimilation of that true utterance and address by which the superior and inferior speak and converse together without intermediary as lover and beloved, as understanding and what is understood, and as sense power and actual sense object whose act is one even more than form and matter are, according to the Commentator.[201] For this reason the Psalm says: "I will listen to what the Lord will speak in me, for he will speak peace unto his people and upon his saints" (Ps. 84:9).

149. Mark that anyone who wishes to hear God speaking must become deaf and inattentive to others. This is what Augustine says in the fourth book of the *Confessions:* "My soul, do not be foolish; let your heart's ear be deaf to the tumult of your folly."[202] And in book nine: "What is like your Word? ... If the tumult of the flesh is silent to a person; if sense images ... and the soul itself are silent; if imaginary revelations, every tongue, every sign, and whatever is transient are silent, ... then he himself may speak through himself so that we hear his Word."[203] "I will lead her into solitude, and I will speak to her heart there" (Hos. 2:14). "Solitude," because solely justice as such speaks to the sole just man and solely the just man as such hears justice, and he hears it solely. "Solitude," because justice and the just man as such are solely one; the just man and justice are solely justice.[204] The just man signifies solely justice, just as something white solely whiteness. And thus one who does not hear other things or anything other hears God. So Paul saw God during the time in which he did not see other things, as Augustine says.[205] Therefore, be deaf that you may hear; "He made the deaf hear" (Mk. 7:37).

150. I can briefly summarize this copious introduction by saying that God's speaking to us is nothing else but God's becoming known to us through his gifts (gifts and inspirations, either of nature or of

grace) that raise us up and irradiate our minds by his light. This is utterance, speech and word in the most proper and pleasing sense; its exterior utterance, speech and word does not measure up to it. For us to speak to God is nothing else but to hear and obey him and his inspiration, to turn away from other things and turn toward him and his likeness, just as some mountains and places answer and speak to those who call out to them in the sound that Aristotle calls an echo.[206] This is what Augustine says in the tenth book of the *Confessions:*

> I asked the earth, . . . the sea and the deeps . . . , heaven, the sun, the moon and the stars. . . . My questioning of them was my contemplation, and their answer was their beauty. . . . They do not change their voice, that is their beauty, if one person is there to see and another to see and to question. . . . Beauty appears to all in the same way, but is silent to one and speaks to the other. . . . They understand it who compare the voice received on the outside with the truth that lies within.[207]

A mirror answering and reflecting the appearance and form of a visible object provides an example.[208] The illustration or begetting of the image is the utterance of the visible object, and the reflection of the mirror is its response or utterance. They speak harmoniously to each other in the image begotten from both as an offspring, so that the two are truly one in the offspring in a spiritual way, just as man and wife are corporeally "two in one flesh" (Gn. 2:24).

151. As we have said of God that he speaks to us and we respond and have conversation with him "just as a friend is wont to speak to his friend" (Ex. 33:11), so too he speaks to everything that exists through all things in exactly the same way. I say that he speaks to all things and he speaks all things. Some things hear and answer him according to the property of existence, namely that by which God is existence and the existence of all things is from him. Other things hear him and receive the Word of God insofar as he is the first and true life. These are all living beings. The highest beings hear God not only through and in existence and through and in life, but also through and in understanding.[209] Intellection and utterance are the same there.

152. For example, any sensible body addresses its whole reality to all the sense faculties, but the eye perceives it only under the aspect of

color or what is colored. In the act of seeing it answers and speaks to the visible body. When a single species has been begotten from both, the two very naturally address each other in the one offspring because each of them, the faculty of sight and the visible object, through that species is the concrete being insofar as it is in act, as Aristotle says.[210] What is more pleasing to a thing than act and its form? Similarly, a visible body, even though it may address the soul's other powers and their organs, is still quite dumb to the ear, which cannot respond to the body under the aspect of color, but hears and perceives it under the aspect of sound. It answers it "face to face," with both partners turned toward each other in a mutual way, mine to yours and yours to mine. "All the things that are mine are yours, and yours are mine" (Jn. 17:10), with the proper restriction. "My beloved speaks to me; . . . my beloved to me and I to him" (Sg. 2:10, 16). "I to my beloved, and his turning is toward me" (Sg. 7:10). The same is true of all the other sensitive and intellective powers of the soul. The more immanent and exalted a thing is (e.g., truth in relation to intellect and goodness in relation to will), the more pleasingly it addresses them.

This is enough to understand the words treated here, as well as many others scattered throughout scripture. On these grounds the entire literal sense of the Songs of Songs can be splendidly interpreted, as I have noted in commenting on the book.[211]

153. Finally, we have to show how these points clearly explain what the first three chapters write about the human race, or about the serpent, the woman and the man. First, let us take the passage from chapter one, "Let us make man to our image and likeness" (Gn. 1:26). This was said of the human race in relation to the intellect that pertains to the superior reason—that by which it is the "head" of the soul and "God's image." Second, there is the passage that follows, "Let him have dominion over the fishes and the fowls and the beasts and every creeping creature" (Gn. 1:26). This pertains to the inferior reason and the sensitive faculty that is more excellent in man than in the other animals, as will be made clear below.

154. Third, we have what it says in chapter two, "The Lord placed the man he had formed in the paradise of pleasure" (Gn. 2:8). "Paradise" means delight and pleasure.[212] It is evident that a person who is ordered to God in such a way, who so adheres and cleaves to God, has a delightful and alluring life. "He who cleaves to God is one spirit with him" (1 Co. 6:17). The intellectual life cannot be compared with any bodily delights, as is especially clear from the seventh chapter

of Wisdom,[213] as well as from the end of the third book of Augustine's *On Free Choice* where he says:

> So great is justice's beauty, so great the pleasure of the eternal light of unchangeable truth, . . . that even if one could only stay there for a day, because of this alone he would still rightly and truly condemn countless years of this life that were full of pleasure and a superabundance of temporal goods.[214]

This is what the text means when it says that man made "to God's image" was placed "in the paradise of pleasure." Paradise is the "garden of delight."[215] In that state man did not contemplate God through things inferior and external in order to understand him through them, but rather he understood them through him. "His knowledge, both natural and gratuitous, began from the illumination of the First Truth,"[216] and he knew God in effects that were internal and intellectual. This is what Augustine says in the second half of the eleventh book of the *Literal Commentary on Genesis:* "God spoke" to man set in such circumstances "internally, whether through words or not, . . . just as he speaks to the angels, illuminating their minds by his unchangeable truth so that the intellect knows at one time all the things that happen at temporally different moments."[217]

155. Finally, fourth, these premises explain the passage at the beginning of the third chapter, "The serpent was more subtle than any of the beasts of the earth." It is evident that man's sensitive faculty signified by the serpent is more excellent than that in any other animal produced on earth. Man's sense-endowed body has a more delicate constitution than any other animal body. Men of delicate flesh are well endowed with intelligence,[218] and the softer and more delicate a person's constitution, the greater the pleasure in the perception of the appropriate sense object. Therefore, our first parents had greater pleasure in every sense insofar as they had a purer nature and a more delicate sense-endowed body. So too now pleasure in food and drink and the like is not less in a sober and temperate man than in one who is a glutton and a drunkard, even though the sober temperate man does not throw himself on the food violently and senselessly and with a burning feeling of concupiscence hang onto pleasure as if he were to find his satisfaction in it. Great pleasure is not excluded from a sober virtuous person, but burning desire and disturbance of soul and disordered passion.[219]

156. From this it follows "that touch, which is the foundation of all the senses," and of the whole sensitive faculty, "is more perfect in man than in any other animal on earth,"[220] and consequently man's taste is more refined, because "taste is a form of touch," as the Philosopher says.[221] The opinion of some that the spider excels man in the sense of touch is completely false.[222] That a spider immediately feels when the edge of its web has been touched does not come from the delicacy of its sense of touch, but from the fact that the whole web and all its parts are so interconnected that when one part is touched all the parts are set in motion. So in our case, whenever any part whatever is touched, even the extremities, we feel it immediately and draw back.

157. It is true that in the case of some of the exterior senses, such as smell, sight, hearing, and also in quickness of movement, and so forth, some animals surpass man. This does not come from the unworthiness, but rather from the nobility of man's sensitive faculty and from the delicacy of a constitution that conforms to the whole soul and its activities, especially the internal ones. For example,

It is necessary that man have a larger brain in comparison to his body than other animals, first, so that the activities of the interior powers that are ordered to the understanding may be more easily completed in him, and second, so that the overflowing heat of his heart may be cooled by the brain's coldness. . . . The humidity of this large brain forms a block to the sense of smell which needs dryness for its operation or coming into action.[223]

That man sees or hears less sharply than many animals, or runs less swiftly, comes from the perfection of his balanced constitution and its delicacy.

158. The ground for what has been said is because in its perfection the rational soul comes closer to and is more like the perfection of heaven's mover than all the other internal forms, and so the body that corresponds to the soul must be more like a celestial body that is totally free of contraries than other bodies are. A total freedom from contraries would not be appropriate for a human body and its soul in its activities. Therefore, nature has seen to it that in its constitution the human body is distanced from the most extreme contraries by being brought back to a mean or state of equality. The delicacy and perfection of the makeup of the sensitive faculty especially ordered to intel-

lect, reason and providence rest in this equality.[224] This is the meaning of "The serpent was more subtle than any of the beasts of the earth," and this is enough for now concerning the third chapter.

159. There are other points in this chapter. First, the serpent's utterance to the woman, and second her response to his words. Third, there is the serpent's second speech to her, and fourth, the woman's testing in which she ate the fruit and gave it to the man. In that act of eating they knew they were naked, made themselves garments and hid themselves from God's face. Fifth, there is God's utterance to Adam and Adam's answer, his speech to the woman and her answer, and his speech to the serpent. There is no response by the serpent, but he is immediately cursed by the Lord. Sixth are the punishments inflicted on the serpent, the woman and Adam, and seventh the casting out of man from paradise and the placing of the cherubim with the flaming sword to guard the path to the tree of life. All these passages are full of teaching about the properties natural to God, and to the superior and inferior reason and sensitive faculty of man. They give instruction about leading a good life and present a picture of the varieties of sins, but to pursue each point in particular would be a lengthy task and can be left to the efforts of the inquisitive reader.

160. Still, at the end of the first three chapters we ought to observe that God's creating or making mentioned in chapter one, and his speaking mentioned in chapters one and three, are and signify the same thing. "He spoke and they were made" (Ps. 32:9, etc.). This holds for his commanding in chapter two, for it says, "He commanded him, saying" (Gn. 2:16).

The first thing you should know is that it is clear on the basis of what has been said that when God brings something such as fire into existence by the very fact that he makes it to be fire he commands, declares and teaches it to heat, to climb upward and rest there, and all the other things that fit and match the form of fire. He gives it no other command or counsel at all; he does not work any other effect through it and in it. He forbids it and bars it from nothing, save what is strange and foreign to fire's form. The same is true in the case of other things. Therefore it is evident that creation, making, universal production and command are the same in God and that what is produced from him is his Word and Commandment. This is why it says "The Word was God" when it speaks of the Son produced from the Father and in the Godhead. The Person of the Son says: "He commanded ... and said to me, 'Let your dwelling be in Jacob' " (Si. 24:12, 13). It also clearly follows that the three things that correspond to these in creatures, namely to become, to be created and to be produced by God, are the same thing as to hear him commanding and to obey, as well as to answer, speak to and converse with him when he speaks.

161. The second conclusion is that these utterances, responses, acts of obedience or attentiveness, are totally pleasing and delightful to creatures, as shown above.[225] What could be more pleasing to the just man insofar as he is just than justice? From justice and from no other source, through and in justice, the just man insofar as he is just is all that he is, knows all that he knows, and loves all that he loves.

162. The third conclusion is that these utterances and "speeches are not words whose voices are heard externally," and for this reason "Their sound has gone forth into the whole earth and their words to the end of the earth" (Ps. 18:4–5). What is outside time is always universal; what is without body and matter is everywhere. In this way, always and everywhere, "The heavens and all the works of his hands proclaim God's glory" (Ps. 18:2), without any external word. For example, the gravitational attraction of a heavy object cannot be checked by time or place in order to be silenced, but "it has no rest day and night in proclaiming and saying, 'Holy, holy, holy is the Lord our God' " (Rv. 4:8; Is. 6:3). "He made us" (Ps. 99:3); "he spoke and we were made" (Ps. 32:9). "He has given his command, and it shall not pass away" (Ps. 148:6). He commanded, and we were created. Even though the external action, such as the fall or downward movement, may be silenced when a heavy object is forcibly held up high so that it does not fall, nevertheless the attraction of gravity that belongs to the form of a stone and by which God addresses, commands, orders and directs it is never silent, but always answers and speaks to God, fulfills his command without neglect. I spoke about utterances, responses, commands, prohibitions, and so forth, of this sort in commenting on the passage in chapter two, "And the Lord God spoke" (Gn. 2:18), and previously in commenting on the verse, "And he commanded him, saying" (Gn. 2:16).[226]

163. This is why evil never totally destroys good, or extinguishes it or renders it dumb. For example, in nature something contrary does destroy and silence a thing's form as far as its external act goes, but the inclination, aptitude, relation, order and appetite to the good that is rooted in the subject's nature it in no way lessens through some detracting or diminishing power that does not strive for and incline toward the form. The reason is that the contrary, or destructive,

tendency of this appetite has a common root and is one with the inclination itself. Nothing destroys itself or its principle. And thus an aptitude of this sort is not more silent or less expressive than others in its quest for form.[227] Think of the case of a heavy object held aloft (as mentioned above), or of a bag full of air held under water.

164. A second point follows from this. Neither the natural desire for existence nor synderesis's opposition to evil is destroyed in the damned.[228] "Their worm will not die" (Is. 66:24). Also, "Natural gifts remain whole and beautiful in the demon."[229] Again, neither in Cain nor in any other sinner is synderesis silent, but it always calls out in opposition to evil and in inclination to good with an appropriate voice that neither time nor place ever interrupts or diminishes. This is so even though its external voice is not audible in time and place, because it is neither temporal nor material. It always addresses the good toward which it tends, and the author or cause of the good. He speaks to it, addresses it, commands and orders it when he grants the nature of a good thing its tendency toward the good.

165. There are four conclusions from what has been said. First, that God does not properly command an exterior act, because it can be hindered.[230] God's word and command cannot be neglected. "He has given his command, and it shall not pass away" (Ps. 148:6); and again, "Your word, O Lord, lasts forever" (Ps. 118:89). Second, that the exterior act is not properly good or divine, and that God does not work it or give birth to it in the proper sense.[231] For the Father works what he works even until now without interruption (Jn. 5:17). Third, it is now clear why the exterior act is heavy and oppressive, but the inner act is never so. God, who gives what he commands, commands the latter; something other than God or at least in company with God can and does command the former. The reason comes from what was said above: God, inasmuch as he is good, commands "the good that all things desire."[232] Everything that is below God, since it is a particular good, does not command the good, but particular goods.[233] Augustine says, "Remove what is particular!"[234] Fourth, the interior act always speaks to God in the proper sense and praises him as its author and active principle, according to the Psalm verse, "Lord, open my lips and my mouth will announce your praise" (Ps. 50:17). As discussed above, an effect is always an act of praise of its cause and of it alone. The subject of my action is always the principle of the act; it is the first of causes and the last. End and principle are the same.[235]

3. SELECTIONS FROM THE COMMENTARY ON JOHN

1. "In the beginning was the Word." "A large eagle with great wings, long-limbed, full of feathers and dappled plumage, came to Lebanon and took away the marrow of the cedar. He cropped off the top of its foliage and carried it away to the land of Chanaan" (Ezk. 17:3–4).[1] John the Evangelist himself is the eagle who "makes the nest" of his attention, contemplation and preaching "among the steep crags and inaccessible rocks" (Jb. 39:27–28). "He came to Lebanon and took away the marrow of the cedar. He cropped off the tops of its foliage and carried it away to the land of Chanaan" when he drank in the Word who was in the Father's breast and manifested him to men with the words "In the beginning was the Word." He is "the first among the evangelists in penetration of the depths of the divine mysteries," as Augustine says:

> In the figure of the four animals of Ezekiel, chapter one, and Revelation, chapter four, he is compared to the eagle which flies higher than other birds and gazes at the sun's rays with undazzled eyes. He rested on the Lord's breast at the Last Supper and drank a draught of heavenly wisdom better than that received by the others from the source itself, the Lord's heart. His concern was to intrust us with Christ's divinity and the mystery of the Trinity.[2]

This is what is said here, "In the beginning was the Word."

2. In interpreting this Word and everything else that follows my intention is the same as in all my works—to explain what the holy

122

Christian faith and the two Testaments maintain through the help of the natural arguments of the philosophers.[3] "God's invisible attributes are seen and understood from the creation of the world in the things that he has made, as well as his everlasting power (that is, the Son), and his divinity (that is, the Holy Spirit)," as the *Gloss* on Romans, chapter one, says.[4] In the seventh book of the *Confessions* Augustine says that he read "In the beginning was the Word" and a large part of this first chapter of John in the works of Plato.[5] In the tenth book of the *City of God* he speaks of a Platonist who used to say that the beginning of this chapter as far as the words "There was a man sent from God" should be written in golden letters and displayed in key locations.[6]

3. Moreover, it is the intention of this work to show how the truths of natural principles, conclusions and properties are well intimated for him "who has ears to hear" (Mt. 13:43) in the very words of sacred scripture, which are interpreted through these natural truths. Now and then some moral interpretations will also be advanced.

CHAPTER ONE[7]

4. The interpretation of "In the beginning was the Word" should be in accord with this intention. First note that "In the beginning was the Word, and the Word was with God," as well as much that follows, are contained in the words: "And God said, 'Let there be light,' and light was made; and God saw the light was good, and he divided the light from the darkness" (Gn. 1:3–4). To clarify the text "In the beginning was the Word" down to "There was a man sent from God," mark first of all that what is produced or proceeds from anything is precontained in it. This is universally and naturally true, both in the Godhead (the topic here) and in natural and artificial things. A fig could as easily come from a vine or a pear tree as a fig tree, if it were not precontained and preexistent in the fig tree.

Second, it is preexistent in it as a seed is in its principle;[8] and this is what the text says, "In the beginning was the Word." "The seed is God's Word" (Lk. 8:11). Third, note that what is produced from something is universally its word. It speaks, announces and discloses whence it comes—hence he says, "In the principle was the Word." The fourth point is that what proceeds is in its source according to the idea and likeness in which and according to which what proceeds is produced by the source.[9] This is in the Greek: "In the principle was the Word," that is, the *Logos*, which in Latin is Word and Idea. You have then four conclusions: What proceeds is in its source; it is in it as a seed is in its principle, as a word is in one who speaks; and it is in it as the idea in which and according to which whatever proceeds is produced by the source.

5. In the fifth place, note that insofar as anything proceeds from another it is distinguished from it. What follows expresses this—"The Word was with God." It does not say "under God," or "descends from God," but says "The Word was with God." The phrase "with God" bespeaks a kind of equality. In things that are analogical what is produced is always inferior, of lower grade, less perfect and unequal to its source. In things that are univocal what is produced is always equal to the source. It does not just participate in the same nature, but it receives the total nature from its source in a simple, whole and equal manner. Thus, the sixth point says that what proceeds is the son of its source. A son is one who is other in person but not other in nature.

6. From this follows the seventh point: That the Son or Word is the same as what the Father or Principle is. This is what follows, "The Word was God." Here it must be noted that in analogical relations what is produced derives from the source, but is nevertheless beneath the principle and not with it. It is of another nature and thus is not the principle itself. Still, insofar as it is in the principle, it is not other in nature or other in supposit.[10] A chest in its maker's mind is not a chest, but is the life and understanding of the maker, his living conception. On this account I would say that what it says here about the procession of the divine Persons holds true and is found in the procession and production of every being of nature and art.

7. The eighth point is that the chest that is or has been brought forth into existence still exists and stays in the maker himself, just as it was in the beginning before it came to be. This is true even if its external existence is destroyed. This is what follows: "This Word was in the beginning with God." He had previously said, "In the beginning was the Word."

8. In the ninth place, note that procession, or production and emanation (our subject here) in the proper, prior and preeminent sense takes place in generation. Generation is without movement or time but is the goal and limit of movement with respect to the substance and the existence of the thing. Therefore, it follows that generation does not fall into nonexistence or sink into the past. If it exists in this way, it is always "In the principle." The same is true with us—take away time, and evening is the same as morning. If generation is always "In

the principle," it is always being born and always being brought forth. It must either never happen or always happen, because the principle or "In the principle" always exists. For this reason the Son in the Godhead, the Word "In the Principle," is always being born and always has been born. This is what the "was" means in "In the principle was the Word." The word "was" signifies three things: Substance, because it is a substantive word;[11] past time; and incomplete time. Because it is substantive, the Word is the very substance of the Principle; because it is past, the Word has always been born; because it is incomplete, it is always being born. This is the reason why John when he speaks about the Word in the first four sentences always uses this substantial, past and incomplete word "was."[12]

9. In the tenth place, note that it is proper to the intellect to receive its object, that is, the intelligible, not in itself, insofar as it is complete, perfect and good, but to receive it in its principles. This is what is meant here: "In the principle was the Word." And again, "This Word was in the principle with God."

In the eleventh place, mark that the word, that is, the mind's concept or the art itself in the maker's mind, is that through which the maker makes all that he does and without which he does nothing as a maker. Hence there follows: "All things were made through him, and without him nothing was made."

10. Twelfth. The chest in the mind or in the art itself is neither a chest nor something already made, but it is art itself, is life, the vital concept of the maker. This is what follows: "What was made in him was life." Thirteenth. The word, as idea, belongs to the rational faculty, which is proper to man. For man is a rational animal, and "The human race lives by art and reason," as the first book of the *Metaphysics* says.[13] Therefore, the word is not only life, but the life is the light of men. Hence there follows: "And the life was the light of men."

11. Fourteenth. The word, the idea and art itself, shines as much by night as by day. It illuminates things hidden within as much as those manifested without. This is what follows: "And the light shines in the darkness," to distinguish it from corporeal light, which is not life, nor properly the light of men, and which does not shine at night or illuminate things hidden within. Further, it is more correct to say that in the case of created things only their ideas shine. "The idea of a thing which the name signifies is its definition," as the Philosopher says.[14] The definition is the way of proving, or rather the entire proof that brings about knowledge.[15] The conclusion is that in created things

nothing shines except their idea alone. This is what is said of the Word here—that it is "the light of men," namely their Idea.[16] So too the text, "And the light shines in the darkness," as if to say that among created things nothing shines, nothing is known, nothing brings about knowledge besides the "what-it-is,"[17] definition and idea of the thing itself.

12. Fifteenth. The word, *Logos* or idea of things exists in such a way and so completely in each of them that it nevertheless exists entire outside each. It is entirely within and entirely without. This is evident in living creatures, both in any species and also in any particular example of the species. For this reason when things are moved, changed or destroyed, their entire idea remains immobile and intact. Nothing is as eternal and unchangeable as the idea of a destructible circle. How can that which is totally outside the destructible circle be destroyed when it is? The idea then is "the light in the darkness" of created beings that is not confined, intermingled or comprehended. This is why when John said, "The light shines in the darkness," he added, "and the darkness did not comprehend it." In the *Book of Causes* it says: "The First Cause rules all things without being intermingled with them."[18] The First Cause of every being is the Idea, the *Logos*, the "Word in the principle."

13. It is evident how the Prologue "In the beginning was the Word" down to "There was a man sent from God" is to be interpreted by means of the ideas and properties of natural beings. It is also clear that these words of the Evangelist, if correctly investigated, teach us the natures and properties of things both in their existence and their operation, and so while they build up our faith, they also instruct us about the natures of things. The Son of God himself, "the Word in the principle," is the Idea, "a sort of 'Art.' . . . full of all the living and unchangeable ideas that are all one in it," as Augustine says in the last chapter of book six of *On the Trinity*.[19]

14. If you consider the just man insofar as he is just in the justice that gives birth to him you will have an example of all that has been said and much else that we shall often mention.[20] First, it is obvious that the just man as such exists in justice itself. How could he be just if he were outside justice, if he were to stand on the outside separated from it? Second, the just man preexists in justice itself, just as a concrete thing does in an abstract one and that which participates in what it participates in.

15. Third. The just man is the word of justice, that by which justice expresses and manifests itself. If justice did not justify, no one

would have knowledge of it, but it would be known to itself alone, as in the text: "No one has ever seen God; the Only-Begotten who is in the Father's heart has made him known" (Jn. 1:18), or "No one knows the Father except the Son" (Mt. 11:27), or "No one knows who does not receive" (Rv. 2:17). It is a universal rule that no one knows divine perfection "who does not receive." Thus justice is known to itself alone and to the just man who has been taken up by justice. This is the meaning of the text that says that the Trinity, God, is known to itself alone and to the man that is taken up in it.[21] The Psalm says: "Blessed is the man you have chosen and taken up" (Ps. 64:5). Fourth, justice has an exemplar in itself, which is the likeness or idea in which and according to which it forms and informs or clothes every just man and thing.

16. Fifth. The just man proceeds from and is begotten by justice and by that very fact is distinguished from it. Nothing can beget itself. Nonetheless, the just man is not different in nature from justice, both because "just" signifies only justice, just as "white" signifies only the quality of whiteness,[22] and because justice would make no one just if its nature changed from one place to another, just as whiteness does not make a man black or grammar make him musical. From this it is clear in the sixth place that the just man is the offspring and son of justice. One is and is called a son in that one becomes other in person, not other in nature. "The Father and I are one" (Jn. 10:30)—we are distinct in person, because nothing gives birth to itself; we are one in nature, because otherwise justice would not beget the just man, nor would the Father beget the Son who became other in person, nor would generation be univocal. This is what is meant by "The Word was God."

17. If the Father and the Son, justice and the just man, are one and the same in nature, it follows in the seventh place that the just man is equal to justice, not less than it, nor is the Son less than the Father. "The Word was with God." The word "with" signifies equality, as said above.[23] Eighth. In bearing or justifying the just man, justice does not cease to be justice and does not cease to be the principle and the idea of the just man. This is what is meant by "This Word was in the principle with God."

18. Ninth. It is clear that justice and the just man as such are no more subject to movement and time than life or light are. For this reason the just man is always being born from justice itself in the same way that he was born from it from the beginning of the time he became just. It is the same in the case of the generation and conservation of light in a medium. It must be continuously generated because it is

not continuously possessed. Tenth. The just man as such is what he is completely and totally from justice itself and in justice itself as his principle. This is what the text means: "In the Principle was the Word." Further, the just man insofar as he is just knows nothing, not even himself, outside justice itself. How could he know that he is just outside justice itself? It is the principle of the just man. It is proper to man and to reason to know things in their principles.

19. Again in the eleventh place. Justice does everything it does by means of "Begotten Justice."[24] Just as nothing just can be begotten without justice, so nothing that has been begotten as just can exist without Begotten Justice. Begotten Justice itself is the word of justice in its principle, the justice that gives birth. This is what it says here: "All things were made through him, and without him nothing was made." Twelfth. The just man in justice itself is not yet begotten nor Begotten Justice, but is Unbegotten Justice itself. This is what is meant by "What was made," or produced by any form of production, "was life in him," that is, "principle without principle."[25] What is without principle lives in the proper sense, for everything that has the principle of its operation from another insofar as it is other does not live in the proper sense.

20. Thirteenth. The just man in justice itself, his principle, because he is unbegotten, "a principle without principle," is life and light. Each individual thing is light and shines in its principles. All knowledge of things is through and in their principles, and until knowledge is reduced to its principles it is always obscure, dark and covered, because it is not sure knowledge.[26] A demonstration, that is, a syllogism, that brings certain knowledge is based on proper principles. This is what the passage means "The life was the light of men." John says "of men" perhaps because man receives his knowledge from what comes later in the order of being and proceeds to the principles by reasoning. This is not the case with the higher intellectual creatures. Perhaps that is why there follows "The light shines in the darkness." Every created being smacks of the shadow of nothingness. "God alone is light, and there is no darkness in him" (1 Jn. 1:5). Therefore, the "light in the darkness" is knowledge *a posteriori*, knowledge that is in and through the phantasm.

21. Put in another way, it is universally true that the principle is the light of what comes from it, and a superior illuminates an inferior. Conversely, what has proceeded and is inferior by the very fact that it is inferior and posterior (that is, as having its existence from another)

is in itself a darkness of privation and negation—privation in the case of corporeal being that can perish, negation in the case of spiritual beings. This is what is meant by "The light shines in darkness." Because the inferior never equals its superior, there follows "The darkness did not comprehend it."

22. The just man of whom we are now speaking by way of example is not light in and of himself. Hence the subsequent passage about that just man John the Baptist, "He was not the light." The fourteenth point is that the just man or just thing in itself is dark and does not shine. It shines in justice itself, its principle, and justice shines in the just man, although what is just, in that it is inferior, does not comprehend justice. Fifteenth, it is evident that justice is present entirely in every just man. Half justice is no justice. If it is entire in every just man, it is also entire outside every just man and thing. This is what the text means: "The darkness did not comprehend it."

23. Very many things in scriptures can be interpreted from the foregoing, especially those that are written about the Only-Begotten Son of God as the image of God (2 Co. 4:4; Col. 1:15). An image insofar as it is an image receives nothing of its own from the subject in which it exists, but receives its whole existence from the object it images.[27] Second, it receives its existence only from the object, and third, it receives the whole existence of the object according to everything by which it is an exemplar. For if the image were to receive anything from another source or did not receive something that was in its exemplar, it would not be an image of that thing but of something else. From which the fourth point follows—that the image of anything is one in itself and is the image of one thing alone. Therefore in the Godhead the Son is one and is of one alone, namely, the Father.

24. From what has been said it is clear in the fifth place that the image is in its exemplar, for there it receives its whole existence. On the other hand, the exemplar insofar as it is an exemplar is in its image because the image has the whole existence of the exemplar in itself. "I am in the Father, and the Father is in me" (Jn. 14:11). Sixth. It follows that the image and that of which it is an image, insofar as they are such, are one. "The Father and I are one" (Jn 10:30). He says "we are" insofar as there is an exemplar that is expressive and begets and an image that is expressed or begotten; he says "one" insofar as the whole existence of the one is in the other and there is nothing alien to it there.

25. Seventh. Such an expression or begetting of the image is a kind of formal emanation.[28] This is why the Commentator on book two

of *On the Soul* holds that the birth of the visible species in the faculty of sight does not need an external light,[29] either because of the visible object, which diffuses itself in many ways by its own power, or because of the faculty of sight, which receives the species of the visible object on its own. It is only because of the transmitting medium that it needs an extrinsic light.[30] Eighth. The image and the exemplar are coeval, and this is what is said here, that "the Word," that is, the image, "was in the beginning with God" in such a way that the exemplar cannot be understood without the image and vice versa. "He who sees me also sees my Father" (Jn. 14:9).

26. Ninth. Only the exemplar knows the image and the image the exemplar. "No one knows the Son except the Father, nor does anyone know the Father except the Son" (Mt. 11:27). The reason is because their existence is one and nothing of one is alien to the other. The principles of knowing and of existence are the same, and nothing is known through what is alien to it.[31]

All of what has been said and many similar points become clear in comparing the just man with justice, a being with its existence, a good man with goodness and in general anything concrete with its abstract form.

27. What we said about the image is clearly summarized in the seventh chapter of Wisdom where it speaks of the Wisdom or Word of God as "a mirror without blemish," "a pure emanation of God." It also says that it is "the image of his goodness," and that "nothing impure touches it"; it is "the heat of his power" and "the brightness of eternal light" (Ws. 7:25–26). Almost everything that is written about the divinity of the Son can be interpreted through these points, as we said before. Let this be enough for now of one way of explaining "In the beginning was the Word" down to "There was a man sent by God."

28. For a second way of understanding "In the beginning was the Word," you should note what Augustine says in the chapter on the Word of God in the *Book of Eighty-Three Questions*:

> In the beginning was the Word. The Greek *Logos* means the same as the Latin "idea" and "word". In this passage we translate it more correctly as "Word" to signify not only the relation to the Father, but also the relation to the things that are made through the Word by means of operative power. "Idea" is a term rightly used even if nothing is made through it.[32]

Thus far Augustine's words. In this connection, it is evident that the science that teaches how to construct arguments in the various sciences and in individual cases is called logic from *Logos*, or idea. Further, logic itself is spoken of as "linguistic" because *Logos* is discourse or word.[33]

29. Second, note that idea is taken in two ways. There is the idea received from things or abstracted by the intellect and this is posterior to the things from which it abstracts, and there is the idea that is prior to things, the cause of things and their idea. This is what definition points to and what the intellect grasps in the intrinsic principles themselves.[34] This is the idea we are speaking of here. Therefore, it is said that *Logos*, that is the Idea, is in the beginning. "In the beginning was the Word," he says.

30. On this basis you should realize that every agent, whether in nature or in art, makes what is like itself and for that reason always has within itself that upon which it models its effect. That is the principle by which an agent acts.[35] Otherwise, it would act by chance and not by art. For example, the architect of a house, insofar as he is an architect, has within him in his mind the form of the house upon which he models the external house. The form is the principle by which the architect makes and produces something externally in matter. It is also the word by whose means he declares and manifests himself and all that is his insofar as he is an architect. Likewise in nature a hot body, such as fire, assimilates what can be heated to it. Heat is the principle by which fire gives warmth, and is the word by which it declares, speaks and manifests itself insofar as it is hot. If an architect were to build by reason of the very substance by which he is a man and this particular man, the external house, his effect, would be the word by which he declares himself, his substance, and his entire self insofar as he is a man and this particular man. His effect, the external house, would be in his substance and thus would be his substance itself, just as now it is the effect of the house that is in his mind or in the operation of his art, and is the art itself, differing from the form of the house only in some foreign elements, such as matter, place, time and the like. This is what is said in the texts, "In the principle was the Word, and the Word was God," and "What was made in him was life."

31. Note further that the effect exists in a different way in the case of a proximate univocal cause. For example, fire in the case of the fire where the effective principle is found (namely generating fire) has the form of the fire that is begotten, but does not have the idea of fire.

Corporeal nature as such does not distinguish between the thing and the idea, because it does not know the idea, which only a rational or intellectual nature grasps and knows. Therefore, the intellect's effect in itself is not only word, but also word and idea, the two meanings of *Logos* mentioned above. This is very clearly put—"The *Logos* was in the principle," and "he was with God," and "he was God," and "he was in the principle with God." The Idea in the proper sense is certainly in the First Intellect. It is also "with God" in every neighboring intellectual being that is its image, or made according to its image as "God's offspring" (Ac. 17:29). It is also "with him" because it is always in the act of understanding and in understanding begets the Idea. The Idea that begets its own understanding is God himself. "The Word was God and was in the principle with God," because it has always understood, has always begotten the Son. Augustine says that if God was always a Father, he always had a Son.[36] Alternatively, "He was from the beginning with God" because he always begets in act just as "he was," that is, just as he was begotten "from the beginning." He gives birth either always or never, because the end and the beginning are the same there, as we said before. An agent like that, one that is a principle in which there is *Logos* and Idea, is an essential agent that precontains its effect in a higher way and exercises causality over the whole species of its effect.

32. "In the beginning was the Word." A third way of explaining these verses notes that among created things the universal rule is that the idea of any particular thing is the principle and cause of all its properties and qualities. Hence Averroes, commenting on the seventh book of the *Metaphysics*,[37] says that the early philosophers always wanted to know the "what-it-is" of things because knowing this, they would know the cause of all, that is, of all that is in the thing itself. The principles of the substance that the terms of its definition disclose are themselves the principles of all the properties and qualities of the subject. So the definition itself (which is the thing's idea) reveals the "what" of the subject and the "why" of its qualities. It is also the means of demonstration and the whole demonstration as productive of knowledge. It is in this way that we expound what it says here, "In the beginning was the *Logos*," that is, the Idea.

33. There is still a fourth way to explain "In the principle was the Word," by noting that the Word, the Son in the Godhead, has four properties. First, that he is innermost—"Receive the innermost Word" (Jm. 1:21). Second, that he is the Firstborn of the whole creation—

"The image of the invisible God, the Firstborn of the whole creation" (Col. 1:15). Third, that he is always being born and always has been born, as was explained above.[38] Fourth, that he proceeds from the Father according to intellect, just as the Holy Spirit proceeds according to love. This is what is said in this passage: The "in" signifies the first property; "the principle" signifies the second; "was" indicates the third, because it is a substantive verb in the past imperfect; and "Word" stands for the fourth, for the Word is the Idea. The idea belongs to the intellect whose property it is to consider one thing under different aspects, to distinguish the things that are one in nature and in existence, and howsoever to grasp the order by which one thing is prior to another, or by which one person derives from another.

34. Here we must make special note of the fact that the intellect is completely and essentially intellect (totally pure understanding), especially in God, and perhaps in him alone insofar as he is the First Principle of all things. Reality and intellect are the same in him. Therefore, "the relations which accompany the activity of the intellect" in the Godhead are real. And so "the Word," that is, the Son, "who proceeds in an intellectual way" from the Father "is not a relation of reason alone, but a real relation, because intellect itself and idea" are realities, or " are a single reality."[39] Thus Augustine says: "The realities that make us blessed . . . are the Father, Son and Holy Spirit."[40]

With reference to the first of these properties, the one denoted by the preposition "in," the point is that to have interior existence and to be innermost pertains to God and to divine things insofar as they are divine. This is very clear from the first proposition of the *Book of Causes,* especially in the commentary.[41] It is also clear from the primary external work of God, which is existence, that which is innermost to all.[42] As Augustine says, "You were within and I was on the outside."[43] The same point is evident in the third place in the powers of the soul, which are the more internal insofar as they are the more divine and perfect.

The second main point, the one indicated by the term "the principle," is clear from what we have said. The idea is what is innermost and first in each thing. The Word is the *Logos* or Idea. What is denoted in the third place by the term "was," and in the fourth by the term "Word," has already been covered. This is the meaning of "In the beginning was the Word."

35. A fifth interpretation of "In the beginning was the Word."

According to the literal sense the Evangelist wants to say that there is an emanation and personal generation of the Son from the Father in the Godhead. This distinguishes the New Testament from the Old, in which there is no open reference to the emanation of the Persons. The New Testament speaks of the Son everywhere, both his divinity and his humanity. According to his divinity, these words denote four things about the Son of God in relation to the Father.[44] First, he is consubstantial with the Father. That is what is meant when it says that he exists in the Father. "In the principle was the Word." Everything that is in the Father is consubstantial with the Father. Second, it notes that there is a personal distinction between them when it says "The Word was with God." Third, they have the purest unity in existence and in nature, one that does not admit of parts in the idea or definition, that is, the genus and difference. This is what it means when it says "The Word was God," that is, the Idea was God. For what is "of the idea" is not the Idea itself. The fourth point is that the Son is coeternal with the Father—"This Word was in the beginning with God." These things show the personal emanation of the Son or Word from the Father. "The Word, however, must possess a Spirit. Even our word is not bereft of spirit" as John Damascene says.[45] And so it is clear that this passage indicates the distinction of three Persons in the Godhead.

36. Because the effect is always an expression and a representation, and is also the word of its principle, the preceding words—"In the principle was the Word, and the Word was with God, and the Word was God; this Word was in the principle with God"—can be explained in a sixth way applying to every work of nature and of art.

37. It is clear first that a painter possesses an inherent form of the figure and its image that he paints externally on the wall. This is what the text means, "The Word was in the principle." Second, it is necessary that the image be with him as an exemplar toward which he looks and according to which he works. As Seneca says in a letter: "It makes no difference whether one has an external exemplar towards which the eyes are turned, or one within that one has conceived oneself."[46] This is what the text "The Word was with God" signifies. Third, the image depicted in the painter's mind is the art itself by which the painter is the principle of the painted image. Thus we have the text, "God was the Word," that is, the principle or cause of the effect, just as the bath in the mind is the principle of the material bath, as Averroes says,[47] and the figure in the mind is the principle of the figure on the wall. Fourth, to cite Aristotle,[48] it is evident that Polycletus is not the prin-

ciple of the statue before he acquires the art to make it, nor would he be able to be its principle if he lost the art. So it is clear from the beginning that the art itself remains with the artist as soon as he is an artist and as long as he is an artist who is able to be the principle of a work of art. This is what the text means: "This Word was in the principle with God," that is, was the art with the artist, coeval with him, as the Son with the Father in the Godhead. I have dealt with this in the second Genesis commentary when treating the verse, "He saw three and adored one" (Gn. 18:2).[49]

38. A seventh interpretation of "In the principle was the Word." There are four natural conditions of any essential principle. First, that in itself it contains what it is the principle of the way a cause contains its effect. This is what "It was in the principle" says. Second, that which it is the principle of is not only in it, but is also in it in a prior and more eminent way than it is in itself. Third, that the principle itself is always pure intellect in which there is no kind of existence save the understanding that has nothing in common with anything, as the citation from Anaxagoras in the third book of *On the Soul* says.[50] The fourth condition is that in and with the principle and by its power the effect is equal in duration to the principle. The three latter conditions are expressed through "the Word," that is, the Idea. The Idea not only has, but also has in a prior and more eminent way, what the effect has in a formal way, because the Idea has it virtually. Again, the Idea is in the intellect; it is formed by understanding and is nothing else than understanding. Again, it is equal in time with the intellect, since it is the act of understanding itself and the intellect itself. This is the meaning of what follows: "The Word was with God, and God was the Word, and this Word was in the principle with God."

39. Please note that the preceding words have been interpreted in many ways so that the reader can freely take now one and now the other as seems useful to him. I use the same method of multiple exposition in my many commentaries.

40. There is still one question about the text "In the beginning was the Word." Because the first property of the Word or Son in the Godhead seems to be that he is begotten from the Father, why does it say here "In the beginning was the Word," rather than "From the beginning"? The explanation seems manifold. First is that the word or art stays in the maker even though it issues forth in the work. The second explanation is that it is proper to divine things to have internal existence and to be innermost. Third, because the Son has been born

from the beginning from the Father in such a way that he is nevertheless always being born. The fourth reason is because it pertains to reason to grasp things in their principles. All four of these points were
demonstrated above.

41. A fifth reason is that the Word itself, the exemplar of created
things, is not something outside God toward which he looks, as in our
case the figure on the wall is related to the painter who looks to its exemplar, but the Word is in the Father himself. "The Word was in the
principle." This is what Boethius says of God in the third book of his
Consolation:

> External causes did not compel him to form
> The work of unstable matter, but rather the
> Innate form of the highest good.[51]

Here it is better to remember that an exemplar that is beheld from
without is never the principle of the artist's work unless it comes with
the idea of the inhering form.[52] Otherwise, a dabbler could make a picture as well as an artist, since both can see the external exemplar equally well. The work that is "with," "outside" and "above" the artist must
become his work "within," by informing him so that he can make a
work of art, as it says in Luke chapter one: "The Holy Spirit will come
upon you" (Lk. 1:35), that is, so that the "upon" may become "within."
This is signified by "was in the principle" and the following statement,
"and the Word was with God." The first clause stands for the formal
cause as it is in the Father; the second for the form or exemplary cause
as it is with the Father.

42. The sixth reason or cause why the Word or the Son is better
said to be "in" the Father than "from" the Father or the principle is
because the term "from" denotes the efficient cause, or it points to and
suggests the property of efficient causality, while the term "in" suggests the nature of the final cause. Although God is as much the efficient as he is final cause of all created things, he is much more truly
in prior and proper fashion the final cause of all caused things, according to that saying of Aristotle that "he moves as the object of love."[53]
He also says that the end is the first cause in the act of causation.[54]
This belongs to what is first, that is, to God, who is simply the First
Cause. Further, the efficient cause does not act except through its intention of the end.[55] It is moved by the end and for the sake of the end,
and is consequently a "moved mover,"[56] and is second in the act of cau-

sation, something that properly does not belong to God. I have remarked on this at length in the treatise "On the End."[57] This is what the text says: "In the principle," that is, in the Father, "was the Word." It does not say "from" the principle or "from" the Father.

43. From what has been said note that things are brought into existence virtually from their end and formally from their efficient cause, and hence they depend on the end rather than the efficient cause in a more radical, prior and noble sense. Similarly, freedom in the will comes from the reason and the intellect. So too the power of generating in the Godhead directly and more principally belongs to the essence rather than to the relation that is paternity.[58]

44. "In the principle was the Word." Every effect possesses existence in a truer and more noble fashion in its cause, but in the First Cause alone it has existence absolutely and simply. This is what the text says, "It was in the principle." In every cause inferior to God the effect has a particular act of existence, just as it is a particular being.[59] In God alone who is simple existence every effect has its existence according to the passage, "All things were made through him," as will be explained below.[60]

Note that the Son in the Father is the Word, that is, the Idea that is not made. The selfsame Son in the world is no longer under the property of Word or Idea and Knowing Intellect, but is under the property of existence.[61] Therefore, the world was made through him, but did not know him. As it says, "In the Principle," that is, the Father, "was the Word." But it says below, "He was in the world, and the world was made through him, and the world did not know him." Later, in the seventeenth chapter, it says: "Just Father, the world has not known you, but I have known you." (Jn. 17:25)

45. "In the beginning was the Word." It is noteworthy that "before the foundation of the world" (Jn. 17:24) everything in the universe was not mere nothing, but was in possession of virtual existence, as I have pointed out in discussing the passage "God saw that the light was good" (Gn. 1:4).[62] Thus, "In the beginning," that is, before the world's foundation, "was the Word," that is, the effect in its primordial, essential and original cause. At this point he wants to say and to teach that there is another beginning of things that is higher than nature. This is the intellect that orders each natural thing to its established end. So the text says: "In the beginning was the Word," that is, the idea belonging to intellect and knowledge.

46. "In the beginning was the Word, and the Word was with God,

and the Word was God. This was in the beginning with God." Augustine in *On the Trinity*, book eight, chapter six, notes that justice or the just intellectual soul is not seen in the soul itself as some image outside that soul, or as something distant, the way a man beholds Carthage or Alexandria in the mind. It is seen in the intellectual soul as something that is present to it, although the intellectual soul still stands outside justice itself. It is in the company of justice, but however similar to it, it still does not attain it.[63] The intellectual soul still strives after justice, and if it attains, grasps and enters it in some way, it becomes one with justice and justice one with it. This happens by "inhering in that same form so that the soul can be informed by it and become a just intellectual soul itself. . . . And how could it inhere in that form (that is, justice) except by loving justice?"[64]

47. From a careful investigation of what Augustine said, we can understand what the second book of the *Posterior Analytics* says: "The questions we ask are equal in number to the things we truly know."[65] We can ask about things whether they are, what sort they are, what they are and why they are.[66] The four passages we have here answer these in order. "In the beginning was the Word" gives you the fact that the thing exists, for he says that it "was." What sort of thing the Word is, is pointed out in what follows, "and the Word was with God." This will be made clear below. What the Word is follows in the text, "the Word was God." The reason why is shown when it says, "this Word was in the beginning with God."

48. An example. When justice is said to be a certain uprightness "by which each person is given his due,"[67] many who stand outside at a distance, "in the land of unlikeness,"[68] hear without hearing or understanding (Mt. 13:13). These are the idols of which the Psalm says, "They have ears, but do not hear" (Ps. 113b:6). And so Matthew in the same passage cited above says: "Let him who has ears to hear, really hear" (Mt. 13:9). Another person, who carefully ponders what he heard, is drawn to justice and his heart softens to it.[69] He now knows what the Word is like, that is, good and pleasant. "Such is my beloved and he is my friend" (Sg. 5:16). What is loved changes the lover. Augustine says, "You are what you love."[70] This is what the statement means, "The Word was with God." He says "with" signifying near and transforming. "You are near, O Lord, and all your ways are truth" (Ps. 118:151). "The soul desires nothing more strongly than truth," as Augustine says in his *Homilies on John*.[71] Book ten of the *Confessions* says, "Truth is loved in such a way that those who love anything else

wish that what they love be the truth."[72] Thus one who is drawn by the Word, which is the Truth, knows its attributes, knows that it is pleasant, but does not yet know what it is. He still seeks what it is.

49. In the tenth book of the *Confessions* Augustine says, "You have introduced me to an internal affection to which I am not at all accustomed, to a sweetness I cannot describe."[73] Hugh of St. Victor, speaking in the person of the soul, asks:

> What is that sweetness that is accustomed to touch me from time to time and affects me so strongly and deliciously that I begin in a way to be completely taken out of myself, and to be carried away I know not where? All at once I am renewed and entirely changed; I begin to feel well in a way that lies beyond description. Consciousness is lifted on high, and all the misery of past misfortunes is forgotten. The intellectual soul rejoices; the understanding is strengthened, the heart is enlightened, the desires satisfied. I already see myself in a different place that I do not know. I hold something within in love's embrace, but I do not know what it is.[74]

50. The third sentence gives the answer to the question of what it is—"And God was the Word." The just man, the word of justice, is justice itself. "The Father and I are one" (Jn. 10:30). The just man signifies justice alone, as we said above.[75] The following sentence, "This was in the beginning with God," teaches us why the Word exists. The end is universally the same as the beginning, or principle. It does not have a why, but is itself the why of all things and for all things.[76] "I am the beginning and the end" (Rv. 1:8). The same is true of every principle and what it is the principle of in art and nature, although it is more or less true depending on how much more truly one thing is a principle than another.

51. "In the beginning was the Word." The moral message is that God ought to be the principle of our every intention and action because "In the beginning was the Word, and God was the Word." Further, if you want to know whether all your internal and external actions are divine or not—whether God works them in you and they are done through him—see if the goal of your intention is God. If it is, the action is divine because its beginning and end are the same thing: God.

We are also taught that our work ought to be reasonable, according to the command and order of reason acting as the principle of the work. John says, "In the principle was the Word," which is Reason. Romans, chapter twelve, speaks of "your reasonable service" (Rm. 12:1), and First Peter, chapter two, of "being reasonable without guile" (1 P. 2:2). In the fourth chapter of *On the Divine Names* Dionysius says that man's good is to exist according to reason, but evil is what is "contrary to reason."[77] In the first book of the *Metaphysics* it says that "the human race lives by art and reason."[78] This is what it says in the Psalm: "Many say, 'Who will show us good things?' " And the response is, "The light of your countenance, O Lord, is signed upon us" (Ps. 4:6–7), that is, the reason that is imprinted on us from God's countenance is that which shows us the good. What is done according to reason is well done, is rightly done, and is good. It comes from God's countenance, as the text says: "Let my judgment come forth from your countenance" (Ps. 16:2). Augustine in *On Free Choice* teaches that every law is just and good in that it comes forth from God's countenance. It is evil and unjust if it does not proceed from that source.[79]

Verse 3. All things were made through the Word.

52. Note: He does not deny that there are other causes of things, but he means that an effect has its existence from God alone and not from any other cause. Addressing God in the first book of the *Confessions* Augustine says: "Existence and life flow into us from no other source, Lord, than from the fact that you create us, . . . for you are the supreme existence and supreme life."[80] The reason for the statement that all things are made through God is that each thing makes what is like it and nothing acts beyond its kind.[81] Everything less than God is a particular being, not being or existence in the absolute sense. This belongs to the First Cause alone, which is God.

The second point to be noted is that the words "all things" can be used only of things that exist. Sin and evil in general are not things that exist, so they are not made through him but without him. This is the meaning of what follows: "Without him was made nothing," that is, sin or evil, as Augustine says.[82] Here it says that all things were made through him, but evil things do not exist and are not made because they are not produced as effects, but as defects of some act of existence. Third, note that the term "all things" denotes division and number. Hence neither the Son nor the Holy Spirit, nor anything divine insofar as it is divine, falls under the term "all things."

53. Fourth. Even though some things are produced and come about from other things that are secondary causes, each and every being whether it be produced by nature or by art possesses its existence or the fact that it is immediately from God alone, so that the text can be read, "All things made exist through him."[83] And so there follows, "Without him nothing was made," that is, everything that is made by any agent whatever is nothing without him. It is clear that anything that lacks existence is nothing. How could anything be without existence? The whole of existence and the existence of all things is from God alone, as was said above.

Verse 3. Without him nothing was made.

54. These words are explained through what has already been said above. A second meaning is that nothing is made by God without cause,[84] wisdom and intellect. The Psalms say: "You have made all things in wisdom" (Ps. 103:24), and "He made the heavens with intellect" (Ps. 135:5). Job says, "Nothing happens on earth without a cause" (Jb. 5:6), and Plato declares, "There is nothing whose origin has not been preceded by an appropriate cause."[85] The *Logos* is the ground or cause, and that is what the text means "without him," that is, without the Word, which is the cause.

Third, "Without him nothing was made," because the ideas of things are eternal in God and they are the existence of everything that is in God or that is made.[86] In book three, chapter four, of *On the Trinity* Augustine says: "There is nothing which comes to be in a visible and sensible way which is not commanded or allowed in the invisible and intelligible inner court of the Supreme Ruler."[87] This is what the Psalm text means, "The heavens were established by the Word of the Lord" (Ps. 32:6), that is, by the Idea. "Heaven and earth will pass away, my words will not pass away" (Mt. 24:35). All created things (that is what is meant by "heaven and earth")[88] are mutable; "the words," that is, the ideas of things in God, are immutable. "You shall change them and they shall be changed; but you are always the same, and your years," that is, the ideas of years and times, "shall not fail" (Ps. 101:27–28), nor shall they "pass away." They are "years without years," as Augustine says on the passage "the number of my days" (Ps. 38:5).[89]

55. Fourth. "Nothing was made without him," that is, without reason, because everything that happens contrary to reason is a sin and is an empty useless nothing. What happens according to reason is made

through God, whether in us or in all things. In book three of *On Free Choice* Augustine says: "Whatever suggests itself to you as the better course by means of a true reason, be assured that it has been made by God as the creator of all good things."[90] "All things were made through him, and nothing was made without him."

56. Again, summarizing what was said above, note that after the Evangelist sets forth the four sentences where the emanation and distinction of the divine Persons are treated he immediately turns his attention to what belongs to the divine nature in an absolute sense. He starts from the same point that Moses put down at the beginning of the Old Law: "In the beginning God created heaven and earth." Just as the Evangelist openly sets forth the distinction of the divine Persons in the foregoing, so too Moses does in that text, but under a veil, as befits the Old Law and its condition. He signifies the Father's Person through the name of "God," the Son's Person by the name "Principle." "In the Principle God created," he says. Concerning the Holy Spirit there follows, "The Spirit of God moved over the waters."[91] Recognize that the message here is very precise and fitting: "All things were made through him," that is, the Son, "and nothing was made without him." The same is true of "In the Principle," that is, in the Son, "God created heaven and earth." The generation of the Son necessarily precedes every action in all things, whether in nature or in art, in being or in knowing, so that "through him," the Son, "all things were made," heaven and earth, "and without him nothing was made," because God made those things from nothing (2 M. 7:28). This is what Moses meant by "creation." "In the beginning God created heaven and earth," he says. Creation is production from nothing. This is what the passage means, "Nothing was made without him."

57. As an example of how the Son's generation precedes every action and how "without him there is nothing," note that in every sensitive or rational power of ours the species, the offspring of the object, must be brought forth first of all so that the faculty of sight in the act of seeing is a different subject but not a different thing from the visible object in act. In the faculty of sight the generating visible object and its offspring are one, as the Philosopher says,[92] father and son, the image and what it images. Insofar as they are actually in act, they are also coeternal. It is the same in art. In order to paint or write artistically, a painter or writer must have generated or formed in his mind some offspring, image or "son" from an external or exemplary house in order to make the "artistic" house. In like manner, the external material

house is formed from the house that exists in the soul. The one is not different from the other, but it is one and the same house existing under different distinguishing properties. As the Commentator says, if it were not for matter, the bath in the soul would be the same as the bath outside the soul.[93]

58. In the same way, it is easy to see this in all the other things that are or have been made in heaven and on earth. One then grasps how proper, clear and precise is the statement "God created heaven and earth in the Principle," that is, in the Son, and that through the Son "all things were made, and without him was made nothing."

59. It is evident that these words denote the unity of substance and the distinction and property of Persons in the Godhead—on the one side, the begetter or Father, on the other, the offspring, image and Son. The same is true in things created or made on the outside, according to the text, "From him all fatherhood in heaven and on earth receives its name" (Ep. 3:15). Whoever denies that the Son is the principle of every action does not understand what he is saying, as the first book of *On Generation and Corruption* remarks of Anaxagoras.[94] Again, he who denies time affirms it, because it is impossible to deny time without an act of speaking that occurs in time.[95] It is the same in the aforementioned case. He who denies that every action takes place through the Son and in the Son affirms that action takes place in the Son. For he cannot utter a denial without a "son," offspring or species of his utterance having been begotten in him, that is, without some preconception of what he is to say. He cannot even be understood by a listener without an offspring, species or "son" begotten in the listener by the speaker himself.

60. At this point we should also note that just as a particular agent acts particularly and a particular patient is formed and produced as particular in the "son" of the particular agent, so too the universe itself, heaven and earth, is produced in the Son of the First Agent that is not particular, but is being and existence itself, which is God. This is the meaning of "In the principle," that is, in the Son, "God created heaven and earth," according to Boethius's poem:

Creator of heaven and earth . . .
You lead all things forth from the Supreme Exemplar . . .
You have the world in your mind and form it to be like the
    image.[96]

Verses 3–4. What was made in him was life.

61. The truth of this proposition is clear from five points. First, because everything that is received is in the one who receives according to the nature in which it finds itself.[97] The acts of active processes are in the recipient that is prepared for them,[98] and the meanings of the categories are determined by their contingent subjects.[99] The second reason is because "The first things are in each other in the way in which one can be in the other," as the *Book of Causes* says. The explanation of that continues: "Existence and life is understanding in the understanding and is simple understanding; existence and understanding in life is life and simple life."[100] God is life: "I am the way, the truth and the life" (Jn. 14:6). This is what is meant by "What was made in him was life."

62. The third reason. In order to understand this text one must know that everything that is moved by itself or by a principle within and in itself is said to be alive or living. What is moved only by something outside itself is neither alive nor said to be living. From this it is clear that nothing that has a maker prior to it or above it, or an end that is beyond it or different from it, is alive in the proper sense. Everything created fits that description. God alone, insofar as he is Final End and First Mover, lives and is life. That is the meaning of "What was made in him was life."

63. The fourth reason. To understand the text, remember first that these three—to live, to exist and to understand—exhaust or complete the totality of being. Second, remember that they have one order when considered abstractly, that is, when we say "to exist, to live and to understand," and another when considered concretely, when we say "being, living thing and intelligent thing."[101] In the abstract, "to exist" is the most perfect among the three, because no mode or perfection of existing can be lacking to it. How could anything be lacking in existence through existence itself? Its lack must rather come from nonexistence or from absence. "To live" is higher than "to understand" on the same grounds.

The situation is reversed in the concrete—being holds the lowest place, living being the second place, and intelligent being the third or highest place. The reason is that in the concrete they are all participating beings. Every participating being as such is empty and imperfect on its own. For this reason it first shares in a more imperfect level of participation because of its own lack of perfection and larger share of the nature of the imperfect. This is the reason why a created thing is a being on the first level, is a living being on a more perfect level, and is an intelligent being on the last and supreme level. And so an intelligent being is more perfect than a mere being because it includes being. Likewise, a living being is more perfect than a mere being because it includes it. Therefore, a living being is more perfect than a mere being, not because it is living, but by reason of the kind of existence it includes. Third, note that something that is inferior exists in a more noble fashion and a more perfect way in what is its superior by essential order.

64. On the basis of these three points it is clear that being in a living being is life in that it exists in the next highest stage. Living being is intellect in its superior, intelligent being. This is perfectly expressed here—"What was made," or being, "was life in him, and life," that is, living being, "was the light of men." Living being is the nearest superior to mere being; intellect is the nearest superior to a living thing. This may be the reason why he says "the light of men," because men's intellect is the nearest superior intellective power to a living thing because it is the lowest intellective power.[102]

65. Two other reasons why he says "the light of men" are given above. Chrysostom holds that it says "the light of men" because John wrote and spoke for men, especially about the Word who was made flesh, that is, man.[103] Therefore he said "the light of men." Origen says that through the words "of men" universal rational nature is to be understood.[104] "The gods and ourselves are rational," as Porphyry says,[105] and the definition of man is "to be a rational animal." Remember that being holds the lowest level in creatures, as we have said. From this it is clear that the first goal of creation is being or existence, as it says in the *Book of Causes*.[106]

66. The fifth reason is that here one must recognize that as a universal rule the effect is in its effective principle according to that by which the agent is formally and necessarily the efficient cause of the effect. Thus in the case of human art, the art itself is that by which the artist formally produces and makes the artifact. Hence the Philosopher says that Polycletus as such is the accidental cause of the statue; he is the necessary cause of the statue insofar as he is a sculptor who possesses the art of making statues.[107] So it makes no difference whether it is Peter or Martin who acts, or even if it is a man or a living creature, as long as it possesses the art. If the artist's substance were his art itself, then the statue in the artist insofar as it is in him would be his very

substance. What is in the One is one; what is in life is life; and universally what is in anything simple is simple itself. This is what the text means, "What was made in him was life." He is life: "I am the life" (Jn. 14:6). "And the life was the light of men." He was the "true light" spoken of later in this first chapter.

67. This is the case in natural things, because the form is that by means of which one who generates does so, as Callias gives birth to Socrates. One man differs from another only because of matter, as the Philosopher says.[108] As far as it can, every agent makes something like itself, and it makes the other itself,[109] that is, makes the other from other into itself. It begins from the other, withdraws from it, and draws it to itself. "The other" is the *terminus a quo*, "the self" is the *terminus ad quem*. Things that are alike are one in quality, things equal one in quantity.[110] What is formal is one in all cases. Nature always begins from the One and returns to the One.[111] In the Godhead it is the same in the case of the notional acts; the one essence is their root, and these three are the one essence.[112] Note that from any one of these five reasons taken in itself "What was made in him was life" can be interpreted. The *Gloss* says here, "What is in the mind lives with the artist; what comes to be, changes with time."[113]

68. "What was made in him was life, and the life was the light of men." From the moral point of view note that the work of virtue always exists and comes to be in virtue. No one works justly outside justice, and so no one performs a work that is divine and good unless he is in God. "Those who work in me shall not sin" (Si. 24:30); "Through God we shall do mightily" (Ps. 59:14). The third chapter of John says of the just man that "his works are in God" (Jn. 3:21); and John, chapter fifteen, "just as the branches cannot bear fruit unless they remain on the vine, so neither can you unless you abide in me" (Jn. 15:4). If you want to know whether your work is virtuous, a divine work, see if it has been done in God. It has been done in God if you are in charity—"He who abides in charity, abides in God" (1 Jn. 4:16).

Second, if you want to know whether your work has been done in God, see if it is living, for it says here, "What was made in him was life." A work is living which has no efficient or final cause outside or contrary to God. Third, if you want to know if your work has been done in God, see if it is your life. "Strive for justice for your soul, and fight for justice unto death" (Si. 4:33); "I live in the faith of the Son of God" (Ga. 2:20); "For to me to live is Christ" (Ph. 1:21). My message is: If you want to act justly and well, may "to fight for justice unto death" be like your life is to you, indeed, may it be dearer and more precious to you than your life is. If this be so, then your work is in God and is a work divine and just. This is the way to explain the text of Matthew, "Take my yoke upon you . . . and you will find rest for your souls" (Mt. 11:29). He who loves God's commandments more than he loves himself takes God's yoke upon himself according to the text "let him deny himself" (Mt. 16:24). Hence for God's love the holy martyrs chose to give up their lives rather than justice.

69. What follows, "The life was the light of men," morally signifies that such a life encourages and enlightens our neighbor more than words do. "Let them see your good works and glorify your Father" (Mt. 5:16). A holy life encourages more people and in a greater way than words do. In the First Book of Kings it says that Saul struck a thousand, and David with his strong hand and splendid appearance struck ten thousand (1 S. 18:7, 16:12, 17:42). In his Letter to Fabiola Jerome says: "A man understands much better what he sees with his eyes than what he hears with his ears."[114] Horace says:

Things received through the ears make a weaker
impression on the soul
Than those that shine upon the faithful eyes.[115]

Seneca says in a letter, "The path through commands is a long one, that through example short and effective."[116] Therefore, "Jesus began to do and to teach" (Ac. 1:1).

Verse 5. The Light shines in the darkness, and the darkness did not comprehend it.

70. These words were interpreted in three ways above.[117] Now we must observe that light does illuminate a medium, but does not send out rays.[118] Therefore, the entire medium receives light immediately from the luminous body, not one end before the other,[119] but both at the same time and immediately from the luminous body. The reason is that light does not send a ray to the end or to any part of the medium. Therefore, light does not inhere in the medium nor does the medium become the "heir" of the light. The luminous body does not make the medium the heir of its action of illuminating. It does impart something to the medium reciprocally and impermanently, in the manner of a reception,[120] something transitory that happens in it so that

it is and is said to be illuminated. It does not impart its light to the medium in the manner of a received quality that is rooted and inherent so that the light would remain and inhere and actively give light in the absence of the luminous body.

71. It is completely different in the case of the heat that is generated in a medium at the same time as light. Heat sends a ray into the medium that inheres and remains in the absence of the luminous body. Third and further, this happens later at one end than at the other, because it is successive and temporal, not immediate and instantaneous. Fourth, not only is each part warmed after another, but also through and by means of another. Therefore, and fifth, no part whatsoever is immediately warmed by the luminous body. Hence, in the sixth place, the medium receives the heat that makes it to be and to be called hot not only as a passing reception, like a loan or a guest, but also as something inhering, like a son and heir whose heredity it is to be and to be called a source of heat. It is the heir of the action of heating, that is, heat in the active sense.

72. This is not the case with light in a medium, as mentioned above. That is the meaning of "The light shines in the darkness, and the darkness did not comprehend it." The "light" is God and everything that is divine and perfect; "darkness" is everything that is created, as mentioned above.[121] Therefore "the light," the divine perfection, "shines in the darkness," but "the darkness did not comprehend it," that is, did not become an active source of illumination as a true heir of God's action of creation, universal governance and things of that sort. I have commented on this in speaking of the text "God sent a sleep upon Adam" (Gn. 2:21) in my second commentary on Genesis.[122]

73. From what has been said, it is quite evident how God speaks once and for all, but two things are heard, as the Psalm says.[123] Job declares, "God speaks once and for all; he does not repeat the same message a second time" (Jb. 33:14), because by means of a single action he both generates the Son who is his heir, light from light, and creates the creature that is darkness, something created and made, not a son or an heir of light, illumination, or the power of creating. Many similar texts in the scriptures can be explained on the basis of this interpretation. "The light shines in the darkness, and the darkness did not comprehend it."

There is yet a fifth interpretation. "The light shines in the darkness, and the darkness did not comprehend it," because the principle always affects what comes from it, but no part of what comes from it affects the principle. Sixth. "The light shines in the darkness," because according to Augustine, during the three days when Paul saw nothing else he was seeing God.[124] I have commented on this in expounding the verse, "Moses went into the dark cloud where God was" (Ex. 20:21).[125]

74. Seventh. "The light shines in the darkness, and the darkness did not comprehend it," because the principle gives a name to what comes from it, and not vice versa. Clearly this is what is meant by "The light shines in the darkness." We say that a medium is illuminated by brightness or light, but we do not say that light is illuminated or participates in brightness. Eighth. "The light shines in the darkness." Note that it is of the nature of light that its transparency is never seen and does not appear to shine unless something dark, such as pitch or lead or the like, is added to it. "God is light, and there is no darkness in him" (1 Jn. 1:5). This is what is expressed here—"The light shines in the darkness," that is, in creatures that have something dark (i.e., nothingness) added to them. This is what Dionysius says: "The divine ray cannot illumine us save as hidden beneath many veils."[126] In the same way, fire in itself, in its sphere, does not give light.[127] Hence it is called darkness in Genesis 1:2, "Darkness (that is, fire according to the doctors)[128] was on the face of the abyss." Fire does give light in foreign material, such as in anything earthly, like coal, or in a flame in air.

75. Ninth. "The light shines in the darkness," because in every case the principle lies hid in itself, but shines out and is manifested in what proceeds from it, namely in its word. This is what Isaiah means: "Truly you are a hidden God" (Is. 45:15). "He dwells in light inaccessible" (1 Tm. 6:16). Later in this first chapter it says, "No one ever saw God, but the Only-Begotten who is in the Father's breast has revealed him." Tenth. "The light shines in the darkness" because evil always exists in something good and is neither seen nor known nor visible without the form of something good. What is false is not recognized outside the truth, privation is not known outside possession, nor negation outside affirmation.[129] Thus good shines in what is evil, truth in falsehood, and possession in privation. So it says, "The light shines in the darkness." There follows, "And the darkness did not comprehend it." Nothing is pure evil or falsehood. Bede says in his *Homilies*, "There is no false teaching that does not have some truth mixed in with it."[130] The same is true of the other examples, such as possession,

affirmation and the like. Again, "the darkness did not comprehend it," because evil does not pervert, ruin, affect or denominate the good that exists in it. The same is true of the other examples.

76. There is still the moral meaning. "The light shines in the darkness" in that virtue shines and is evident in difficult and contrary circumstances. "Power is perfected in weakness" (2 Co. 12:9); "You have tried me by fire and iniquity has not been found in me" (Ps. 16:3). Gregory says, "Reproach that is inflicted brings out what a person is really like on the inside."[131] In his *Book of Resemblances* Anselm gives the example of a copper coin gilded on the outside, which when it is thrown in the fire cannot blame the fire that it is made of copper.[132] The fire would respond, "I did not make you copper, but I uncovered what you were in your hidden nature, according to the text, 'The furnace tries the potter's vessels' " (Si. 27:6). As a universal rule, every power glows and receives existence insofar as it is a power not from its subject but from its object or contrary.[133] Thus virtue glows from its contrary. Therefore Matthew says, "Love your enemies" (Mt. 5:44), and, "A man's enemies are those of his own household" (Mt. 10:36). The more a person is contrary to us and is our enemy, the more virtue is evident in us, especially patience and the love of God, which are "the things of our own household." We can interpret the Psalm text, "You will feed us with the bread of tears" (Ps. 79:6) in this way, and also, "My tears were my bread" (Ps. 41:4). For good men are fed, nourished, supported, helped and gladdened by the difficult circumstances signified by the tears. And so Matthew says, "Blessed are those who suffer persecution" (Mt. 5:10), not "will suffer" or "have suffered." Patience really gleams when one is actually suffering. Augustine in his book *On Patience* says: "Job was more wary in the midst of pain than Adam in the midst of plenty. The one was overcome in pleasures; the other overcame in pains. The one gave in to delights, the other did not yield to tortures."[134] In the letter to Marcellinus he says that the virtue of patience is greater than everything that can be taken away from a man against his will.[135]

77. When it says, "The light shines in the darkness," the moral message is that God himself consoles and shines upon those who bear with difficulties and tribulations. "The Lord is near those whose heart is in tribulation" (Ps. 33:19), and "I am with him in tribulation" (Ps. 90:15). "And the darkness did not comprehend it," because ". . . the sufferings of the present time are not worthy to be compared with the glory to come" (Rm. 8:18). So Genesis says, "I . . . am your very great

reward" (Gn. 15:1). God always rewards more than he should and punishes less than he should.[136]

78. A third moral sense. Even though a man may be suffering some trial because of evil he has done (think of a thief and robber), as long as he accepts death voluntarily, dying for justice's sake because it is just for such a person to die, he will certainly be saved, as Chrysostom says on the fifth chapter of Matthew.[137] The proof is clear in the case of the thief of Luke's Gospel who says: "We indeed suffer justly, for we are receiving what our deeds deserved," and who hears the reply, "This day you will be with me in paradise" (Lk. 23:41, 43). This is what is meant here, "The light shines in the darkness." Fourth. It often happens that a person hopes and prays to be freed from difficulties while ignorant of the fact that by them he is preserved from greater evils and prepared for better things. Thus once more, "The light shines in the darkness," although it is not known or comprehended. This is how Chrysostom explains the verse in Matthew seven, "If he asks . . . for bread, will you hand him a stone?" (Mt. 7:9)[138]

79. Fifth. "The light shines in the darkness," because God gives even when he does not give, as when a person knows how to give up something that he wants for God's sake, according to the text in Romans, "I wanted to be anathema from Christ for the sake of my brethren" (Rm. 9:3). I have commented on this text more fully.[139] Perhaps this is what Matthew means: "Your will be done on earth as it is in heaven" (Mt. 6:10). Earth is to be understood as darkness, heaven as light. Daniel says, "Bless the Lord, light and darkness" (Dn. 3:72).

Sixth. "The light shines in the darkness," because "He calls the things that are not as though they are" (Rm. 4:17). "He stands at the door and knocks" (Rv. 3:20); "He makes his sun to rise on the good and the evil" (Mt. 5:45). So, too, the genus "animal" is univocal for both irrational and rational animals. He speaks all things to all beings, but all beings do not hear all things, as Augustine says in the *Confessions* when he treats the verse, "I am the Principle who is also speaking to you" (Jn. 8:25).[140] In the *Book of Causes* it says, "The First Cause exists in all things according to a single disposition, but all things are not in the First Cause according to a single disposition."[141]

80. Seventh. "It shines in the darkness," that is, in a silence and stillness apart from the commotion of creatures. The Creator "makes the deaf hear" (Mk. 7:37). In the fourth book of the *Confessions* Augustine says, "My soul, make your heart's ear deaf to the commotion of your vanity and hear the Word."[142] Addressing God in book nine he

says: "What is similar to your Word . . . if the commotion of the flesh is silent to a person, images are silent . . . and the soul is silent to itself and passes beyond itself by not thinking on itself?"[143] "When a deep silence held all things" (Ws. 18:14). I have discussed this in commenting on this verse.[144]

81. Finally, what is expressed in "The light shines in the darkness" is not only verified because opposites are more evident when placed next to each other,[145] as we said above, but also because darkness itself, privations, defects and evils praise and bless God. This is seen first in an example. Judas damned praises God's justice; Peter saved praises God's mercy. These two, justice and mercy, are one thing.[146] Second, the light that is God, his power and might, shines and gleams in the act of creation as much from nothing (the *terminus a quo*) as it does from the *terminus in quem* that is existence. Creation would not be a divine action and light unless it were from nothing.

Third. "The light shines in the darkness," because detestation and hatred of evil always come from and are born of love of the good.[147] So Augustine says that in the same measure that someone delights in his own justice, he is displeased with that alien injustice that belongs to others,[148] according to the verse in Matthew, "When the wheat sprang up . . . then the weeds appeared too" (Mt. 13:26). Thus, the darkness glorifies God, and the light shines in it, not so much as opposites placed next to each other, but rather as opposites placed within each other. Hatred of evils itself is the love of good or of God. It is one habit, one act.

82. "In the beginning was the Word" and the rest down to "There was a man sent from God."

Finally, I want to say in summary that the beginning of this chapter teaches the general features of all being, both uncreated and created. Regarding uncreated being, when it says, "In the beginning was the Word," its initial teaching is that there is an emanation of Persons in the Godhead, that there are three Persons, and that they have an order of origin one to another. Under the name "Beginning" or "Principle," understand the Father, under "Word" the Son, and because a word cannot exist without a breath, consequently also understand the Holy Spirit. There is no generation without love; the generation is that of the Son, the love that of the Holy Spirit. In the second place the text teaches the divine properties of the proceeding Persons, especially of the Son whose Incarnation is the subject here in the passages, "The Word was with God" (signifying his personal distinction), "God was the Word" (signifying the unity of essence), and "This Word was in the beginning with God" (signifying his coeternity with the Father). Third, it teaches the universal causality of the whole Trinity when it says, "All things were made through him" (signifying the creation of all things), "and without him nothing was made" (signifying the conservation of created beings in existence).

83. In relation to created being, it distinguishes four grades of beings in the universe. The first grade is those that are mere beings, the second grade is living beings, the third grade is the human intellect, the fourth grade is the angelic intellect and any other that might be separated, free from matter and image. This is expressed in the passage "What was made" (the first grade), "in him was life" (the second grade), "and life was the light of men" (the third grade), and "the light shines in the darkness" (the fourth grade).

Note that the highest and finest of the elements, that is, fire, is invisible in its proper matter and sphere, and for this reason is understood as darkness in the first chapter of Genesis, "Darkness was over the face of the earth" (Gn. 1:2). So it is fitting that what is highest and finest in the realm of intellect is as it were invisible and unknown to us and denoted by darkness, as in the text, "The light shines in the darkness." John says "shines," because the intellect, which begins in the senses, is clouded by the images through which and in which it knows.

84. You can say quite fittingly that the "light of men" is the inferior reason signified by the woman with veiled head (1 Co. 11:6–7). The man with unveiled head is the image of God, the superior reason, signified through the darkness when it says, "The light shines in the darkness."[149] Augustine teaches about the two kinds of reason and their properties, especially in *On the Trinity*, book twelve, chapters fourteen and fifteen, and in the three following books in many places.[150] The passage that follows, "And the darkness did not comprehend it," is well put. If the highest intellects denoted by "darkness" cannot comprehend the light that is God, then it is clear that he is absolutely "incomprehensible to thought," as the thirty-second chapter of Jeremiah says (Jr. 32:19).

Verses 6–7. There was a man sent from God whose name was John. This man came as a witness, to bear witness concerning the light.

85. The text of Plato that Augustine introduces into the seventh book of the *Confessions* has it that "The soul of man, although it bears testimony to the light, is not the light itself."[151] Note that the just man, insofar as he is just, participates in justice itself. As such, he is sent or has been sent by justice, and he is the one who bears witness to the existence and character of justice itself. He is not justice, but is sent and begotten by it. No one but the just man knows justice—"No one knows the Father except the Son" (Mt. 11:27), and "No one knows who has not received" (Rv. 2:17). Therefore, no one bears testimony to justice except the just man, the son begotten from it. "Wisdom is justified by her children" (Mt. 11:19). This is what it says below in the third chapter concerning the one "who comes down from heaven." "No one receives his witness. He who receives his witness has set his seal on this, that God is true. He whom God has sent speaks the words of God" (Jn. 3:31–34). The author wants to say that no one who is not just knows or can bear witness to justice and its properties. The just man who comes "down from heaven" and from the height of justice sees, hears or knows, and consequently testifies to what "he has seen and heard" and received from that justice that is present as a teacher and source of illumination in the just man himself. It seals and impresses the truth of what it says and the truthfulness of God who seals and imparts justice.

Verse 9. He was the true light.

86. Note first that God is called "true light" because in the Godhead light is not taken in a metaphorical or figurative sense, as corporeal things are, such as stone, lion or the like. This is what Augustine says in book four of his *Literal Commentary on Genesis.*[152] But Ambrose puts "brilliance" among the words that are used metaphorically of God.[153] Remember that the absolute sense of the perfections signified by the terms we use truly and properly belongs to God. Indeed, they belong to God in a more proper and prior way than they do to any creature, even though in relation to the mode of signifying and to some of their implications and connotations the case is otherwise.[154] For every perfection is "from above, from the Father of lights" (Jm. 1:17), and

leaves aside everything that connotes even the smallest imperfection in any way.

87. Second. Note that each thing is said to be true on two grounds: first, if it attains the substantial form of its nature; and second, if it has nothing foreign mixed in with it. Both are true of God. "God is light, and there is no darkness in him" (1 Jn. 1:5). Third, God is "true light," that is, not coming from the outside, not something illuminated (as is true of creatures and was discussed above),[155] but he is the illuminating light. Fourth, note that as a universal rule what is higher in essential order as such is "light," and what is lower as such is always "darkness," as said above.[156] Therefore God, as the Supreme Being, is light simply and absolutely, fully and truly, and hence the true "light, and there is no darkness in him" (1 Jn. 1:5). The case is different with every creature—it has something above it (that is, God), and so the prior text, "The light shines in the darkness," namely God in creatures. This is what the next text means.

Verse 9. He enlightens every man who comes into this world.

88. Note that this passage is ably interpreted in different ways by various saints in Thomas's *Gloss on John*,[157] especially because it seems that many in this world are not enlightened. From what has been set down already, we can briefly say that because God is light, as the Supreme Being and the First of all things, it is necessary that he enlighten everything under him, both "man" and also "each one who comes into the world." For the world was "made through him," and "all things were made through him," as said above. If anyone or anything is not enlightened by him, then it is not under him and inferior to him, and he is not above all things and the First. For "The First is rich through itself,"[158] and exercises influence on all things. If it does not influence all things, it is no longer the First, because it does not exist through itself.[159] It pertains to the nature of the First to be able to exercise influence through itself. That is universally true of anything insofar as it is a cause. It cannot be a cause of things it has no influence on. Again, "The first of any kind whatever is the cause of all that follows."[160] Then it is clear that God enlightens all men and the things that come about or come into this world, or that are in this world, that is, the whole universe.

89. It is indeed true that he enlightens and influences different people and different things in different ways: some by light according

to the property of existence (this is the way he enlightens every being in the universe); others in more restricted numbers by light as life (this is the case with living beings). He enlightens other more perfect beings fewer in number insofar as he is "the light of men," according to the Psalm text, "The light of your countenance, Lord, is signed upon us" (Ps. 4:7), that is, reason, which points to and shows what is good. In the fourth way, he enlightens beings that are more perfect than men by illuminating them himself without shadow of phantasms. In the fifth way, he enlightens others by grace, the supernatural light.

90. From what has been said it is clear that a sinner without grace counts for nothing among the just and is not subject to God as the light of grace. God does not influence or enlighten him; every cause only influences its inferior. This is why Christ especially, and the saints and doctors in general, recommend humility as that which subjects man to God. "Learn of me because I am meek and humble of heart" (Mt. 11:29); "Everyone who humbles himself will be exalted" (Lk. 14:11). On the basis of this virtue the virgin herself was worthy to conceive and bear God's Son—"He has regarded the humility of his handmaid" (Lk. 1:48). In his *Sermon on the Assumption of the Blessed Virgin* Augustine says that humility is the ladder by which God comes to man and men to God.[161] In the third book of *On Consideration* Bernard says: "Humility is the good foundation on which the whole spiritual structure is erected and grows into a temple holy to the Lord."[162] This "tower of strength in the face of the enemy" (Ps. 60:4) is as brilliant as any gem. You can have no virtue without it, as Augustine says,[163] because it alone makes man subject to God and has him look upon God the way an inferior does a superior.

91. The same can be said concerning the other ways by which God enlightens different things in different ways. Those he does not enlighten insofar as he is life do not live and are not living beings, though they can be beings. God enlightens them as such with the light of his existence. If they are not subject to him insofar as he is existence, they are not beings, but are nothing existing at all. All privations, evils, corruptions and defects are of this nature. All of these and things like them are not beings, but lack all existence. They are not effects, but defects, and therefore do not have God as cause. Cause and effect are naturally related to each other as superior and inferior. Without this relation the one does not enlighten, nor is the other enlightened. When this relation is established, the superior enlightens everything that comes into the "world" of its order of activity. This is what is signified

by "He was the true light that enlightens every man that comes into the world." The things that are not beings, but that lack all existence, do not come into the world. They are evils, vices, privations, negations and the like, as we have said.

92. "He enlightens every man coming into the world." Briefly put: Every influence is a form of enlightenment on the part of that which exerts the influence, and the influence given is a light for that which receives it. From this point of view, God, the light, the First Cause of all, either has an influence on all things and on each one in particular, or else he has none on each and all. If he has no influence, he is neither a cause nor the First Cause of each and all. If he has some influence on individual things, my case is proved, for every form of influence is a light, especially if the cause and principle of influence are themselves entirely light. This is what is signified here, "He was the true light which enlightens every man coming into this world."

93. To the third point I speak thus: God, the true and pure light, enlightens all or none. But he does not enlighten none; therefore, he enlightens all. The obvious conclusion follows: He regards all things equally, uniformly and immediately, and is present to all before anything else. An example and explanation of this is evident in the soul. As the substantial form of the body it is immediately and totally present to each part and therefore gives existence and life to all the members. It is different with the other perfections that the soul does not communicate to each part, such as sight, hearing, speech, and so forth. Since life and existence are light, by the essence by which it is a form and a type of light, the soul must enlighten every part of the body and everything included under this form and in this body, that is, in this world of the animated body.

Yet another example is taken from bodies composed of homogeneous parts. The substantial form of fire, because it is first and most immediately present to its matter prior to quantity, or any extension and distinction that belong to the genus of quantity or accident, by fire's light necessarily informs and enlightens either every part of the matter or none. But it does not enlighten none, and therefore it must enlighten every part. As the First Cause, God is present before any secondary cause and departs after it, as the first proposition in the *Book of Causes* and its Commentator say.[164] And this is what is meant here: "He was the true light that enlightens every man who comes into the world."

94. Note that the fact that it says that God enlightens "every man

who comes into the world" has created and continues to create a difficulty for many because of a twofold false mental image. First, they imagine that things are not present equally and immediately to God at the same time,[165] and so they seek a difficulty where there is none by looking for a medium in what is immediate, a space where there is no quantity. The second cause and false mental image is because they think that grace alone is an illumination, when every perfection, especially existence itself, is an illumination and a source of each enlightening perfection. Aristotle in the third book of *On the Soul* calls the agent intellect an illumination.[166] Much the same can be found in sacred scripture and in the books of the philosophers. "I fill heaven and earth, says the Lord" (Jr. 23:24). In the Psalm it says: "His going out is from one end of heaven and his circuit is to the other end; and there is no one who can hide himself from his heat" (Ps. 18:7). This is what it says here, God enlightens "every man who comes into the world."

95. Comment briefly that God "enlightens every man who comes into this world," but one who is not humble ("from the ground") is not a man, for the word "man" (*homo*) is taken from "ground" (*humus*).[167] Again, he is not a man who does not live according to reason, for man is a rational animal. And so "he enlightens every man," although not every man is enlightened, just as he addresses all, although all do not listen, as Augustine says when he treats John 8:25: "I am the Principle who is also speaking to you."[168] Further, one is not a man who does not have all things subject to him. The Psalm asks, "What is man?" and answers, "You have placed all things under his feet" (Ps. 8:5, 8). Man's affections are his feet. When the first man was created or formed he heard the message, "Fill the earth and subdue it, and rule over all the creatures that move on the earth" (Gn. 1:28).

Verse 11. He came to his own.

96. In the first place, note that God, although he is everywhere and in all things as existence, and is also everywhere and in all things through his essence, is still said to "come" when his presence is evident through some new effect. Second, note that Augustine in the seventh book of the *Confessions* says that he did not find the passage from "He came to his own" down to "those who believe in his name" in the books of Plato.[169] It is nevertheless a probable opinion that natural reason has an incontestable exemplary proof for these words, "He came to his own" and for others like them in the things of nature. Remember

that nothing is so much its own as a being's act of existence or a creature's creator. But God is existence itself and is also the creator. This is the meaning of "He came to his own."

97. The passage can be taken in a second way as follows. The things that are his own into which God came are Existence or Being, the One, the True and the Good. These four things are God's own, for he is "the First which is rich through itself."[170] He possesses these because he is "rich"; he possesses them as his own because he exists "through himself." In the case of everything that is below the First these four things are "guests and strangers" (Ep. 2:19); with God they are "members of the household." Therefore, we teach first that God exists and works in all things and comes to all men and all things insofar as they exist, insofar as they are one, and insofar as they are true and good. Second, we teach that through his coming and presence God immediately and with no other agent causes being, unity, truth and goodness in all things in an analogical fashion.

98. "He came to his own." Third. In a more theological sense it can be said that these "own" to which God the Word came are the act of having mercy, according to that saying of Gregory, "God, whose property it is always to have mercy and to spare,"[171] and the act of saving, according to the text of Augustine, "He is called Savior of the world so that he may save the world; . . . if you do not wish to be saved, you will judge yourself by your own action."[172] God the Word possesses both these attributes. They are proper to him as God yet they are held in common with the Father and the Holy Spirit. Because he is the Son, he also certainly possesses what is intrinsically proper to him. So John says that God the Word, the Son, "came to his own," that is, to those who are God's sons through the grace of adoption. "Because you are sons, God has sent his Son's Spirit into your hearts" (Ga. 4:6). This is what it says here: "He gave them the power to become God's sons, to those who believe in his name." His proper name is that he is the Son.

99. The following passage, "His own received him not," can be explained according to the three interpretations of "He came to his own" just given. Neither things that exist nor things that are one, true or good possess their being, unity, truth and goodness from themselves (this is what the text "His own received him not" means), but they possess them from the Word himself, the Son of God (this is what follows, "As many as received him, he gave them the power"). The very power to receive him comes from him, just as Augustine in the twelfth book

of the *Confessions* says that prime matter's own receptive capacity comes from God.[173] In *On the Trinity*, book fifteen, chapter fifteen, he says that the capacity to conceive a word is already to be called a word.[174] And thus the text, "His own received him not." First, because they possess nothing from themselves or from what is their own; second, because they do not have any capacity which is not from God; third, because what is received does not take root in them, as we discussed above in the case of light;[175] and fourth, because indistinct existence is proper to God and he is distinguished by his indistinction alone, while distinct existence is proper to a creature. It does not belong to what is distinct to receive what is indistinct.[176] So Augustine addressing God says: "You were with me, and I was not with you."[177]

100. In full agreement with this is the fact that in nature the form of what is generated by means of the generation as received "comes to its own," that is, to its proper matter. The acts of active agents are in the recipient that is prepared for them,[178] and in nature there is a proper passive recipient corresponding to every agent. As long as matter possesses something of its own, whether it be some act or some property of the prior form—and thus is not pure receptive power—it never receives the substantial form itself, the "son" of the generating cause that brings it into existence. This existence is the gift of the substantial form, or rather is the substantial form itself, even though in coming into existence or coming to be it must tolerate the dispositions and properties of the form that perishes. Clearly this is the meaning of "He came to his own," and the following text, "His own received him not," that is, everything that still possesses something of its own.

For example, if the eye possesses some color or something pertaining to color, it will see neither that color nor any other.[179] Yet further: If the sense of sight is informed by any act whatsoever, even its own act, it is not as such capable of receiving what is visible insofar as it is visible.[180] What is active as such cannot be passive, and inversely what is passive as such can in no way be active. Therefore, the intellect has no actual existence of its own so that it can understand all things.[181] It understands itself the way it understands other things. Therefore, it has nothing of itself, nothing of its own, before it understands. Understanding is a reception.[182] The formal property of what receives something is to be naked.[183] This is all clear from the third book of *On the Soul* and is the way it is with matter and substantial form in nature. Matter itself, in which there is nothing distinct, as the

Philosopher says,[184] is the foundation of nature. Every act creates a distinction.

101. In relation to the passage "He came to his own," it is even more appropriate to say that these words teach first that "the Word made flesh" assumed a pure human nature, that is, one without the vices that the Enemy sowed (Mt. 13:25). These are not God's seed; he did not plant them; they are not his work. They are not made by God nor are they proper to him, but are the Enemy's. God made man righteous (Si. 7:30). Thus John says, "He came to his own," that is, he assumed the nature he made, his own work, without vice and without sin. "Without him was made nothing," that is, sin.[185] This is what John Damascene says—God the Word assumed what he planted.[186]

102. Second. We are taught in these words how "the Word made flesh" assumed human nature out of pure grace and not from any prior merits of the nature.[187] This is "He came to his own," because it was not from something that belonged to the nature, but from the grace that belongs to God alone, that "the goodness and kindness . . . of God appeared, not from the works of justice, but according to his mercy" (Tt. 3:4–5). This is what follows in the first chapter of John, "to those who were born not from blood, . . . but from God." We can also say "He came to his own" in the sense of what belongs to man and human nature. He assumed the mortality and passibility that belong to man, not to God.[188] Therefore, perhaps it says "The Word was made flesh" because he assumed the defects to which the flesh is heir, that is, the punishments due to original sin, but not the defects that are personal sins and belong to the soul.[189]

103. Again, "He came to his own." Note that everything created, because it is a particular being, something distinct, belongs to some genus, species or individual thing. God is not anything distinct or proper to some nature, but is common to all.[190] He is outside and above every genus.[191] The proof of this is that being, God's effect, is not in a genus and does not belong to any genus, but is common to every genus.[192] When God came into this world, assumed a created nature and was made man, it was as if he came to what is proper from the height of what is common. This is what the text clearly means, "He was the true light that enlightens every man," for this light is common and superior to all. There follows, "He was in the world, and the world," that which contains every genus, "was made through him." Finally, John concludes, "He came to his own." "I came forth from the Father and have

161

come into the world" (Jn. 16:28). "I came out of the mouth of the Most High, the Firstborn before all creatures" (Si. 24:5); and below, "I came forth from Paradise," that is, divinity; "I said, I will water my garden of plants," that is, by creating the world (Si. 24:41–42).

104. The literal meaning of these words, "He came to his own, and his own received him not," is that the Word assumed flesh in his chosen Jewish people to whom "the oracles of God were entrusted" (Rm. 3:2) and the Law was given in which Christ, his Incarnation and like things were prefigured. God's "people, the sheep of his pasture" (Ps. 99:3) did not receive him through faith.[193]

105. "He came to his own, and his own received him not." The moral meaning is that God comes to the minds of men who dedicate themselves totally to him and who make themselves so much his that they no longer live for themselves, but for him. This is what is meant by "His own received him not," where "his own" are those who live for themselves, seeking what is theirs and not what is God's. This is what the next passage signifies.

Verses 12-13. As many as received him he gave the power of becoming sons of God; to those who believe in his name, who were born not from blood, nor of the will of the flesh, nor of the will of man, but of God.

106. In order to explain these words and many others in scripture four things must be noted. First, that the first fruit of the Incarnation of Christ, God's Son, is that man may become by the grace of adoption what the Son is by nature, as it says in the text here, "He gave them the power of becoming sons of God," and in the third chapter of Second Corinthians, "with faces unveiled reflecting as in a mirror the glory of the Lord, we are being transformed in the same image from glory to glory" (2 Co. 3:18). Second, everything that receives something or participates in something as such is empty and is in the passive power alone, according to the text, "As many as received him."

107. Third, the passive or receptive power through its being a power naturally and in every case receives its whole existence from the object alone, and no more from its subject than it does from any other subject foreign to it. Insofar as it is a power, it receives the same act of existence as that of the object. The Philosopher says that not only in things that are separate from matter is the intellective power the same as the intelligible object, but even in corporeal beings the sense

faculty and sense object are identical in act.[194] For even though the sense object does not give existence to the eye insofar as it is an eye or a being, and the eye does not give existence to the sense object insofar as it is a being (for in this respect the sense faculty and sense object are two), nevertheless, insofar as they are in act as the eye seeing and the object being seen, they are still one. In one and the same act they are the eye seeing and the object being seen. So Augustine in *On the Trinity* 9.12 says, "It must be held with certainty that everything we know begets its knowledge of itself in us."[195] This from Augustine. Take seeing away from the eye, and you take away being seen from the object. On the other hand, take away being seen from the object, and you take away seeing from the eye. To see and to be seen are one and the same thing, that is, they begin at the same time, and continue, cease and revive—originate and die—all at the same time. Neither nature, nor intellect, nor God can separate them.

Therefore as the Savior puts it so clearly and well, "This is eternal life, to know you alone" (Jn. 17:3). And Matthew teaches us to pray, "Hallowed be your name" (Mt. 6:9). The name, that is, the knowledge of God, is hallowed when he alone is acknowledged. Since man, as said above, receives his total existence entirely from God as from an object, existence for him is not "existence-for-himself" but "existence-for-God." It is existence-for-God, I say, insofar as God is the principle that gives existence, and insofar as he is the end for which man exists and lives. It is ignorance of self and of anything that is not God or is not in God insofar as it is in him and is divine. In speaking to God in the sixth book of the *Confessions* Augustine says, "Unfortunate is the man who knows everything else, but does not know you; blessed the man who knows you, even if he is ignorant of all those things. He who knows you and other things is not more blessed because of them, but blessed because of you alone."[196]

108. From what has been said the error of those who claim that the intellect and the will would be distinct powers even if they had one formal object is evident. Also clear is the error of those who say that beatitude consists in a reflective act of the intellect by which man actually knows that he knows God. I have treated these points in detail in the *Work of Questions*.[197]

109. Fourth. Note that it follows from what has been said that the known object begets itself or its species and gives birth in the knowing power. The begotten species is one common offspring in the object known and in the knowing power, as Augustine says in the passage

from the ninth book of *On the Trinity* cited above. As we said, because the knowing power receives its existence from what is known, and receives the very existence of the thing known, the Truth gives us good advice by prohibiting having or acknowledging any other father than God—"Call no one on earth your father, for one is your Father who is in heaven" (Mt. 23:9); and "I have come to set a man against his father," (Mt. 10:35), that is, so that he has no other father than God and knows no other except God. If a man has anything beyond God as his father, something that bears itself in him and is known by him, then he would be formed and given existence by that thing, indeed, given its very existence. Hence, he would not be perfect and would not truly be a son of God alone. "Be perfect, just as your Father is perfect" (Mt. 5:48). He would not be God's son at all. No one can have two fathers. Therefore, Matthew clearly says, "Your Father is one" (Mt. 23:9).

110. This is what our passage says, "As many as received him," namely, as many as were empty of every form begotten and impressed by creatures, "he gave the power to become sons of God." He gave it "to those who believe in his name," that is, his knowledge (for name is derived from knowledge) "so that they may know God alone" (Jn. 17:3), as we said above. John says "those who believe," because knowing and recognizing "is justice perfected and the root of immortality" (Ws. 15:3), as well as "eternal life" (Jn. 17:3). "We walk by faith" (2 Co. 5:7); "He who draws near to God must have belief" (Heb. 11:6). This is what the text signifies by "those who believe in his name." Now we see "through a glass darkly, but then it will be face to face; now we know in part, but then we shall know even as we have been known" (1 Co. 13:12). "Who were not born from blood, nor of the will of the flesh, nor of the will of man, but of God." "That which is born of the flesh is flesh; and that which is born of the Spirit is spirit" (Jn. 3:6). So what is born of God is God, God's son. "Everything born from God overcomes the world" (1 Jn. 5:4), and in the sixteenth chapter the Son says, "I have overcome the world" (Jn. 16:33).

111. Remember that there are three faculties in man: The first an irrational one that does not obey reason; the second an irrational one, but born to obey reason (the positive and negative appetites)[198]—"The appetite thereof shall be under you" (Gn. 4:7); and Aristotle calls it rational by participation[199]—and the third essentially rational. The first of these is signified when it says "not from blood," the second under "not from the will of the flesh," and the third with the words that follow, "not from the will of man." He wants to say that nothing human

and therefore nothing worldly or created ought to beget itself in us so that we are born from it, but that we are to be born from God alone. This is the meaning of the text "who were not born from blood, nor of the will of the flesh, nor of the will of man, but of God."

In distinguishing the three Augustine says that Latin does not use the plural "bloods," but Greek does.[200] The translator preferred to be a bit less grammatical to serve the truth better. Man is born "from the bloods" of husband and wife. Through "the will of the flesh" understand the wife, whose role is to obey and serve, just as through the spirit we sometimes understand the husband, whose role it is to rule. Corrupt is the household where the woman rules over the man. There is nothing worse.

112. In the first exegesis of the passage, "He came to his own," we said that God is everywhere and in all things.[201] Second we said its moral message is that in order to be divine and godlike a man should behave uniformly everywhere and in all things.[202] "God is one" (Ga. 3:20), and from this fact we derive the word "uniform." Again, as the *Book of Causes* says, God himself "exists in all things according to a single disposition, but all things do not exist in him according to a single disposition."[203] It follows that he who is not "in all things according to a single disposition" is not uniform to the one God and is not deiform in things. Rather, he is not deiform in things and in God, but is in them according to the nature and properties of creatures. He who is nowhere, who, I say, is not tied down by love of any place, homeland or household, is really everywhere. He who is not affected by any particular created being is thus in all things.

113. Again, on the basis of the second exegesis of "He came to his own,"[204] note in the third place the moral message that the further a thing is removed from the many and aims toward the One the more perfect and divine it is. "You are troubled about many things, . . . yet only one thing is necessary" (Lk. 10:41–42). Again, "If your eye," that is, your intention, "is simple, your whole body will be full of light" (Lk. 11:34). Because of this Ecclesiasticus says, "My son, meddle not with many matters" (Si. 11:10); and the Psalm, "I have asked the One from the Lord" (Ps. 26:4). (The text uses the feminine instead of the neuter here, according to Hebrew usage, as Jerome says.)[205] In book one of *On Order* Augustine says:

> The soul which enters multiplicity eagerly strives after the
> loss that it does not know can only be avoided by shunning

multiplicity. . . . The greater the desire to embrace multiplicity, the greater the loss it suffers. Just as no matter how big the circle is, there is one midpoint where all the radii meet . . . and that is the source of their equal length and the ground in which everything in any part of the circle loses that which makes it multiple, so too the intellectual soul, when it pours itself out, is beaten down by a kind of vastness and is uprooted by a real indigence since its nature impels it to seek the One in all things but multiplicity forbids it.[206]

This is what Augustine says. In *On True Religion* he also says, "The principle of everything that is one is the One alone, that from which comes everything that is one."[207] And later, "We certainly seek that One which is simpler than anything else." Therefore, "Let us seek him 'in simplicity of heart' " (Ws. 1:1). "The phantasms of the whirl and swirl of life do not let us see the unchanging unity."[208] Further below he says, "We naturally reject anything that falls from unity and strives towards unlikeness. Unity allows us to understand that a thing is a thing. . . . On this principle unity belongs to that which is in any way one, . . . the Word in the Principle, and God the Word with God."[209]

114. The ground for what has been said is that the One, Being, the True and the Good are interchangeable.[210] To depart from the One is to fall from the True, from the Good, from God. "God is one" (Ga. 3:20). He who falls from the True falls into a lie. "You love vanity and seek after lying" (Ps. 4:3). To fall from the Good is to fall into malice— "You have loved malice more than goodness" (Ps. 51:5). To leave God is to approach the devil—"The devil is your father" (Jn. 8:44). On this basis you can explain the text "We have all things in you, the One" (Tb. 10:5). Everything that exists and that is true and good is possessed in the One itself. On this basis the text in chapter two of James is clear that anyone who offends "against the One is guilty in all things" (Jm. 2:10). By the very fact that anyone departs from the One, offends against the One itself and abandons it, he incurs guilt in all things. Guilt and stain in all things is vanity: "All is vanity" (Si. 1:2). Guilt in all things is division, number and multitude: "We have all offended in many things" (Jm. 3:2). Multitude, the opponent and adversary of the One, is always a sin, either of nature or of morality. "You will pardon my sin for it is many" (Ps. 24:11). Every sin in itself is "many," even if it happens only once, because the many is a fall from the One and therefore from the Good, which is interchangeable with it. Hence Je-

rome in his *Commentary on Ecclesiastes* says that a plural number is always taken as an evil.[211] I have commented on this at length in speaking of the work of the second day in the first chapter of Genesis.[212]

115. From the third exegesis of "He came to his own" take note of a fourth moral meaning: He who wants to find God in himself must be God's son.[213] The Father and the Son exist at one and the same time and are mutually related. The Holy Spirit proceeds from the Son in the Trinity, and hence he does not proceed into us nor is he presented except to sons. "Because you are sons, God has sent his Son's Spirit into your hearts" (Ga. 4:6). We are sons if we do each of our works from the love of the good alone insofar as it is good. Son comes from *philos*, which in Greek means love.[214]

Verse 14. The Word was made flesh and dwelt among us.

116. Note first that "flesh" here stands for man figuratively, according to Matthew's text, "No flesh would be saved" (Mt. 24:22), and "No flesh will be justified from the works of the law" (Rm. 3:20). The Evangelist preferred to say "The Word was made flesh," rather than man, to commend the goodness of God who assumed not only man's soul, but also his flesh. In this he strikes at the pride of all those who when asked about their relatives respond by pointing to one who holds an important position, but are silent about their own descent. When asked, they say they are nephews of such and such a bishop, prelate, dean or the like. There is the story of the mule who when asked who his father was answered that his uncle was a thoroughbred, but out of shame hid the fact that his father was an ass.[215]

117. Second. As mentioned above,[216] note that the first fruit of the Incarnation of the Word, who is the natural Son of God, is that we should be God's sons through adoption. It would be of little value for me that "the Word was made flesh" for man in Christ as a person distinct from me unless he was also made flesh in me personally so that I too might be God's son. "If son, then also heir" (Ga. 4:7). Perhaps this is what we pray for at the Lord's command: "Your will be done on earth as it is in heaven" (Mt. 6:10). That is, just as the Father's will that he be a Son has been done in Christ, the "heaven" (for by nature it is the will of a father as father to bear and have a son), so also may the Father's will that we be sons of God be done on "earth," that is, in us who live upon the earth. "You have received the spirit of adoption of

the sons of God" (Rm. 8:15); and below, "If we are sons, we are heirs also: Heirs indeed of God and joint heirs with Christ" (Rm. 8:17). Further on it says, "He has predestined them to become conformed to his Son's image so that he should be the firstborn among many brethren" (Rm. 8:29). This is the meaning of "The Word was made flesh" in Christ the firstborn, "and dwelt among us" when we are born God's sons through adoption. In the sixteenth chapter it says, "I will see you again, and your heart shall rejoice, and your joy no one shall take from you" (Jn. 16:22). God has "seen us" when he was made man for us in Christ; he sees us again in adopting us as sons and dwelling in us like a Father in his sons. That is, "The Word was made flesh and dwelt among us."

118. "The Word was made flesh" in Christ who is outside us. He does not make us perfect by being outside us; but afterwards, through the fact that "he dwelt among us," he gives us his name and perfects us "so that we are called and truly are God's sons" (1 Jn. 3:1). For then the Son of God, "The Word made flesh," dwells in us, that is, in our very selves—"Behold God's dwelling with man, and he will dwell with them . . . and God himself will be with them as their God" (Rv. 21:3). "His name shall be Emmanuel, that is God with us" (Is. 7:14; Mt. 1:23); and "Rejoice and give praise, habitation of Sion, for great is the Holy One of Israel who is in your midst" (Is. 12:6). He says, "He dwelt among us," that is, he made man his dwelling.[217] Again, "He dwelt among us" because we have him in us. Anything takes its name and existence from what it has in it. This is what the Bride prays for in the Song of Songs: "Let him kiss me with the kiss of his mouth" (Sg. 1:1). After she received it, "The winter is past and gone, . . . the vines in flower yield their sweet smell, . . . for his lips are like a dripping honeycomb" (Sg. 2:11, 2:13, 4:11). John says therefore, "The Word was made flesh" in Christ, "and dwelt among us" when in any one of us the Son of God becomes man and a son of man becomes a son of God. "See what manner of love God has given us, that we should be called and truly be God's sons" (1 Jn. 3:1).

119. What is said here, "The Word was made flesh and dwelt among us," in the sixteenth chapter is expressed as "Again I will see you" (Jn. 16:22). He saw us when he was "made flesh"; he sees us again when he dwells in us. "The kingdom of heaven is within you" (Lk. 17:21); and "A virgin shall conceive and bear a son" (this is said of Christ), "and his name shall be called Emmanuel, that is, God with us" (this is said of each of us as a son of man becomes a son of God). "We

are being transformed into the same image from glory to glory, as through the Spirit of the Lord" (2 Co. 3:18). We should not falsely suppose that it is by one son or image that Christ is the Son of God and by some other that the just and godlike man is a son of God, for he says, "We are being transformed into the same image."[218] Furthermore, just as when many mirrors held up to a person's face and countenance are all informed by the same one face, so too each and every just person is completely and perfectly justified by the same justice. They are formed, informed and transformed into the same justice.[219] Otherwise they would not be just in a univocal sense, and no single just person would be truly just if justice were one thing in itself and another in the just person.

120. The text in Hebrews, "It was right that he should in all things be made like his brethren" (Heb. 2:17), can be interpreted in a good and true fashion on this basis. Earlier it says, "Both he who sanctifies and they who are sanctified are all from one, for which cause he is not ashamed to call them brethren" (Heb. 2:11). In the text from Corinthians when he said, "We are being transformed into the same image," he added, "as through the Spirit of the Lord," as if to say that just as we are all sanctified by the same Holy Spirit who comes upon us (Lk. 1:35), so too all of us who are just and godlike are called and truly are God's sons in the same Son of God who is "the Word made flesh" in Christ living among us and conforming us to himself through grace. He does not merely say, "that we may be called," but he says, "that we may be called and may truly be" (1 Jn. 3:1)—"in order that we may be"—"in order that he might be the firstborn among many brethren" (Rm. 8:29).[220] Immediately before this, it has, "He predestined them to be conformed to the image of his Son." This is what our text means, "The Word was made flesh," and the very same Word, the Son, "dwelt among us."

121. With us no matter how close the object of sight approaches the faculty of sight, we never see unless the visible image itself (the same image as that of the visible thing) is imprinted on and transferred to or "dwells in" the one who sees. If there were a different image in the one and the other, the person who sees would not see the visible object through the image that is in him, and the visible object would not be seen through or in the image in the one who sees. And so the object and the faculty of sight would not be one in act, as Aristotle says.[221] This is "the grace upon grace" (Si. 26:19) and "the grace for grace" (Jn. 1:16), so that not only may "the Word be made flesh," but

"what is made flesh may also dwell among us." This is what the Son says further on—"I have come," that is, by taking on flesh, "that they may have life" (Jn. 10:10), that is, by my living among them. This is said right below, "And of his fullness we have all received, grace for grace."

Verse 14. We saw his glory, glory as of the Only-Begotten of the Father.

122. The literal interpretation. According to Chrysostom, the Evangelist wished to demonstrate in brief fashion that the glory of the Word made flesh is totally ineffable in itself in all aspects, and so he says that his glory is of the kind that befits the Father's Only-Begotten.[222] Such a Person by nature has everything that the Father has. "All the things that the Father has are mine" (Jn. 16:15); and "knowing that the Father had given all things into his hands" (Jn. 13:3); and "All things that are mine are yours and yours are mine" (Jn. 17:10). Also, "What my Father has given me is greater than all" (Jn. 10:29), because "All things were made through him"; but he himself was not made but received something greater from the Father, namely the Father's uncreated nature, which is truly something greater than everything, for as creator it is the beginning and end of all things.

123. It also can be said quite fittingly that in this passage the Evangelist wanted to show that those who had received the power to become God's sons and "to be born from God," and to have the Word made flesh dwell among them are seeing his "glory as of the Only-Begotten." This glory is "as of the Only-Begotten" ("Only-Begotten" in the sense of first of many), that is, it is like that of the Only-Begotten, because the term "as of" signifies likeness. "We shall be like him, for we shall see him just as he is" (1 Jn. 3:2). Like is always known by like.[223] This is as if he were to say, "We see the glory of the Only-Begotten of the Father," as if we also were only-begotten. He is the Only-Begotten, coming from the Father alone; we are begotten, but not from one father. He is a Son through the generation that leads to existence, species and nature, and therefore he is the natural Son; we are sons through the rebirth that leads to conformity with this nature. He is "the Father's image" (Col. 1:15); we are made to the image of the whole Trinity[224]—"Let us make man to our image" (Gn. 1:26). He is the one to whom witness is given; we are the witnesses (Ac. 2:32).

"The Word was made flesh and dwelt among us. And we saw his

glory, glory as of the Only-Begotten of the Father, full of grace and truth."

124. In the seventh book of the *Confessions* Augustine says that everything from the beginning of the chapter down to and including "full of grace and truth" he had read and found in Plato's books.[225] The exceptions were the part discussed above from "He came to his own" down to "those who believe in his name," and what is said here, "The Word became flesh and dwelt among us."

125. But there is still good reason to say (always presupposing the historical truth of the text) that everything that is said here, the whole verse, is contained in and taught by the properties of the things of nature, morality and art. The word universally and naturally becomes flesh in every work of nature and art and it dwells in things that are made or in which word becomes flesh. This is the case with the soul, spirit or word become flesh when it is united to flesh in a human being or in any animal. The soul itself dwells in the flesh or in the person composed of body and soul. The person himself sees the "glory," that is, every perfection and all the soul's properties, as something begotten and "only-begotten" from it, that is, from the soul as the father and begetter of the living being. This happens inasmuch as there is the same act of existence for everything that belongs to a person as man, as flesh and as soul.

126. Just as the flesh receives, possesses and sees by experience the very existence of the soul, it does the same with every property and operation of soul, so that the act of existence and all its operations are not proper to the soul but to the joint body and soul. The flesh and its soul share the modes of predication that are proper to each,[226] that is, their properties, modes of address and language, so that we do not say that the soul exists, senses and understands, but we say that the whole composite of body and soul exists, senses and understands, as it says in the first book of *On the Soul*.[227]

127. The same holds true in the case of every substantial form and its matter, in the case of an accident and its subject, and also in the case of the form of art in the artist's soul and what he makes. That is what this text means: "Full of grace and truth," that is, of every perfection of "grace and truth." Anyone who is informed by a form possesses the full act of its existence. By having it within him he sees every "grace" and every "truth" or every perfection and power of the form, in accord with the texts, "All good things came to me together with her" (Ws. 7:11) and "He has given us all things with him" (Rm. 8:32).

128. On the level of sense we see that an iron bar that is well and fully heated in fire does what fire does and more. Avicenna says that molten lead burns a hand worse than fire does,[228] according to the passage "The works that I do he shall also do, and greater than these he shall do" (Jn. 14:12). This is true in the case of everyone who is born from the Spirit or from God (Jn. 3:6). The Word made flesh dwells in him. Informed by that Word, like its only-begotten he sees its glory, since he is full of grace and truth, that is, of its every perfection and glory. "Your face is full of graces" (Est. 15:17). This is the meaning of "The Word was made flesh and dwelt among us, and we saw his glory, glory as of the Only-Begotten of the Father, full of grace and truth."

129. The Savior speaks of this fullness in chapter sixteen when he says, "Ask and receive, that your joy may be full" (Jn. 16:24). As long as a fire is being ignited from a piece of wood, it is not fully hot.[229] But after the wood has gained the form of fire, then through and in that form it attains and gains full heat perfectly. Heat is no longer something that precedes and prepares fire's form, but is rather something that follows after and comes from the form of fire itself. Thus the grief that accompanies birth, change and motion ceases, and the wood rejoices and delights completely in the full heat of the form of fire. Since it is completely hot, nothing can be added to it, but it rests in that heat when every grief and resistance accompanying change and movement has ceased. Hence the text in chapter sixteen, "A woman about to give birth has grief . . ., but when she has brought forth the child, she no longer remembers the anguish for her joy that a man is born into the world" (Jn. 16:21). And immediately below, "You grieve now, but I will see you again and your heart will rejoice" (Jn. 16:22). As long as anything is becoming something else, it always has the grief of unlikeness and restlessness. When it has received existence through the form, it is at rest and is content. Fire, by heating and changing pieces of wood, "sees" them. It prepares them for the form of fire, but accompanied by a painful unlikeness that resists change. It "sees" the pieces of wood once again when they receive the form of fire through generation after the unlikeness has been cast off. This generation takes place in complete stillness of motion, time and unlikeness, so that while the form of fire remains, the heat and natural delight in it cannot be taken away. This is what follows, "Your joy no one shall take from you," a passage introduced by, "I will see you again, and your heart shall rejoice" (Jn. 16:22).

130. This is the case in what we are discussing: As long as we are

not like God and are still undergoing the birth by which Christ is formed in us (Ga. 4:19), like Martha (Lk. 10:41) we are restless and troubled about many things.[230] But when Christ, God's Son, has been formed in us so that "we are in his true Son" (1 Jn. 5:20), and we are God's sons after every unlikeness has been cast off, "We shall be like him, for we shall see him just as he is, having been made one in him and through him" (1 Jn. 3:2; Jn. 17:21). At that time we shall have full and perfect delight and we shall be at rest, as Augustine says, "You have made us for Yourself, and our heart is restless until it rests in you."[231] Thus in Luke, chapter ten, after he said that Martha was troubled about many things, he says, "yet only one thing is necessary" (Lk. 10:42). Giving birth always involves plurality and disturbance; what has been born and begotten is always one, something that remains and holds fast as an heir. So there follows, "Mary has chosen the best part and it will not be taken away from her" (Lk. 10:42). This is the same as the text from John, chapter sixteen, cited above, "Your joy no one will take from you" (Jn. 16:22). Galatians says, "If a son, then also an heir" (Ga. 4:7). Heir is derived from "holding fast" and "remaining." "The Son remains in the house forever" (Jn. 8:35) in accordance with the texts, "Your joy no one shall take from you," and "The best part will not be taken away." In chapter sixteen below when the Savior says, "Ask that your joy may be full," the sense is, ask that you may be sons. Immediately prior he said, "Hitherto you have not asked anything in my name" (Jn. 16:24), who am the Son. One who is not yet a son does not ask in the Son's name.

131. This is what our text means, "We (yes *we!*) have seen his glory, like the Only-Begotten of the Father (that means the Son)." Then follows, "full of grace and truth." Only he who is a Son is full of grace and truth. I have much more on this in my comments on verse seventeen below ("The law was given through Moses; grace and truth came through Jesus Christ").[232]

Part Two

German Works

translated by
Edmund Colledge, O.S.A.

1. SELECTED SERMONS

Sermon 2: Intravit Jesus in quoddam castellum et mulier quaedam,
Martha nomine, excepit illum in domum suam (Lk. 10:38).[1]

I have begun with a few words in Latin that are written in the gospel; and in German this means: "Our Lord Jesus Christ went up into a little town, and was received by a virgin who was a wife."[2]

Now notice carefully what this says. It must necessarily be that the person by whom Jesus was received was a virgin. "Virgin" is as much as to say a person who is free of all alien images, as free as he was when he was not. Observe that people may ask how a man who has been born and has advanced to the age of reason could be as free of all images as when he was nothing; he who knows so many things that are all images: How then can he be free? Keep in mind this distinction, which I want to make clear for you. If I were so rational that there were present in my reason all the images that all men had ever received,[3] and those that are present in God himself, and if I could be without possessiveness in their regard, so that I had not seized possessively upon any one of them, not in what I did or what I left undone, not looking to past or to future, but I stood in this present moment free and empty according to God's dearest will, performing it without ceasing, then truly I should be a virgin, as truly unimpeded by any images as I was when I was not.

But I say that because a man is a virgin, that does not deprive him at all of any of the works he has ever done; but all this permits him to remain, maidenly and free, without any obstacles between him and supreme truth, just as Jesus is empty and free and maidenly in himself. As the authorities say that only between equals can unity be produced, so must a man be a maid and a virgin who is to receive the maidenly Jesus.[4]

177

Now mark what I say and pay careful attention! For if a man were to be a virgin forever, no fruit would come from him. If he is to become fruitful, he must of necessity be a wife. "Wife" is the noblest word one can apply to the soul, much nobler than "virgin." That a man conceives God in himself is good, and in his conceiving he is a maiden. But that God should become fruitful in him is better; for the only gratitude for a gift is to be fruitful with the gift, and then the spirit is a wife, in its gratitude giving birth in return, when he for God gives birth again to Jesus into the heart of the Father.

Many good gifts are received in virginity and are not born again in wifely fruitfulness with grateful praise to God. The gifts all spoil and turn to nothing, so that the man is no better or more blessed because of them. So his virginity is no profit to him, because he is not, in addition to his virginity, a wife with all her fruitfulness. That is where the trouble is. That is why I have said: "Jesus went up into a little town, and was received by a virgin who was a wife." This must necessarily be so, as I have shown.

Married people seldom produce in a year more than one fruit.[5] But I am now talking about a different kind of married people, about all those who are possessively attached to prayer, to fasting, to vigils and to all kinds of exterior exercises and penances. Every attachment to every work deprives one of the freedom to wait upon God in the present and to follow him alone in the light with which he would guide you in what to do and what to leave alone, free and renewed in every present moment, as if this were all that you had ever had or wanted or could do. Every attachment or every work you propose deprives you again and again of this freedom, and is what I now call a "year," because your soul produces no fruit unless it performs the work to which you have been so attached; and you have no trust, not in God or in yourself, unless you have performed the work on which you seized with such possessiveness, and otherwise you have no peace. That is why you too produce no fruit, unless you perform your work. This is what I reckon as a "year," and your fruit is small indeed, because it has been produced out of attachment to the work and not out of freedom. And I call these married people, because they are pledged to possessiveness. They produce little fruit, and what they do produce is small indeed, as I have said.

A virgin who is a wife is free and unpledged, without attachment; she is always equally close to God and to herself. She produces much fruit, and it is great, neither less nor more than is God himself. This virgin who is a wife brings this fruit and this birth about, and every day she produces fruit, a hundred or a thousand times, yes, more than can be counted, giving birth and becoming fruitful from the noblest ground of all—or, to put it better, from that same ground where the Father is bearing his eternal Word, from that ground is she fruitfully bearing with him. For Jesus, the light and the reflection of the Fatherly heart—Saint Paul says that he is the glory and the reflection of the Fatherly heart, and with his power he illumines completely the Fatherly heart (Heb. 1:3)—this Jesus is united with her and she with him, and she shines and glows with him as one in oneness and as a pure bright light in the Fatherly heart.

And I have often said that there is a power in the soul that touches neither time nor flesh. It flows from the spirit and remains in the spirit and is wholly spiritual. In this power God is always verdant and blossoming in all the joy and the honor that he is in himself. That is a joy so heartfelt, a joy so incomprehensible and great that no one can tell it all. For it is in this power that the eternal Father ceaselessly brings his eternal Son so to birth, that this power also is bearing the Son of the Father, and bearing itself, that same Son, in the single power of the Father. If a man possessed a whole kingdom, or all the riches of the earth, and gave up the whole of it for the love of God and became one of the poorest men that ever lived on earth, and if God then gave him as much to suffer as he has ever given any man, and if he suffered it all until his death, and if God then gave him one single glimpse of what he is in this power, his joy would be so great that all this suffering and poverty would be too little. Yes, even if after this God never gave him the kingdom of heaven, he still would have received a reward great enough for all that he had ever suffered, for God is present in this power as he is in the eternal now. If the spirit were always united with God in this power, the man could never grow old; for that now in which God made the first man, and the now in which the last man will have his end, and the now in which I am talking, they are all the same in God, and there is not more than the one now. Now you can see that this man lives in one light with God, and therefore there is not in him either suffering or the passage of time, but an unchanging eternity. From this man, truly, all wonderment has been taken away, and all things are essentially present in him. Therefore nothing new will come to him out of future events or accidents, for he dwells always anew in a now without ceasing. Such a divine lordship is there in this power.

There is another power that is also not of the body; it flows out of the spirit and remains in the spirit and is wholly spiritual. In this power God is ceaselessly gleaming and burning with all his riches, with all his sweetness and with all his joy. Truly, there is such delight and such great, immeasurable joy in this power that no one can tell or reveal it all. But I say: If there were a single man who were to contemplate rationally and truly in this for an instant the joy and the delight that is there, everything that he could have suffered and that God would have wished him to suffer would be for him too little and, indeed, nothing; and I say more—it would always be his joy and his ease.

If you really want to know whether your sufferings are your own or are God's, this is what you should observe. If you suffer for your own sake, however this may be, the suffering hurts you and is hard for you to bear. But if you suffer for God's sake and for his sake alone, the suffering will not hurt you and will not be hard for you, because God is carrying the burden. This is really true! If there were a man who wanted to suffer for the love of God and purely for God alone, if all the suffering came down on him at once that all men have ever suffered and the whole world has as its common lot, that would not hurt him or be hard for him, because it would be God who was carrying the burden. If someone loaded a hundredweight on my neck and then someone else supported it on my neck, I should be as glad to carry a hundred of them as one, because it would not be hard for me, nor would it hurt me at all. In a few words: Whatever a man suffers for the love of God and for him alone, God makes this easy and sweet for him, as I said at the beginning, when we started our sermon: "Jesus went up into a little town, and was received by a virgin who was a wife." Why? It must necessarily be that she was a virgin and also a wife. Now I have told you that Jesus was received, but I have not said to you what the little town is; but now I want to talk about that.

I have sometimes said that there is a power in the spirit that alone is free. Sometimes I have said that it is a guard of the spirit; sometimes I have said that it is a light of the spirit; sometimes I have said that it is a spark. But now I say that it is neither this nor that, and yet it is a something that is higher above this and that than heaven is above the earth. And therefore I now give it finer names than I have ever given it before, and yet whatever fine names, whatever words we use, they are telling lies, and it is far above them. It is free of all names, it is bare of all forms, wholly empty and free, as God in himself is empty and free. It is so utterly one and simple, as God is one and simple, that man cannot in any way look into it. The same power of which I have spoken, in which God is verdant and growing with all his divinity, and the spirit in God—with this same power is the Father bringing to birth his Only-Begotten Son as truly as in himself, for he truly lives in this power, and the spirit with the Father brings to birth the same Only-Begotten Son, and it begets itself the same Son, and is the same Son in this light, and it is the truth. If you could look upon this with my heart, you would well understand what I say, for it is true, and it is Truth's own self that says it.

And now see and pay heed! This little town, about which I am talking and which I have in mind, is in the soul so one and so simple, far above whatever can be described, that this noble power about which I have spoken is not worthy even once for an instant to look into this little town; and the other power too of which I spoke, in which God is gleaming and burning with all his riches and with all his joy, it also does not ever dare to look into it. This little town is so truly one and simple, and this simple one is so exalted above every manner and every power,[6] that no power, no manner, not God himself may look at it. It is as true that this is true and that I speak truly as that God is alive! God himself never for an instant looks into it, never yet did he look on it, so far as he possesses himself in the manner and according to the properties of his Persons.[7] It is well to observe this, because this simple one is without manner and without properties. And therefore, if God were ever to look upon it, that must cost him all his divine names and the properties of his Persons; that he must wholly forsake, if he is ever once to look into it. But as he is simply one, without any manner and properties, he is not Father or Son or Holy Spirit, and yet he is a something that is neither this nor that.

Observe that as he is one and simple, so he comes into the one, which in the soul I have called a little town, and he does not come into it in any other way; but so he comes there, and so he is there. In this part the soul is like to God, and otherwise not. What I have said to you is true; I call the truth to witness this, and I lay my soul as a pledge.

That we may also be a little town into which Jesus may come and be received, and remain forever in us in the way that I have said, may God help us to this. Amen.

Sermon 5b: In hoc apparuit charitas dei in nobis.[1]

"In this God's love for us has been revealed and has appeared to us, because God has sent his Only-Begotten Son into the world, so that we live with the Son and in the Son and through the Son," because those who do not live through the Son are not living as they should (1 Jn. 4:9).

Suppose that there were a mighty king who had a fair daughter whom he gave to the son of a poor man. All who were of that man's family would be ennobled and honored by this. Now one authority says: "God became man, and through that all the human race has been ennobled and honored. We may well all rejoice over this, that Christ our brother has through his own power gone up above all the choirs of angels and sits at the right hand of the Father."[2] This authority has said well, but really I am not much concerned about this. How would it help me if I had a brother who was a rich man, if I still remained poor? How would it help me if I had a brother who was a wise man, if I still remained a fool?

I shall say something else that has more application to us: God did not only become man—he took human nature upon himself.

The authorities commonly say that all men are equally noble by nature.[3] But truly I say: Everything good that all the saints have possessed, and Mary the mother of God, and Christ in his humanity, all that is my own in this human nature.[4] Now you could ask me: "Since in this nature I have everything that Christ according to his humanity can attain, how is it that we exalt and honor Christ as our Lord and our God?" That is because he became a messenger from God to us and brought us our blessedness. The blessedness that he brought us was ours.[5]

Where the Father gives birth to his Son in the innermost ground, there this nature is suspended.[6] This nature is one and simple. Something may well look forth from it and somehow depend on it, but that is not this, which is one.

I shall say something else that is harder: Whoever is to remain in the nakedness of this nature without any medium must have gone out beyond all persons to such an extent that he is willing to believe as well of a man far beyond the seas, whom he never set eyes on, as he does of the man who lives with him and is his closest friend. For so long as you think better of your own people than you do of the man whom you never saw, you are going quite astray, and you have never had a single glimpse into this simple ground. You may well have seen in some derivative image the truth in a similitude, but that was not the best that could be.

Next, you should have a pure heart, for only that heart is pure which has annihilated everything that is created. Third, you must become naked of what is nothing. People ask, "What is it that burns in hell?" The authorities commonly say that it is self-will.[7] But I say truly that what burns in hell is nothing. Take a comparison. Suppose that someone takes a burning coal and puts it in my hand. If I were to say that it was the coal that was burning my hand, I should be doing the coal an injustice; but if I were to say properly what it is that is burning me, it is nothing, because the coal has something in it that my hand does not have. You must see that it is this nothing that is burning me. But if my hand had everything in it that is in the coal and that the coal can do, my hand would have all the nature of fire. If someone then took all the fire that has ever burned and put it on my hand, that could not hurt me. And in the same way I say: Since God and all those who are in God's sight have in them, according to their proper blessedness, something that those who are separated from God do not have, that "nothing"[8] alone torments the souls who are in hell, more than self-will or any fire. I say truly: So long as "nothing" holds you bound, so long are you imperfect. Therefore, if you want to be perfect, you must be naked of what is nothing.

That is what the text means with which I began: "God has sent his Only-Begotten Son into the world." You must not by this understand the external world in which the Son ate and drank with us, but understand it to apply to the inner world. As truly as the Father in his simple nature gives his Son birth naturally, so truly does he give him birth in the most inward part of the spirit, and that is the inner world. Here God's ground is my ground, and my ground is God's ground.[9] Here I live from what is my own, as God lives from what is his own. Whoever has looked for an instant into this ground, to such a man a thousand marks of red, minted gold are no more than a counterfeit penny. It is out of this inner ground that you should perform all your works without asking, "Why?" I say truly: So long as you perform your works for the sake of the kingdom of heaven, or for God's sake, or for the sake of your eternal blessedness, and you work them from without, you are going completely astray. You may well be tolerated, but it is not the best. Because truly, when people think that they are acquiring more of God in inwardness, in devotion, in sweetness and in various approaches than they do by the fireside or in the stable, you are acting just as if you took God and muffled his head up in a cloak and pushed him under a bench. Whoever is seeking God by ways is finding ways and losing God, who in ways is hidden.[10] But whoever seeks for God without ways will find him as he is in himself, and that man will live with the Son, and he is life itself. If anyone went on for a thousand years asking of life: "Why are you living?" life, if it could answer, would only say: "I live so that I may live." That is because life lives out of its own ground and springs from its own source, and so it lives without asking why it is itself living. If anyone asked a truthful man who works out of his own ground: "Why are you performing your works?" and if he were to give a straight answer, he would only say, "I work so that I may work."[11]

Where the creature stops, there God begins to be. Now God wants no more from you than that you should in creaturely fashion go out of yourself, and let God be God in you. The smallest creaturely image that ever forms in you is as great as God is great. Why? Because it comes between you and the whole of God. As soon as the image comes in, God and all his divinity have to give way. But as the image goes out, God goes in. God wants you to go out of yourself in creaturely fashion as much as if all his blessedness consisted in it. O my dear man, what harm does it do you to allow God to be God in you? Go completely out of yourself for God's love, and God comes completely out of himself for love of you. And when these two have gone out, what remains there is a simplified One. In this One the Father brings his Son to birth in the innermost source. Then the Holy Spirit blossoms forth, and then there springs up in God a will that belongs to the soul. So long as the will remains untouched by all created things and by all creation, it is free. Christ says: "No one comes into heaven except him who has come from heaven" (Jn. 3:13). All things are created from nothing; therefore their true origin is nothing, and so far as this noble will inclines toward created things, it flows off with created things toward their nothing.

Now the question is: Does this noble will flow off in such a manner that it can never return? The authorities commonly say that it will never return, so far as it has flowed away in time. But I say: If this will turns away from itself and from all creation for one instant, and back to its first source, then the will stands in its true and free state, and it is free, and in this instant all lost time is restored.

People often say to me: "Pray for me." Then I think: Why are you coming out? Why do you not stay in yourself and hold on to your own good? After all, you are carrying all truth in you in an essential manner.

That we may so truly remain within, that we may possess all

truth, without medium and without distinction, in true blessedness, may God help us to do this. Amen.

Sermon 6: *Justi vivent in aeternum (Ws. 5:16)*[1]

"The just will live forever, and their reward is with God." See exactly what this means; though it may sound simple and commonplace, it is really noteworthy and excellent.

"The just will live." Which are the just? Somewhere it is written: "That man is just who gives everyone what belongs to him";[2] those who give God what is his, and the saints and the angels what is theirs, and their fellow man what is his.

Honor belongs to God.[3] Who are those who honor God? Those who have wholly gone out of themselves, and who do not seek for what is theirs in anything, whatever it may be, great or little, who are not looking beneath themselves or above themselves or beside themselves or at themselves, who are not desiring possessions or honors or ease or pleasure or profit or inwardness or holiness or reward or the kingdom of heaven, and who have gone out from all this, from everything that is theirs, these people pay honor to God,[4] and they honor God properly, and they give him what is his.

People ought to give joy to the angels and the saints. What, does this amaze you? Can a man in this life give joy to those who are in everlasting life? Yes, indeed, he can! Every saint has such great delight and such unspeakable joy from every good work; from a good will or an aspiration they have such great joy that no tongue can tell, no heart can think how great is the joy they have from this. Why is that? Because their love for God is so immeasurably great, and they have so true a love for him, that his honor is dearer to them than their blessedness. And not only the saints or the angels, for God himself takes such delight in this, just as if it were his blessedness; and his being depends upon it, and his contentment and his well-being. Yes, mark this well: If we do not want to serve God for any other reason than the great joy they have in this who are in everlasting life, and that God himself has, we could do it gladly and with all our might.

And one ought also to give help and support to those who are in purgatory, and improvement and edification[5] to those who are still living.

Such a man is just in one way, and so in another sense are all those who accept all things alike from God, whatever it may be, great or small, joy or sorrow, all of it alike, less or more, one like the other. If you account anything more than something else, you do wrong. You ought to go wholly out from your own will.

Recently I had this thought: If God did not wish as I do, then I would still wish as he does. There are some people who want to have their own will in everything; that is bad, and there is much harm in it. Those are a little better who do want what God wants, and want nothing contrary to his will; if they were sick, what they would wish would be for God's will to be for them to be well. So these people want God to want according to their will, not for themselves to want according to his will. One has to endure this, but still it is wrong. The just have no will at all; what God wills is all the same to them, however great distress that may be.

For just men, the pursuit of justice is so imperative that if God were not just, they would not give a fig for God; and they stand fast by justice, and they have gone out of themselves so completely that they have no regard for the pains of hell or the joys of heaven or for any other thing. Yes, if all the pains that those have who are in hell, men or devils, or all the pains that have ever been or ever will be suffered on earth were to be joined on to justice, they would not give a straw for that, so fast do they stand by God and by justice. Nothing is more painful or hard for a just man than what is contrary to justice.[6] In what way? If one thing gives them joy and another sorrow, they are not just; but if on one occasion they are joyful, then they are always joyful; and if on one occasion they are more joyful and on others less, then they are wrong. Whoever loves justice stands so fast by it that whatever he loves, that is his being; nothing can deflect him from this, nor does he esteem anything differently. Saint Augustine says: "When the soul loves, it is more properly itself than when it gives life."[7] This sounds simple and commonplace, and yet few understand what it means, and still it is true. Anyone who has discernment in justice and in just men, he understands everything I am saying.

"The just will live." Among all things there is nothing so dear or so desirable as life. However wretched or hard his life may be, a man still wants to live. It is written somewhere that the closer anything is to death, the more it suffers. Yet however wretched life may be, still it wants to live. Why do you eat? Why do you sleep? So that you live. Why do you want riches or honors? That you know very well; but— why do you live? So as to live; and still you do not know why you live. Life is in itself so desirable that we desire it for its own sake. Those in hell are in everlasting torment, but they would not want to lose their lives, not the devils or the souls of men, for their life is so precious that it flows without any medium from God into the soul. And because it flows from God without medium they want to live. What is life? God's being is my life. If my life is God's being, then God's existence must be my existence and God's is-ness is my is-ness,[8] neither less nor more.

They live eternally "with God,"[9] directly close to God, not beneath or above. They perform all their works with God, and God with them. Saint John says: "The Word was with God" (Jn. 1:1). It was wholly equal, and it was close beside, not beneath there or above there, but just equal. When God made man, he made woman from man's side, so that she might be equal to him. He did not make her out of man's head or his feet, so that she would be neither woman nor man for him, but so that she might be equal. So should the just soul be equal with God and close beside God, equal beside him, not beneath or above.

Who are they who are thus equal? Those who are equal to nothing, they alone are equal to God. The divine being is equal to nothing, and in it there is neither image nor form. To the souls who are equal, the Father gives equally, and he withholds nothing at all from them. Whatever the Father can achieve, that he gives equally to this soul, yes, if it no longer equals itself more than anything else, and it should not be closer to itself than to anything else. It should desire or heed its own honor, its profit and whatever may be its own, no more than what is a stranger's. Whatever belongs to anyone should not be distant or strange to the soul, whether this be evil or good. All the love of this world is founded on self-love. If you had forsaken that, you would have forsaken the whole world.

The Father gives birth to his Son in eternity, equal to himself. "The Word was with God, and God was the Word" (Jn. 1:1); it was the same in the same nature. Yet I say more: He has given birth to him in my soul. Not only is the soul with him, and he equal with it, but he is in it, and the Father gives his Son birth in the soul in the same way as he gives him birth in eternity, and not otherwise. He must do it whether he likes it or not. The Father gives birth to his Son without ceasing; and I say more: He gives me birth, me, his Son and the same Son. I say more: He gives birth not only to me, his Son, but he gives birth to me as himself and himself as me and to me as his being and nature. In the innermost source, there I spring out in the Holy Spirit, where there is one life and one being and one work. Everything God performs is one; therefore he gives me, his Son, birth without any distinction.[10] My fleshly father is not actually my father except in one little portion of his nature, and I am separated from him; he may be dead and I alive. Therefore the heavenly Father is truly my Father, for I am his Son and have everything that I have from him, and I am the same Son and not a different one. Because the Father performs one work, therefore his work is me, his Only-Begotten Son without any difference.

"We shall be completely transformed and changed into God" (2 Co. 3:18). See a comparison. In the same way, when in the sacrament bread is changed into the Body of our Lord, however many pieces of bread there were, they still become one Body. Just so, if all the pieces of bread were changed into my finger, there would still not be more than one finger. But if my finger were changed into the bread, there would be as many of one as of the other. What is changed into something else becomes one with it. I am so changed into him that he produces his being in me as one, not just similar.[11] By the living God, this is true! There is no distinction.[12]

The Father gives his Son birth without ceasing. Once the Son has been born he receives nothing from the Father because he has it all, but what he receives from the Father is his being born. In this we ought not to ask for something from God as if he were a stranger. Our Lord said to his disciples: "I have not called you servants, but friends" (Jn. 15:14). Whoever asks for something from someone else is a servant, and he who grants it is a master. Recently I considered whether there was anything I would take or ask from God. I shall take careful thought about this, because if I were accepting anything from God, I should be subject to him as a servant, and he in giving would be as a master. We shall not be so in life everlasting.[13]

Once I said here, and what I said is true: If a man obtains or accepts something from outside himself, he is in this wrong. One should not accept or esteem God as being outside oneself, but as one's own and as what is within one; nor should one serve or labor for any recompense, not for God or for his honor or for anything that is outside oneself, but only for that which one's own being and one's own life is within one. Some simple people think that they will see God as if he were standing there and they here. It is not so. God and I, we are one. I accept God into me in knowing; I go into God in loving. There are some who say that blessedness consists not in knowing but in willing. They are wrong; for if it consisted only in the will, it would not be one. Working and becoming are one. If a carpenter does not work, nothing becomes of the house. If the axe is not doing anything, nothing is becoming anything. In this working God and I are one; he is working and I am becoming. The fire changes anything into itself that is put into it and this takes on fire's own nature. The wood does not change the fire into itself, but the fire changes the wood into itself. So are we changed into God, that we shall know him as he is (1 Jn. 3:2). Saint Paul says: "So shall we come to know him, I knowing him just as he knows me" (1 Co. 13:12), neither less nor more, perfectly equal. "The just will live forever, and their reward is with God," perfectly equal.

That we may love justice, for its own sake and for God, without asking return, may God help us to this. Amen.

Sermon 15: Homo quidam nobilis abiit in regionem longinquam accipere regnum et reverti (Lk. 19:12).

These words are written in the gospel, and in German they mean: "There was a noble man who went into a foreign land, away from himself, and he came back home richer." Now in one gospel we read that Christ said, "No one can be my disciple unless he follow me" (Lk. 14:27), and forsake himself and keep nothing for himself, and then he will have everything, for to have nothing is to have everything. But to submit oneself to God with one's desire and one's heart, to make one's will wholly God's will, never once to look upon created things—anyone who had so forsaken himself, he would truly be given back to himself.

Goodness in itself, only goodness, does not bring peace to the soul. . . .[1] If God were to give me anything without his will, I should not esteem it; but the very least that God gives me by his will, that gives me blessedness.

All created things have flowed out of God's will. If I were able only to long for God's goodness, his will is so noble that the Holy Spirit is flowing from his will without a medium.[2] All good flows out from the overflowing of the goodness of God. Yes, God's will has savor for me only in his unity where God's peace is for the goodness of all created things. In this unity goodness and everything that ever gained being and life have peace, as in their last end. There you must love the Holy Spirit, as he is there, in unity, not in himself, but there where he alone with God's goodness has savor in that unity from which all

189

goodness flows out of the overflowing of the goodness of God. Such a man "comes back home richer" than he went out. Whoever had so gone out of himself would be given back again to himself, more his own, and all the things he had in multiplicity and forsook will be wholly given back again to him in unity, for he will find himself and all things in the present now of unity. And anyone who had so gone out would come back home far more noble than he went out. This man lives now in utter freedom and a pure nakedness, for there is nothing that he must make subject to himself or that he must acquire, be it little or much, for everything that is God's own is his own.

The sun in its highest part corresponds to God in his unfathomable depths, in his depths of humility.[3] Yes, the humble man does not need to entreat, but he can indeed command, for the heights of the divinity cannot look down except into the depths of humility, for the humble man and God are one and not two. This humble man has as much power over God as he has over himself; and all the good that is in all the angels and in all the saints is all his own, as it is God's own. God and this humble man are wholly one, and not two; for what God performs he performs too, and what God wishes he wishes too, and what God is he is too—one life and one being. Yes, by God! If this man were in hell, God would have to come down to him in hell, and hell would have to be for him the kingdom of heaven. God must of necessity do this, he would be compelled so that he had to do it; for then this man is divine being, and divine being is this man. For here, from the unity of God and from the humble man, there comes the kiss, for the virtue that is called humility is a root in the ground of the divinity in which it was planted, so that the virtue has its being only in the eternal One and nowhere else. I said in Paris in the schools that all things would be perfected in the truly humble man; and therefore I say that for the truly humble man nothing can be harmful, nothing can lead him astray. For there is nothing that does not flee what can annihilate it. All created things flee this, for they are nothing at all in themselves;[4] and therefore the humble man flees everything that could lead him astray from God. This is why I flee from burning coals, because they want to destroy me, because they want to rob me of my being.

Scripture said: "A man went out." Aristotle began to write a book in which he wanted to discuss all things.[5] Now observe what Aristotle said about this man. *Homo* means as much as a "man" who has been endowed with form, and this gives him being and life with all created things, rational and irrational—irrational with all corporeal creatures and rational with the angels. And he says: "Just as all created things, with their images and forms, are comprehended in the rational angels, and the angels know with reason every differentiated thing—which gives the angel such delight that it would be amazing for those who had not experienced and tasted this—so man understands rationally the image and form of all created differentiated things."[6] Aristotle said that the attribute of a man that makes him to be a man is that he understands all images and forms;[7] because of this a man is a man, and that was the highest characteristic with which Aristotle could characterize a man.

Now I too want to demonstrate what a man is. *Homo* means as much as a "man" to whom substance has been given, which gives him being and life and a rational being. A rational man is one who comprehends himself rationally, and who is himself separated from all matter and forms. The more he is separated from all things and turned into himself, the more he knows all things clearly and rationally within himself, without going outside; and the more he is a man.

Now I ask: How can it be that separation of the understanding from form and image understands all things in itself, without going out from or changing itself? I reply: This comes from its simplicity, for the more purely simple a man's self is in itself, the more simply does he in himself understand all multiplicity, and he remains unchangeable in himself. Boethius says that God is an immovable good, standing still in himself, untouched and unmoved and moving all things.[8] A simple understanding is in itself so pure that it understands the pure, naked divine being without a medium.[9] And in the inflowing it receives divine nature just as do the angels, and in this the angels receive great joy. For anyone to be able to see an angel, he should be willing to be a thousand years in hell; but this understanding is in itself so pure and so clear that whatever one might see in this light would be an angel.

Now notice carefully what Aristotle says about separated spirits in the book called *Metaphysics*.[10] He is the greatest of the authorities who ever spoke about the natural sciences, and he deals with these separated spirits and says that they are not the form of anything, and that they accept their being as it flows without medium from God; and so they flow back in again, and receive the outflowing from God without medium, above the angels, and they contemplate God's naked being without distinction. This pure naked being Aristotle calls a "something."[11] This is the most sublime thing that Aristotle ever said about the natural sciences, and no authority can say anything more sublime than this, unless he were to speak in the Holy Spirit. Now I say that for this noble man the substance which the angels understood without form and on which they depend without medium is not sufficient; nothing but the Simple One suffices him.

I have also said more about the first beginning and the last end. The Father is a beginning of the divinity, for he understands himself in himself, and out of this the Eternal Word proceeds and yet remains within, and the Holy Spirit flows from them both, remaining within and unbegetting, for insofar as he remains within he is an end of the divinity and of all created things; he is a pure repose and a resting of all that being ever acquired. The beginning is for the sake of the end, for in the last end is the repose of everything that rational being ever acquired. The last end[12] of being is the darkness or the unknownness of the hidden divinity, in which this light shines that the darkness does not comprehend. Therefore Moses said, "He who is sent me" (Ex. 3:14), he who is without name, who is a denial of all names and who never acquired a name; and therefore the prophet said: "Truly you are the hidden God" (Is. 45:15), in the ground of the soul, where God's ground and the soul's ground are one ground. The more one seeks you, the less one finds you. You should so seek him that you find him nowhere. If you do not seek him, then you will find him. That we may so seek him that we may eternally remain with him, may God help us to this. Amen.

Sermon 22: Ave, gratia plena (Lk. 1:28).[1]

The Latin text that I have read is written in the holy gospel, and its meaning in German is: "Greetings to you, full of grace, the Lord is with you" (Lk. 1:28). The Holy Spirit will come down from above the highest throne, and will enter into you from the light of the eternal Father.[2]

There are three things here to understand. First, the lowliness of the angelic nature; second, that he acknowledged himself unworthy to name the mother of God; third, that he did not speak the word only to her, but that he spoke it to a great multitude, to every good soul that longs for God.

I say this: If Mary had not first given spiritual birth to God, he would never have been born bodily from her.[3] A woman said to our

Lord: "Blessed is the womb which bore you" (Lk. 11:27). Then our Lord said: "It is not only the womb which bore me which is blessed; they are blessed who hear God's word and keep it" (Lk. 11:28). It is more precious to God to be born spiritually from every such virgin or from every good soul than that he was bodily born of Mary.

In this we must understand that we must be an only son whom the Father has eternally begotten. When the Father begot all created things, then he begot me, and I flowed out with all created things, and yet I remained within, in the Father. In the same way, when the word that I am now speaking springs up in me, there is a second process as I rest upon the image,[4] and a third when I pronounce it and you all receive it; and yet properly it remains within me. So I have remained within the Father. In the Father are the images of all created things.[5] This piece of wood has a rational image in God. It is not merely rational, but it is pure reason.[6]

The greatest good that God ever performed for man was that he became man. I ought to tell a story now that is very apposite here. There were a rich husband and wife. Then the wife suffered a misfortune through which she lost an eye, and she was much distressed by this. Then her husband came to her and said: "Madam, why are you so distressed? You should not distress yourself so, because you have lost your eye." Then she said: "Sir, I am not distressing myself about the fact that I have lost my eye; what distresses me is that it seems to me that you will love me less because of it." Then he said: "Madam, I do love you." Not long after that he gouged out one of his own eyes and came to his wife and said: "Madam, to make you believe that I love you, I have made myself like you; now I too have only one eye."[7] This stands for man, who could scarcely believe that God loved him so much, until God gouged out one of his own eyes and took upon himself human nature. This is what "being made flesh" (Jn. 1:14) is. Our Lady said: "How should this happen?" Then the angel said: "The Holy Spirit will come down from above into you" (Lk. 1:34–35), from the highest throne, from the Father of eternal light.[8]

"In the beginning" (Jn. 1:1). "A child is born to us, a son is given to us" (Is. 9:6), a child in the smallness of its human nature, a Son in its everlasting divinity. The authorities say: "All created things behave as they do because they want to give birth and they want to resemble the Father."[9] Another authority says: "Every being which acts, acts for the sake of its end, that in its end it may find rest and repose."[10] One authority says: "All created things act according to their first purity and according to their highest perfection."[11] Fire as fire does not burn; it is so pure and so fine that it does not burn; but it is fire's nature that burns and pours its nature and its brightness according to its highest perfection into the dry wood. God has acted like this. He created the soul according to the highest perfection, and poured into it in its first purity all his brightness and yet he has remained unmixed.[12]

Recently I said in another place: "When God created all things, even if God had not before begotten anything that was uncreated, that carried within itself the images of all created things; that is the spark"—as I said before in the Machabees' church (as you heard, if you were listening)[13]—"and this little spark is so closely akin to God that it is an undivided simple one,[14] and bears within itself the images of all created things, images without images and images beyond images."[15]

Yesterday in the school among the important clerics there was a disputation.[16] "I am surprised," I said, "that scripture is so rich that no one can fathom the least word in it." Now if you ask me, since I am an only son whom the heavenly Father has eternally born, if then I have eternally been a son in God then I say: "Yes and no. Yes, a son, as the Father has eternally borne me, and not a son, as to being unborn."[17]

"In the beginning." Here we are given to understand that we are an only son whom the Father has eternally borne out of the concealed darkness of the eternal concealment, remaining within in the first beginning of the first purity, which is a plenitude of all purity. Here I had my everlasting rest and sleep, in the eternal Father's hidden knowledge, remaining unspoken within. Out of the purity he everlastingly bore me, his only-born Son, into that same image of his eternal Fatherhood, that I may be Father and give birth to him of whom I am born. It is just as if someone were to stand before a high cliff and were to shout: "Are you there?" The echo of his voice would shout back: "Are you there?" If he were to say: "Come out of there!" the echo too would say: "Come out of there!" Yes, if someone saw a piece of wood in that light, it would become an angel and a rational being, and not merely rational; it would become pure reason in primal purity, for there is the plenitude of all purity. God acts like that: He gives birth to his Only-Begotten Son in the highest part of the soul. And as he gives birth to his Only-Begotten Son into me, so I give him birth again into the Father. That was not different from when God gave birth to the angel while he was born of the Virgin.

I wondered—this is many years ago—whether I would be asked how it is that each blade of grass can be so different from the others; and it happened that I was asked how they could be so different. I said: "What is more surprising is how they are all so alike." An authority said that the fact that all blades of grass are so different comes from the superabundance of God's goodness, which he pours superabundantly into all created things, so that his supremacy may be the more revealed.[18] When I said: "It is more surprising that all the blades of grass are so alike," I went on, "just as all angels in the primal purity are all one angel, so are all blades of grass one in the primal purity, and all things there are one."

As I was coming here, I was thinking that in temporal existence man can reach the point where he is able to compel God. If I were up here,[19] and I said to someone, "Come up here," that would be difficult. But if I were to say, "Sit down there," that would be easy. God acts like that. If a man humbles himself, God cannot withhold his own goodness but must come down and flow into the humble man, and to him who is least of all he gives himself the most of all, and he gives himself to him completely. What God gives is his being, and his being is his goodness, and his goodness is his love. All sorrow and all joy come from love. On the way, when I had to come here, I was thinking that I did not want to come here because I would become wet with tears of love. If you have ever been all wet with tears of love, let us leave that aside for now. Joy and sorrow come from love. A man ought not to fear God, for whoever fears him flees from him. This fear is a harmful fear. There is a rightful fear, when someone fears that he may lose God. A man should not fear him, he should love him, for God loves man with all his supreme perfection. The authorities say that all things work with the intention of giving birth and want to resemble the Father. They say: "The earth flees the heavens. If it flees downward, it comes down to the heavens; if it flees upward, it comes to the lowest part of the heavens."[20] The earth can flee nowhere so deep that the heavens will not flow into it and impress their powers on it and make it fruitful, whether it likes this or not. This is how a man acts when he thinks that he can flee from God, and yet he cannot flee from him; every corner where he may go reveals God to him. He thinks that he is fleeing God, and he runs into his lap. God bears his Only-Begotten Son in you, whether you like it or not. Whether you are sleeping or waking, he does his part. Recently I asked whose fault it is if a man does not taste this,[21] and I said that the fault was that his tongue was coated with some impurity, that is, with created things, just as with a man to whom all food is bitter and for whom nothing tastes good. Whose fault is it that food does not taste good to us? The fault is that we have no salt. The salt is divine love. If we had divine love, God would taste good to us, and all the works God ever performed, and we should receive all things from God, and we should perform all the same works that he performs. In this likeness we are all one single Son.

When God created the soul, he created it according to his highest perfection, so that it might be a bride of the Only-Begotten Son. Because he knew this, he wanted to come forth from the secret treasure chamber of the eternal Fatherhood, in which he had eternally slept, unspoken, remaining within. "In the beginning." In the first beginning of the primal purity the Son had set up the pavilion of his everlasting glory, and he came out from there, from what was most exalted of all, because he wanted to exalt his beloved, whom the Father had eternally betrothed with him, so that he might bring her back again into the exaltation from which she came. Elsewhere it is written: "See! Your king is coming to you" (Zc. 9:9). This is why he came out, and came leaping like a young hart (Sg. 2:9), and suffered his torments for love, and he did not go out without wishing to go in again into his chamber with his bride. This chamber is the silent darkness of the hidden Fatherhood. When he went out from the highest place of all, he wanted to go in again with his bride to the purest place of all, and wanted to reveal to her the hidden secret of his hidden divinity, where he takes his rest with himself and with all created things.[22]

In principio means in German as much as a beginning of all being, as I said in the school. I said more: It is an end of all being, for the first beginning is for the sake of the last end. Yes, God never takes rest there where he is the first beginning; he takes rest there where he is an end and a repose of all being, not that this being should perish, but rather it is there perfected in its last end according to its highest perfection. What is the last end? It is the hidden darkness of the eternal divinity, and it is unknown, and it was never known, and it will never be known. God remains there within himself, unknown, and the light of the eternal Father has eternally shone in there, and the darkness does not comprehend the light (Jn. 1:5). May the truth of which I have spoken help us that we may come to this truth. Amen.

GERMAN WORKS

Sermon 48: Ein meister sprichet: alliu glîchiu dinc minnent sich under einander.

An authority says: "All things that are alike love one another and unite with one another, and all things that are unlike flee from one another and hate one another."[1] And one authority says that nothing is so unlike as are heaven and earth.[2] The kingdom of earth was endowed by nature with being far off from heaven and unlike it. This is why earth fled to the lowest place and is immovable so that it may not approach heaven. Heaven by nature apprehended that the earth fled from it and occupied the lowest place. Therefore heaven always pours itself out fruitfully upon the kingdom of earth; and the authorities maintain that the broad and wide heaven does not retain for itself so much as the width of a needle's point, but rather bestows it upon the earth.[3] That is why earth is called the most fruitful of all created things that exist in time.

I say the same about the man who has annihilated himself in himself and in God and in all created things; this man has taken possession of the lowest place, and God must pour the whole of himself into this man, or else he is not God. I say in the truth, which is good and eternal and enduring, that God must pour out the whole of himself with all his might so totally into every man who has utterly abandoned himself that God withholds nothing of his being or his nature or his entire divinity, but he must pour all of it fruitfully into the man who has abandoned himself for God and has occupied the lowest place.

As I was coming here today I was wondering how I should preach to you so that it would make sense and you would understand it. Then I thought of a comparison: If you could understand that, you would understand my meaning and the basis of all my thinking in everything I have ever preached. The comparison concerns my eyes and a piece of wood. If my eye is open, it is an eye; if it is closed, it is the same eye. It is not the wood that comes and goes, but it is my vision of it. Now pay good heed to me! If it happens that my eye is in itself one and simple (Mt. 6:22), and it is opened and casts its glance upon the piece of wood, the eye and the wood remain what they are, and yet in the act of vision they become as one, so that we can truly say that my eye is the wood and the wood is my eye. But if the wood were immaterial, purely spiritual as is the sight of my eye, then one could truly say that in the act of vision the wood and my eye subsisted in one being.[4] If this is true of physical objects, it is far truer of spiritual objects.

You should know that my eye has far more in common with the eye of a sheep which is on the other side of the sea and which I never saw, than it has in common with my ears, with which, however, it shares its being; and that is because the action of the sheep's eye is also that of my eye. And so I attribute to both more in common in their action than I do to my eyes and my ears, because their actions are different.

Sometimes I have spoken of a light that is uncreated and not capable of creation and that is in the soul.[5] I always mention this light in my sermons; and this same light comprehends God without a medium, uncovered, naked, as he is in himself; and this comprehension is to be understood as happening when the birth takes place.[6] Here I may truly say that this light may have more unity with God than it has with any power of the soul,[7] with which, however, it is one in being. For you should know that this light is not nobler in my soul's being than is the feeblest or crudest power, such as hearing or sight or anything else which can be affected by hunger or thirst, frost or heat; and the simplicity of my being is the cause of that. Because of this, if we take the powers as they are in our being, they are all equally noble; but if we take them as they work, one is much nobler and higher than another.

That is why I say that if a man will turn away from himself and from all created things, by so much will you be made one and blessed in the spark in the soul, which has never touched either time or place. This spark rejects all created things, and wants nothing but its naked God, as he is in himself. It is not content with the Father or the Son or the Holy Spirit, or with the three Persons so far as each of them persists in his properties. I say truly that this light is not content with the divine nature's generative or fruitful qualities. I will say more, surprising though this is. I speak in all truth, truth that is eternal and enduring, that this same light is not content with the simple divine essence in its repose,[8] as it neither gives nor receives; but it wants to know the source of this essence, it wants to go into the simple ground, into the quiet desert, into which distinction never gazed, not the Father, nor the Son, nor the Holy Spirit. In the innermost part, where no one dwells, there is contentment for that light, and there it is more inward than it can be to itself, for this ground is a simple silence, in itself immovable, and by this immovability all things are moved, all life is received by those who in themselves have rational being.

May that enduring truth of which I have spoken help us that we may so have rational life. Amen.

GERMAN WORKS

Sermon 52: Beati pauperes spiritu, quoniam ipsorum est regnum caelorum (Mt. 5:3). [1]

Blessedness opened its mouth to wisdom and said: "Blessed are the poor in spirit, for the kingdom of heaven is theirs" (Mt. 5:3).

All angels and all saints and all who were ever born must keep silent when the Wisdom of the Father speaks, for all the Wisdom of the angels and of all created beings is mere folly before the unfathomable Wisdom of God. It has said that the poor are blessed.

Now there are two kinds of poverty. There is an external poverty, which is good and is greatly to be esteemed in a man who voluntarily practices it for the love of our Lord Jesus Christ, for he himself used it when he was on earth. I do not now want to say anything more about this poverty. But there is a different poverty, an inward poverty, and it is of this that we must understand that our Lord is speaking: "Blessed are the poor in spirit."

Now I beg you to be disposed to what I say;[2] for I say to you in everlasting truth that if you are unlike this truth of which we want to speak, you cannot understand me. Various people have asked me what poverty may be in itself and what a poor man may be. Let us try to answer this.

Bishop Albert says that a poor man is one who does not find satisfaction in all the things God created;[3] and this is well said. But we can put it even better, and take poverty in a higher sense. A poor man wants nothing, and knows nothing, and has nothing. Let us now talk about these three points; and I beg you for the sake of God's love that you understand this truth, if you can, and if you do not understand it, do not burden yourself with it, for the truth I want to expound is such that there will be few good people to understand it.

First let us discuss a poor man as one who wants nothing. There are some people who do not understand this well. They are those who are attached to their own penances and external exercises, which seem important to people.[4] God help those who hold divine truth in such low esteem! Such people present an outward picture that gives them the name of saints; but inside they are donkeys, for they cannot distinguish divine truth. These people say that a man is poor who wants nothing; but they interpret it in this way, that a man ought to live so that he never fulfills his own will in anything, but that he ought to comport himself so that he may fulfill God's dearest will. Such people are in the right, for their intention is good. For this let us commend

199

them. May God in his mercy grant them the kingdom of heaven. But I speak in the divine truth when I say that they are not poor men, nor do they resemble poor men. They have great esteem in the sight of men who know no better, but I say that they are donkeys who have no understanding of divine truth. They deserve the kingdom of heaven for their good intention, but of the poverty of which we want to talk they know nothing.

If someone asks me now what kind of poor man he is who wants nothing, I reply in this way. So long as a man has this as his will, that he wants to fulfill God's dearest will, he has not the poverty about which we want to talk. Such a person has a will with which he wants to fulfill God's will, and that is not true poverty. For if a person wants really to have poverty, he ought to be as free of his own created will as he was when he did not exist. For I tell you by the truth that is eternal, so long as you have a will to fulfill God's will, and a longing for God and for eternity, then you are not poor; for a poor man is one who has a will and longing for nothing.

When I stood in my first cause, I then had no "God," and then I was my own cause. I wanted nothing, I longed for nothing, for I was an empty being,[5] and the only truth in which I rejoiced was in the knowledge of myself. Then it was myself I wanted and nothing else. What I wanted I was, and what I was I wanted; and so I stood, empty of God and of everything. But when I went out from my own free will and received my created being, then I had a "God," for before there were any creatures, God was not "God," but he was what he was.[6] But when creatures came to be and received their created being, then God was not "God" in himself, but he was "God" in the creatures.

Now I say that God, so far as he is "God," is not the perfect end of created beings. The least of these beings possesses in God as much as he possesses. If it could be that a fly had reason and could with its reason seek out the eternal depths of the divine being from which it issued, I say that God, with all that he has as he is "God," could not fulfill or satisfy the fly. So therefore let us pray to God that we may be free of "God," and that we may apprehend and rejoice in that everlasting truth in which the highest angel and the fly and the soul are equal—there where I was established, where I wanted what I was and was what I wanted. So I say: If a man is to become poor in his will, he must want and desire as little as he wanted and desired when he did not exist. And in this way a man is poor who wants nothing.

Next, a man is poor who knows nothing. Sometimes I have said that a man ought to live so that he did not live for himself or for the truth or for God. But now I say something different and something more, that a man who would possess this poverty ought to live as if he does not even know that he is not in any way living for himself or for the truth or for God. Rather, he should be so free of all knowing that he does not know or experience or grasp that God lives in him. For when man was established in God's everlasting being, there was no different life in him. What was living there was himself. So I say that a man should be set as free of his own knowing as he was when he was not. Let God perform what he will, and let man be free.

Everything that ever came from God is directed into pure activity. Now the actions proper to a man are loving and knowing. The question is: In which of these does blessedness most consist? Some authorities have said that it consists in knowing, others say that it consists in loving; others that it consists in knowing and loving, and what they say is better. But I say that it does not consist in either knowing or loving, but that there is that in the soul from which knowing and loving flow; that something does not know or love as do the powers of the soul. Whoever knows this knows in what blessedness consists.[7] That something has neither before nor after, and it is not waiting for anything that is to come, for it can neither gain nor lose. So it is deprived of the knowledge that God is acting in it; but it is itself the very thing that rejoices in itself as God does in himself. So I say that a man ought to be established, free and empty, not knowing or perceiving that God is acting in him; and so a man may possess poverty. The authorities say that God is a being, and a rational one, and that he knows all things. I say that God is neither being nor rational, and that he does not know this or that.[8] Therefore God is free of all things, and therefore he is all things. Whoever will be poor in spirit, he must be poor of all his own knowledge, so that he knows nothing, not God or created things or himself. Therefore it is necessary for a man to long not to be able to know or perceive God's works. In this way a man can be poor of his own knowledge.

Third, a man is poor who has nothing. Many people have said that it is perfection when one possesses no material, earthly things, and in one sense this is indeed true, if a man does this voluntarily. But this is not the sense in which I mean it.

I have said just now that a man is poor who does not want to fulfill God's will, but who lives so that he may be free both of his own will and of God's will, as he was when he was not. About this poverty I say that it is the highest poverty. Second, I say that a man is poor who knows nothing of God's works in him. A man who is so established is as free of knowing and perceiving as God is free of all things, and this is the purest poverty. But a third form is the most intimate poverty, on which I now want to speak; and this is when a man has nothing.

Now pay great attention and give heed! I have often said, and great authorities say, that a man should be so free of all things and of all works, both interior and exterior, that he might become a place only for God, in which God could work. Now I say otherwise. If it be the case that man is free of all created things and of God and of himself, and if it also be that God may find place in him in which to work, then I say that so long as that is in man, he is not poor with the most intimate poverty. For it is not God's intention in his works that man should have in himself a place for God to work in. Poverty of spirit is for a man to keep so free of God and of all his works that if God wishes to work in the soul, he himself is the place in which he wants to work; and that he will gladly do. For if he finds a man so poor as this, then God performs his own work, and the man is in this way suffering God to work, and God is his own place to work in, and so God is his own worker in himself. Thus in this poverty man pursues that everlasting being which he was and which he is now and which he will evermore remain.

It is Saint Paul who says: "All that I am, I am by God's grace" (1 Co. 15:10). But if what I say[9] transcends grace and being and understanding and will and longing, how then can Paul's words be true? People show that what Paul said is true in this way. That the grace of God was in him was necessarily so, for it was God's grace working in him that brought what was accidental to the perfection of the essential. When grace had finished and had perfected its work, then Paul remained what he was.

So I say that man should be so poor that he should not be or have any place in which God could work. When man clings to place, he clings to distinction. Therefore I pray to God that he may make me free of "God," for my real being is above God if we take "God" to be the beginning of created things. For in the same being of God where God is above being and above distinction, there I myself was, there I willed myself and committed myself to create this man. Therefore I am the cause of myself in the order of my being, which is eternal, and not in the order of my becoming, which is temporal. And therefore I am unborn, and in the manner in which I am unborn I can never die. In my unborn manner I have been eternally, and am now, and shall eternally remain. What I am in the order of having been born, that will die and perish, for it is mortal, and so it must in time suffer corruption. In my birth all things were born and I was the cause of myself and of all things;[10] and if I would have wished it, I would not be nor would all other things be. And if I did not exist, "God" would also not exist. That God is "God," of that I am a cause; if I did not exist, God too would not be "God." There is no need to understand this.

A great authority says that his breaking through is nobler than his flowing out;[11] and that is true. When I flowed out from God, all things said: "God is." And this cannot make me blessed, for with this I acknowledge that I am a creature. But in the breaking-through, when I come to be free of will of myself and of God's will and of all his works and of God himself, then I am above all created things, and I am neither God nor creature, but I am what I was and what I shall remain, now and eternally. Then I received an impulse that will bring me up above all the angels. Together with this impulse, I receive such riches that God, as he is "God," and as he performs all his divine works, cannot suffice me; for in this breaking-through I receive that God and I are one. Then I am what I was, and then I neither diminish nor increase, for I am then an immovable cause that moves all things. Here God finds no place in man, for with this poverty man achieves what he has been eternally and will evermore remain. Here God is one with the spirit, and that is the most intimate poverty one can find.

Whoever does not understand what I have said, let him not burden his heart with it; for as long as a man is not equal to this truth, he will not understand these words, for this is a truth beyond speculation that has come immediately from the heart of God. May God help us so to live that we may find it eternally. Amen.

Sermon 53: Misit dominus manum suam et tetigit os meum et dixit mihi . . . Ecce constitui te super gentes et regna (Jr. 1:9).

When I preach, I am accustomed to speak about detachment, and that a man should be free of himself and of all things; second, that a man should be formed again into that simple good which is God; third, that he should reflect on the great nobility with which God has endowed his soul, so that in this way he may come to wonder at God;[1] fourth, about the purity of the divine nature, for the brightness of the divine nature is beyond words. God is a word, a word unspoken.

Augustine says: "All writings are in vain. If one says that God is a word, he has been expressed; but if one says that God has not been spoken, he is ineffable."[2] And yet he is something, but who can speak this word? No one can do this, except him who is this Word. God is a Word that speaks itself. Wherever God is, he speaks this Word; wherever he is not, he does not speak. God is spoken and unspoken. The Father is a speaking work, and the Son is speech working.[3] Whatever is in me proceeds from me; if I only think it, my word manifests it, and still it remains in me. So does the Father speak the unspoken Son, and yet the Son remains in him.[4] And I have often said: "God's going out is his going in." To the extent that I am close to God, so to that extent God utters himself into me. The more that all rational creatures in their works go out of themselves, the more they go into themselves. This is not so with merely corporeal creatures; the more they work, the more they go out of themselves. All creatures want to utter God in all their works; they all come as close as they can in uttering him, and yet they cannot utter him. Whether they wish it or not, whether they like it or not, they all want to utter God, and yet he remains unuttered.

David says: "The Lord is his name" (Ps. 67:5). "Lord" signifies being promoted in power, "servant" means subjection. There are some names that are proper to God and inappropriate to all other things, such as "God." "God" is the name most proper to God of all names, as "man" is the name of men. A man is a man, be he foolish or wise. Seneca says: "That man is a pitiful creature who cannot rise above other men."[5] Some names denote a connection with God, such as "fatherhood" and "sonship." When one says "father," one understands "son." No one can be a father if he does not have a son, nor can a son be a son if he has no father; both of them have an eternal relationship that is beyond time. Third, there are some names that signify a lifting up to God and a regard to time. In scripture God is called by many names. I say that whoever perceives something in God and attaches thereby some name to him, that is not God. God is above names and above nature. We read of one good man who was entreating God in his prayer and wanted to give names to him. Then a brother said: "Be quiet—you are dishonoring God."[6] We cannot find a single name we might give to God. Yet those names are permitted to us by which the saints have called him and which God so consecrated with divine light and poured into all their hearts. And through these we should first learn how we ought to pray to God. We should say: "Lord, with the same names that you have so consecrated in the hearts of your saints and have poured into all their hearts, so we pray to you and praise you." Second, we should learn not to give any name to God, lest we imagine that in so doing we have praised and exalted him as we should; for God is "above names" and ineffable.

The Father speaks the Son out of all his power, and he speaks in him all things. All created things are God's speech. The being of a stone speaks and manifests the same as does my mouth about God; and people understand more by what is done than by what is said.[7] The work that is performed by the highest nature in its greatest power is not understood by an inferior nature.[8] If the inferior nature performed the same work, it would not be subject to the highest nature—they would be the same. All creatures would like to echo God in their works, but there is little indeed they can manifest. Even the highest angels, as they mount toward and touch God, are as unlike that which is in God as white is unlike black. What all creatures have received is quite unlike him, except only that they would gladly express him as closely as they can. The prophet says: "Lord, you say one thing, and I hear two things" (Ps. 61:12).[9] As God speaks into the soul, the soul and he are one; but, as soon as this goes, there is a separation. The more that we ascend in our understanding, the more are we one in him. Therefore the Father speaks the Son always, in unity, and pours out in him all created things. They are all called to return into whence they have flowed out. All their life and their being is a calling and a hastening back to him from whom they have issued.

The prophet says: "The Lord stretched out his hand" (Jr. 1:9), and he means the Holy Spirit. Now he says: "He has touched my mouth," and goes on at once, "and has spoken to me." The soul's mouth is its highest part, which the soul means when it says: "He has put his word in my mouth" (*ibid.*). That is the kiss of the soul, there mouth touches mouth, there the Father bears his Son into the soul, and there the soul is spoken to.[10] Now he says: "Take heed; today I have chosen you, and have placed you above peoples and above kingdoms" (Jr. 1:10). In a "today" God vows that he will choose us where there is nothing, and where yet in an eternity there is a "today." "And I have placed you above peoples," that is, above all the world, of which you must be free, "and above kingdoms," that is, whatever is more than one, which is too much, for you must die to all things and be formed again into the heights, where we dwell in the Holy Spirit.

May God the Holy Spirit help us to that end. Amen.

Sermon 83: Renovamini spiritu (Ep. 4:23).

"Be renewed in your spirit" (Ep. 4:23), which is here called *mens,* [1] that is, your disposition. This is what Saint Paul says.

Augustine says that in the highest part of the soul, which he calls *mens* or disposition, God created together with the soul's being a power, which the authorities call a store or a coffer of spiritual forms or formal images.[2] This power makes the soul resemble the Father in his outflowing divinity, out of which he has poured the whole treasure of his divine being into the Son and into the Holy Spirit, differentiating between the Persons, just as the soul's memory pours the treasure of its images into the soul's powers. So when the soul with these powers contemplates what consists of images, whether that be an angel's image or its own, there is for the soul something lacking. Even if the soul contemplates God, either as God or as an image or as three, the soul lacks something. But if all images are detached from the soul, and it contemplates only the Simple One, then the soul's naked being finds the naked, formless being of the divine unity, which is there a being above being, accepting and reposing in itself. Ah, marvel of marvels, how noble is that acceptance, when the soul's being can accept nothing else than the naked unity of God!

Now Saint Paul says: "Be renewed in the spirit." Renewal happens to all created beings under God; but no renewal comes to God, but evermore only eternity. What is eternity? Pay heed! It is the property of eternity that in it being and youth are one because eternity would not be eternal if it could be renewed, if it did not always exist. So I say: Renewal happens to the angels, as the future is intimated to them, for an angel knows about future things, though only so much as God reveals to him. And renewal happens also to the soul, so far as "soul" is its name, for it is called soul because it gives life to the body and is a form of the body. To a soul, too, renewal happens, so far as "spirit" is its name. It is called spirit because it is detached from here and now and from the whole natural order. But when it is an image of God and as nameless as God, then no renewal happens to it, but only eternity, as in God.

Now pay attention: God is nameless, because no one can say anything or understand anything about him. Therefore a pagan teacher says: "Whatever we understand or say about the First Cause, that is far more ourselves than it is the First Cause, for it is beyond all saying and understanding."[3] So if I say: "God is good," that is not true.[4] I am good, but God is not good. I can even say: "I am better than God," for whatever is good can become better, and whatever can become better can become best of all. But since God is not good, he cannot become better. And since he cannot become better, he cannot be best of all. For these three degrees are alien to God: "good," "better," and "best," for he is superior to them all. And if I say: "God is wise," that is not true. I am wiser than he. If I say: "God is a being," it is not true; he is a being transcending being and a transcending nothingness. About this, Saint Augustine says: "The best that one can say about God is for one to keep silent out of the wisdom of one's inward riches."[5] So be silent, and do not chatter about God; for when you do chatter about him, you are telling lies and sinning. But if you want to be without sin and perfect, you should not chatter about God. And do not try to understand God, for God is beyond all understanding. One authority says: "If I had a God whom I could understand, I should never consider him God."[6] If you can understand anything about him, it in no way belongs to him, and insofar as you understand anything about him, that brings you into incomprehension, and from incomprehension you arrive at a brute's stupidity; for when created beings do not understand, they resemble the brutes. So if you do not wish to be brutish, do not understand the God who is beyond words. "Then what ought I to do?" You ought to sink down out of all your your-ness, and flow into his his-ness, and your "yours" and his "his" ought to become one "mine," so completely that you with him perceive forever his uncreated is-ness, and his nothingness, for which there is no name.

Now Saint Paul says: "You should be renewed in the spirit." If we want to be renewed in the spirit, each of the soul's six powers, the superior and the inferior powers, must have a ring of gold, gilded with the gold of divine love. Now pay heed! There are three inferior powers.[7] The first is called "rational," and it is discretion, and on it you ought to wear a golden ring, which is the light, a divine light, with which your powers of discretion should always be illumined. The next is called "irascible," the "angry power," and on it you ought to have a ring, which is your peace. "Why?" Because as much as you are at peace, so much are you in God, and as much as you lack peace, so much do you lack God. The third power is called "appetitive," and on it you ought wear a ring, which is contentment; that is, you should be content with all creatures who are under God, but you should never be content with God, because you can never be content with God. The more you have of God, the more you long for him, for if you could be content with God, and such a contentment with him were to come, God would not be God.

And you must also wear a golden ring on each of the superior powers. There are, too, three superior powers. The first is called a retentive power, "memory." This power one compares with the Father in the Trinity, and on it you should have a golden ring, that is, a retention so that you hold on to everything that is eternal. The second power is called "intellectual," understanding. This power one compares with the Son, and you ought to wear on it a golden ring, that is, an understanding so that you should always perceive God. "And how?" You should perceive him without images, without a medium, and without comparisons. But if I am to perceive God so, without a medium, then I must just become him, and he must become me. I say more: God must just become me, and I must just become God, so completely one that this "he" and this "I" become and are one "is," and, in this is-ness, eternally perform one work, for this "he," who is God, and this "I," which is the soul, are greatly fruitful. But let there be a single "here" or a single "now," and the "I" and the "he" will never perform anything or become one.[8] The third power is called "voluntary," the will, and one compares it with the Holy Spirit. On it you should wear a golden ring, that is, love: You should love God. You should love God apart from his loveableness, that is, not because he is loveable, for God is unloveable. He is above all love and loveableness. "Then how should I love God?" You should love God unspiritually, that is, your soul should be unspiritual and stripped of all spirituality, for so long as your soul has a spirit's form, it has images, and so long as it has images, it has a medium, and so long as it has a medium, it has not unity or simplicity. Therefore your soul must be unspiritual, free of all spirit, and must remain spiritless; for if you love God as he is God, as he is spirit, as he is person and as he is image—all this must go! "Then how should I love him?" You should love him as he is a non-God, a nonspirit, a nonperson, a nonimage,[9] but as he is a pure, unmixed, bright "One," separated from all duality; and in that One we should eternally sink down, out of "something" into "nothing."[10]

May God help us to that. Amen.

2. TREATISES

A. The Book of "Benedictus":
The Book of Divine Consolation

BENEDICTUS DEUS ET PATER DOMINI NOSTRI IESU
CHRISTI, ETC. (2 Co. 1:3).

The noble apostle Saint Paul says these words: "Blessed be the God and Father of our Lord Jesus Christ, a Father of mercy and God of all comfort, who comforts us in all our tribulations." There are three kinds of tribulation that touch and oppress a man in this sorrowful life. One is the harm that may come to his material possessions. The second is what may happen to his kinsfolk and his friends. The third is what may happen to him, disgraces and sufferings, the pains of his body and the sorrows of his heart.

That is why I want in this book to write some counsels with which a man can console himself in all his sufferings, afflictions and sorrow; and the book has three parts. In the first he will find various true sayings, and in them he will find the ready and complete comfort he ought to have for all his sorrows. Then next there are some thirty topics and precepts from each of which he can always gain great consolation. Then in the third part of the book he will find examples of what wise men have done and have said when they were suffering.

1

First of all we ought to know that a wise man and wisdom, a truthful man and truth, a just man and justice, a good man and goodness, have a mutual relationship, and depend on one another, in this way. Goodness is not created, not made, not born; rather it is what gives birth and bears the good man; and the good man, insofar as he is good,

209

is unmade and uncreated, and yet he is born, the child and the son of goodness. In the good man goodness gives birth to itself and to everything that it is. Being, knowing, loving and working—goodness pours all this into the good man, and the good man accepts all his being, knowing, loving and working from the innermost heart of goodness, and from it alone. That which is good and goodness are nothing else than one single goodness in everything, apart from the one bearing and the other being born; but that goodness does bear and that it is born in the good man, this is all one being, one life. Everything the good man has, he receives both from goodness and also in goodness. That is where he is and lives and dwells. That is where he knows himself and everything that he knows, and loves everything that he loves, and he works with goodness in goodness, and goodness with him and in him works all its works, according to what the Son says, as it is written: "The Father, who remains and abides in me, does the works" (Jn. 14:10). "The Father works until now, and I work" (Jn. 5:17). "Everything which is the Father's is mine, and everything which is mine and of me is my Father's" (Jn. 17:10), his in giving and mine in taking.

Then next we ought to know that the name or the word that we use when we say "good" names and comprises in itself nothing else, neither less nor more, than bare and pure goodness; and yet it gives itself. When we say "good," people understand that their goodness has been given to them, poured in and given birth by unborn goodness. That is why the gospel says: "As the Father has life in himself, so he has given to the Son, that he also may have life in himself" (Jn. 5:26). He says "in himself," not "from himself," because the Father has given it to him.

Everything I have just now said about the good man and goodness is just as true of the truthful man and truth, of the just man and justice, of the wise man and wisdom, of the Son of God and God the Father, of everything that is born of God and has no earthly father here, everything in which nothing created and nothing that is not God is born, in which there is no image except God, bare, pure, alone. For as Saint John says in his gospel: "To all those the power and might is given to become the sons of God, who are born not of blood nor of the will of the flesh nor of the will of man, but of God" (Jn. 1:12), and from God alone.

By "blood" he means everything in man that is not subject to man's will. By "the will of the flesh" he means everything that in man is subject to his will, but that yet offers resistance and opposition, inclining to the desires of the flesh, and that is common to the soul and the body, and is not properly in the soul alone; and so it is that man's powers grow weary and sick and old. By "the will of man" Saint John means the highest powers of the soul, whose nature and works are unmixed with the flesh, residing in the soul's purity, separated from time and place and all that, which neither regard nor take delight in time and place, which have nothing in common with anything, and in which man is formed after God's image, in which man is one of God's family and of his kin.[1] And yet, because these powers are not themselves God, and are created in the soul and with the soul, they must lose their own image, and be transformed above themselves into the image of God alone, and be born in God and from God, so that God alone may be their Father; for in this way they too are the sons of God and God's Only-Begotten Son. For I am the son of everything that forms and bears me to be like it and in its likeness. Such a man, God's son, good and the son of goodness, just and the son of justice, so far as he is their son alone, is the begotten son of what is unbegotten and begetting, and he shares that one same being which justice has and is, and he enters into all the attributes of justice and of truth.

From all this teaching, which is written in the holy gospel and is recognized with certainty in the natural light of the rational soul, we find true consolation in all our sufferings.

Saint Augustine says: "God is not distant or far off. If you want nothing to be distant or far off from you, submit yourself to God,"[2] for there a thousand years are but as today. And so I say: In God there is no sorrow or suffering or affliction. If you want to be free of all affliction and suffering, hold fast to God, and turn wholly to him, and to no one else. Indeed, all your suffering comes from this, that you do not turn in God and to God and no one else. If you preserved yourself as you were formed, in justice alone, and as you were born, then truly nothing could cause you suffering, any more than justice can cause suffering to God himself. Solomon says: "Whatever may happen to one who is just, it will not sadden him" (Pr. 12:21). He does not say "to a man who is just," or "to an angel who is just," or this or that.[3] He says "to *one* who is just." Apart from his justice and that he is just, what makes him this particular just man is that he is a son and has an earthly father, and is a creature, made and created because his father is a creature, made or created. But only his attribute of being just has no created or made father, and God and justice are wholly one, and justice alone is his father. Therefore he can be injured as little by sorrow or affliction as can God himself. Justice cannot cause him sorrow, for justice is all joy and love and delight; and what is more, if justice were to make the just man sorrowful, it would make itself sorrowful. Not unlikeness, not injustice, not anything made or created can cause suffering to one who is just, for everything that is created is as far beneath him as it is beneath God; it makes no impression, it has no influence on those who are just, it does not come to birth in them, for God alone is their Father. Therefore a man must do all he can to lose the image of himself and of all creatures, and to know no Father except God alone, and so nothing can cause him suffering or sadness, not God or his creatures, nothing created or uncreated, and all his being, living, knowing and loving is from God, is in God, is God.

There is something else that we ought to know, that also comforts a man in all his afflictions. It is certain that a just and good man rejoices in his works of justice, more than will bear comparison or can be told, finding in them more delight and joy than he or even the highest angel finds in his natural being or life. And that is why the saints joyfully gave their lives for the sake of justice.

Now I say this: If outward harms come to the good and just man, and if then he remains unperturbed with equanimity and peace of heart, then what I have said is true, that nothing that happens to the just man afflicts him. But if it happens that he is afflicted by outward harms, it is very just and proper that God decreed that harm came to a man who wished and believed himself to be just, and who yet could be afflicted by such little things. If then this is God's decree, truly the man ought not to be saddened by it, but he ought rather to rejoice over it, far more than over his own life, which yet every man delights in and values more than he does this whole world; for what use would this whole world be to a man who did not exist?

The third counsel that we can and should know is that in natural truth God alone is the single source and channel of all good, of essential truth and of consolation, and that everything that is not God possesses from its own nature bitterness, sadness and suffering. It contributes nothing to the goodness that is from God and that is God, but it saps and obscures and conceals the sweetness, joy and consolation God gives.

And what is more, I say that all suffering comes from love for that which harm has taken from me. If I sorrow for the harm done to external things, that is a true sign that I love external things, and that, in truth, I love sorrow and desolation. Is it then surprising that I am afflicted, I who love and yearn for sorrow and desolation? My heart and my love are squandering upon created things the good things that are God's own possession. I run after created things, from which by their nature desolation comes, and I run away from God, from whom all consolation flows. Is it then surprising that I suffer and that I am sad? Truly, God and the whole world make it impossible for a man to find true consolation who seeks his consolation in created things. But he who would in created things love God alone, and who would love created things only in God, he would find true, just and unchanging consolation everywhere. And let this be enough for the first part of this book.

2

Here now in the second part are some thirty topics, each single one of which ought readily to console a rational man in his sorrow.

The first is that there is no affliction and harm that is without consolation, nor is there any harm that is nothing but harm. That is why Saint Paul says that God's faithfulness and goodness do not suffer any temptation or sorrow to become unendurable (1 Co. 10:15). He always makes and gives some comfort with which a man can help himself; for the saints and the pagan philosophers also say that God and nature do not permit unmixed evil or suffering to exist.

I give you an example: A man has a hundred marks, of which he loses forty and retains sixty. If he is going to think day and night about the forty he has lost, he will never stop feeling aggrieved and sorry for himself. How could anyone find consolation and forget his sorrow who keeps coming back to his loss and his grief, thinking about what it has done to him and what he has become through it, staring at affliction while affliction stares back at him, moaning over it whilst it moans in reply, as they sit there, affliction and he, gazing into each other's eyes? But if he would just turn his mind to the sixty marks he still has, and turn his back on the forty that are lost, and think of what the sixty are to him, and if he would look at them face to face and chat with them, he would certainly find consolation. What exists and what is good can console me; but what is nonexistent and is not good, what is not mine and what I have lost, that must of necessity bring desolation and sorrow and affliction. Solomon says about this: "In the day of evils do not be unmindful of the day of good things" (Si. 11:27). That is to say: When you are in sorrow and affliction, think of the good things

213

and the comfort you still have and possess. And it ought to console a man if he will think how many thousands of people there are who, if they had the sixty marks he still has, would consider themselves fine ladies and gentlemen and that they were very rich and would be glad of heart.

But there is something else that should console a man. If he is sick and in great bodily pain, he still has a house and what he needs to eat and drink, doctors to treat him, his servants to look after him, his friends to sympathize and be with him. What more does he want? What do poor people do when they have times when they are as sick or even sicker, and have no one to give them a cup of cold water? They have to go out begging a crust of bread in the rain and the snow and the cold from house to house. So if you want consolation, forget those who are better off and think of all those for whom things are worse.

What is more, I say this: All sorrow comes from love and from holding dear.[4] Therefore, if I feel sorrow because of perishable things, my heart and I will still love and hold dear perishable things, and God still does not have the love of my whole heart, and I still do not love such things as God would have me love with him. Is it then any wonder that God decrees that I so justly suffer harm and sorrow?

Saint Augustine says: "Lord, I did not want to lose you, but I wanted to possess, along with you, the created things which I crave; and that is why I lost you, because you do not want anyone to possess, along with you who are the truth, the falsehood and deceits of created things."[5] And in another place he says that "The man who is not content with God alone is too greedy by far."[6] And somewhere else he says: "How could God's gifts to his creatures content a man who is not content with God himself?"[7] Everything that is alien to God, and that is not God himself alone, ought to be for a good man not consolation but a torment. He ought always to say: "Lord, my God and my comfort, if you turn me away from yourself to anything, give me another you, so that I pass from you to you, for I want nothing except you." When the Lord promised Moses everything that is good and sent him into the Holy Land, which signifies the kingdom of heaven, Moses said: "Lord, do not send me anywhere if you are not willing to come with me yourself" (Ex. 33:15).

All attraction and desire and love come from that which is like, because all things are attracted by and love what is like them.[8] The pure man loves everything that is pure, the just man loves and is attracted to justice; a man's lips speak the things that are in the man, as our Lord says: "Out of the abundance of the heart the mouth speaks" (Lk. 6:45); and Solomon says: "All the labor of man is in his mouth" (Qo. 6:7). Therefore it is a true sign that not God but created things are in a man's heart when he is still attracted and consoled by what is outside him.

This is why a good man ought to feel great shame before God and in his own eyes if he is made aware that God is not within him, and that it is not God the Father who is performing his works in him, but that miserable creatures still live in him and attract him and perform his works in him. That is why King David in the Psalms says and laments: "My tears have been my comfort day and night; all the time, men could still say to me: 'Where is your God?' " (Ps. 41:4). For to be attracted by external things and to find consolation in what is desolation and to take delight in much talk about it is a true sign that God does not appear in me, does not watch over me, does not work in me. And what is more, a good man should feel shame before good men, that they should detect this in him. He should never complain about his harm and griefs; all that he ought to complain about is that he does complain, and that he is aware of complaint and grief in himself.

The teachers say that under the sky there is a great fire, far and wide, immediate and powerful in its heat, and yet the sky is never affected by it at all.[9] Now one treatise says that the lowest part of the soul is finer than the highest heaven.[10] How then can a man misjudge himself, thinking that he is a heavenly being with his heart in heaven, if he can still be oppressed and suffer about such little things?

Now I shall say something else. There can be no good man who does not will what is the particular will of God, for it is impossible for God to will anything but good; and precisely because it is God's will, it becomes and necessarily is good, and, what is more, it is the best. And that is why our Lord taught the apostles, and us through them, that we should pray every day for God's will to be done (Mt. 6:10). And all the same, when God's will comes to pass and is achieved, then we complain.

Seneca, a pagan philosopher, asks: "What is the best consolation in sorrow and in misfortune?" And he says: "It is for a man to accept everything as if he had wished for it and had asked for it; for you would have wished for it, if you had known that everything happens by God's will, with his will and in his will."[11] A pagan philosopher says: "Leader and commander, Father and Lord of high heaven, I am ready for everything which is your will; give me the will to will according to your will."[12]

A good man ought to have trust and faith and certainty in God, and know him to be so good that it would be impossible to him and to his goodness and to his love to suffer any sorrow or harm to come to a man, unless he should wish to take a greater harm away from him, or to give him greater consolation on earth, or, using the harm as instrument and material, to make something better with it, so that God's glory becomes more widely and more deeply revealed. But, however this may be, in that alone, that it is God's will that it should happen so, a good man's will ought to be so wholly one and united with God's will that he and God have only one will, though that should be for the man's harm or even for his damnation. This is why Saint Paul wished that he might be separated from God, for the love of God, by the will of God, and to the glory of God (Rm. 9:3). For a truly perfect man should be accustomed to regard himself as dead, and his self as transformed in God, and so supernaturally changed in God's will that all his blessedness consists in knowing nothing of himself or of anything, and in knowing God alone, in willing and wanting to know nothing but God's will, and in wanting to know God as God knows him, as Saint Paul says (1 Co. 13:12). God knows everything that he knows, he loves and wills everything that he loves and wills, in himself in his own will. Our Lord himself says: "This is eternal life, to know God alone" (Jn. 17:3).

This is why the teachers say that the blessed in heaven perceive creatures free from every creaturely image, and that they perceive them in that one image which is God, and in which God knows and loves and wills himself and all things.[13] And that is what God himself teaches us to pray and long for, when we say: "Our Father . . . hallowed be your name," that is, let us know you alone; "your kingdom come," that is, that I may possess nothing that I regard as riches except only you who are rich.[14] The gospel says about this: "Blessed are the poor in spirit" (Mt. 5:3), that is, in the will; and we pray to God that "his will be done on earth," that is, in us, "as it is in heaven," that is, in God himself. Such a man is so much of one will with God that he wills everything that God wills, and in the fashion in which God wills it. And therefore, because in some way or other it is God's will that I should have sinned, I should not want not to have done so, for in this way God's will is done "on earth," that is, in misdeeds, "as it is in heaven," that is, in good deeds. Thus a man wishes to be deprived of God for God's own sake and for God's own sake to be separated from God, and that alone is true repentance for my sins.[15] And so my sins are to me a painless pain, just as God suffers all wickedness without suffering. I do suffer, and I suffer as much as I can over sin, because I would not commit a sin for the sake of everything that has been or could be created, even if a thousand worlds could exist for evermore; but I suffer without suffering. And I take and draw the suffering in God's will and from God's will. Only such sorrow is perfect sorrow, because it proceeds and springs from a pure love of God's purest goodness and joy. So it is made true, and men come to know, as I have said in this little book, that the good man, insofar as he is good, becomes possessed of all the properties of goodness itself, which God is in himself.

Now see what a wonderful and joyful life man has, "on earth as it is in heaven," in God himself. Misfortune serves him as if it were good fortune, and sorrow as much as joy. And see too that there is in this a special consolation, for if I have the grace and the goodness of which I have now spoken, I shall always be completely consoled and joyful, at all times and under all circumstances; and if I do not have this, I ought to do without it for the love of God and in his will. If God wills to give what I ask for, I thereby have it and rejoice; and if God does not will to give it, let me accept that I lack it in that same will of God, for this is something that is not his will. And so I obtain, not by obtaining but by lacking. For what is it that I then lack? And truly, man obtains God more truly in lacking than in obtaining; for when a man receives something, the gift possesses in itself that by which he is glad and comforted. But if he does not receive it, he does not have, he does not find, he does not know any cause for joy except God and God's will alone.

But then there is another consolation. If a man has lost some material possession, or a friend or a kinsman, an eye, a hand or whatever it may be, then he should be sure that if he accepts this patiently for the love of God, then by the loss he did not want to suffer he has in God's reckoning gained at least as much. Suppose that a man loses an eye; he would not for a thousand marks or six thousand marks or more wish to be without the eye. Certainly in God's sight and in God he has saved up for him at least as much as he did not want to lose through such a harm or sorrow. And perhaps this is what is meant when our Lord said: "It is better for you to enter into everlasting life having one eye than to have two eyes and to be lost" (Mt. 18:9). It is perhaps also what is meant when God said: "Everyone who has left father and mother, sister and brother, house or land or whatever it may be, will receive a hundredfold, and life everlasting" (Mt. 19:29). I am sure that I can say in God's truth, and as I hope to be blessed, that whoever for the love of God and goodness leaves father and mother, brother and sister or whatever it may be, he receives a hundredfold in two different ways. One is that his father, mother, brother and sister will become a hundred times dearer to him than they now are. The second way is that not only a hundred people but all people, to the extent that they are people and human beings, will become far dearer to him than his father, mother or brother now are by his natural inclinations. A man is not aware of this, simply and solely because he has not yet forsaken father and mother, sister and brother and everything else, purely and only for the love of God and goodness. How has a man left father and mother, sister and brother for the love of God, who still here on earth finds them occupying his heart, who still becomes oppressed and thinks and searches after that which is not God? How has he forsaken everything for the love of God who still is caring and seeking for one good thing or another? Saint Augustine says: "Get rid of these and those goods, and what will remain is pure goodness, moving in its own bare and limitless orbit, and that is God."[16] For as I have already said, goods of any sort do not add anything to goodness, but they conceal and hide the goodness in us. Anyone who sees and contemplates in the light of truth knows and perceives that this is so, because it is true in truth and therefore one must perceive it there and nowhere else.

Yet one should know that possessing virtues and willingness to suffer exist in a wide variety of degrees, just as we can see in nature that one man is bigger and finer than another in stature, in complexion, in knowledge and in accomplishments. And so I say too that a good man may well be good, and still be moved and swayed by his natural love for his father, mother, sister, brother, sometimes less, sometimes more, and yet not be wanting in his love for God and for goodness. Yet he becomes good and better in the measure, small or great, to which he is consoled and touched by and is conscious of his natural love and attraction to his father and mother, sister and brother, and to himself.

Yet even so, as I have already written, if a man could accept this as being in God's will—insofar as it is God's will—that human nature should have these deficiencies, through God's particular justice, as a consequence of the sin of the first man, and also, even if that were not so, if he would gladly accept it as God's will for him that he should renounce such natural love, everything would then be well with him, and he would certainly find consolation for his sorrows. That is what is meant when Saint John says that the true "light shines in darkness" (Jn. 1:5) and Saint Paul says that "virtue is made perfect in infirmity" (2 Co. 12:9). If a thief were able to suffer death with a true, complete, pure, glad, willing and joyful love of divine justice, in which and according to which God and his justice will that the evildoer be put to death, truly he would be saved and blessed.[17]

But another consolation is that probably one will find no one who does not love some living person so dearly that he would not gladly sacrifice an eye or go blind for a year, provided that he could have the eye back again, if in this way he could save his friend from death. So if a man would sacrifice his eye for a year, to save from death someone who must still die in a few years' time, he ought rightly and more gladly to sacrifice the ten or twenty or thirty years he might still have to live so as to make himself eternally blessed, possessing the everlasting vision of God in his divine light, seeing, in God, himself and all created beings.

But there is a further consolation: To a good man, insofar as he is good and born of goodness alone and an image of goodness, everything that is limited and created is of no value and a bitter sorrow and pain. And so for him to be deprived of them is to be deprived of and freed from sorrow, affliction and loss. To be deprived of sorrow is indeed a real consolation. For this reason, a man should not complain about loss. He ought to complain far more that he does not know consolation, that consolation cannot console him, just as sweet wine tastes sour to a sick man. He ought to complain, as I have written before, that he is not wholly free of creaturely images, and has not been transformed with all that he is into the image of the good.

A man in his sorrow ought also to remember that God speaks the truth and swears by himself, who is the Truth. If God were to fall short of his word, his Truth, he would fall short of his divinity and would not be God, for he is his word, his Truth. His word is that our sorrow will be turned into joy (Jn. 16:20). Truly, if I knew for certain that every piece of stone that I had would be turned into gold, the more stones I possessed and the bigger they were, the gladder I should be; yes, I should go around begging for stones and collecting them, as big and as many as possible; and the more of them there were and the bigger, the happier they would make me. This surely would give a man mighty comfort in all his sorrow.

And there is another like this: No cask can hold two different kinds of drink. If it is to contain wine, then they must of necessity pour the water out; the cask must become empty and free. Therefore, if you are to receive God's joy and God, you are obliged to pour out created things. Saint Augustine says: "Empty yourself, so that you may be filled. Learn not to love, so that you may learn how to love. Draw back, so that you may be approached."[18] In a few words, everything that is to receive and be capable of receiving should and must be empty. The authorities say that if the eye had some color in it when it was observing, it would recognize neither the color it had nor the color it had not;[19] but because it is free of all colors, it therefore recognizes all colors. A wall has its own color, and therefore it recognizes neither its color nor any other color, and it takes no pleasure in colors, no more in that of gold or lapis lazuli than in that of charcoal. The eye has no color and yet truly possesses color, because it recognizes it with pleasure and delight and joy. And as the powers of the soul become more perfect and unmixed, so they apprehend more perfectly and comprehensively whatever they apprehend, receiving it more comprehensively, having greater joy, becoming more united with what they apprehend, to the point where the highest power of the soul, bare of all things and having nothing in common with anything, receives into itself nothing less than God himself, in all the vastness and fulness of his being. And the authorities show us that there is no delight and no joy that can be compared with this union and this fulfilling and this joy.[20] This is why our Lord says so insistently: "Blessed are the poor in spirit" (Mt. 5:3). A man is poor who has nothing. To be poor in spirit means that as the eye is poor and deprived of color, and is able to apprehend every color, so he is poor in spirit who is able to apprehend every spirit, and the Spirit of all spirits is God. The fruit of the spirit is love, joy and peace (Ga. 5:22). To be naked, to be poor, to have nothing, to be empty transforms nature; emptiness makes water flow uphill, and many other marvels of which we need not now speak.

Therefore, if you want to have and to find complete joy and consolation in God, make sure that you are naked of all created things, of all comfort from created things; for truly, so long as created things console you and can console you, never will you find true consolation. But when nothing but God can console you, then truly God does console you, and with him and in him everything that is joy consoles you. If what is not God consoles you, then you will have no consolation, neither now nor later. But if creatures do not console you and give you no delight, then you will find consolation, both now and to come.

If a man were able and knew how to make a goblet quite empty, and to keep it empty of everything that could fill it, even of air, doubtless the goblet would forgo and forget all its nature, and its emptiness would lift it up into the sky. And so to be naked, poor, empty of all created things lifts the soul up to God. Likeness and heat too draw up above. We attribute likeness in the divinity to the Son, heat and love to the Holy Spirit. Likeness in all things, but more so and first of all in the divine nature, is the birth of the One and the likeness of the One, in the One and with the One; it is the beginning and origin of flowering, fiery love. The One is the beginning without any beginning. Likeness is the beginning of the One alone, and it receives that it is and that it is beginning from the One and in the One.[21] It is the nature of love that it flows and springs up out of two as one. One as one does not produce love, two as two does not produce love; two as one perforce produces natural, consenting, fiery love.

Solomon says that all waters, that is all created things, flow and run back to their beginning (Qo. 1:7). That is why what I have said is necessarily true. Likeness and fiery love draw up the soul and lead it and bring it to the first source of the One, which is "the Father of all," "in heaven and earth" (Ep. 4:6 and 3:15).[22] And so I say that likeness, born of the One, draws the soul into God, as he is one in his hidden union, for that is what "One" signifies. Of this we have a plain example: When material fire kindles wood, a spark receives the nature of fire, and it becomes like pure fire, and without any medium sticks to the lower heavens. At once it forgets and denies father and mother, brother and sister down upon earth, and hastens up to the heavenly father. The father of the spark down here is the fire, and its mother is the wood, its brothers and sisters are the other sparks; but the first small spark does not wait for them. Swiftly it hastens up to its true father, which is the heavens; for anyone who recognizes truth knows very well that the fire is not the real true father of the spark, once it is fire. The real true father of the spark and of all fiery things is the heavens. And it should also be carefully observed that this little spark not only forsakes and forgets father and mother, brother and sister here upon earth; it forsakes and forgets and denies its own self out of its love to come to its lawful father, the heavens, because it must perforce be extinguished in the coldness of the air; and yet it wants to show its natural love, which it has for its true, heavenly father.

And as it has already been said about emptiness or nakedness, as the soul becomes more pure and bare and poor, and possesses less of created things, and is emptier of all things that are not God, it receives God more purely, and is more totally in him, and it truly becomes one with God, and it looks into God and God into it, face to face, as it were two images transformed into one. This is what Saint Paul says,[23] and this is what I say now about likeness and about the heat of love; because as one thing becomes more like another, so it hastens always faster toward it, and travels with greater speed, and its course is sweeter and more joyful to it. And the further it goes away from itself and from everything that is not the object of its pursuit, the less like it becomes to itself and to everything that is not that object, and the more it becomes like the object toward which it drives. And because likeness flows from the One and draws and attracts by the power and in the power of the One, this does not pacify or satisfy that which is drawing or that which is being drawn, until they become united into one. Therefore the Lord said through the prophet Isaias and meant that "no likeness, however exalted, and no loving peace will satisfy me, until I shine out myself in my Son" (Is. 62:1), and until I myself am set on fire and enkindled in the love of the Holy Spirit. And our Lord prayed his Father that we might become one with him and in him (Jn. 17:11), not merely that we should be joined together. Of what this says, and of its truth, we have a plain example and proof even in the external natural order: When fire works, and kindles wood and sets it on fire, the fire diminishes the wood and makes it unlike itself, taking away its coarseness, coldness, heaviness and dampness, and turns the wood into itself, into fire, more and more like to it. But neither the fire nor the wood is pacified or quieted or satisfied with any warmth or heat or likeness until the fire gives birth to itself in the wood, and gives to the wood its own nature and also its own being, so that they both become one and the same unseparated fire, neither less nor more. And therefore, before this may be achieved, there is always smoke, contention, crackling, effort and violence between fire and wood. But when all the unlikeness has been taken away and rejected, then the fire is stilled and the wood is quiet.[24] And I say something else that is true, that nature's hidden power secretly hates likeness insofar as it carries within itself distinction and duality, and nature seeks in likeness the One it loves for its own sake alone in likeness. So the mouth seeks and loves in the wine and from the wine its flavor or its sweetness. If water had the flavor that wine has, the mouth would love the wine no more than the water.

And that is why I have said that the soul hates likeness in likeness and does not love it in itself and for its own sake, but it loves likeness for the sake of the One that is concealed in likeness, and is the true "Father," beginning without beginning, "of all in heaven and on earth" (Ep. 4:6 and 3:15). And therefore I say: So long as likeness can still be perceived and appears between fire and wood, there is never true delight or silence or rest or contentment. That is why the authorities say: Fire comes about in strife and contention and unrest, and it happens in time; but the birth of the fire and joy is timeless, placeless. It seems to no one that delight and joy are slow or distant. Everything I have now said is signified when our Lord says: "When a woman gives birth to a child she has pain and anguish and sorrow; but when the child is born, she forgets the pain and anguish" (Jn. 16:21). Therefore too God says in the gospel and admonishes us that we should pray to the heavenly Father that our joy may be complete (Jn. 15:11); and Saint Philip said: "Lord, show us the Father, and it is enough for us" (Jn. 14:8). For "Father" implies birth, not likeness, and it signifies the One in which all likeness is stilled, and everything is silenced that longs for being.

Now a man may plainly see why and because of what he is unconsoled in all his sorrow, distress and hurt. This all comes from nothing else than that he is far away from God, that he is not emptied of created things, that he is unlike to God, cold toward divine love.

Yet there is another matter; and anyone who would observe it and see it for what it is would soon be consoled in any worldly hurt and sorrow. Suppose that a man goes on a journey or undertakes some action or stops something else he is doing, and he suffers an injury. He breaks a leg, an arm, or loses an eye, or becomes sick. If then he keeps on thinking: If you had taken another road, or if you had done something different, that would not have happened to you, he will remain unconsoled, and he is of necessity unhappy. That is why he should think: If you had taken another road or if you had started or stopped doing something different, some much worse injury or harm could easily have happened to you. And so he would rightly be consoled.

And I will put another case: If you have lost a thousand marks, you ought not to lament the thousand marks that are lost. You should thank God who gave you a thousand marks to lose, and who permits you to exercise the virtue of patience and so to gain that eternal life which many thousands of men will not possess.

Here is something else that can console a man. I put the case of someone who has enjoyed honors and ease for many years, and now loses it through God's decree. Then he should reflect wisely and thank God. When he feels his present harm and hurt, he realizes for the first time the profit and ease he used to have. He should thank God for the ease he enjoyed for so many years and never acknowledged truly, when he was so well off, and he should not complain. He ought to reflect that a man of his own true nature has nothing of his own except sinfulness and weakness. Everything that is good and is goodness God has loaned him, not given him. Anyone who sees the truth knows that God, the heavenly Father, gives everything that is good to the Son and to the Holy Spirit; but to his creatures he gives nothing good, he lets them have it as a loan. The sun gives heat to the air, but makes a loan of light; and that is why, as soon as the sun goes down, the air loses the light, but the heat remains there, because the heat is given to the air to possess as its own. And that is why the authorities say that God, the heavenly Father, is Father and not Lord of the Son, nor is he the Lord of the Holy Spirit. But God, Father, Son and Holy Spirit—this is one Lord, and the Lord of created things. We say that God was everlastingly the Father; but in time, in which he made created things, he is the Lord.

Now I say: Since it is so, that everything which is good or comforting or temporal is only loaned to man, what cause has he to complain when he who has loaned it to him wishes to take it back? He ought to thank God, who has loaned it to him for so long. And he ought also to thank him that he does not take back everything he has loaned to him, as he well might take all his loan back, when the man becomes enraged because God takes from him a part of what was never his and of which he was never the owner. And that is why Jeremias the prophet truly says of when he was in great sorrow and distress: "Many are the mercies of the Lord, that we are not wholly consumed" (Lm. 3:22). If anyone had loaned me his coat and jerkin and cloak, and were to take back his cloak and leave me the coat and the jerkin against the cold, I ought to thank him greatly and be glad. And one ought to see clearly how very unjust I am if I storm and complain if I lose something; because if what I want is for the possessions I have to be given to me and not loaned, that means that I want to be Lord, and God's

Son by nature, I who am not yet even God's son by grace, for it is the property of the Son of God and of the Holy Spirit to be unchanging in all circumstances.

One ought also to know that beyond any doubt even natural, human virtue is so excellent and so strong that there is no external work too difficult for it or great enough for it to manifest itself in it and through it and to form itself in it. And there is an interior work, which cannot be confined or comprehended by time or place; and in this work is what is divine and like to God, whom neither time nor place confine, for he is everywhere and present in all time, and this work is also like to God in this, that no creature can perfectly receive him nor form God's goodness in himself. And so there must be something, more inward, more exalted, uncreated, lacking all measure, lacking all manner, in which the heavenly Father can form and pour and manifest his whole self; and that is the Son and the Holy Spirit. And no one can hinder this interior working of virtue, any more than anyone can hinder God. The work gleams and shines day and night. It lauds and sings God's praise and a new song, as David says: "Sing to God a new song" (Ps. 95:1). God does not love that work whose praise is of the earth, for it is external, it is confined by time and place, it is narrow, men can hinder and force it, and it grows weary and old through time and labor. This work[25] is to love God, to want good and goodness, and in this all that man wants and would do with a pure and perfect will in all good works has already been done, and in this he is like God, of whom David writes: "Whatever he pleased, he has already done and made" (Ps. 134:6).

Of this teaching we have a clear example in stones, the external function of which is to fall down and to lie on the ground. This function can be prevented, and a stone does not keep on falling all the time. There is another function, more essential to the stone, and that is its propensity to fall, and that was made with it; neither God nor his creatures can take that away. The stone fulfills that function unceasingly, day and night. It can lie on the ground for a thousand years, but it will have the same propensity, neither less nor more, as on the first day.[26]

This is what I mean when I say that virtue has an interior work, to want and to incline to everything that is good, to flee and oppose everything that is corrupt and evil and unlike goodness and God. And the worse that a deed is and the more unlike God, the greater is the opposition; and the greater a deed and the more like to God, the easier and more willing and joyful virtue finds it. And all its lament and sorrow, if sorrow could find any place in virtue, is that what is suffered for God is too little, and that all external works performed in time are too little, so that in them virtue cannot wholly show itself or fully manifest itself or form itself in them. Exercising itself, virtue grows strong, and in its generosity it becomes mighty. It would not wish to have finished suffering or to have vanquished sorrow and pain. It wishes and would always want unceasingly to continue suffering for the love of God and of doing good. All its blessedness is in suffering now, not in having suffered, for the love of God. And therefore our Lord says very plainly: "Blessed are they who suffer for the sake of justice" (Mt. 5:10). He does not say "who have suffered." Such a man hates "having-suffered," for having-suffered is not the suffering he loves; it is a release from and a loss of suffering that he alone loves for the sake of God. And therefore I say that such a man also hates "shall-suffer," for that also is not suffering. But he hates shall-suffer less than having-suffered, because having-suffered is further away from suffering and more unlike it, because it is wholly finished. If a man is yet to suffer, that does not entirely deprive him of the suffering he loves.

Saint Paul says that he would be willing to be deprived of God, for God's sake, so that God's glory might be increased (Rm. 9:3). They say that Saint Paul said this at the time when he was not yet perfect; but I think that this saying came from a heart that was perfect. They say too that he meant that he wanted to be deprived of God for a time; but I say that a perfect man would be as loath to be deprived of God for one hour as for a thousand years. Yet if it were the will of God and to God's glory for him to be deprived of God, that would be as easy for him for a thousand years or for all eternity as for a day or an hour.

And the interior work is divine and of God and tastes of divinity in the sense that, just as all created beings, even if there were a thousand worlds, are not one hair's breadth better than is God alone, so I say now as I have said before that this external work does not at all add, not in its quantity or size or length or breadth, to the goodness of the interior work, which possesses its goodness in itself. Thus the external work can never be trivial if the interior work is great, and the external work can never be great or good if the interior work is trivial or worthless. The interior work contains in itself all time, all vastness, all breadth and all length. The interior work receives and creates its whole being out of nowhere else than from and in the heart of God. It receives the Son, and is born Son in the bosom of the heavenly Father.[27]

It is not so with the external work, for it has its divine goodness brought and poured into it by means of the interior work, as the divine nature stoops and clothes itself in distinction, in quantity, in division, all of which, and everything like it, and likeness itself, are far from God and alien to him. They seize upon and are seized and silenced by that which is good, enlightened, creaturely. They are wholly blind to what is in itself the good and the light and to the One in which God brings to birth his Only-Begotten Son, and in all who are God's children, his begotten sons. Here is the flowing out and the springing up of the Holy Spirit, from whom alone, as he is God's Spirit and himself Spirit, God the Son is conceived in us. Here is the flowing out of all those who are the sons of God, to the measure, greater or less, in which they are purely born of God alone, formed in God's likeness and in God, and strangers to all multiplicity, even though one does find multiplicity in the highest angels by their nature. And if we will see things truly, they are strangers to goodness, truth and everything that tolerates any distinction, be it in a thought or in a name, in a notion or just a shadow of a distinction. They are intimates of the One that is bare of every kind of multiplicity and distinction. In the One, "God-Father-Son-and-Holy Spirit" are stripped of every distinction and property, and are one.[28] And the One makes us blessed, and the further we are away from the One, the less we are sons and the Son, and the less perfectly does the Holy Spirit spring up in us and flow out from us. And the closer we are to the One, the more truly are we God's sons and his Son, and also the more truly does God the Holy Spirit flow from us. This is what our Lord, God's Son in the divinity, means when he says: "Whoever drinks from the water which I shall give, in him will spring a fountain of water, springing up into life everlasting" (Jn. 4:14). And Saint John says that he said that referring to the Holy Spirit (Jn. 7:39).

The Son in the divinity according to his proper attribute[29] gives nothing else than being son, nothing else than being born of God, source, the springing up and flowing out of the Holy Spirit, the love of God, nothing else than the full, true and complete tasting of the One, of the heavenly Father. Therefore the Father's voice said from heaven to the Son: "You are my beloved Son, in whom I am loved and am well pleased" (Mt. 3:17). For beyond doubt, no one loves God sufficiently and purely who is not God's son. For love, the Holy Spirit, springs and flows from the Son, and the Son loves the Father for the Father's sake, and loves the Father in himself, and loves himself in the Father. And therefore indeed our Lord says that "the poor in spirit are blessed" (Mt. 5:13), that is, those who have nothing of their own and of human spirit, and who come naked to God. And Saint Paul says: "God has manifested it to us in his Spirit" (Col. 1:8).

Saint Augustine says that that man understands the scriptures best of all who is free of all intellectual ambition,[30] and seeks for the sense and truth of the scriptures in scripture itself, that is, in the Spirit, in whom the scriptures were written and uttered, in the Spirit of God.[31] Saint Peter says that all holy men have spoken in the Spirit of God (2 P. 1:21). Saint Paul says: "No man knows what things may be in a man but the Spirit which is in him, and no man can know what is the Spirit of God and is in God except the Spirit, who is of God and is God" (1 Co. 2:11).

Therefore one commentary, a gloss, says very truly that no one can understand or teach Saint Paul's writings if he does not possess the Spirit in which Saint Paul spoke and wrote.[32] And this is what I always complain about, that crude men, empty of the Spirit of God and not possessing it, want to judge according to their crude human understanding what they hear or read in holy scripture, which was spoken and written by and in the Holy Spirit, and that they forget what is written: That what is impossible to man is possible to God (Mt. 19:26). That is also true in common things and in the natural order: What is impossible to our lower nature is commonplace and natural to our higher nature.

Understand too what I have just said, that a good man, a son of God born in God, loves God for himself and in himself, and much else that I have already said. To understand it better one should know, as I have also often said, that a good man, born of goodness and in God, enters into all the attributes of the divine nature.[33] Now it is one attribute of God, according to the words of Solomon, that he forms all things for his own sake (Pr. 16:4), that is, that he does not look around outside himself for any reason other than himself; he loves and performs all things for his own sake. Therefore, if a man loves him and all things and performs all his works not for reward or honor or ease, but for God's sake and for his glory alone, that is a sign that he is God's Son.

What is more: God loves for his own sake and performs all things for his own sake; that is, he loves for love, and he works for working's sake. For without doubt, God would never have begotten in eternity his Only-Begotten Son, were not having begotten the same as begetting. That is why the saints say that as the Son was eternally begotten, so is he still being begotten without ceasing.[34] Nor would God ever have created the world, were not having been created the same as creating. Therefore, God so created the world that he still without ceasing creates it. Everything that is past and that is yet to come is unknown to God and remote from him. And therefore, whoever, born of God, is God's son loves God for his sake alone. That is, he loves God for the sake of loving God, and performs all his works for the sake of working.[35] God never wearies of loving and working, and everything he loves is to him one love. And therefore it is true that God is love (1 Jn. 4:16). And that is why I said before that a good man wants and would always want to suffer for God's sake, not to have suffered; for, suffering, he has what he loves. He loves suffering for God's sake, and he suffers for the sake of God. Therefore and thereby is he God's son, formed in God's likeness and in God, who loves for his own sake. That is, he loves for love, works for working; and therefore God loves and works without ceasing. And God's working is his nature, his being, his life, his blessedness. So truly, for God's son, a good man, inasmuch as he is God's son, to suffer and to work for the love of God is his being, his life, his working, his blessedness; for so our Lord says: "Blessed are they who suffer for justice's sake" (Mt. 5:10).

Furthermore, I make a third point: A good man, insofar as he is good, has God's attributes not only in that he loves and works everything that he loves and works for the sake of God, whom he loves in everything and for love of whom he works, but he also loves and works for the sake of himself, who is the one loving. For what he loves, that is God, Father, Unbegotten; and he who loves is God, Son, Begotten.[36] Now the Father is in the Son, and the Son is in the Father (Jn. 17:21). Father and Son are one. Seek at the end of this book for how the innermost and the highest part of the soul creates and receives God's Son and becoming-God's-Son in the bosom and heart of the heavenly Father, in what I write about "the nobleman who traveled far into a distant land to accept a kingdom and to return" (Lk. 19:12)[37]

One ought also to know that in nature the impression and the influence of the highest and most exalted nature upon every man is to him more joyful and delightful than his self's own nature and being. By its own nature water flows downhill, and in its flowing downhill is its being. But by the impression and the influence of the moon up above in the heavens, it denies and forgets its own nature, and flows uphill, and to flow uphill is much easier for it than flowing downhill.[38] Through this a man ought to know whether it be proper that he should delight and rejoice in wholly abandoning and denying his own natural will, and in completely forsaking himself in everything God wants him to suffer. This is the best understanding of what our Lord said: "If any man will come to me, he should forsake and deny himself and take up his cross" (Mt. 16:24), that is, he should lay down and put away everything that is a cross and suffering. For truly, if anyone had denied himself and had wholly forsaken himself, nothing could be for him a cross or sorrow or suffering; it would all be a delight to him, a happiness, a joy to his heart, and he would truly be coming to God and following him. For just as nothing can grieve or afflict God, so nothing can make such a man rueful or sad. And, therefore, when our Lord says: "If any man will come to me, he should deny himself and take up his cross and follow me," it is not merely a command, as people usually say and think. It is a promise and a divine teaching about how all a man's suffering, all his work, all his life can become joyful and happy for him, and it is more a reward than a command. For such a man has everything he wants, and he wants nothing that is wrong; and that is blessedness. And that is indeed why our Lord says: "Blessed are they who suffer for the sake of justice" (Mt. 5:10).

Furthermore, when our Lord, the Son, says, "Let him deny himself and lift up his cross and come to me," that means: Let him become a Son, as I am Son,[39] God-begotten, and let him become that same one which I am, which I, being and remaining in the bosom and the heart of the Father, create. "Father," the Son also says, "I wish the man who follows me, who comes to me, to be where I am" (Jn. 12:26). No one truly comes to the Son as he is Son except the one who becomes son, and no one is where the Son is, who is one in the One in the Father's bosom and heart, except him who is son.

The Father says: "I will lead her into the wilderness and there speak to her heart" (Hos. 2:14). Heart to heart, one in the One, so God loves.[40] Everything that is alien to the One and far from it God hates. God invites and draws to the One. All creatures seek the One, the very meanest of created things seek the One, and the highest creatures find the One; drawn above their natures and transformed, they seek the One in the One, the One in its self. Perhaps this is why the Son says: "In the Son of divinity in the Father, where I am, he shall be who serves me, who follows me, who comes to me."

But there is yet another consolation. One ought to know that it is impossible to the whole of nature for it to break, spoil or even touch anything in which it does not intend something better for the thing it touches. It is not enough for it to make something just as good; always it wants to make something better. How? A wise physician never touches a man's ailing finger so as to hurt the man if he cannot produce an improvement in the finger itself or in the whole man, and do him good. If he can cure the man and the finger too, he does so; if he cannot, he amputates the finger to cure the man. And it is much better to lose the finger and to save the man than to lose both finger and man. One hurt is better than two, especially when one would be much greater than the other. One ought also to know that the finger and the hand and every member are naturally more concerned for the man to whom they belong than they are for themselves, and will gladly and unhesitatingly accept hardship and injury for the man's sake. I say with certainty and truth that the member does not love itself at all except insofar as it is a member. Therefore it would be very proper and would by nature be right for us not to love ourselves at all except for God's sake and in God. And if that were so, everything God wanted from us and in us would be easy and joyful for us, especially if we were convinced that God could not so easily allow our loss or harm, if he did not know and intend that it would bring us a much greater benefit. Truly it is only too right for a man to suffer and be sad if he does not trust God.

There is another consolation. Saint Paul says that God chastises all those whom he receives and accepts as sons (Heb. 12:6). It is part of our being a son for us to suffer. Because God's Son could not suffer in his divinity and in eternity, the heavenly Father therefore sent him into time, to become man and to be able to suffer. So if you want to be son of God and you do not want to suffer, you are all wrong. In the Book of Wisdom it is written that God tests and tries whether a man is just, as men test and try gold and melt it in a furnace (Ws. 3:5–6). It is a sign that the king or a prince has great trust in a knight when he sends him into battle. I knew a lord who, when he had accepted a knight into his service, would send him out by night and charge at him and fight with him. And once it happened that he was nearly killed by a man whom he wanted to test in this way, and he was much fonder of this soldier afterward than he had ever been.

We read that Saint Anthony in the desert was once in particular torment from evil spirits, and when he had overcome his distress, our Lord appeared joyfully to him in bodily form. Then the holy man said: "O, dear Lord, wherever were you when I was in such need?" Then our Lord said: "I was here, just where I am now; but it was my will and my pleasure to see how valiant you might be."[41] A piece of silver or gold may be quite pure; but if they want to make a vessel out of it for the king to drink from, they will melt it down more thoroughly than another. That is why it is written of the apostles that they rejoiced that they were worthy to suffer contempt for the love of God (Ac. 5:41).

God's Son by nature wanted to become man as a favor, so that he could suffer for your sake; and you want to become God's son and not man, so that you cannot and need not suffer, either for love of God or of yourself.

Then, too, if a man knew and would consider what great joy, truly, God himself in his fashion and all the angels and all who know and love God have in the patience of the man who for God's sake suffers sorrow and harm, indeed through that alone he should rightly be comforted. For a man sacrifices his possessions and suffers harm so that he can bring joy to his friend and show some love for him.

And one might also think: If a man had a friend who for his sake was suffering and in sorrow and distress, it would certainly be the right thing to be with him and console him with his presence and with the consolations he could bring him. Of this the Lord says in the Psalms that he is with a good man in his sufferings (Ps. 33:19). From these words one can draw seven teachings and a sevenfold consolation.

First, Saint Augustine says that patience in suffering for God's sake is better, dearer, higher, nobler than everything men can take away from a man against his will;[42] for that is only his external possessions. God knows, one does not find anyone who loves this world who is so rich that he would not willingly and gladly suffer even for a long time great sorrow and pains, if afterward he might be the mighty lord of all this world.

Second, I do not deduce from what God says merely that he is with man in his sufferings; but from what he says and in its spirit I deduce and say this: If God is with me in my suffering, what more or what else do I want? If I think rightly, I want nothing else and I want nothing more than God. Saint Augustine says: "He is too greedy and foolish who is not satisfied with God"; and elsewhere he says: "How can God's gifts, material or spiritual, satisfy the man who is not satisfied with God's own self?"[43] And that is why he says in another place: "Lord, if you send us away from you, then give us another you, because we want nothing else than you."[44] This is why the Book of Wisdom says: "All good things come to me together with God, eternal

Wisdom" (Ws. 7:11). In one sense that means that nothing is good or can be good that comes without God, and everything that comes with God is good, and good only because it comes with God. About God I will not speak; but, if one were to take away from all the creatures of this whole world the being God gives, they would remain a mere nothing, displeasing, worthless and hateful. This saying contains much else of most excellent meaning about how all good things come with God, but it would take too long to talk about it now.

The Lord says: "I am with a man in suffering" (Ps. 90:15). About this Saint Bernard says: "Lord, if you are with us in suffering, give me suffering always, so that you are always with me, so that I always have you."[45]

Third, I say: That God is with us in suffering means that he himself suffers with us. Indeed, anyone who sees the truth knows that what I say is true. God suffers with man, he truly does; he suffers in his own fashion, sooner and far more than the man suffers who suffers for love of him. Now I say, if God himself is willing to suffer, then I ought fittingly to suffer, for if I think rightly, I want what God wants. I pray every day as God commands me to pray: "Lord, may your will be done," and yet, if God's will is for suffering, I want to complain about suffering; and that is not right at all. And I say too with certainty that since God suffers so willingly with us and for our sake, if we suffer only for love of him, he suffers without suffering. Suffering is for him so joyful that it is for him not suffering. And therefore, if we thought rightly, suffering would not be suffering for us; it would be our joy and consolation.

Fourth, I say that a friend's compassion naturally makes this suffering less. If then the compassion that a man has for me can console me, God's compassion should console me far more.

Fifth, If I should suffer with a man whom I loved and who loved me, and I wanted this, then I ought gladly and fittingly to suffer with God, who is suffering in this with me and suffers for my sake, out of the love that he has for me.

Sixth, I say that if God has suffered already, before ever I suffer, and if I suffer for the love of God, truly all my sufferings will easily turn into my consolation and joy, however great and varied my suffering may be. This is true in the natural order: If a man does something for something else's sake, that for the sake of which he does it is closer to his heart, and what he does is further from his heart, and only touches his heart through that which is the object and cause of what he does.

If someone is building, hewing wood and breaking stone with the intention of making a house as a shelter against the summer's heat and the winter's frost, his heart is set, chiefly and wholly, on the house; he is not cutting the stone or doing the labor except for the sake of the house. We see well that if a sick man drinks sweet wine, it seems to him bitter and he says that it is, and this is true, because the wine loses all its sweetness outside, on the bitterness of the tongue, before it can penetrate to where the soul recognizes and judges its flavor. This is so, far more and more truly, of a man who performs all his works for the love of God. Then God is the medium, and he is what is closest to the soul. Nothing can touch a man's heart and soul that for God's sake and through his sweetness does not lose and must lose its bitterness and become wholly sweet, before it can ever touch a man's heart.

There is another token and simile that signifies this: The authorities say that beneath the heaven there is a vast extent of fire, and that therefore no rain or wind or any kind of storm or tempest from below can reach so close to the heaven that anything can touch it; everything is burned up and consumed by the fire's heat before it can reach heaven. So I say that everything a man suffers and performs for God's sake becomes wholly sweet in God's sweetness, before it can reach the heart of the man who works and suffers for the love of God. That is what we mean when we say "for the love of God,"[46] for nothing can ever come to the heart except by flowing through God's sweetness, in which it loses its bitterness. And it is also consumed in the fiery heat of the divine love, which has wholly enclosed the good man's heart.

Now one can plainly see how fittingly and variously a good man is comforted on all sides in suffering, in sorrow and in working. One way is for him to suffer and work for the love of God; another way is for him to be in the divine love. And a man can see and know whether he performs all his works for the love of God and whether he is in God's love, for when a man finds himself sorrowful and unconsoled, to that extent his work was not done for God alone, and you may be sure that to that extent he is not wholly in God's love. King David says that a fire comes with God and before him, consuming everything God finds opposed to him and unlike him (Ps. 96:3), that is, sorrow, despair, strife and bitterness.

And the seventh teaching from the saying that God is with us in suffering and suffers with us is that we should be mightily comforted by God's attribute, that he is the purely one, without any accidental admixture of distinction, even in thought;[47] that everything that is in

234

him is God himself. And because that is true, therefore I say, everything the good man suffers for God's sake, he suffers in God, and God is suffering with him in his suffering. But if my suffering is in God and God is suffering with me, how then can suffering be sorrow to me, if suffering loses its sorrow, and my sorrow is in God, and my sorrow is God? Truly, as God is Truth and as I find the Truth, I find my God, the Truth, there; and too, neither less nor more, as I find pure suffering for the love of God and in God, I find God my suffering. If anyone does not recognize this, let him blame his blindness, not me, and not God's truth and loving generosity.

So suffer in this way for God's sake since this is so greatly profitable and brings such blessedness. "Blessed are they," our Lord said, "who suffer for the sake of justice" (Mt. 5:10). How can God, who loves goodness, suffer his friends, who are good men, not to be in suffering always and without ceasing? If a man had a friend who could, by suffering for a few days, so earn great profit and honor and ease and possess it for a long time, and he wanted to hinder that or let it be hindered by anyone else, no one would say that he could be the other man's friend or that he loved him. Therefore, far less could God suffer in any way that his friends, good men, should ever be without suffering, unless they were able to suffer without suffering. Any good in external suffering proceeds and flows from the goodness of the will, as I have already written. And therefore everything a good man wished and is ready and longs to suffer for God's sake, he suffers in God's sight, and, for God's sake, in God. King David says in the Psalms: "I am ready for every hardship, and my suffering is continually before me" (Ps. 37:18), in my heart and in my sight. Saint Jerome says that a piece of pure wax, quite pliable and serviceable to have this or that made out of it according to someone's intention and wish, contains within it everything anyone can make with it, even though no one actually makes anything from it.[48] And I have written before that the stone does not weigh any less if one cannot see it lying on the ground; all its weight is completely present because it is in itself capable of falling and ready to fall. And I have also written already that the good man has already performed in heaven and on earth everything he wished to do, and in this too he is like God.

Now one can see and know how stupid the people are who are always surprised when they see good men suffering pain and harm; and often in their folly they wrongly imagine that this must be for such men's secret sins, and then sometimes they say: "Oh, I thought he was a very good man! How can it be that he is suffering such great sorrow and harm, when I thought that he was perfect?" And I agree with them: Certainly, if this were suffering, and if they did suffer sorrow and misfortune, then they would not be good or free from sin. But if they are good, then suffering for them is not sorrow or misfortune, but it is their great good fortune and blessedness. "Blessed," said God, who is Truth, "are all those who suffer for the sake of righteousness." Therefore the Book of Wisdom says that "The souls of the just are in the hand of God. The unwise think and imagine that they die and perish, but they are in peace" (Ws. 3:1), in joy and blessedness. When Saint Paul writes how many of the saints have suffered so many great torments, he says that the world was not worthy of this (Heb. 11:36–38); and for anyone who understands this saying, it has a threefold meaning. One is that this world is not worthy that many good men live in it. Another and better meaning tells us that what counts as goodness in the world is base and worthless; God alone has worth, and therefore they are worthy before God and of God. The third meaning, which is the one I now have in mind and wish to say, is that this world, that is, the people who love this world, are not worthy to suffer sorrow and hardship for God's sake. Of this it is written that the holy apostles rejoiced that they were worthy to suffer torment for the name of God (Ac. 5:41).

Let what I have said now be enough, because in the third part of this book I want to write of various consolations with which a good man can and should comfort himself in his sorrow, and which one can find not only in the words but also in the deeds of good and wise men.

3

We read in the Book of Kings that a man cursed King David and said what was deeply shameful to him (2 S. 16:5 sqq). Then one of David's friends said that he would strike this vile dog dead. But the king said: "No! because perhaps it is God's will through this shame to do what is best for me."

We read in the *Lives of the Fathers* that a man complained to a holy father that he was suffering. Then the father said: "My son, do you want me to pray to God to take it away from you?" Then the other said: "No, father, because it is profitable to me—that I see well. But pray to God to give me his grace so that I suffer it willingly."[49]

Once someone asked a sick man why he did not pray to God to

make him well. Then the man said that there were three reasons why he would be sorry to do that. The first was because he wanted to be sure that our loving God would never allow him to be sick, if that were not the best thing for him. The second reason was that if a man is good, he wants everything God wishes, and not that God should wish what he may want, for that would be wholly wrong. And therefore if it is his will that I should be sick—and if he did not will it so, it would not be so—then I ought not to wish to be well. For without any doubt, if it could be that God might make me well against his will, it would seem to me unworthy and base that he should make me well. Willing comes from loving, unwilling comes from unloving. It is dearer and better and more profitable to me that God should love me and that I should be sick than for me to be well in my body and for God not to love me. What God loves, that is something; but what God does not love, that is nothing, as the Book of Wisdom says (Ws. 11:25). And it is also true that everything God wills, in that and because God wills it, is good. Truly, to speak in ordinary language, I should rather that some rich and mighty man, a king, maybe, should love me and yet leave me for a while without any gift than that he should straight away order me to be given something, and that he should not in fact love me. Let him now not give me anything because of his love, and yet not give me anything now because he wishes later to make me richer and greater gifts. And even if I suppose that the man who loves me and who gives me nothing now does not propose to give me anything later, perhaps he will think better of this afterward and will give me something. I ought to wait patiently, especially because his gift is gratuitous and unmerited. And certainly, if I do not esteem someone's love, and if my will is opposed to his will, unless I receive a gift from him, it is very right that he give me nothing, and that he hate me and leave me as wretched as I am.

The third reason why it would not be of value and importance to me to want to ask God to make me well is because I do not wish to and I should not ask our mighty, loving, merciful God for so small a thing. If I were to go a hundred or two hundred miles to see the pope, and I were to come into his presence and say: "Lord, holy father, I have come all of two hundred miles, a hard journey that has cost a lot, and I ask your Holiness, because this is what I have come for, to give me a bean"—truly, he and anyone else who heard it would say, and rightly, that I was a perfect idiot. Now what I say is gospel truth: All possessions and indeed all created things are in comparison with God less than is a bean in comparison with all this physical world. Therefore I should do well, if I were a good and wise man, to be ashamed of asking that I might get well.

On this topic I say too that it is the sign of a sick heart if a man becomes glad or sorry over the transitory things of this world. We should feel shame for this in our hearts in the sight of God and his angels, and in the sight of men, that we should detect this in ourselves. We are ashamed soon enough of some facial disfigurement which is there for people to see. What more do I need to say? The books of the Old Testament and the New, and those of the saints and even the pagans are full of this, how pious men for God's sake and also for the sake of natural virtue have given their lives and have willingly sacrificed themselves.

A pagan philosopher, Socrates, says that virtue makes impossible things possible, and even easy and delightful.[50] And I must not forget that the blessed woman of whom the Book of the Machabees tells that in a single day she saw enacted before her own eyes the horrifying and horrible torments, intolerable even to hear about, that were inflicted and imposed upon her seven sons, and she watched this cheerfully and encouraged and particularly admonished them not to be afraid, and to surrender willingly their bodies and their spirits for the sake of God's justice. This could be the end of the book, but there are two more things that I want to say.

The first thing is that truly a good and pious man ought to be bitterly and greatly ashamed that suffering ever moved him, when we see how a merchant, for the sake of earning a little money, of which, too, he cannot be sure, will travel so far overland on arduous tracks, up hill and down dale, across wildernesses and oceans, risking robbery and assault on his person and his goods, going in great want of food and drink and sleep and suffering other hardships, and yet he is glad and willing to forget all this for the sake of his small and uncertain profit. A knight in a battle risks possessions and body and life for the sake of a transient and very fleeting honor; and yet we think it such a great matter that we should suffer a little for God's sake, who is everlasting blessedness.

The second thing is that I expect that many stupid people will say that much that I have written in this book and elsewhere is not true. To that I reply with what Saint Augustine says in the first book of his *Confessions.* He says that God has already made every single thing, everything that is still to come for thousands and thousands of years, if this world should last so long, and everything that is past during many thousands of years he will make again today.[51] Is it my fault if people do not understand this? And he says in another place that a man's self-love is too blatant when he wants to blind other men so that his own blindness may be hidden.[52] It is enough for me that what I say and write be true in me and in God. If anyone sees a stick pushed down into the water, it seems to him that the stick is bent, although it is quite straight; and the reason for this is that water is cruder than air. But yet the stick is straight and not bent, both in itself and also in the eyes of anyone who looks at it only through the pure air.

Saint Augustine says: "Whoever without thought of any kind, or without any kind of bodily likeness and image, perceives within himself what no external vision has presented to him, he knows that this is true."[53] But the man who knows nothing of this will laugh at me and mock me, and I can only pity him. But people like this want to contemplate and taste eternal things and the works of God, and to stand in the light of eternity, and yet their hearts are still fluttering around in yesterday and tomorrow.

A pagan philosopher, Seneca, says: "We must speak about great and exalted matters with great and exalted understanding and with sublime souls."[54] And we shall be told that one ought not to talk about or write such teachings to the untaught. But to this I say that if we are not to teach people who have not been taught, no one will ever be taught, and no one will ever be able to teach or write. For that is why we teach the untaught, so that they may be changed from uninstructed into instructed. If there were nothing new, nothing would ever grow old. Our Lord says: "Those who are healthy do not need medicine" (Lk. 5:31). That is what the physician is there for, to make the sick healthy. But if there is someone who misunderstands what I say, what is that to the man who says truly that which is true? Saint John narrates his holy gospel for all believers and also for all unbelievers, so that they might believe, and yet he begins that gospel with the most exalted thoughts any man could utter here about God; and both what he says and what our Lord says are constantly misunderstood.

May our loving and merciful God, who is Truth, grant to me and to all those who will read this book that we may find the truth within ourselves and come to know it. Amen.

B.   The Book of "Benedictus": Of the Nobleman

Our Lord says in the gospel: "A nobleman went out into a far country to obtain for himself a kingdom and returned" (Lk. 19:12). Our Lord teaches us in these words how noble man has been created in his nature, and how divine that is which he can attain by grace, and also how man should attain to it. And in these words much of holy scripture is touched upon.

In the first place we should know what is very evident, that man has in himself a twofold nature, body and spirit. Therefore it is said in a treatise that whoever knows himself knows all created things, because all created things are either body or spirit.[1] That is why scripture says about what is human that there is in us one outward man and a second inner man (2 Co. 4:16).[2] To the outer man belongs everything that cleaves to the spirit, but that is captive to and mixed with the flesh and that works in common with and in every bodily member, such as the eye, the ear, the tongue, the hand and all others like them. And scripture calls all this the old man, the earthly man, the outer man, the hostile man, a subject man.[3]

The second man who is in us is the inner man, whom scripture calls a new man, a heavenly man, a young man, a friend and a noble man.[4] And this is what our Lord says, that "A nobleman went into a far country, and obtained a kingdom for himself and returned."

Now we should know that Saint Jerome says,[5] and the authorities generally say, that every man from the moment that he is a man has a good spirit, an angel, and an evil spirit, a devil. The good angel counsels and unceasingly inclines him to what is good, what is divine, what is virtue and heavenly and eternal. The evil spirit constantly counsels and inclines the man to what is temporal and transient, to what is vice and evil and devilish. The same evil spirit is always talking to the outer man, and through him he is always lying in wait for the inner man, just as the serpent spoke to Mother Eve and through her talked to the man Adam.[6] Adam is the inner man, the man in the soul,[7] who is the good tree that never ceases to produce good fruit of which our Lord also speaks (Mt. 7:17). This is also the field in which God has sowed his image and likeness (Gn. 1:26), and has sowed the good seed (Mt. 13:24), the root of all wisdom, all knowledge, all virtues, all goodness, the seed of the divine nature. The seed of the divine nature is the Son of God, God's Word (Lk. 8:11).

The outer man is the hostile, evil man, who has sowed and strewn weeds on the field (Mt. 13:25). Saint Paul says about him: "I find that in me which hinders me and fights against what God commands and what God counsels and what God has spoken and still speaks in the highest place, in the ground of my soul" (Rm. 7:23). And elsewhere he says and laments: "Alas, unhappy man that I am! Who will deliver me from this deadly flesh and body?" (Rm. 7:24). And he also says in another place that a man's spirit and his flesh are at constant war with one another. The flesh counsels vice and wickedness; the spirit counsels the love of God, joy, peace and every virtue (Ga. 5:17–23). Whoever follows and lives according to the spirit, obeying its counsels, belongs to everlasting life. The inner man is he of whom our Lord says that "A nobleman went out into a far country to obtain for himself a kingdom." That is the good tree of which our Lord says that it always produces good fruit and never bad, for that man wants goodness and is inclined toward goodness, goodness as it is moved of itself, untouched by anything particular.[8] The outer man is the bad tree that can never produce good fruit.

The pagan teachers Cicero and Seneca also speak about the nobility of the inner man, of the spirit, and of the inferiority of the outer man, of the flesh.[9] They teach that there is no rational soul without God; God's seed is in us. If it were tended by a good, wise and industrious laborer, it would then flourish all the better, and would grow up to God, whose seed it is, and its fruits would be like God's own nature. The seed of a pear tree grows into a pear tree, the seed of a nut tree grows to be a nut tree, the seed of God grows to be God. But if it happens that the good seed has a foolish and evil laborer, then weeds grow up and overgrow and smother the good seed, so that it cannot grow up to the light and to its full size. Yet Origen, a great teacher, says: "Because God himself has sowed and planted and given life to this seed, even though it may be overgrown and hidden, it will never be destroyed or extinguished completely; it will glow and shine, gleam and burn, and it will never cease to turn toward God."[10]

The first stage of the inner and new man, Saint Augustine says, is when a man lives according to the model of good and holy people, though he still staggers from chair to chair and leans against the walls and still feeds himself on milk.[11]

The second stage is when he not only observes external models, even of good people, but he runs and hastens to God's teaching and counsel and to divine wisdom, turns his back on humanity and his face to God, creeps out of his mother's lap and laughs up at his heavenly Father.

The third stage is when the man withdraws himself more and more from his mother, is further and further away from her lap, escapes from care, rejects his fears, so that even if he could without angering everyone do what is wicked and wrong, he would have no desire for this; for he is constrained by love and with a great zeal for God, until God places and leads him into joy and sweetness and blessedness, where everything that is unlike and alien to God becomes worthless for him.

The fourth stage is when he grows and becomes rooted more and more in love and in God, so that he is ready to accept all opposition, all temptation and downheartedness, and willingly and gladly to endure sorrow, welcoming it and rejoicing in it.

The fifth stage is when he lives in peace in all his being, reposing silently in the wealth and in the overflowing riches of supreme and ineffable wisdom.

The sixth stage is when the man becomes free of images and is transformed into the image of God's everlastingness and has attained to a complete and perfect oblivion of this transient life in time, and has been drawn and wholly changed into a divine image and has become God's child. Truly, there is no higher stage than this, and there is in it eternal repose and blessedness, for the end of the inner man and of the new man is eternal life.

The great master Origen describes a simile of this inner noble man, in whom God's seed and God's image have been impressed and sowed, of how the seed and the image of the divine nature and the divine being that is the Son of God will appear, and man will apprehend him, though it may be that he is sometimes hidden. He says that God's image, God's Son, is in the ground of the soul as a fount of living water (Jn. 4:14). But if anyone throws earth, which is earthly desire, on it, that impedes and conceals it, so that we do not perceive or grow aware of it; but the fount itself goes on living, and when they take the earth away that was thrown over it, then it appears, and we know that it is there. And he says that this truth is signified in the first book of Moses, where it is written that Abraham had excavated in his field living fountains, and that evil-doers had filled them up with earth; and afterward, when the earth was thrown out, then the fountains appeared, living yet.[12]

And there is still another simile: The sun never stops shining; but if there is a cloud or mist between us and the sun, we are not aware that it is shining. And if the eye is diseased in itself or is ailing or covered, it knows nothing of the sunshine. And sometimes I have made an evident comparison: If a master craftsman makes figures out of wood or stone, he does not introduce the figure into the wood, but he cuts away the fragments that had hidden and concealed the figure; he gives nothing to the wood, rather he takes away from it, cutting away its surface and removing its rough covering, and then what had lain hidden beneath shines out.[13] This is the treasure that lay hidden in the field, as our Lord says in the gospel (Mt. 13:44).

Saint Augustine says: "When all of man's soul mounts into eternity to God alone, the image of God appears and shines";[14] but if the soul is distracted toward external things, even to the outward exercise of virtues, then this image is wholly concealed. And that, according to Saint Paul's teaching, is why women have their heads covered and men's heads are bare (1 Co. 11:4). And therefore everything in the soul that declines receives a covering, a head veil, from that toward which it declines; but that in the soul which ascends is a bare image of God, a birth of God, uncovered and bare in the bare soul.[15] Of the nobleman, as an image of God, God's Son, the seed of the divine nature that is never destroyed in us, but only covered over, King David says in the Psalms: "Though a man may be afflicted by all kinds of vanity, sorrow and distress, still he remains in the image of God, and the image in him."[16] The true light shines in the darkness, but we are not aware of it (Jn. 1:5).

"Do not consider," says the Book of Love, "that I am brown, for I am beautiful and well-formed, but the sun has changed my color" (Sg. 1:4–5). The sun is the light of this world and signifies that the highest and the best that has been created and made covers and discolors in us the image of God. "Take away," Solomon says, "the rust from the silver, and there will gleam and shine out the most pure vessel" (Pr. 25:4), the image, God's Son, in the soul. And that is what our Lord means by these words when he says, that "A nobleman went out," because man must go out of every image and out of himself and out of everything, he must go far off indeed, and become quite unlike all this, truly, if he wishes to and shall receive the Son, and become son in the bosom and heart of the Father.

Every kind of medium is alien to God. "I am," God says, "the first and the last" (Rv. 22:13). There is no distinction in God's nature or in the Persons, according to the unity of the nature. The divine nature is one, and each Person is also one, and it is the same one the nature is.[17] Distinction between being and essence[18] is apprehended as one and is one. Only when it is no longer contained within itself does it accept and possess and bestow distinction. Therefore man finds God in the One, and he who will find God must be one. "One man,"[19] our Lord says, "went out." In distinction we do not find either one, or being, or God, or rest, or blessedness or satisfaction. Be one, so that you may find God! And truly, if you were indeed one, you would also remain one in distinction, and distinction would be one to you, and there would be nothing that could in any way hinder you. One always remains one, in a thousand times a thousand stones just as in four stones, and a thousand times a thousand is as truly a single number as is four.[20]

A heathen philosopher says that the One is born from the highest God.[21] Its property is that of being one with One. Whoever looks for it anywhere beneath God is deceiving himself. And the same philosopher says as his fourth point that this One has no more real friendship than with virgins or maidens. As Saint Paul says: "I have betrothed and espoused you as chaste virgins to the One" (2 Co. 11:12). And this is as men should be, for so our Lord says: "One man went out."

The true meaning of the Latin word for "man" is in one sense he who subjects himself wholly to God,[22] and surrenders everything that he is and that is his, and looks upward to God, not to what is his, which he knows to be behind him, below him, beside him. This is perfect and real humility, which has its name from "earth."[23] But of this I do not want to say more now. And when one says "man," the word also means something that is above nature, above time, and above everything that has inclination toward time or tastes of time, and I say the same about place and about corporeality. Nor, indeed, has man in one sense anything in common with anything, that is, he is not formed or made like this thing or that thing, and he knows nothing about nothing, so that one finds nowhere anything of this nothing in him, and this nothing is thus wholly taken away from him so that in him there is found only life, being, truth and goodness. Thus he who is such a man is "a nobleman," indeed neither less nor more.

And in what our Lord calls a "nobleman" there is another sense and teaching. We ought also to know that those who know God alone[24]

244

also know along with him created things; for knowledge is a light of the soul, and all men naturally long for knowledge,[25] for even the knowledge of bad things is good.[26] The authorities say that when one knows creatures in themselves, that is called an "evening knowledge," and then we see created things in images of various distinctions; but when one knows created things in God, that is called and is a "morning knowledge,"[27] and then we can see created things without distinction and transformed from every form and made unlike every likeness in the One that is God himself. This is also the nobleman of whom our Lord says: "One nobleman went out," noble because he is one and because he knows God and created things in one.

Now I want to discuss and touch upon another sense "the nobleman" may have. I say that as man, the soul, the spirit, contemplates God, he also knows and perceives himself perceiving; that is, he perceives that he is contemplating and perceiving God. Now some people have thought, and it seems quite plausible, that the flower and core of blessedness consists in knowledge, when the spirit knows that it knows God. For if I possessed all joy, and I did not know it, how could that help me and what joy would that be to me? Yet I say certainly that this is not so. It is only true that without that the soul would not be blessed; but blessedness does not consist in this, for the first thing in which blessedness consists is when the soul contemplates God directly.[28] From there, out of God's ground, it takes all its being and its life and makes everything that it is, and it knows nothing about knowing or about love or about anything at all.[29] It comes to rest completely and only in the being of God, and it knows nothing there except being and God. But when the soul knows and perceives that it contemplates, perceives and loves God, this is in the natural order a going out and a return to the starting point; for no one knows himself as being white except the man who is in fact white.[30] Therefore whoever knows himself as being white is building and erecting his knowledge upon being white, and he does not receive his knowledge without a medium or without previous knowledge of the color; but he derives his perception of it and his knowledge about it from things that are white, and so he forms his perception not purely from the color as such, but his perceiving and knowledge are formed from what is colored, that is, what is white, and he then recognizes himself as white. But "white" is far inferior to, more external than "being white."[31] The wall is something very different from the foundation on which the wall is built.[32]

The authorities say that there is one power with which the eye sees, and another with which it knows that it sees.[33] The first, that it sees, it takes wholly from the color, not from that which is colored. Therefore it is all the same whether what is colored is a stone or a piece of wood, a man or an angel; its essential property is only that it is something that has color.

So I say that the nobleman takes and draws all his being, life and blessedness from God, by God and in God, simply and solely, not from knowing God, contemplating or loving him or anything like that. Therefore our Lord says well from his whole heart that everlasting life is to know God alone as the one true God (Jn. 17:3), not to know that we know God.[34] How could a man know himself to be knowing God who does not know himself? For certainly that man does not know himself or other things in any way, but only God, God in whom he becomes blessed and is blessed, in the root and the ground of blessedness. But when the soul knows that it knows God, then it has knowledge of God and of itself.

And so there is one distinct power, as I have already said, by which man sees, and another power by which he knows and recognizes that he sees. It is true that the power here in us now by which we know and recognize that we see is nobler and higher than the power by which we see; for nature begins its work in what is feeblest, but God begins his work in what is most perfect. Nature forms the man from the child and the hen from the egg, but God makes the man before the child and the hen before the egg. Nature makes the wood first warm, then hot, and so it forms the being of the fire; but God first gives being to all created things, and thereafter gives in time, and yet gives outside time and outside everything that pertains to it.[35] And God gives the Holy Spirit before the gifts of the Holy Spirit.

So I say that there is no blessedness unless man perceives and knows well that he contemplates and perceives God, and yet God forbid that my blessedness should consist in that. If someone is satisfied with something else, let him keep it for himself, but I pity him. The heat of the fire and the being of the fire are quite different, utterly separated in nature from one another, and their only proximity is in terms of time and of place. God's contemplating and our contemplating are wholly separate and different from one another.

Therefore our Lord says very truly that "A nobleman went out into a far country to obtain for himself a kingdom and returned." For man must be one in himself, and must seek that in himself and in One, and he must receive it in One, that is to contemplate God alone; and

246

to return is to know and perceive that we perceive and know God. And everything I have said was foretold by the prophet Ezechiel, when he said that a mighty eagle with great wings, long-limbed, full of various feathers, came to the pure mountain and took the marrow or the kernel of the highest tree, tore off the tops of its branches, and carried it down (Ezk. 17:3–4). What our Lord calls a nobleman the prophet names a great eagle. Who is then nobler[36] than he who on one side is born of the highest and the best among created things, and on the other side from the inmost ground of the divine nature and its desert? "I," says our Lord through the prophet Osee, "will lead the noble soul out into a desert,[37] and there I will speak to her heart" (Os. 2:14), one with One, one from One, one in One, and in One, one everlastingly. Amen.

C. Counsels on Discernment

These are the conversations that the vicar of Thuringia, the prior of Erfurt, Friar Eckhart of the order of Preachers, held with those young men who, conversing, asked him about many things as they sat with each other at Collation.[1]

Counsel 1. First, about true obedience.

True and perfect obedience is a virtue above all virtues, and no work is so great that it can be achieved or done without this virtue; and however little and however humble a work may be, it is done to greater profit in true obedience, be it saying Mass, hearing it,[2] praying, contemplating or whatever else you can think of. But take as humble a work as you like, whatever it may be, true obedience makes it finer and better for you. Obedience always produces the best of everything in everything. Truly, obedience never perturbs, never fails, whatever one is doing, in anything that comes from true obedience, for obedience neglects nothing that is good. Obedience need never be troubled, for it lacks no good thing.

When a man in obedience goes out of himself and renounces what he possesses, God must necessarily respond by going in there, for if anyone does not want something for himself, God must want it as if for himself. If I deny my own will, putting it in the hands of my superior, and want nothing for myself, then God must want it for me, and if he fails me in this matter, he will be failing himself. So in all things, when I do not want something for myself, God wants it for me. Now pay good heed. What is it that God wants for me that I do not want for myself? When I empty myself of self, he must necessarily want everything for me that he wants for himself, neither more nor less, and in the same manner as he wants it for himself. And if he were not to do this, by that truth which is God, he would not be just, nor would he be the God that it is his nature to be.

In true obedience there should be no trace of "I want it so, or so," or "I want this or that," but there should be a pure going out from what is yours. And therefore in the best of all prayers that a man can pray, there should not be "Give me this virtue, or that way of life," or "Yes, Lord, give me yourself, or give me everlasting life," but "Lord, give me nothing but what you will, and do, Lord, whatever and however you will in every way." That is superior to the first way of praying as the heavens are above the earth. And when one has concluded that prayer, one has prayed well, for then one has in true obedience wholly entered into God. And just as true obedience should have no "I want it so," so also one should not hear from obedience "I do not want," because "I do not want" is a sure poison of all obedience. That is what Saint Augustine says: "God's faithful servant has no desire for people to say or to give to him, or what he likes to hear or see, for his first and his greatest aim is to hear what is most pleasing to God."[3]

Counsel 2. Of the most powerful prayer, and of the highest work of all.

The most powerful prayer, and almost the strongest of all to obtain everything, and the most honorable of all works, is that which proceeds from an empty spirit.[4] The emptier the spirit, the more is the prayer and the work mighty, worthy, profitable, praiseworthy and perfect. The empty spirit can do everything.

What is an empty spirit?

An empty spirit is one that is confused by nothing, attached to nothing, has not attached its best to any fixed way of acting, and has no concern whatever in anything for its own gain, for it is all sunk deep down into God's dearest will and has forsaken its own. A man can never perform any work, however humble, without it gaining strength and power from this.

We ought to pray so powerfully that we should like to put our every member and strength, our two eyes and ears, mouth, heart and all our senses to work; and we should not give up until we find that we wish to be one with him who is present to us and whom we entreat, namely God.

Counsel 3. Of people who have not denied themselves and are full of their own will.

People say: "O Lord, how much I wish that I stood as well with God, that I had as much devotion and peace in God as others have, I wish that it were so with me!" Or, "I should like to be poor," or else, "Things will never go right for me till I am in this place or that, or till I act one way or another. I must go and live in a strange land, or in a hermitage, or in a cloister."

In fact, this is all about yourself, and nothing else at all. This is just self-will, only you do not know it or it does not seem so to you. There is never any trouble that starts in you that does not come from your own will, whether people see this or not. We can think what we like, that a man ought to shun one thing or pursue another—places and people and ways of life and environments and undertakings—that is not the trouble, such ways of life or such matters are not what impedes you. It is what you are in these things that causes the trouble, because in them you do not govern yourself as you should.

Therefore, make a start with yourself, and abandon yourself. Truly, if you do not begin by getting away from yourself, wherever you run to, you will find obstacles and trouble wherever it may be. People who seek peace in external things—be it in places or ways of life or people or activities or solitude or poverty or degradation—however great such a thing may be or whatever it may be, still it is all nothing and gives no peace. People who seek in that way are doing it all wrong; the further they wander, the less will they find what they are seeking. They go around like someone who has lost his way; the further he goes, the more lost he is. Then what ought he to do? He ought to begin by forsaking himself, because then he has forsaken everything. Truly, if a man renounced a kingdom or the whole world but held on to himself, he would not have renounced anything. What is more, if a man renounces himself, whatever else he retains, riches or honors or whatever it may be, he has forsaken everything.

About what Saint Peter said: "See, Lord, we have forsaken everything" (Mt. 19:27)—and all that he had forsaken was just a net and his little boat—there is a saint who says: "If anyone willingly gives up something little, that is not all which he has given up, but he has forsaken everything which worldly men can gain and what they can even long for; for whoever has renounced his own will and himself has renounced everything, as truly as if he had possessed it as his own, to dispose of as he would."[5] For what you choose not to long for, you have wholly forsaken and renounced for the love of God. That is why our Lord said: "Blessed are the poor in spirit" (Mt. 5:3), that is, in the will. And no one ought to be in doubt about this; if there were a better form of living, our Lord would have said so, as he also said: "Whoever wishes to come after me, let him deny himself" (Mt. 16:24), as a beginning; everything depends on that. Take a look at yourself, and whenever you find yourself, deny yourself. That is the best of all.

Counsel 4. Of the profits of self-abandonment, which one should practice inwardly and outwardly.

You should know that there was never any man in this life who forsook himself so much that he could not still find more in himself to forsake. There are few people who see this to be true and stick by it. This is indeed a fair exchange and an honest deal: By as much as you go out in forsaking all things, by so much, neither less nor more, does God go in, with all that is his, as you entirely forsake everything that is yours. Undertake this, and let it cost you everything you can afford. There you will find true peace, and nowhere else.

People ought never to think too much about what they could do, but they ought to think about what they could be. If people and their way of life were only good, what they did might be a shining example. If you are just, then your works too are just. We ought not to think of building holiness upon action; we ought to build it upon a way of being, for it is not what we do that makes us holy, but we ought to make holy what we do. However holy the works may be, they do not, as works, make us at all holy; but, as we are holy and have being, to that extent we make all our works holy, be it eating, sleeping, keeping vigil or whatever it may be. It does not matter what men may do whose being is mean; nothing will come of it. Take good heed: We ought to do everything we can to be good; it does not matter so much what we may do, or what kinds of works ours may be. What matters is the ground on which the works are built.

Counsel 5. See what can make our being and our ground good.

A man's being and ground—from which his works derive their goodness—is good when his intention is wholly directed to God. Set all your care on that, that God become great within you, and that all your zeal and effort in everything you do and in everything you renounce be directed toward God. Truly, the more you do this in all your works, whatever they are, the better they are. Cleave to God, and he will endow you with all goodness. Seek God, and you will find God and every good thing as well. Yes, truly, with such an attitude you could tread upon a stone, and that would be a more godly thing for you to do than for you to receive the Body of our Lord, if then you were thinking more of yourself with less detachment. If we cling to God, then God and all virtues cling to us. And what once you were seeking now seeks you; what once you hunted after now hunts you, and what you once wished to shun now avoids you. Therefore to him who clings greatly to God, everything clings that is godly, and from him everything takes flight that is unlike God and alien to him.

Counsel 6. Of detachment and of the possession of God.

I was asked: "Since some people keep themselves much apart from others, and most of all like to be alone, and since it is in this and in being in church that they find peace, would that be the best thing to do?" Then I said: "No! and see why not!" If all is well with a man, then truly, wherever he may be, whomever he may be with, it is well with him. But if things are not right with him, then everywhere and with everybody it is all wrong with him. If it is well with him, truly he has God with him. But whoever really and truly has God, he has him everywhere, in the street and in company with everyone, just as much as in church or in solitary places or in his cell. But if a man really has God, and has only God, then no one can hinder him.

Why?

Because he has only God, and his intention is toward God alone, and all things become for him nothing but God. That man carries God in his every work and in every place, and it is God alone who performs all the man's works; for whoever causes the work, to him it belongs more properly and truly than it does to the one who performs it. Then let our intention be purely and only for God, and then truly he must perform all our works, and no person, no crowds, no places can hinder him in all his works. In the same way, no one can hinder this man, for he intends and seeks and takes delight in nothing but God, for God has become one with the man in all his intention. And so, just as no multiplicity can disturb God, nothing can disturb or fragment this man, for he is one in that One where all multiplicity is one and is one unmultiplicity.

A man should accept God in all things, and should accustom himself to having God present always in his disposition and his intention and his love. Take heed how you can have God as the object of your thoughts whether you are in church or in your cell. Preserve and carry with you that same disposition when you are in crowds and in uproar and in unlikeness. And, as I have said before, when one speaks of likeness, one does not mean that we should pay like attention to all works or all places or all people. That would be quite wrong, because praying is a better work than spinning, and the church is a better place than the street. But you ought in your works to have a like disposition and a like confidence and a like love for your God and a like seriousness. Believe me, if you were constant in this way, no one could come between you and the God who is present to you.

But a man in whom truly God is not but who must grasp God in this thing or in that from outside, and who seeks God in unlike ways, be it in works or people or places, such a man does not possess God. And it may easily be that something hinders such a man for he does not possess God, and he does not seek him alone, nor does he love and intend him alone; and therefore it is not only bad company that hinders him. Good company can also hinder him—not just the street, but the church too, not only evil words and deeds, but good words and deeds as well, for the hindrance is in him, because in him God has not become all things. Were that so, everything would be right and good for him, in every place and among all people, because he has God, and no one can take God away from him or hinder him in his work.

On what does this true possession of God depend, so that we may truly have him?

This true possession of God depends on the disposition, and on an inward directing of the reason and intention toward God, not on a constant contemplation in an unchanging manner, for it would be impossible to nature to preserve such an intention, and very laborious, and not the best thing either. A man ought not to have a God who is just a product of his thought, nor should he be satisfied with that, because if the thought vanished, God too would vanish. But one ought to have a God who is present, a God who is far above the notions of men and of all created things. That God does not vanish, if a man does not wilfully turn away from him.

The man who has God essentially present to him grasps God divinely, and to him God shines in all things; for everything tastes to him of God, and God forms himself for the man out of all things. God always shines out in him, in him there is a detachment and a turning away, and a forming of his God whom he loves and who is present to him. It is like a man consumed with a real and burning thirst, who may well not drink and may turn his mind to other things. But whatever he may do, in whatever company he may be, whatever he may be intending or thinking of or working at, still the idea of drinking does not leave him, so long as he is thirsty. The more his thirst grows, the more the idea of drinking grows and intrudes and possesses him and will not leave him. Or if a man loves something ardently and with all his heart, so that nothing else has savor for him or touches his heart but that, and that and nothing but that is his whole object: Truly, wherever he is, whomever he is with, whatever he may undertake, whatever he does, what he so loves never passes from his mind, and he finds the image of what he loves in everything, and it is the more present to him the more his love grows and grows. He does not seek rest, because no unrest hinders him.

Such a man finds far greater merit with God because he grasps everything as divine and as greater than things in themselves are. Truly, to this belong zeal and love and a clear apprehension of his own inwardness, and a lively, true, prudent and real knowledge of what his disposition is concerned with amid things and persons. A man cannot learn this by running away, by shunning things and shutting himself up in an external solitude; but he must practice a solitude of the spirit, wherever or with whomever he is. He must learn to break through things and to grasp his God in them and to form him in himself powerfully in an essential manner. This is like someone who wants to learn to write. If he is to acquire the art, he must certainly practice it hard and long, however disagreeable and difficult this may be for him and however impossible it may seem. If he will practice it industriously and assiduously, he learns it and masters the art. To begin with, he must indeed memorize each single letter and get it firmly into his mind. Then, when he has the art, he will not need to think about and remember the letters' appearance; he can write effortlessly and easily—and it will be the same if he wants to play the fiddle or to learn any other skill. It will always be enough for him to make up his mind to do the hard work the art demands; and even if he is not thinking about it all the time, still, whatever he may be thinking when he does perform it, this will be from the art he has learned.

So a man must be penetrated with the divine presence, and be shaped through and through with the shape of the God he loves, and be present in him, so that God's presence may shine out to him without any effort. What is more, in all things let him acquire nakedness, and let him always remain free of things. But at the beginning there must be attentiveness and a careful formation within himself, like a schoolboy setting himself to learn.

Counsel 7. How a man should perform his work in the most reasonable way.

One often finds people who are not impeded by the things that are around them—and this is easy to attain if one wishes—nor do they have any constant thought about them. For if the heart is full of God, created things can have and find no place in it. But, what is more, this alone should not satisfy us. We ought to turn everything into great profit, whatever it may be, wherever we may be, whatever we see or hear, however strange or unlikely it may be. Then for the first time all is well with us and not until then, and one will never come to an end in this. One can always go on increasing in this, gaining more and more from it in true growth.

And in all his activities and under all circumstances a man should take care to use his reason, and in everything he should have a reasonable consciousness of himself and of his inwardness, and find God in all things, in the highest degree that is possible. For a man ought to be as our Lord said: "You should be like men who are always watching and waiting for their master" (Lk. 12:36). Truly, people who wait stay awake and look around them for whence he for whom they are waiting may be coming; and they are on the lookout for him in whatever may come, however unknown it may be to them, for perhaps he might somehow be in it. So we should have in all things a knowing perception of our master. We must show zeal in this, and it must cost us everything we are capable of in mind and body, and so it will be well with us, and we shall find God in everything alike, and find God always alike in all things.

Certainly, one work differs from another; but whoever undertakes all his works in the same frame of mind, then, truly, all that man's works are the same. Indeed, for the man for whom God shines forth as directly in worldly things as he does in divine things and to whom God would be so present, for such a man things would be well. Not indeed that the man himself would be doing worldly things, unlike to God; rather, whatever external matters he chanced to see and hear, he would refer it all back to God. Only he to whom God is present in everything and who employs his reason in the highest degree and has enjoyment in it knows anything of true peace and has a real kingdom of heaven.

For if things are to go well with a man, one of two things must always happen to him. Either he must find and learn to possess God in works, or he must abandon all works. But since a man cannot in this life be without works, which are proper to humans and are of so many kinds, therefore he must learn to possess his God in all things and to remain unimpeded, whatever he may be doing, wherever he may be. And therefore if a man who is beginning must do something with other people, he ought first to make a powerful petition to God for his help, and put him immovably in his heart and unite all his intentions, thoughts, will and power to God, so that nothing else than God can take shape in that man.

Counsel 8. Of constant zeal for the highest growth.

A man should never be so satisfied with what he does or accomplish it in such a way that he becomes so independent or overconfident in his works that his reason becomes idle or lulled to sleep. He ought always to lift himself up by the two powers of reason and will, and in this to grasp at what is best of all for him in the highest degree, and outwardly and inwardly to guard prudently against everything that could harm him. So in all things he will lack nothing, but he will grow constantly and mightily.

Counsel 9. How the inclination to sin always helps a man.

You must know that when vices attack us, this is never for the just man without great profit and utility. See carefully. There are two men, and one of them may be so disposed that shortcomings never or seldom touch him; but it is the other man's nature that they do. The outward presence of things so stirs the outer man in him that he is easily moved to anger or to vain ambition or it may be to bodily lusts, whatever the circumstance may be. But in his highest powers he always stands firm and unmoved, never willing to commit sin, not anger or any other, and he puts up great resistance against sin, because the sin is perhaps a weakness of his nature, as many men are naturally wrathful or proud or whatever it may be, and yet he does not want to sin. This man is far more to be praised, and his reward is much greater and his virtue is much more excellent than that of the first man, for the perfection of virtue comes from fighting, as Saint Paul says: "Virtue is made perfect in infirmity" (2 Co. 12:9).

The inclination to sin is not sin, but to want to sin is sin, to want to be angry is sin. Indeed, if a man thought rightly, and if he had the power to choose, he would not want to choose that his inclination to sin should die in him, because without it he would lack decision in everything and in all that he did he would be without care in these matters, and, too, he would lose the honor of the battle and of the victory and of the reward; for it is the assault and the force of vice that bring virtue and the reward for striving. It is this inclination that makes a man ever more zealous to exercise himself valiantly in virtue and impels him mightily toward virtue, and it is a stern whip driving a man on to caution and virtue. For the weaker a man finds himself, the more should he protect himself with strength and victory. For virtue and vice too are a question of the will.

Counsel 10. How the will can do all things, and how all virtues are a question of the will, if only it is just.

A man should not be too afraid of anything, so long as he sees that he has good will, nor should he be depressed if he cannot accomplish his will in his deeds; but he should not consider himself deprived of virtue if he finds in himself a will that is just and good, because the virtues and everything that is good are a question of good will. You can want for nothing if you have a true and just will, not love or humility or any virtue. But what you desire with all your might and all your will, that you have, and God and all created things cannot take it away from you, if only your will is wholly just and godly and is directed toward the present. So do not say: "One day I should like . . . ," because that would be for the future, but "I want it to be so now." Pay good attention: If something is more than a thousand miles away and I want to have it, I really have it—more than what is lying in my lap and what I do not want.

What is good has not less power to draw toward good than what is evil has to draw toward evil. Pay heed: Though I might never perform any evil deed, if I have the will to evil, I have the sin, as if I had performed the deeds; and I could commit as great sins only in my will as if I had murdered the whole human race, even if I had actually never done anything of the kind. So why should the same thing not be true of a good will? Truly, and far more so!

Indeed, with my will I can do everything. I can take on myself every man's toil, I can feed every poor man, I can do every man's work and anything else that you could think of. If you are not lacking in will but only in power, in truth in God's sight you have done it all, and no one can take it away from you, or stop you for a moment from doing it; for wanting to do something as soon as I can and having done it are the same in the sight of God. What is more, if I wanted to have as great a will as the whole world has, and if my longing for that is great and complete, then indeed I have it; for what I want to have, I have. And, too, if I truly wanted to have as much love as all men have ever gained, or to praise God as much, or anything else you can think of, then, indeed, you have it all, if only your will is complete.

Now you might ask, "When is the will a just will?"

The will is complete and just when it is without any self-seeking, and when it has forsaken itself, and has been formed and shaped into God's will. And the more this is so with a man, the more is his will just and true. And in that will you can accomplish everything, be it love or whatever you want.

Now you ask: "How could I have this love, whilst I do not feel it and am not aware of it, and yet I see many people who accomplish great deeds, and I see in them great devotion and marvelous qualities I do not have?"

Here you ought to observe two properties that love possesses; one is the being of love, the other is the deeds or the manifestation of love. The place where love has its being is only in the will; the man who has more will, he also has more love. But no one knows about anyone else, whether he has more of it; that lies hidden in the soul, so long as God lies hidden in the soul's ground. This love lies wholly in the will; whoever has more will, he also has more love.

Yet there is something else, which is a manifestation and a deed of love. Often this appears plainly as inwardness and devotion and jubilation; and yet this is not always the best that could be. For it may be that it does not come from love, but perhaps it only comes from nature that a man experiences such savor and sweetness. It may be sent down from heaven, or it may be borne in from the senses. And those who have more of this are not always the best men; for even if such a gift be truly from God, our Lord often gives it to such people to entice and draw them on, and also to make them, through it, very withdrawn from others. Yet these same people, when later they have obtained more love, may then well not experience so much emotion and feeling, and from that it is well seen that they have love, if they cleave faithfully and steadily to God without such a prop.

And even if this really be love, it still is not the very best love. That can be seen when sometimes a man must abandon this kind of jubilation because of a better kind of love, and sometimes to perform a work of love, whether spiritual or bodily, when someone has need of him. I have said before: If a man were in an ecstasy, as Saint Paul was, and knew that some sick man needed him to give him a bit of soup, I should think it far better if you would abandon your ecstasy out of love and show greater love in caring for the other in his need.[6]

Nor should a man think that in doing so he will be deprived of grace, for whatever he willingly abandons out of love will become a much greater reward for him, as Christ said: "Whoever has given up something for love of me, he will receive in return a hundred times as much" (Mt. 19:29). Yes, truly, when a man forsakes something and denies it to himself for the love of God, yes, even if it be that a man has a great desire to experience such consolations and inwardness and does everything he can to obtain this and God does not give it to him, and he willingly relinquishes and forgoes this for God's love, then such a man will find in God what he seeks, just as if he had possessed as his own all the riches that ever were and had willingly relinquished, abandoned and denied them for God's sake. He will receive a hundred times as much. For whatever a man would gladly have that he relinquishes and goes without for God's love, be it something material or spiritual, he will find all of it in God, just as if he had possessed it and had willingly abandoned it; for a man ought gladly be robbed of all that he has for the love of God, and out of love he should wholly abandon and deny love's consolations.

That a man ought sometimes out of love to forgo such sensations, Saint Paul in his love admonishes us when he says: "I have wished that I might be separated from Christ for the love of my brothers" (Rm. 9:3). By that he means not the pure love of God,[7] for from that he did not wish to be separated for one instant, not for the sake of everything that might be in heaven and on earth. He means the consolations of love.

But you must know that God's friends are never without consolation, for whatever God wills is for them the greatest consolation of all, whether it be consolation or desolation.

Counsel 11. What a man should do when God has hidden himself and he seeks for him in vain.

You ought also to know that a man with good will can never lose God. Rather, it sometimes seems to his feelings that he loses him, and often he thinks that God has gone far away. What ought you to do then? Just what you did when you felt the greatest consolation; learn to do the same when you are in the greatest sorrow, and under all circumstances behave as you did then. There is no advice so good as to find God where one has left him; so do now, when you cannot find him, as you were doing when you had him; and in that way you will find him. But a good will never loses or seeks in vain for God. Many people say: "We have a good will," but they do not have God's will. They want to have their will and they want to teach our Lord that he should be doing this and that. That is not a good will. We ought to seek from God what is his very dearest will.

This is what God looks for in all things, that we surrender our will. When Saint Paul had done a lot of talking to our Lord, and our Lord had reasoned much with him, that produced nothing, until he surrendered his will, and said: "Lord, what do you want me to do?" (Ac. 9:6). Then our Lord showed him[8] clearly what he ought to do. So too, when the angel appeared to our Lady, nothing either she or he had to say would ever have made her the Mother of God, but as soon as she gave up her own will, at that moment she became a true mother of the everlasting Word and she conceived God immediately; he became her Son by nature. Nor can anything make a true man except giving up his will. Truly, without giving up our own will in all things, we never accomplish anything in God's sight. But if it were to progress so far that we gave up the whole of our will and had the courage to renounce everything, external and internal, for the love of God, then we would have accomplished all things, and not until then.

We find few people, whether they know it or not, who would not like this to be so for them: to experience great things, to have this way of living and this treasure. But all this is nothing in them except self-will. You ought to surrender yourself wholly to God in all things, and then do not trouble yourself about what he may do with his own. There are thousands of people, dead and in heaven, who never truly and perfectly forsook their own wills. Only a perfect and true will could make one enter perfectly into God's will and be without will of one's own; and whoever has more of this, he is more fully and more truly established in God. Yes, one Hail Mary said when a man has abandoned himself is more profitable than to read the Psalms a thousand times over without that. With that, one pace forward would be better than to walk across the sea without it.

The man who in this way had wholly gone out of himself with everything that he possessed would indeed be established wholly in God, so that if anyone wanted to move him, he would first have to move God. For he is wholly in God, and God is around him as my cap is round my head. If anyone wanted to seize hold of me, first he would have to seize hold of my coat. In the same way, if I want to drink, the drink must first pass over my tongue; in this way the drink gives its flavor. If the tongue is coated with bitterness, then truly, however sweet the wine itself may be, it must become bitter through the means by which it comes to me. In truth, if a man had completely abandoned everything that is his, he would be so surrounded by God that no created thing could move him, unless it had first moved God. Whatever would reach him would first have to reach him by means of God. So it will find its savor from God, and will become godlike. However great a sorrow may be, if it comes by means of God, then God has suffered it first. Yes, by that Truth which is God, however little a sorrow may be that comes upon a man, as he places it in God, be it some displeasure or contradiction, it moves God immeasurably more than the man, and if it is grievous for the man it is more so for God. But God suffers it for the sake of some good thing that he has provided in it for you, and if you will suffer the sorrow that God suffers and that comes to you through him, it will easily become godlike—contempt, it may be, just as respect; bitterness just as sweetness; the greatest darkness just as the brightest light. It takes all its savor from God, and it becomes godlike, for it forms itself wholly in his image, whatever comes to this man, for this is all his intention and nothing else has savor for him; and in this he accepts God in all bitterness, just as in the greatest sweetness.

The light shines in darkness, and there man perceives it. What is the use to people of teaching or light, unless they use it? If they are in darkness or sorrow, they ought to see the light.

Yes, the more that we possess ourselves, the less do we possess.[9] The man who has gone out of what is his own could never fail to find God in anything he did. But if it happened that a man did or said something amiss, or engaged in matters that were wrong, then God, since he was in the undertaking at the beginning, must of necessity take this harm upon him too; but you must under no circumstances abandon your undertaking because of this. We find an example of this in Saint Bernard and in many other saints. One can never in this life be wholly free from such mishaps. But because some weeds happen among the corn, one should not for that reason throw away the good corn. Indeed, if it were well with a man and he knew himself well with God, all such sorrows and mishaps would turn into his great profit. For to good men all things come to good, as Saint Paul says (Rm. 8:28); and, as Saint Augustine says, "Yes, even sins."[10]

Counsel 12. Of sins and of how we should act when we find ourselves in sin.

Indeed, to have committed sins is not sin, if we have sorrow for them. A man should never wish to commit sin, not for anything that could be in time or in eternity, not mortal sins, not venial, not any sins at all. A man who knew himself well with God ought always to see that our faithful and loving God has brought man out of a sinful life into a life that is divine, and out of him who was his enemy God has made a friend, and that is more than to create a new earth. This would be one of the greatest reasons for a man to become wholly established in God; and it would be astonishing how greatly it would kindle the man to a stronger and greater love, so that he would wholly abandon what is his own.

Yes, that man would indeed be established in God's will who would not wish that the sin into which he had fallen had never been committed;[11] not because it was against God, but since, through that, you are obliged to greater love, and, through that, brought low and humbled. He should only wish that he had not acted against God. But you should indeed trust God, that he would not have inflicted this on you, had he not wished to produce from it what is best for you. But when a man with all his resolution rises up from his sins and turns wholly away from them, our faithful God then acts as if he had never fallen into sin. For all his sins, God will not allow him for one moment to suffer. Were they as many as all men have ever committed, God will never allow him to suffer for this. With this man God can use all the simple tenderness that he has ever shown toward created beings. If he now finds the man ready to be different, he will have no regard for what he used to be. God is a God of the present. He takes and receives you as he finds you—not what you have been, but what you are now. All the harms and the insults that could come upon God for all sins he is gladly willing to suffer and to have suffered for many years so that a man thereafter may come to a greater knowledge of his love and so that man's love and gratitude may be so much greater and his zeal may be so much more ardent, which properly and frequently follows after our sins.

Therefore God gladly suffers the harm of sins, and has often suffered it, and most often he has permitted it to happen to men for whom he has provided that he would draw them to great things. Notice well: Who was dearer or closer to our Lord than were the apostles? But there was no one of them who did not fall into mortal sin; they had all been mortal sinners. In the Old Law and the New he often showed this through men who afterward were by far the dearest to him. And even now one seldom finds that people attain to anything good unless first they have gone somewhat astray. Our Lord's intention in this is that we should recognize his great mercifulness; and through it he wishes to exhort us to a greater and truer humility and devotion. For when repentance is renewed, so too love should be greatly increased and renewed.

Counsel 13. Of a twofold repentance.

Repentance is of two kinds; one is of time and of the senses, the other is divine and supernatural. Repentance in time always declines into greater sorrow and plunges a man into lamentation, as if he must now despair; and there repentance remains in its sorrow, and can make no progress; nothing comes of it.

But divine repentance is quite different. As soon as a man has achieved self-loathing, at once he lifts himself up to God, and establishes himself in an eternal turning away from all sin in an immovable will; and there he lifts himself up in great confidence to God, and achieves a great security. And from this there comes a spiritual joy that lifts the soul up out of all sorrow and lamentation, and makes it secure in God. For the weaker a man finds himself and the more have been his misdeeds, the more cause he has to bind himself to God with an undivided love in which there is no sin or weakness. Therefore the best path up which a man can proceed when he wants to go to God in all devotion, is for him to be sinless, made strong by a godly repentance.

And the heavier a man's sins are as he weighs them, the readier is God to forgive them, and to come to the soul, and to drive the sins out. Every man does his utmost to get rid of what most irks him. And the greater and the more the sins are, still immeasurably more is God glad and ready to forgive them, because they are irksome to him. And then, as godly repentance lifts itself up to God, sins vanish into God's abyss, faster than it takes me to shut my eyes, and so they become utterly nothing, as if they had never happened, if repentance is complete.

Counsel 14. Of true confidence and of hope.

One ought to test whether love be true and perfect by asking if one has great hope and confidence in God, for there is nothing by which one can better see whether one's love is total than by trust. For if one man loves another greatly and completely, that causes him to have trust; for everything that we dare trust to be in God we find in him truly and a thousand times more. And so, since no man could ever love God too much, so also no man could ever trust him too much. Nothing that a man can do is so fitting as to have great trust in God. God never ceased to achieve great things through those who ever gained great confidence in him. He has truly shown to all men that this trusting comes from love, for love not only has trust, it also has true knowledge and unshakeable certainty.

MEISTER ECKHART

Counsel 15. Of a twofold certainty of everlasting life.

In this life we have a twofold knowledge of everlasting life. One knowledge is when God himself imparts it to a man or sends it to him through an angel or shows it through a special illumination; this happens seldom and to few people.

The second knowledge, which is incomparably better and more profitable and happens often to all who are perfect in their love, is when a man, through the love and the intimacy that exist between his God and him, trusts in him so fully and is so certain of him that he cannot doubt. What makes him so certain is that he loves God in all his creatures without any distinction. And even if all God's creatures were to deny him and abjure him, yes, if God himself were to deny him, he would not mistrust; for love cannot mistrust, love has trust in everything that is good. There is no need for one to say anything to the lover and to his beloved, for once the lover knows that his beloved loves him, he knows at once everything that is for his good and makes for his happiness.[12] For however great your love for him may be, of this you are sure: His love for you is greater beyond measure, and his trust in you is incomparably more. For he is Trust himself; one should be sure of this with him, and they are all sure of it who love him.

This certainty is by far greater, more complete and true than is the first, and it cannot deceive. To be told it in words could deceive, and could easily be a false light.[13] But this certainty one receives in all the powers of the soul, and it cannot deceive those who truly love God; they doubt as little as a man doubts in God, because love drives out all fear. "Love has no fear," as Saint Paul says,[14] and as it is also written: "Love covers a multitude of sins" (1 P. 4:8). For when sins occur, there cannot be complete trust or love, for love completely covers sin over; love knows nothing about sin. It is not as if a man had not sinned, but that love wholly destroys and drives out sin, as if it had never been. For all God's works are wholly perfect and superabundant, so that whomever he forgives, he forgives wholly and completely, and great sinners more gladly than the lesser ones, and this makes a perfect trust. I estimate this to be far and incomparably better than the first knowledge; and it brings a greater reward and is more true, for it is not hindered by sin or by anything else. For if God finds a man to be in such a state of love, he judges him just as lovingly, whether or not the man may have done something greatly amiss. But the man who receives greater forgiveness should love more, as Christ our Lord said: "To whom more is forgiven, let him love more" (Lk. 7:47).

Counsel 16. Of true penitence and a blessed life.

Many people think that they ought to perform great exterior works, such as fasting, going barefoot and such things as that, which are called "penitence." But the true and very best of all penitence, which greatly improves men and raises them to the highest, is for a man to have a great and perfect aversion from everything in himself and in all creatures that is not wholly God and godly, and for him to have a great and perfect and complete conversion to his dear God in a love so unshakeable that his devotion to God and his longing for him be great. The more you have of this in any work, the more you are justified; and as this grows and grows, so you have more and more true penitence, and this will the more blot out sin and even sin's punishment. Yes, you could in a short time with great resolution turn away from all sin with a true disgust for it, and with equal resolution betake yourself to God, so that even if you had committed all the sins that have ever been done since the days of Adam and will ever be done, all that would be completely forgiven you and its punishment remitted, so that if you were to die this moment you would come into the presence of God.

This is true penitence, and it comes, particularly and most perfectly, from what our Lord Jesus Christ suffered so fruitfully in his perfect penitence. The more that a man forms himself in that, the more do all sins and the pains of sin fall away from him. And it ought to be a man's habit at all times and in all his works to form himself in the life and the works of our Lord Jesus Christ, in everything he does and refrains from and suffers and experiences. And let him think constantly of him as our Lord thought of us.

This penitence is a complete lifting up of the mind away from all things into God, and whatever the works may be in which you have found and still find that you can most perfectly achieve this, do them with no constraint; and if you are impeded in this by any exterior works, whether it be fasting, keeping vigil, reading or whatever else, give it up and do not be afraid that in this you may be forgoing any of your penitence, because God has no regard for what your works are, but for what your love and devotion and intention in the works are.

Our works do not greatly matter to him, but only our intention in all our works, and that we love him alone in all things. For the man is far too greedy who is not satisfied with God.[15] All your works will be rewarded in your God's knowledge of them, and that in them he was your intention; and always be content with that. And the more that your intention is directed wholly and simply toward him, the more truly will all your works atone for all your sins.

And you must also reflect that God was the general redeemer of all the world, and I owe him far more gratitude for that than if he had redeemed me alone. So too ought you to be a general redeemer of everything in you that you have spoiled with your sins; and, doing that, put your whole confidence in him, for with your sins you have spoiled everything there is in you: Your heart, your intellect, your body, your soul, your powers, everything about you and in you, all of it is sick and spoiled. So take refuge in him in whom there is nothing lacking, but everything that is good, so that he may be the general redeemer of all your shortcomings both internal and external.

Counsel 17. How a man should preserve himself in peace, if he does not find himself severely tried as Christ and many saints were; and how he ought to follow God.

People may become anxious and distressed because the lives of our Lord Jesus Christ and of the saints were so harsh and laborious, and a man may be able to perform little like this and may not feel himself forced to do so. Therefore, when people find themselves unequal to this, they think that they are far away from God, and that they cannot follow him. No one ought to think this. No man ought ever under any circumstances to think himself far away from God, not because of his sins or his weakness or anything else. If it should ever be that your great sins drive you so far off that you cannot think of yourself as being close to God, still think of him as being close to you. For a man does himself great harm in considering that God is far away from him; wherever a man may go, far or near, God never goes far off. He is always close at hand, and even if he cannot remain under your roof, still he goes no further away than outside the door, where he stands.[16]

And it is the same with the labor of following God. Take heed of how you ought to follow him. You ought to know and to have taken heed of what it is that God is requiring most of you; for not everyone is called to come along the same way to God, as Saint Paul says.[17] So if you find that your shortest way does not consist of many external works and great labors or mortifications—which, to look at things simply, are not so very important unless a man is especially called to them by God and has the strength to perform them all without damage to his spiritual life—and if you find that you are not like this, keep quite calm and do not let yourself be too concerned about it.

But you may say: "If this is not so important, why have so many of our forebears, so many saints practiced it?"

But consider: Our Lord gave them this manner of life,[18] and he also gave them the strength to act like that, so that they could follow this way of life, and what they did was very pleasing to him, and it was in so doing that they were to achieve their very best. But God has not made man's salvation depend on any such particular way of life. What is peculiar to one way of life is not found in another; but it is God who has endowed all holy practices with the power of fulfillment, and it is denied to no good way of life. For one good thing is not in opposition to another. And from this people ought to learn that they are doing wrong if they see or hear that some good man is not following their way of life and they decide that what he is doing is useless. If they do not like what he does, immediately they shut their eyes to what is good in what he does and his intention in doing it. That is not right. People should have regard to the true devotion that is to be found in men's practices, and they should not despise what anyone does. It is not possible for everyone to live alike, for all men to follow one single way of life or for one man to adopt what everyone else or what some one other man may be doing.

So let every man keep to his own pious practices, let him mix in it any other practice, accepting into what he does everything that is good and all practices. To change from one to another makes for instability in one's piety and in one's intention. What one such practice could give you, you could also obtain from another, if they are both good and praiseworthy and have only God as their intention; everyone cannot follow one single way. And it is the same with imitating the mortifications of such saints. You may well admire and be pleased by practices you still are not required to imitate.

But now you may say: "Our Lord Jesus Christ always practiced what was the very best, and it is always he whom we should imitate."

That is very true. One ought indeed to imitate our Lord, but still not in everything he did. Our Lord, we are told, fasted for forty days. But no one ought to undertake to imitate this. Many of his works

Christ performed with the intention that we should imitate him spiritually, not physically. And so we ought to do our best to be able to imitate him with our reason, for he values our love more than our works. Each of us ought in our own ways to imitate him.

"And how?"

Take good heed: in everything.

"How, and in what way?"

As I have often said: "I esteem a work of the reason far higher than a work of the body."

"And how?"

Christ fasted for forty days. Imitate him by considering what you are sure that you are most inclined and ready to do; apply yourself to this and observe yourself closely. It is often more profitable for you to refrain from these things than to go without any food. Similarly, it is sometimes harder for you to suppress one word than to keep completely silent. So it is harder at times for a man to endure one little word of contempt, which really is insignificant, when it would be easy for him to suffer a heavy blow to which he had steeled himself, and it is much harder for him to be alone in a crowd than in the desert, and it is often harder for him to abandon some little thing than a big one, harder for him to carry out a trifling enterprise than one that people would think much more important. Thus a man in his weakness can very well imitate our Lord, and he need never consider himself far off from him.

*Counsel 18. The way for a man to make proper use of the delicate
food and fine clothing and pleasant companions to which his
natural disposition inclines him.*

You must not concern yourself about food or clothing, by worrying if they seem too good for you, but train the ground of your being and your disposition to be far above all this; and nothing ought to move your disposition to delight or to love except God alone. It should be far above everything else.

Why?

Because a man's interior life would indeed be deficient if he needed outer garments to guide it for him; it is the interior that should guide the exterior, so far as that is in your power. But if something different comes your way, in the ground of your being you can be content that you are so disposed that even if another time something else should be given to you, you would receive that just as willingly and gladly.[19] And it is the same with food and friends and relatives and everything else that God may give or take away.

And that is why I think it better than everything that a man should abandon himself wholly to God, whatever it may be his will to impose on him, be it contempt or heavy labors or any other kind of suffering, so that he accepts it joyfully and thankfully, and lets himself be guided by God rather than trying to arrange things for himself. So if you will learn gladly from God and follow him, things will be all right for you. With such a disposition one can well accept honors and ease. But if hardships and disgrace come to a man, he must bear it and be glad to bear it. And so people can with every justification and right judgment eat well, if in the same spirit they would be prepared to fast.

And this is probably the reason why God spares his friends many great sorrows; for his immeasurable faithfulness to them could not otherwise suffer it to be so, because so great and so many profits are contained in suffering, and he does not wish, nor would it be fitting, to let them lack such benefits. But he is content when their will is good and just. Were it not so, he would not permit them to escape any suffering because of the innumerable benefits suffering brings.

Therefore, so long as God is well content, be at peace; but if it pleases him that something different should happen with you, still be at peace. For inwardly a man ought to entrust himself so completely to God with his whole will that he is not greatly concerned about his way of life or the works he performs. And you ought especially to avoid anything extraordinary, whether in clothing or food or speech— such as indulging in fine talk—or extraordinary gestures,[20] because this leads to nothing. But still you must know that not everything extraordinary is forbidden to you. There are many extraordinary things one has to do at certain times and among certain people, because if a man is extraordinary he must act in various extraordinary ways on many occasions.

A man ought to have formed his inward disposition in our Lord Jesus Christ in all respects, so that people can see in him a reflection of all our Lord's works and of his divine image; and within himself a man ought, so far as he can, to carry out a perfect imitation of all these works. You must work, and he ought to receive. Perform your works with all your devotion and all your intention; let this always be your disposition, and may you in all your works form yourself into him.

Counsel 19. Why God often permits good men, who are genuinely good, to be often hindered in their good works.

Our faithful God often permits his friends to weaken so that any support on which they might depend or rely should be taken from them. For to a man who loves God it would be a great joy if he could perform many great deeds, perhaps keeping vigil or fasting or other exercises, and such remarkable, great and difficult matters. To be able to do this is a great joy and a prop and gives hope, and it lends people support and help and confidence in their undertakings. But our Lord's will is to take this away from them, because he wants to be their only support and confidence. And his only reason for doing this is simply his goodness and mercy. God is not moved to perform any deed by anything else than his own goodness. Our deeds do not move him to give us anything or to do anything for us. Our Lord wants his friends to forget such false notions, and this is why he takes this support away from them so that he may be their only support. For he wants to endow them richly, and this only out of his generous goodness; and he should be their support and comfort, and they should see and consider themselves as a mere nothing among all God's great gifts. For the more man's spirit, naked and empty, depends upon God and is preserved by him, the deeper is the man established in God, and the more receptive is he to God's finest gifts. For man should build upon God alone.

Counsel 20. Of the Body of our Lord: how one should often receive it, and with what manner and devotion.

Whoever would gladly receive the Body of our Lord ought not to wait until he discovers certain emotions or sensations in himself, or until his inwardness and devotion are great; but he ought to make sure that he has the proper will and intention. You should not attach such importance to what you feel; rather, consider important what you love and what you intend.

The man who freely wants and is able to go to our Lord should as the first condition have a conscience free from every reproach of sin. The second condition is that his will be turned to God, that he intends nothing and delights in nothing except in God and what is wholly godly, and that everything should displease him that is unlike God. And it is in this way too that a man should test how far away from God or

270

how close to him he may be, and this will tell him how near or far away from God he is.[21] The third condition is that his love for the blessed sacrament and for our Lord ought to grow in him more and more, and that his reverent awe for it should not decrease because of his frequent receiving; because often what is life for one man is death for another. Therefore you should observe whether your love for God grows and your reverence does not decrease; and then the oftener that you go to the sacrament, the better by far will you be, and the better and more profitable by far will it be for you. So do not let people talk and preach you away from your God; the oftener, the better, and the dearer to God. For it is our Lord's delight to dwell in man and with him.

Now you may say: "Alas, sir, I know how empty and cold and inert I am, and that is why I dare not go to our Lord!"

But what I say is, all the more reason for you to go to your God; for it is in him that you will be warmed and kindled, and in him you will be made holy, to him alone will you be joined and with him alone made one, for you will find that the sacrament possesses, as does nothing else, the grace by which your bodily strength will be united and collected through the wonderful power of our Lord's bodily presence, so that all man's distracted thoughts and intentions are here collected and united, and what was dispersed and debased is here raised up again and its due order restored as it is offered to God. The senses within are so informed by our indwelling God, and weened from the outward distractions of temporal things, and all at once become godly; and as your body is strengthened by his Body it becomes renewed. For we shall be changed into him and wholly united, so that what is his becomes ours, and all that is ours becomes his, our heart and his one heart, our body and his one Body. Our senses and our will, our intention, our powers and our members shall be so brought into him that we sense him and become aware of him in every power of our bodies and our souls.

Now you may say: "Alas, sir, I can find nothing better than poverty in myself. How could I dare to go to him?"

Be sure of this, if you want all your poverty to be changed, then go to that abundant treasury of all immeasurable riches, and so you will be rich; for in your heart you should know that he alone is the treasure that can satisfy and fulfill you. So say: "This is why I want to come to you, that your riches may replenish my poverty, that your immeasurable wealth may fill out my emptiness, that your boundless and incomprehensible divinity may make good my so pitiful and decayed humanity."

"Alas, sir, I have committed so many sins that I cannot atone for them!"

Go to him for this, for he has made fitting atonement for all guilt. In him you may well offer up to the heavenly Father an offering worthy enough to atone for all your sins.

"Alas, sir, I should like to utter my praises, but I cannot!"

Go to him, for he only is the thanks the Father will accept and he alone is the immeasurable, truth-revealing, perfect praise of all the divine goodness.

In short, if you want all your sins to be wholly taken from you and to be clothed in virtues and graces, if you want to be led back joyfully to the source and to be guided by every virtue and grace, see to it that you are able to receive that sacrament worthily and often; so you will become one with him and be ennobled through his Body. Yes, in the Body of our Lord the soul is joined so close to God that not even the angels, not the cherubim or seraphim, can find or tell the difference between them. For as the angels approach God they approach the soul, as they approach the soul they approach God. There was never union so close; for the soul is far more closely united with God than are the body and soul that form one man. This union is far closer than if one were to pour a drop of water into a cask of wine;[22] there, we still have water and wine, but here we have such a changing into one that there is no creature who can find the distinction.

Now you may say: "How can this be? I don't feel anything of the kind."

What does that matter? The less that you feel and the more that you believe, the more praiseworthy is your faith, the more regarded, and the more praise will it receive, for a perfect faith is far more in a man than a mere supposing. In God we have true knowledge. In truth, all that we lack is true faith. We may think that what we feel benefits us more than faith, but that is only because we obey external rules. There is no more in the one than in the other. If a man believes constantly, he will receive constantly and possess constantly.

Now you say: "How could I have faith in greater things, when I am not disposed to this, but know myself to be deficient and distracted by many things?"

Well, you ought to be aware of two properties in yourself that our

Lord too had in him. He possessed superior and inferior powers, which in their turn performed two works; for his superior powers possessed and enjoyed everlasting blessedness, but at the same time here on earth his inferior powers were engaged in the greatest suffering and strife. Yet this working of the inferior powers did not deter the superior powers from attaining their object. It ought to be so in you; your superior powers should be elevated to God, wholly offered and bound to him. But beyond doubt we ought to consign all our sufferings to the body and the inferior powers and the senses; but the spirit ought with all its might to lift itself up, and then, liberated, sink down into its God. But the sufferings of the senses and of the inferior powers, and the opposition they meet, is not the spirit's concern; for the greater and the more violent the conflict is, the greater and more praiseworthy is the victory and its glory. For the greater the opposition, the more violent the onslaughts of vice, the more does man possess virtue if he conquers, and the dearer he is to God. And therefore, if you wish to receive your God worthily, be sure that your superior powers are directed toward your God and that your will is seeking his will, that you are intending him, and that your trust is based on him.

When a man is so disposed, he never receives the precious Body of our Lord without receiving extraordinary and great graces, and the oftener, the greater profit to him. Yes, a man might receive the Body of our Lord with such devotion and intention that if it were already ordained for him to come into the lowest order of angels, he might by so receiving on that one occasion be raised up into the next rank. Yes, you could receive him with such devotion that you might be seen in the eighth or in the ninth choir. And therefore, if there were two men alike in their whole lives, and one of them had received the Body of our Lord once more often than the other, through that he could appear like a shining sun in comparison with the other, and could receive a singular union with God.

This receiving and this blessed enjoyment of the Body of our Lord does not consist only in an external enjoyment. Its enjoyment is also spiritual, with a heart that yearns and in a union in devotion. A man may receive it in such faith that he becomes richer in graces than any other man on earth. A man may receive spiritually, whatever he may be, a thousand times and more in a day, whether he be sick or well. But one ought to approach such spiritual communion as the sacrament itself, according to the dictates of good order and with great longing. But even if one does not have the longing, one should incite it and prepare for it and act as it requires, and so one will become holy here in time and blessed there in eternity; for to go after God and to follow him, that is eternity. May the teacher of truth and the lover of chastity and the life of eternity grant us this.[23] Amen.

Counsel 21. Of zeal.

If a man wishes to receive the Body of our Lord, that should be done without any great anxiety. So it is fitting and very profitable to go to confession first, even if we have not incurred any blame, so that we may have the fruits of the sacrament of penance. But if it were the case that a man had incurred some blame, and it is difficult for him to go to confession, then let him have recourse to his God, and admit his guilt with great contrition, and then let him be at peace until he can make his confession. And if recollection of his sins or of their punishment intrude, then let him think that God too has forgotten them. It is God to whom we should confess sooner than to men, and if we are guilty of sin, it is our confession and our self-reproaches before God to which we should attend carefully. And if we want to go to the sacrament, we ought not to neglect this confession before God in favor of external penance, for it is what is in our intention as we perform our works that is just and godly and good.

People ought to learn to be free of their works as they perform them. For a man who has not practiced this, it is hard, learning to attain to a state in which the people around him and the works he performs are no hindrance—and much zeal is needed to achieve this—so that God is present to him and his light shines in him undiminished, whatever the occasion, whatever the environment. For this a lively zeal is needed, and, particularly, two things. One is that a man should have his inwardness well protected, and that his mind be on its guard against the images that surround him outside, keeping them out, never letting them intrude to occupy him and accompany him, never letting them find a home in him. The second is that a man does not allow himself to be weakened or distracted or alienated by any multiplicity, not by his own inward images, whether these be his own imaginings or an exaltation of his perceptions, nor by outward images or whatever else it may be that he has present to him. To this he ought to apply and turn all his power.

Now you may say: "If a man is to perform outward works he must go outside himself, for no work can be accomplished except in the form that is proper to it."

That is indeed true. But to practiced men the outwardness of images is not outward because to inward men all things possess a divine inwardness.

Above all things, it is necessary that a man should apply and exercise his reason, firmly and constantly directing it toward God, and so always inwardly it will become divinized. To reason, nothing is so proper or so present or so close as God. Reason never turns itself in any other direction. It does not have recourse to creatures, unless it suffers violence and injustice, and it is then all broken down and distracted. If, in someone young—or whoever he may be—reason has suffered injury, great zeal must be used, and he must do all he can to coax reason back again and to tend and foster it. For however proper or natural God may be to reason, if people begin by misdirecting reason and making it rely upon creatures, perverting it into their forms and applying it to them, reason will lose some of its health and its power, and its noble intentions will be so hindered that all the zeal men can use is not too much for him to restore himself. When he has done all this, still he must be on constant guard.

Above everything else a man should see to it that he applies himself vigorously and well. If someone who does not apply and exercise himself wants to be and act like a man who applies himself, he will go completely astray, and nothing will become of him. Even if a man has begun by freeing and separating himself from all things, after that he can still perform all his works discerningly, learning to use them without possessiveness or to forgo them without distress. But if a man finds all his love and delight in something, and pursues it with all his will, whether it be food or drink or whatever else, this cannot but bring harm to an inexperienced man.

A man should accustom himself to seeking and wanting nothing for himself in anything, and to finding and accepting God in everything. For God does not give, he has never given any gift so that we might have it and then rest upon it; but all the gifts he ever gave in heaven and on earth he gave so that he might give us the one gift that is himself. With all these other gifts he wants to prepare us for the gift that he himself is. All the works God has ever performed in heaven and in earth he performed for the sake of one work, so that he might perform that, and it is to be himself blessed, so that he may make us blessed. Therefore I say: In every gift, in every work, we ought to learn to look toward God, and we should not allow ourselves to be satisfied or be detained by any thing. Whatever our way of life may be, we must not cease to progress; this has been true for everyone, however far he might have advanced. Above all else, we should always be preparing ourselves, always renewing ourselves to receive God's gifts.

Let me tell you briefly about someone who greatly longed to obtain something from our Lord; but I said she was not nearly ready for it, and if God were to give her the gift, unready as she was, it would have been the ruin of her.

One may ask, "Why was she not ready? She had a good enough will; and do you not say that this can accomplish all things, and that in this everything and every perfection consist?"

That is true, but "will" is to be understood in two senses. There is one will that is accidental and inessential, another will that is determining, creative, habitual.

Indeed, it is not enough for a man's disposition to be detached just for the present moment when he wants to be bound to God, but he must have a well-exercised detachment from what is past and from what is yet to come. Then one is able to receive from God great things and, in the things, God. But if a man is not ready, the gift is ruined, and God with the gift. This is the reason why God cannot always give us as we ask from him. This is no fault in him, for he is a thousand times swifter to give than we are to receive. But we do him violence and injustice, because we with our unreadiness are obstacles to the works that belong to his nature.

A man with all his gifts should learn to take himself out of himself, to keep nothing for himself, to seek nothing, not profit or delight or inward joy or sweetness or reward or the kingdom of heaven or his own will. God never gave himself or gives himself according to anyone else's will. He gives himself only by his own will. When God finds someone who is of one will with him,[24] he gives himself to him and lets himself be in him, with everything that he is. And the more that we cease to belong to ourselves, the more truly do we belong to this. Therefore it is not enough for God that we should once surrender ourselves and all that we possess and can do, but we should renew this in us again and again, uniting ourselves with him and emptying ourselves of self in all things.

And it is also very profitable for a man not to be content because he is disposed toward virtues such as obedience, poverty and other such, but he should exercise the works and the fruits of these virtues, trying himself often, and he should wish and long for other people to exercise and try him. For it is not enough for a man to perform the works of virtue, or to practice obedience, or to accept poverty or contempt, or that he should in other ways humble or detach himself; but one must persist in this, never giving up, until one has gained the essence and the foundation of these virtues. And we can test if we have them by this: When a man finds himself inclined above all else to virtue, and if one performs the works of virtue without preparing one's will, and if one carries them out without any special intention of obtaining some just or important matter, acting virtuously for virtue's own sake, for the love of virtue and no other reason—then one possesses the virtues perfectly, and not until then.

Let us go on learning to abandon ourselves until we hold on to nothing that is our own. All our tempests and strife come only from self-will, whether we see this or whether we do not. We should put ourselves and all that we are in a pure cessation of will and desire, into God's good and dearest will, with everything that we might will and desire in all things.

A question: "Ought one willingly to forgo even God's sweetness? Could that not come from inertia and from too little love for him?"

Yes, provided that one can recognize the distinction. If we want to know whether this comes from inertia, or from a true detachment, or from surrender to God's will, we ought to observe, when we experience such inward surrender, whether we find ourselves as faithful to God as ever we could be in times of great emotion, whether then we do all that we would at other times do, and not less, and that we keep ourselves as detached from all consolations and helps as we would if we were to feel God himself present to us.

Then no time can be too short for a just man who is in perfect good will. For when the will is so disposed that it wants to accomplish every single thing of which it is capable—not just now, but if the man were to live for another thousand years, he would want to do all he was capable of—then the will gains as much as a thousand years of works could do; in God's eyes, he has all this.

Counsel 22. How man should follow God and of a good manner of living.

A man who wants to establish himself in a new life or a new way of working must go to his God, and with great force and with all devotion he must entreat of him that he will furnish him with what is best of all, with what is dearest and the greatest honor to God, and he must want and intend nothing for himself, but only God's dearest will and nothing else. Whatever God may then send him, let him accept it directly[25] from God himself and let him regard it as the best of all that could come to him, and let him be wholly and utterly at peace in it.

And if later some other manner of living pleases him better, he ought to think: God gave you this manner; and so let it be the best that he could wish. In this he should have faith in God, and he should draw all that is good in other manners of living into this one manner, and accept everything, whatever its nature be, in this and according to this. For whatever good God has performed and endowed one manner with may also be found in all good manners; for one ought to take from one manner of living the good that is common to all of them and not what is peculiar to that one. For a man must always accomplish some one thing; he cannot do everything. It has to be one thing and in that one thing we ought to find everything. Because if a man wanted to do everything, this, that and the other, leaving his own manner of living and taking on another that for the moment pleased him better, in truth that would produce great instability. For a man who has renounced the world and entered a religious order is more likely to achieve perfection than is someone who has left one order to join another, however holy he may have been. That is what changing one's way of life does. Let a man decide on one good way and persist in it, and introduce into it all ways that are good, and let him consider that he has received this way of life from God, and not set off today on one way and then tomorrow on another, and let him never be afraid that in doing this he is missing anything. Because with God one cannot miss anything; as little as God himself can, so little can man miss anything with God. Therefore accept some one thing from God, and into it bring everything that is good.

But if it happens that it cannot be that one thing be reconciled with another, that is a certain sign for you that it is not from God. One good is not in opposition to another; for, as our Lord said: "Every kingdom which is divided in itself must perish" (Lk. 11:17); and as he also said: "Who is not with me is against me, and he who does not gather with me scatters" (Mt. 12:30). So let this be a certain sign for you; if something good cannot tolerate another good thing, or, it may be, a less good thing, then that is not from God. It ought to bring in and not disperse.

So it was said in a few true words that were added here: "Our faithful God disposes the best of all for every man, of that there is no doubt."

This is certainly true, and he never takes anyone lying down whom he could have found standing upright, for God's goodness intends all things for the very best.

Then I was asked why God did not therefore dispose for men who, he knew, would fall from the grace of baptism to die in childhood before they had reached years of discretion, since he knew that they would fall and not rise again—would not that be the very best for them?

So I said: God is no destroyer of any good thing, but rather he brings it to perfection. God does not destroy nature, he perfects it. And grace too does not destroy nature, but perfects it. If in the beginning God had destroyed nature, it would have suffered violence and injustice; and this God does not do. Man has a free will, with which he may choose good and evil, and God offers death in return for evil deeds, and in return for good deeds he offers life. Man must be free, and the master of all his actions, unimpeded and unconstrained. Grace does not destroy nature, it perfects it. Glory does not destroy grace, it perfects it, for glory is perfected grace. Therefore it is not in God to destroy anything that has being, but rather he is a perfecter of all things. So we should not destroy in ourselves any good thing, however small it may be, even for the sake of something great, but we should rather bring it to the greatest perfection.

Then we talked about one man who was supposed to be beginning a completely new life, and I said something like this: He ought to become a man who seeks for God and finds God in all things, always, everywhere, with everyone, in every way. Doing this, we can always go on growing and increasing, and never come to the end of our increasing.

Counsel 23. Of interior and exterior works.

If a man wished to withdraw into himself with all his powers, interior and exterior, and if he could maintain this state in such a way
that there was neither imagining nor activity[26] in him, and he could
remain free of all activities, interior or exterior, he ought to be on his
guard in case this very state itself may become a form of activity. But
if a man is not attracted toward works and does not want to be engaged
in them, he ought to force himself to do something, whether it be an
interior or exterior work, because he should not allow himself to become self-complacent in anything, however good it may seem or may
be. If he experiences such struggle or compulsion that it seems that he
is being acted upon rather than himself acting, so let him learn to cooperate with his God. He ought not to flee or deny or suspect his own
inwardness. He should learn to work in it and with it and from it, so
that he can transform inwardness into activity and bring his activities
into his inwardness, and so that he can train himself to act in freedom.
For we ought to keep our eye on this interior work and on what we
produce from it, reading, praying, or, if need be, exterior activities. But
if an exterior activity is hindering our interior work, we should prefer
what is interior. But if both could exist together in one form of working, that would be the best, for man and God to work together.

Now if it be asked: "How could a man cooperate in this way when
he is detached from himself and from all works—as Saint Dionysius
said, that man says the finest things about God who has learned out
of the fullness of his inward riches to keep silence about him[27]—and
when for such a man images and works, praises and thanks, or anything else he could do have departed?"

The answer is that there is still one work that remains proper and
his own, and that is annihilation of self. Yet this annihilation and dim-
inution of the self, however great a work it may be, will remain un-
completed unless it is God who completes it in the self. Humility
becomes perfected only when God humbles man with man's cooperation. When this happens, it is sufficient for the man and for the virtue, and not until then.

A question: "How should God annihilate a man, even with his cooperation? It would seem that man's annihilation would be his exaltation by God, for the gospel says: 'Whoever humbles himself will be exalted'" (Mt. 23:12).

Answer: yes, and no! A man ought to humble himself, and even that cannot be enough if God does not do it; and he ought to be exalted. Not that humbling is one thing and exaltation another; but rather the most exalted exaltedness of exaltation lies in the very depths of humility. The deeper and lower the depth is, the higher and more immeasurable the exaltation and the heights, and the deeper the fount, the higher it springs; height and depth are the same. Therefore, the more a man can humble himself, the higher he will be, and that is why our Lord said: "Whoever wants to be the greatest, let him become the least among you" (Mk. 9:34). Whoever wants to be the one must become the other. Being this is learned only by becoming that. He who will become the least will in truth be the greatest, but he who has become the least is here and now the greatest of all. And so the words of the evangelist become true and fulfilled: "Whoever humbles himself will be exalted." For all our being consists in nothing but becoming nothing.

It is written: "You have become rich in all virtues" (1 Co. 1:5). Truly that can never happen until first one has become poor in all things. Whoever wants to receive everything must also renounce everything. That is a fair bargain and an equal return, as I said a while ago. Therefore, because God wants to give us himself and all things as our own free possessions, so he wants to deprive us, utterly and completely, of all possessiveness. Yes, truly, God in no way wants us to possess even as much as I could hold in my eye. For none of the gifts he ever gave us, neither gifts of nature nor gifts of grace, did he give for any other reason than that he wishes us to have nothing that is our own; and he never gave anything as their own to his mother or to any man or to any creature in any way at all. And so that he may teach us and make us aware of this, he often takes away from us both earthly and spiritual possessions, for it should not be for us but for him alone to possess them as honors. But we ought to have everything as if it were loaned to us and not given, without any possessiveness, whether it be our bodies or our souls, our minds, powers, worldly goods or honors, friends, kinsmen, houses, lands, all things.

What is God's intention in this which he considers so important?

Because he wants himself to be, solely and wholly, what we possess. This is what he wants, this is what he intends, this alone is important to him, that he may be and he must be this. In this consists his greatest delight and pleasure; and the more fully and generously he may be this, the greater is his delight and joy. For the more that we possess all things, the less do we possess him, and the less the love we have for all things, the more do we have him and all that he has to bestow. Therefore when our Lord wanted to speak about every form of blessedness, he put poverty of spirit at the head of them all; and it was put first as a sign that all blessedness and perfections together have their beginning in poverty of spirit.[28] And truly, wherever that was the foundation, all good things could be built upon it, and without this there would be nothing.

If we strip ourselves of everything that is external, in return God wishes to give us as our own everything that is in heaven, and heaven itself with all its powers, yes, everything that ever flowed out from him and that all the angels and saints possess, that it may be our own as much as it is theirs, and more our own than any external thing can be. In return for my going out of myself for love of him, God will wholly become my own, with all that he is and all that he can bestow, as much my own as his own, neither less nor more. He will be my own a thousandfold more than any man ever owned anything that he has in his coffer, more than he ever owned himself. Nothing was ever owned so much as God will be my own, with everything he can do and is.

We ought to earn the owning of this by living here without ownership of ourselves and of anything that is not God, and the more perfect and unimpeded this poverty is, so is our owning it more our own. We ought not to intend or look for such a return as this, we ought never to give one glance at whether we are going to gain or receive anything, but all should be for the love of virtue alone. The less we own, the more it is our own, as the great Paul says: "Possessing, we should be as if we possess nothing, and still we should possess all things" (2 Co. 6:10). A man is free of possessiveness who covets nothing, who wants to have nothing, not of himself, not of everything that is external to him, yes, not even of God or of all things.

Do you want to know what a truly poor man is like?

That man is truly poor in spirit who can well forgo everything that is not necessary. That is why the man who sat naked in the barrel said to the great Alexander, who had all the world subject to him: "I am," he said, "a far greater lord than you, for I have despised more than you have possessed. All the things that you thought so great that you wanted them were too little for me to despise."[29] He is more blessed who can forgo all things and has no need of them than is the man who possessed everything and needed it. The best man is the one who can forgo what he does not need. Therefore the man who can best of all forgo and despise has forsaken most of all. We think it something great that a man should for the love of God give a thousand gold marks and with his riches build convents and monasteries and feed all the poor; that would be something great. But a man would be far more blessed who for the love of God despised all this. A man would possess a truly heavenly kingdom who knew how to renounce everything for God, whatever God might or might not give him.

Then you say: "Yes, sir, but would not I, with my shortcomings, be an occasion of possessiveness or a hindrance to true poverty?"[30]

If you have shortcomings, ask God earnestly to take them away, if that be to his glory and pleasing to him, because without him you can do nothing. If he takes them away, then thank him; and if he does not do this, suffer it for his love, but not as a shortcoming through sin, but rather as a good exercise through which you will gain reward and exercise patience. You must be at peace, whether he gives you his gifts or not.

God gives to every man according to what is best and most fitting for him. If you are making a coat for someone, you must make it to his measure; what fits one man will not fit another at all. You take everyone's measure, and then it fits him. And so God gives to everyone the very best that he sees to be closest to his needs. Truly, anyone who trusts God completely in this accepts and receives as much from his smallest gift as from the greatest of all. If God wanted to give me what he gave Saint Paul, I should be glad to accept it, if that were his will. But since he does not want to give me that—for there are very few people whom he wishes to know so much in this life—he is as dear to me, I pay him as much thanks and I am as much at peace because God does not give it to me, that he withholds it from me, as if he were giving it to me. I am as satisfied and well pleased with that as if he were to give it to me, if either be acceptable to me.[31] Truly, this is how God's will ought to content me: Everything God might wish to do or to give ought to be to me so dear and so precious, because it is so according to his will, that for him not to give me the gift, not to do the thing, would be as pleasing to me as if he did. So all God's gifts and all his deeds would be mine, and let every created thing do its best, or its worst, they could deprive me of nothing of this. So what do I have to complain about if all men's gifts are mine? In truth, I am so well contented with what God does or does not give to me and do for me that I would not pay a copper penny for being able to live the finest life I could think of.

Now you say: "I am afraid that I am not working as hard as I ought at this and I am not keeping it up as I could."

Accept it as suffering, suffer it patiently, take it as an exercise, and be at peace. God is glad to suffer shame and adversity and is happy to forgo service and praise so that they who intend and obey him should possess him in peace. Why should we not be at peace, whatever he may give us or whatever we may lack? It is written and our Lord says that "They are blessed who suffer for the sake of justice" (Mt. 5:10). Truly, if there was a thief whom they were about to hang who deserved to hang because he had stolen, and if there were another who had committed murder and whom justly they were going to break on the wheel—if these two found it in themselves to say: "Look, what you will suffer is for the sake of justice, for they are treating you justly," they would at once be blessed.[32]

In truth, however unjust we may be, if we accept from God whatever he may or may not do to us as justice, and suffer it for justice's sake, then we shall be blessed. So do not complain about anything; all you need to complain about is that you go on complaining and that nothing satisfies you. All that you should complain about is that you have too much. Anyone properly disposed would accept want as if it were plenty.

Now you say: "Alas, God does such great things in lots of people, and they become so transmuted in the divine life, and God does all this in them and they do nothing."

Thank God for what he does in them, and if he gives this to you, take it, for God's sake; and if he does not give it, then you ought willingly to lack it, and intend nothing but him, and do not be upset, whether God does your works for you or whether you perform them yourself; because if you intend God alone, he must perform them, whether he like it or not.

Do not upset yourself, whatever form of life or devotion God may give to anyone. If I were so good and holy that they had to raise me to the altars with the saints, still people would be talking and worrying about whether this were grace or nature working in me, and puzzling themselves about it. They are all wrong in this. Leave God to work in you, let him do it, and do not be upset over whether he is working with nature or above nature; for nature and grace are both his. What has that to do with you, what it suits him to work with, or what he may work in you or in someone else? He must work how or where or in what way it is fitting to him.

There was a man who would dearly have liked to make a stream flow through his garden, and he said: "If the water could be mine, I should not care what sort of channel brought it to me, iron or timber, bone or rusty metal, if only I could have the water." And so anyone is quite wrong who worries about the means through which God is working his works in you, whether it be nature or grace. Just let him work, and just be at peace.

For as much as you are in God, so much are you at peace, and as far as you are distant from God, so far are you from peace. Whatever is in God, it has peace. As much in God, so much in peace. So see by this how much you are in God, or if you are not, whether you are or are not at peace; for if you are not at peace, there cannot then be peace in you, for lack of peace comes from created things and not from God. And there is nothing in God that is to be feared; everything that is in God is only to be loved. And so there is nothing in him that is to be mourned.

He who has all his will and his wish has all his joy; and no one has this whose will is not wholly one with the will of God. May God grant us this union. Amen.

D. On Detachment

I have read many writings both by the pagan teachers and by the prophets and in the Old and the New Law, and I have inquired, carefully and most industriously, to find which is the greatest and best virtue with which man can most completely and closely conform himself to God, with which he can by grace become that which God is by nature, and with which man can come most of all to resemble that image which he was in God, and between which and God there was no distinction before ever God made created things. And as I scrutinize all these writings, so far as my reason can lead and instruct me, I find no other virtue better than a pure detachment from all things; because all other virtues have some regard for created things, but detachment is free from all created things. That is why our Lord said to Martha: "One thing is necessary" (Lk. 10:42), which is as much as to say: "Martha, whoever wants to be free of care and to be pure must have one thing, and that is detachment."

The teachers have great things to say in praise of love, as had Saint

Paul, who says: "Whatever I may practice, if I do not have love, I am worth nothing at all" (1 Co. 13:1–2). And yet I praise detachment above all love.[1] First, because the best thing about love is that it compels me to love God, yet detachment compels God to love me. Now it is far greater for me to compel God to come to me than to compel myself to come to God; and that is because God is able to conform himself, far better and with more suppleness, and to unite himself with me than I could unite myself with God. And I prove that detachment compels God to come to me in this way; it is because everything longs to achieve its own natural place.[2] Now God's own natural place is unity and purity,[3] and that comes from detachment. Therefore God must of necessity give himself to a heart that has detachment. Second, I praise detachment above love because love compels me to suffer all things for God's love, yet detachment leads me to where I am receptive to nothing except God. Now it is far greater to be receptive to nothing except God than to suffer all things for God's love, for man when he suffers has some regard for the created things from which he receives the suffering, but detachment is wholly free of all created things. And that detachment is receptive to nothing at all except God—that I prove in this way: Whatever is to be received must be received by something; but detachment is so close to nothingness that there is nothing so subtle that it can be apprehended by detachment, except God alone. He is so simple and so subtle that he can indeed be apprehended in a detached heart. And so detachment can apprehend nothing except God.

The authorities also praise humility above many other virtues. But I praise detachment above all humility, and that is because, although there may be humility without detachment, there cannot be perfect detachment without perfect humility, because perfect humility proceeds from annihilation of self. Now detachment approaches so closely to nothingness that there can be nothing between perfect detachment and nothingness. Therefore perfect detachment cannot exist without humility. Now two virtues are always better than one. The second reason why I praise detachment above humility is that perfect humility is always abasing itself below all created things, and in this abasement man goes out of himself toward created things, but detachment remains within itself. Now there can never be any going out of self so excellent that remaining within self is not itself much more excellent. The prophet David said of this: "All the glory of the king's daughter is from her inwardness."[4] Perfect detachment has no looking up to, no abasement, not beneath any created thing or above it; it wishes to be neither beneath nor above, it wants to exist by itself, not giving joy or sorrow to anyone, not wanting equality or inequality with any created thing, not wishing for this or for that. All that it wants is to be. But to wish to be this thing or that,[5] this it does not want. Whoever wants to be this or that wants to be something, but detachment wants to be nothing at all. So it is that detachment makes no claim upon anything.

Now a man could say: "All virtues were most perfectly present in our Lady, so that she must have had perfect detachment." But if detachment is more excellent than humility, why did our Lady single out not her detachment but her humility when she said: "Because he has regarded the humility of his handmaid" (Lk. 1:48)? Why did she not say: "He has regarded the detachment of his handmaid?" To this I answer and say that detachment and humility are in God, so far as we can speak of virtues as present in God. Now you must know that it was loving humility that brought God to abase himself into human nature; yet when he became man, detachment remained immovable in itself as it was when he created the kingdoms of heaven and earth, as afterward I intend to say to you. And when our Lord, wishing to become man, remained immovable in his detachment, our Lady knew well that this was what he desired also from her, and that on that account it was to her humility that he was looking, not to her detachment. So she remained immovable in her detachment, and praised in herself not detachment but humility. And if she had by so much as a word mentioned her detachment, and had said: "He has regarded my detachment," detachment would have been troubled by that, and would not have remained wholly perfect, for there would then have been a going out. There can be no going out, however small, in which detachment can remain unblemished. And so you have the reason why our Lady singled out her humility and not her detachment. The prophet spoke about that: "I shall hear what the Lord God will say in me" (Ps. 84:9), that is, I shall be silent and hear what my God and my Lord may say in me, as if he were to say: "If God wishes to speak to me, let him come in here to me; I do not want to go out."

I also praise detachment above all mercifulness, because mercifulness is nothing else than man's going out of himself to the shortcomings of his fellow men, and through this his heart becomes troubled. But detachment remains free of this, and remains in itself, and allows nothing to trouble it, for nothing can ever trouble a man unless things are not well with him. In a few words, if I regard all virtues, I find not one so much without shortcomings and so leading us to God as detachment.

An authority called Avicenna says: "The excellence of the spirit which has achieved detachment is so great that whatever it contemplates is true, and whatever it desires is granted, and whatever it commands one must obey."[6] And you should know that this is really so; when the free spirit has attained true detachment, it compels God to its being; and if the spirit could attain formlessness, and be without all accidents, it would take on God's properties. But this God can give to no one but to himself; therefore God cannot do more for the spirit that has attained detachment than to give himself to it. And the man who has attained this complete detachment is so carried into eternity that no transient thing can move him, so that he experiences nothing of whatever is bodily, and he calls the world dead, because nothing earthly has any savor for him. This is what Saint Paul meant when he said: "I live, and yet I do not; Christ lives in me" (Ga. 2:20).

Now you may ask what detachment is since it is in itself so excellent. Here you should know that true detachment is nothing else than for the spirit to stand as immovable against whatever may chance to it of joy and sorrow, honor, shame and disgrace, as a mountain of lead stands before a little breath of wind. This immovable detachment brings a man into the greatest equality with God, because God has it from his immovable detachment that he is God, and it is from his detachment that he has his purity and his simplicity and his unchangeability. And if man is to become equal with God, insofar as a creature can have equality with God, that must happen through detachment. It then draws a man into purity, and from purity into simplicity, and from simplicity into unchangeability, and these things produce an equality between God and the man; and the equality must come about in grace, for it is grace that draws a man away from all temporal things, and makes him pure of all transient things. And you must know that to be empty of all created things is to be full of God, and to be full of created things is to be empty of God.

Now you must know that God has been in this immovable detachment since before the world began, and he still remains so; and you must know that when God created heaven and earth and all created things, that affected his immovable detachment as little as if no creature had ever been made. And I say more: All the prayers and good works that man can accomplish in time move God's detachment as little as if no single prayer or good work were ever performed in time, and yet for this God is never any less gentle or less inclined toward man than if he had never achieved prayer or good works. And I say more: When the Son in his divinity wished to become man, and became man, and suffered his passion, that affected God's immovable detachment as little as if the Son had never become man. Now you may say: "If I hear rightly, all prayers and good works are wasted, because God does not accept them in such a way that anyone could move him through them; and yet people say that God wants to be asked for everything." But here you must pay me good attention, and understand properly, if you can, that God, in his first everlasting glance—if we can think of his first glancing at anything—saw all things as they were to happen, and in that same glance he saw when and how he would make all created things, and when the Son would become man and would suffer. He also saw the smallest prayer and good work that anyone would ever perform, and he took into his regard which prayers and devotion he would or should give ear to. He saw what you will earnestly pray and entreat him for tomorrow; and it will not be tomorrow that he will give ear to your entreaty and prayer, because he has heard it in his everlastingness, before ever you became man. But if your prayer is not insistent and lacks earnestness, it will not be now that God refuses you, because he has refused you in his everlastingness. And so God has looked upon all things in his first everlasting glance, and God does not undertake anything whatever afresh, because everything is something already accomplished. And so God always remains in his immovable detachment, and yet men's prayers and good works are not on this account wasted; for whoever does well will also be well rewarded, whoever does evil will be rewarded accordingly. This is the meaning of what Saint Augustine says in the fifth book of *On the Trinity*, in the last chapter, where he begins: "Yet God . . ."[7] which has this sense:

> God forbid that anyone should say that God loves anyone in time, because with him nothing is past, and nothing is to come, and he had loved all the saints before ever the world was created, when he foresaw that they would be. And when it comes to pass in time that he in time regards what he has looked upon in eternity, then people think that God has turned to them with a new love; yet it is so that whether God be angry or confer some blessing, it is we who are changed,

and he remains unchangeable, as the light of the sun is painful to sick eyes and good for healthy ones, and yet the light of the sun remains in itself unchangeable.

And he touches on the same meaning in the twelfth book of *On the Trinity*, in the fourth chapter, where he says: "God does not see in temporal fashion, and nothing new happens in his sight."[8] Isidore also means this, in his book about the highest good where he says: "Many people ask what God did before he created heaven and earth, or when did the new will in God, to make created things, come about?"[9] He answers this so: "No new will ever came about in God, because when it was so that the creature was in itself nothing"—of what it now is—"still it was before the world began, in God and in his mind." God did not create heaven and earth in the temporal fashion in which we describe it—"Let there be!"—because all created things were spoken in the everlasting Word. We must also deduce this from the Lord's colloquy with Moses, when Moses said to the Lord: "Lord, if Pharaoh asks me who you are, what shall I say to him?" and the Lord said: "Say, 'He who is has sent me' " (Ex. 3:10–14), which is as much as to say: He who is in himself unchangeable, he has sent me.

Now someone might say: "Did Christ have immovable detachment, even when he said: 'My soul is sorrowful even to death' (Mt. 26:38), and did Mary, when she stood beneath the cross—and people tell us much about her lamentations. How can all this be reconciled with immovable detachment?" Here you must know that the authorities say that in every man there are two kinds of man: One is called the outer man, which is our sensuality, with the five senses serving him, and yet the outer man works through the power of the soul. The second man is called the inner man, which is the man's inwardness. Now you should know that a spiritual man who loves God makes no use in his outer man of the soul's powers except when the five senses require it; and his inwardness pays no heed to the five senses, except as this leads and guides them, and protects them, so that they are not employed for beastly purposes, as they are by some people who live for their carnal delight, as beasts lacking reason do. Such people deserve to be called beasts rather than men. And whatever power the soul possesses, beyond that which it gives to the five senses, it gives wholly to the inner man, and if he has a high and noble object, the soul draws to itself all its powers it had loaned to the five senses. Then the man is called senseless and rapt, for his object is an image which the reason can apprehend, or, it may be, something reasonable which has no image. Yet know that God requires every spiritual man to love him with all the powers of his soul. Of this he said: "Love your God with your whole heart" (Dt. 6:5, etc.). But there are people who squander all the soul's powers on the outer man. They are those who apply all their intelligence and reason to perishable goods, and who know nothing about the inner man. Now you must know that the outer man may be active whilst the inner man remains wholly free and immovable. In Christ, too, there was an outer man and an inner man, and also in Our Lady; and whatever Christ and Our Lady may have said about outward affairs, they acted according to the outer man, and the inner man remained in an immovable detachment. And Christ spoke in this sense when he said: "My soul is sorrowful even to death"; and however much Our Lady lamented, and whatever else she may have said, still always her inwardness remained in an immovable detachment. Consider a simile of this: A door, opening and shutting on a hinge. I compare the planks on the outside of the door with the outer man, but the hinge with the inner man. As the door opens and shuts, the outside planks move backwards and forwards, but the hinge remains immovable in one place, and the opening and shutting does not affect it. It is just the same here, if you can understand it rightly.

And now I ask, what is the object of this pure detachment? My answer is that neither this nor that is the object of pure detachment. It reposes in a naked nothingness, and I shall tell you why that is: Pure detachment reposes in the highest place. If a man has repose in the highest place, God can work in him according to his whole will. But God cannot work according to his whole will in every man's heart, for though it may be that God is omnipotent, still he cannot work except where he finds or creates a willing cooperation. And I say "or creates" because of Saint Paul, for in him God did not find willing cooperation, but he made Paul willing by the inpouring of grace.[10] So I say: God works according as he finds willingness. He works in one way in men, and another in stones. We can find an analogy of this in nature: If someone heats a baker's oven, and puts in one loaf of oats and another of barley and another of rye and another of wheat, there is only one temperature in the oven, but it does not have the same effect upon the different doughs, because one turns into fine bread, another is coarse and a third even coarser. And that is not the fault of the temperature but of the materials, which are not the same. In the same way, God does not work alike in every man's heart; he works as he finds willingness and receptivity.[11] There may be one thing or another in some heart, on which one thing or another God cannot work to bring it up to the highest place. And if the heart is to be willing for that highest place, it must repose in a naked nothingness; and in this there is the greatest potentiality that can be. And when the heart that has detachment attains to the highest place, that must be nothingness, for in this is the greatest receptivity. See an analogy of this in nature. If I want to write on a wax tablet, it does not matter how fine the words may be that are written on the tablet, they still hinder me from writing on it. If I really want to write something, I must erase and eliminate everything that is already there; and the tablet is never so good for me to write on as when there is nothing on it at all. In the same way, if God is to write on my heart up in the highest place, everything that can be called this or that must come out of my heart, and in that way my heart will have won detachment. And so God can work upon it in the highest place and according to his highest will. And this is why the heart in its detachment has no this or that as its object.

But now I ask: "What is the prayer of a heart that has detachment?" And to answer it I say that purity in detachment does not know how to pray, because if someone prays he asks God to get something for him, or he asks God to take something away from him. But a heart in detachment asks for nothing, nor has it anything of which it would gladly be free. So it is free of all prayer, and its prayer is nothing else than for uniformity with God.[12] That is all its prayer consists in. To illustrate this meaning we may consider what Saint Dionysius said about Saint Paul's words, when he said: "There are many of you racing for the crown, but it will be given only to one" (1 Co. 9:24). All the powers of the soul are racing for the crown, but it will be given only to the soul's being—and Dionysius says: "The race is nothing but a turning away from all created things and a uniting oneself with that which is uncreated."[13] And as the soul attains this, it loses its name and it draws God into itself, so that in itself it becomes nothing, as the sun draws up the red dawn into itself so that it becomes nothing. Nothing else will bring man to this except pure detachment. And we can also apply to this what Augustine says: "The soul has a secret entry into the divine nature when all things become nothing to it."[14] This entry here on this earth is nothing else than pure detachment. And when this detachment ascends to the highest place, it knows nothing of knowing, it loves nothing of loving, and from light it becomes dark. To this we can also apply what one teacher says: "The poor in spirit are those who have abandoned all things for God, just as they were his when we did not exist."[15] No one can do this but a heart with pure detachment. We can see that God would rather be in a heart with such detachment than in all hearts. For if you ask me: "What is it God seeks in all things?" then I answer you out of the Book of Wisdom, where he says: "In all things I seek rest" (Si. 14:11). Nowhere is there complete rest, except only in the heart that has found detachment. Hence God would rather be there than in other virtues or in any other things. And you should also know that the more a man applies himself to becoming susceptible to the divine inflowing, the more blessed will he be; and whoever can establish himself in the highest readiness, he will also be in the highest blessedness. Now no one can make himself susceptible to the divine inflowing except through uniformity with God, for as each man becomes uniform with God, to that measure he becomes susceptible to the divine inflowing. And uniformity comes from man's subjecting himself to God; and the more a man subjects himself to created things, the less is he uniform with God. Now a heart that has pure detachment is free of all created things, and so it is wholly submitted to God, and so it achieves the highest uniformity with God, and is most susceptible to the divine inflowing. This is what Saint Paul means when he said: "Put on Jesus Christ" (Rm. 13:14). He means through uniformity with Christ, and this putting-on cannot happen except through uniformity with Christ. And you must know that when Christ became man, it was not just a human being he put on himself; he put on human nature.[16] Therefore, do you too go out of all things, and then there will be only what Christ accepted and put on, and so you will have put on Christ.

Whoever now wishes to see properly what is the excellence and the profit of perfect detachment, let him take good heed of Christ's words, when he spoke about his human nature and said to his disciples: "It is expedient for you that I go from you, for if I do not go, the Holy Spirit cannot come to you" (Jn. 16:7). This is just as if he were to say: "You have taken too much delight in my present image, so that the perfect delight of the Holy Spirit cannot be yours. So detach yourselves from the image, and unite yourselves to the formless being, for God's spiritual consolation is delicate; therefore he will not offer it to anyone except to him who disdains bodily consolations."

Now, all you reasonable people, take heed! No one is happier than a man who has attained the greatest detachment. No one can accept fleshly and bodily consolations without spiritual damage, "because the flesh longs in opposition to the spirit and the spirit to the flesh" (Ga.

5:17). Therefore whoever sows in the flesh inordinate love will reap everlasting death, and whoever in the spirit sows a well-ordered love will from the spirit reap everlasting life (Ga. 6:8). So it is that the sooner a man shuns what is created, the sooner will the creator come to him. So take heed, all you reasonable people! Since the delight we might have in Christ's bodily image deprives us of receptivity for the Holy Spirit, how much more shall we be deprived of God by the ill-ordered delight that we take in transient consolations! So detachment is the best of all, for it purifies the soul and cleanses the conscience and enkindles the heart and awakens the spirit and stimulates our longings and shows us where God is and separates us from created things and unites itself with God.

Now, all you reasonable people, take heed! The fastest beast that will carry you to your perfection is suffering, for no one will enjoy more eternal sweetness than those who endure with Christ in the greatest bitterness. There is nothing more gall-bitter than suffering, and nothing more honey-sweet than to have suffered; nothing disfigures the body more than suffering, and nothing more adorns the soul in the sight of God than to have suffered. The firmest foundation on which this perfection can stand is humility, for whichever mortal crawls here in the deepest abasement, his spirit will fly up into the highest realms of the divinity, for love brings sorrow, and sorrow brings love. And therefore, whoever longs to attain to perfect detachment, let him struggle for perfect humility, and so he will come close to the divinity.

That we may all be brought to this, may that supreme detachment help us which is God himself. Amen.

NOTES

PREFACE

1. *The Transformation of Nature in Art* (Cambridge: Harvard University Press, 1934), p. 61.
2. Claude Levi-Strauss, *Myth and Meaning* (New York: Schocken Books, 1979), p. 14.
3. *The Autobiography of Malcolm X* (New York: Grove Press, 1964), p. 205.

INTRODUCTION: 1. HISTORICAL DATA

1. See *Sermon* 9 (DW I, pp. 152–54).
2. For bibliographies of discussions of Eckhart's biographical data, see Thomas Kaeppeli, *Scriptores ordinis praedicatorum medii aevi* (Rome, 1970) I, p. 354 sqq.; Josef Koch, *Kleine Schriften* (2 vols., Rome, 1973); R. M. Kully, "Eckhart," in W. Kosch and B. Berger, ed., *Deutsche Literatur-Lexikon* 3 (Berlin-Munich, 1972), pp. 872–87; Kurt Ruh, "Meister Eckhart" (Verfasserlexikon). Edmund Colledge is much indebted to Professor Ruh for an advance view of proofs of his article.
3. Koch, "Kritische Studien zum Leben Meister Eckharts," in *Kleine Schriften*, vol. 2, p. 249.
4. D. Prümmer, ed., *Fontes vitae S. Thomae* (Toulouse, 1912), no. LXXXII.
5. Koch, "Kritische Studien," pp. 245–47.
6. See below, p. 86.
7. See "Defense," p. 72.
8. Adolar Zumkeller, "Ein Zeitgenosse Eckharts zu Fehlentwicklung in der damaligen mystischen Bewegung: kritische Bemerkungen in neuentdeckten mystischen Traktaten Heinrichs von Friemar des Älteren O.S.A.," *Würzburger Diözesangeschichtsblätter* 37/38, *Kirche und Theologie in Franken* (Würzburg, 1975), pp. 229–38. Edmund Colledge is indebted to Fr. Adolar Zumkeller for drawing his attention to this important article.

9. See Edmund Colledge, "Liberty of the Spirit: *The Mirror of Simple Souls*," in L. K. Shook, ed., *Congress on the Theology of Renewal in the Church* (Montreal, 1968), 2, pp. 100–17; and Edmund Colledge and Romana Guarnieri, "The Glosses by 'M.N.' and Richard Methley to *The Mirror of Simple Souls*," *Archivio Italiano per la Storia della Pietà* 5 (1968): 357–82.

10. P. Glorieux, *Répertoire des maîtres en théologie de Paris au xiiie siècle* (Paris, 1933), I, no. 65.

11. The best study of the manifestations and origins of such movements remains that of Herbert Grundmann, *Religiöse Bewegungen im Mittelalter*, 2nd ed. (Darmstadt, 1970); and an excellent recent survey will be found in Robert E. Lerner, *The Heresy of the Free Spirit in the Later Middle Ages* (Berkeley, 1972). See also Edmund Colledge and J. C. Marler, "*Tractatus Magistri Johannis Gerson De Mistica Theologia:* St. Pölten, Diözesanarchiv MS. 25," *Mediaeval Studies* 41 (1979): 354–86.

12. See Edmund Colledge, "Meister Eckhart: His Times and His Writings," *The Thomist* 42 (1978): 240–41.

13. Ibid., quoting from Koch, *Kleine Schriften*, p. 202.

14. Translated with an introduction in A. Maurer, *Meister Eckhart, Parisian Questions and Prologues* (Toronto, 1974).

15. G. Thery, "Édition critique des pièces relatives au procès d'Eckhart contenues dans la manuscrit 33b de la Bibliothèque de Soest," *Archives d'histoire doctrinale et littéraire du moyen âge* 1 (1926): 129–268.

16. F. Pelster, "Ein Gutachten aus dem Eckehart-Prozess in Avignon," *Festschrift Martin Grabmann* (Münster, 1935), pp. 1099–1124.

17. M.-H. Laurent, "Autour du procès de Maître Eckhart: les documents des Archives Vaticanes," *Divus Thomas* 39 (1936): 331–48, 430–47.

18. See J. Koch's important essay, "Philosophische und theologische Irrtumslisten von 1270–1329," reprinted from *Mélanges Mandonnet* 2 (1930) in *Kleine Schriften* 2, pp. 423–50.

19. Described in greater detail in Colledge, "Meister Eckhart: His Times and His Writings," pp. 245–48.

20. Information on this was generously supplied by Damasus Trapp, O.S.A., who is preparing for publication an edition of the *Ten Responses*.

21. The Bull is edited in Denzinger-Schönmetzer, *Enchiridion symbolorum*, nos. 950–80.

22. Koch's chief contribution on this matter is the paper he read to a Strassburg conference, "Meister Eckharts Weiterwirken im deutsch-niederländischen Raum im 14. und 15. Jahrhundert," published in *La mystique rhénane* (Paris, 1968), pp. 133–56.

23. Denzinger-Schönmetzer, no. 979. See below, p. 80.

24. Koch, "Weiterwirken," p. 135.

25. "Die Gottesgeburt: die Lehre der Kirchenväter von der Geburt Christi aus dem Herzen der Kirche und der Gläubigen," *Zeitschrift für katholische*

NOTES

Theologie 59 (1935): 333–418; reprinted in his *Symbole der Kirche* (Salzburg, 1964), pp. 13–87.

26. Denzinger-Schönmetzer, no. 964. See below, p. 79.

27. See below, pp. 216–17.

28. See below, p. 261.

29. Colledge, "Meister Eckhart: His Times and His Writings," pp. 251–52.

30. Denzinger-Schönmetzer, no. 980. See below, p. 81.

31. F. Vetter, ed., *Die Predigten Taulers* (Berlin, 1910), p. 69.

32. "Weiterwirken," p. 142 sqq.

33. See Colledge, "Meister Eckhart: His Times and His Writings," p. 254, n. 45. This character is usually called in English "the Wild Man." Romana Guarnieri pointed out that it is a "Thing," not only nameless but sexless, as she doubtless observed from Josef Koch's commentaries.

34. On this passage in *The Little Book of Truth*, see Karl Bihlmeyer, *Heinrich Seuse: Deutsche Schriften* (Stuttgart, 1907, repr. Frankfurt, 1961), pp. 352–57; Koch, "Weiterwirken," pp. 142–43; Colledge, "Meister Eckhart: His Times and His Writings," pp. 253–54.

35. Denzinger-Schönmetzer, no. 963; see below, p. 79.

36. Bihlmeyer, *Deutsche Schriften*, p. 355.

37. F. Pelster, "Ein Gutachten," p. 1120.

38. This translation of *Sermon* 5a will appear in a subsequent volume; see in this volume *Sermon* 5b, p. 182.

39. Bihlmeyer, *Deutsche Schriften*, p. 356.

40. Bihlmeyer, *Deutsche Schriften*, p. 22, n. 28.

41. Kaepelli, *Scriptores* I, pp. 358–60.

42. Bihlmeyer, *Deutsche Schriften*, "Introduction," pp. 132–34.

43. MHG: *selig*, which, as in modern German, need mean no more than "departed."

44. MHG: *blos vergotet.*

45 That is, Suso himself.

46. Bihlmeyer, *Deutsche Schriften*, pp. 22–23.

47. B. M. Reichert, ed., *Acta capitulorum generalium ordinis praedicatorum* 2 (*Monumenta ordinis fratrum praedicatorum historica* 4, 1889), p. 258.

48. *De viribus illustribus ordinis praedicatorum* (Bologna, 1517).

49. Quétif-Echard: *Scriptores ordinis praedicatorum* (Paris, 1719–1721), I, p. 593.

50. Koch, "Weiterwirken," p. 139; and see Colledge, "Meister Eckhart: His Times and His Writings," pp. 255–56.

51. Koch, "Weiterwirken," pp. 139–40.

52. See M. G. Sargent, "The Transmission by the English Carthusians of Some Late Medieval Spiritual Writings," *Journal of Ecclesiastical History* 27 (1976): 225–40.

53. Koch, "Weiterwirken," pp. 137–38.

54. Colledge, "Meister Eckhart: His Times and His Writings," p. 256, where the sources for this are quoted. Reprinted with the kind permission of the editor, *The Thomist*.

55. *Bibliotheca dominicana neerlandica manuscripta 1224–1500* (Louvain, 1970).

56. Albert Ampe, ed., *Den Tempel onser Sielen* (Antwerp, 1968).

57. Ibid., pp. 300–301.

58. See below, p. 202.

59. Edmund Colledge and J. C. Marler hope soon to publish their account of *Beati pauperes spiritu*, of Eckhart's sources for his doctrine of "poverty of the will," and of Ruysbroek's trenchant criticism of the doctrine in *The Twelve Beguines*.

INTRODUCTION: 2. THEOLOGICAL SUMMARY

1. For a general introduction to the relation between thought and style in Eckhart, see J. Quint, "Mystik und Sprache: Ihr Verhältnis zueinander, insbesondere in der spekulativen Mystik Meister Eckeharts," in *Altdeutsche und altniederländische Mystik* (Darmstadt: Wissenschaftliche Buchgesellschaft, 1964), pp. 113–51. In English, see F. Tobin, "Eckhart's Mystical Use of Language: The Contexts of *eigenschaft*," *Seminar* 8 (1972): 160–68.

2. J. Quint, *Meister Eckehart. Deutsche Predigten und Traktate* (Munich: Carl Hanser, 1955), pp. 22–23.

3. For the history of the interpretations of Eckhart, both old and new, see I. Degenhardt, *Studien zum Wandel des Eckhartbildes* (Leiden: E. J. Brill, 1967); and T. Schaller, "Die Meister Eckhart-Forschung von der Jahrhundertwende bis zur Gegenwart," *Freiburger Zeitschrift für Philosophie und Theologie* 15 (1968): 262–316, 403–26; and "Zur Eckhart-Deutung der letzten 30 Jahre," *Freiburger Zeitschrift* 16 (1969): 22–39.

4. The *Work of Propositions* was to consist of a thousand or more propositions divided into fourteen treatises. Only a brief account of the first proposition ("Existence is God") survives in the General Prologue to the *Three-Part Work* and in the Prologue to the *Work of Propositions* itself. See LW I, pp. 148–84; and the translation by A. Maurer, *Parisian Questions and Prologues* (Toronto: Pontifical Institute, 1974), pp. 78–104.

5. J. Koch, "Sinn und Struktur der Schriftauslegungen," in *Meister Eckhart der Prediger* (Freiburg: Herder, 1960), pp. 73–103.

6. In this connection we might advert to the special role of "communications" as one of the functional specialties of theology in B. Lonergan's *Method in Theology* (New York: Longmans, 1972), pp. 355–68.

7. E.g., the birth of the Son in the soul; see below pp. 50–52.

8. E.g., the key notion of the negation of negation appears explicitly only in *Sermon* 21 (DW I, pp. 361–62).

9. *STh* Ia.1.1.

10. E.g., *Comm. Jn.* nn. 6, 23, 36, 96 (pp. 124, 129, 134, 158). Such intermingling occurs throughout the work, e.g., nn. 137, 142, 444 and 509 (LW III, pp. 110, 119–20, 380, and 441). See also the natural arguments for the Trinity in n. 160 (LW III, p. 132).

11. See *Sermon* XL.2 (LW IV, p. 343).

12. C. F. Kelley, in his *Meister Eckhart on Divine Knowledge* (New Haven: Yale University Press, 1977), argues that Eckhart is a "pure metaphysician" (e.g., pp. 106–10), though it is difficult to understand exactly what Kelley means by this.

13. As noted by H. Fischer in "Die theologische Arbeitsweise Meister Eckharts in den lateinischen Werken," *Miscellanea Mediaevalia 7. Methoden in Wissenschaft und Kunst des Mittelalters* (Berlin: De Gruyter, 1970), pp. 68–69.

14. *Comm. Jn.* n. 185 (LW III, pp. 154–55).

15. *Comm. Jn.* nn. 96 and 124–25 (pp. 158, 171).

16. On Christ as the Truth, see *Par. Gen.* nn. 2–3 (pp. 94–95), and *Comm. Jn.* n. 109 (pp. 163–64). That truth and science pertain to the supernatural realm and only the likeness of truth to the natural is found in *Comm. Wis.* n. 274 (LW II, p. 604).

17. E.g., *Sermon* 15 (pp. 191–92). See also *Sermon* 9 (DW I, p. 152).

18. *Comm. Jn.* n. 361 (LW III, p. 307). On the relation between knowledge by faith and knowledge by science, see *Comm. Jn.* n. 405 (LW III, pp. 343–44).

19. *Comm. Jn.* n. 2 (p. 123). See also nn. 3, 13, and 36–37 (pp. 123, 126, 134–35).

20. K. Weiss, "Meister Eckharts Biblische Hermeneutik," in *La mystique rhénane* (Paris: Presses Universitaires, 1963), pp. 107–08, has speculated that Eckhart consciously abandoned work on the other two parts of the *Three-Part Work* to concentrate on the *Work of Expositions,* but this cannot be proven.

21. *Sermon* 51 (DW II, pp. 465–66). The image is a patristic one, the lambs being humble souls, the cows crude souls, and the elephants clever ones.

22. *Par. Gen.* nn. 1–6 (pp. 92–95). On Eckhart's exegesis, besides the works of Weiss and Koch (see notes 5 and 20), see E. Winkler, *Exegetische Methoden bei Meister Eckhart* (Tübingen: Mohr, 1965).

23. On Maimonides' influence on Eckhart, see J. Koch, "Meister Eckhart und die jüdische Religionsphilosophie des Mittelalters," *Jahresbericht der Schlesischen Gesellschaft für vaterländische Kultur 1928* 101 (1929): 134–48.

24. See Weiss, pp. 96–104; and Winkler, pp. 51–54.

25. E.g., *Par. Gen.* n. 1 (p. 92). See also *Comm. Jn.* n. 3 (p. 123).

26. The division of science into theological, natural, and moral truth appears to be a mixture of the Aristotelian division of speculative philosophy into

physics, mathematics, and theology (*Met.* 6.1), and the traditional Platonic-Stoic division of physics, logic, and ethics found in Augustine, among others (e.g., *City of God* 8.4.6–8).

27. *Comm. Ex.* n. 211 (LW II, p. 178).

28. *Par. Gen.* n. 2 (p. 93).

29. *Par. Gen.* nn. 135–36 (p. 108). For the attack, see G. Théry, "Edition critique des pièces relatives au procès d'Eckhart," *Archives d'histoire littéraire et doctrinal du moyen âge* 1 (1926): 170, 193. (Hereafter referred to as Théry.)

30. *Par. Gen.* nn. 4–6 (p. 105).

31. *Sermon* 53 (p. 203). For a presentation of Eckhart's mysticism based on this sermon, see R. Schürmann, "The Loss of Origin in Soto Zen and in Meister Eckhart," *The Thomist* 42 (1978): 281–312.

32. *Sermon* 52 (p. 203).

33. *Sermon* 15 (pp. 189–92).

34. *Sermon* 22 (p. 196).

35. *Sermon* 53 (pp. 204, 205). In the treatises, see *Bened.* 2 (p. 245).

36. LW IV, p. 237.

37. *Sermon LVI* (LW IV, p. 466).

38. On *bullitio/ebullitio*, see below pp. 37–41.

39. Eckhart cites Augustine's reflection on the paradox of speaking about the ineffable God (*Christ. Doct.* 1.6) in several places, e.g., *Sermon* 53 (p. 204).

40. E.g., *Sermons* 15, 22, 53 and 83 (pp. 192, 196, 204–05, 206–08).

41. "That God is neither good, nor better, nor best; hence I speak as incorrectly when I call God good as if I were to call white black" (p. 80). The Bull places the article in the category of statements only doubtfully ascribed to Eckhart, but both at Cologne and at Avignon the Meister accepted this text as his own—it comes from *Sermon* 9 (DW I, p. 148)—and defended it as a legitimate expression of negative theology. See also *Sermon* 83 (p. 207).

42. LW I, pp. 166–82 (trans. in Maurer, pp. 93–104). On Eckhart's doctrine of *esse*, see K. Albert, *Meister Eckharts These vom Sein* (Saarbrücken: Universitäts- und Schulbuchverlag, 1976).

43. LW V, pp. 37–48 (trans. in Maurer, pp. 43–50). On this text, see R. Imbach, *Deus est Intelligere.* Studia Friburgensia, N.F. 53 (Freiburg, Switzerland: Universitätsverlag, 1976); and in English, J. Caputo, "The Nothingness of the Intellect in Meister Eckhart's 'Parisian Questions,' " *The Thomist* 39 (1975): 85–115.

44. God is *esse simpliciter* or *luter wesen*: e.g., *Comm. Jn.* n. 60 (p. 143), *Sermon IV.*1 (LW IV, pp. 24–25), and throughout the *Comm. Ex.*; as well as in such German works as *Sermon* 39 (DW III, p. 266), *Bened.* 1 (p. 220), and *Detach.* (p. 293). God is above *esse* in some way: e.g., *Sermons XI.*2 and *XXIX* (LW IV, pp. 112 and 270); and *Sermons* 52 and 83 (pp. 201, 206) and *Detach.* (p. 291).

45. Among the texts given here, see *Comm. Gen.* n. 11 (p. 86), *Comm. Jn.*

n. 34 (p. 133). On the characteristics of *intelligere* in Eckhart, see Imbach, *Deus est Intelligere* pp. 173–80.

46. See B. McGinn, "The God beyond God: Theology and Mysticism in the Thought of Meister Eckhart," *Journal of Religion* 61 (1981): 1–19. I do not see my conclusions as fundamentally different from those of the most detailed and insightful study of Eckhart's negative theology, V. Lossky's *Théologie négative et connaissance de Dieu chez Maître Eckhart* (Paris: Vrin, 1960).

47. On Eckhart's doctrine of analogy, see especially J. Koch, "Zur Analogielehre Meister Eckharts," *Mélanges offerts à Etienne Gilson* (Paris: Vrin, 1959), pp. 327–50; and F. Brunner, "L'analogie chez Maître Eckhart," *Freiburger Zeitschrift für Philosophie und Theologie* 16 (1969): 333–49.

48. *Sermons and Lectures* n. 53 (LW II, p. 282).

49. Art. 26 taken from *Sermon* 4 (DW I, pp. 69–70), an extract condemned as suspect of heresy. See Eckhart's defense of this position, both at Cologne (Théry, pp. 247–48) and at Avignon, in F. Pelster, "Ein Gutachten aus dem Eckehart-Prozess in Avignon," *Aus der Geisteswelt des Mittelalters. Festgabe Martin Grabmann* (*Beiträge* Supplement III. Münster, 1935), pp. 1112–113. (Hereafter referred to as Pelster.)

50. *Sermon* 6 (p. 187). For a similar text in the Latin works, see *Comm. Jn.* n. 96 (pp. 158–59).

51. Théry, p. 193. For an interpretation of the meaning of this distinction in Eckhart, see B. Muller-Thym, *The Establishment of the University of Being in the Doctrine of Meister Eckhart of Hochheim* (New York: Sheed and Ward, 1939), pp. 84–88, 110–13.

52. *Par. Quest.* q. 1 n. 8 (LW V, p. 45; trans. of Maurer, p. 48).

53. Of the previous studies of Eckhart's dialectic I would note especially Lossky's book and the article of M. de Gandillac, "La 'dialectique' du Maître Eckhart," in *La mystique rhénane*, pp. 59–94.

54. *Comm. Wis.* nn. 144–57 (LW II, pp. 481–94). The two other major dialectical texts are to be found in *Comm. Ex.* nn. 110–26 (LW II, pp. 109–17), and *Sermons and Lectures on Ecclesiasticus* nn. 42–61 (LW II, pp. 270–90).

55. The dialectic of distinction/indistinction has been studied by Lossky, *Théologie negative*, pp. 254–75. In English, there is a discussion in K. Kertz, "Meister Eckhart's Teaching on the Birth of the Divine Word in the Soul," *Traditio* 15 (1959): 342, n. 53, and 351–53. Kertz's stress on seeing "not-separate" as one of the crucial components in the meaning of indistinct is well taken, but he misses the dialectical character of the term.

56. *Comm. Wis.* n. 144 (LW II, p. 482).

57. *Comm. Wis.* n. 147 (LW II, p. 485).

58. *Comm. Wis.* n. 148 (LW II, p. 486).

59. Among the texts given here, see *Comm. Jn.* n. 99 (p. 160) on the divine indistinction. On God as Absolute Unity, see, e.g., *Comm. Gen.* nn. 12, 26 (pp.

87, 91); *Par. Gen.* nn. 13–15 (pp. 96–99); *Sermons* 2, 15, and 83 (pp. 180–81, 191, 206, 208); as well as *Bened.* 1 (pp. 221–23, 227, 230).

60. See note 8 above. Although Aquinas had spoken of *unum* as the negation of negation, Eckhart was probably more influenced by the *Commentary on the Parmenides* of Proclus, available to him in William of Moerbeke's translation. On this comparison, see W. Beierwaltes, *Proklos. Grundzüge seiner Metaphysik* (Frankfurt: Klostermann, 1965), pp. 395–98.

61. E.g., *Sermon* XXIX (LW IV, pp. 263–70), and *Comm. Jn.* n. 34 (p. 133) and *Comm. Gen.* n. 11 (p. 86). On the relation of *unum* and *intelligere*, see Imbach, *Deus est Intelligere*, pp. 188–94.

62. *Comm. Jn.* nn. 511–13 (LW III, pp. 442–45). It is important to note, however, that an earlier text, commenting on Jn. 3:34, identified *unum* with the divine substance, and *ens, verum,* and *bonum* with the three divine Persons (LW III, pp. 304–06).

63. *Comm. Jn.* n. 562 (LW III, p. 489).

64. On the coincidence of opposing predicates in God, see *Sermon* XVIII (LW IV, p. 171).

65. I have investigated this in my article "The God beyond God: Theology and Mysticism in the Thought of Meister Eckhart," especially pp. 11–15. A discussion of the key texts can be found in S. Ueda, *Die Gottesgeburt in der Seele und der Durchbruch zur Gottheit* (Gütersloh: Mohn, 1965), pp. 103–07, though I would not agree with all his conclusions.

66. "In agro dominico," arts. 23 and 24, both centering on the crucial notion of distinction/indistinction. Note that these articles, however, are only "suspect of heresy."

67. *Sermon* XI.2 (LW IV, p. 112).

68. *Comm. Ex.* nn. 58 and 61 (LW II, pp. 64, 66). The combination of these two passages, largely a quotation from Maimonides, made up art. 23 of the Bull. Compare with Aquinas, *STh* Ia.13.4.

69. *Comm. Ex.* n. 65 (LW II, p. 70). See Thomas's rejection of this in *STh* Ia.28.2. Eckhart does stress that substance and relation are the only two Aristotelian categories that may be applied (though in transcendental fashion) to God; see *Comm. Ex.* n. 62 (LW II, pp. 66–67), and *Comm. Jn.* 198 (LW III, p. 167).

70. *Sermon* 48 (p. 198). See also *Sermons* 2, 52, 83 (pp. 181, 200, 202, 206). Among sermons not available here, see also 67 and 80 (DW III, pp. 132, 379).

71. E.g., *Comm. Jn.* n. 67 (p. 146). Among the German works, see *Sermon* 24 (DW I, p. 419).

72. DW I, p. 178. The text refers to the Latin sermons II–IV for Trinity Sunday (LW IV, pp. 5–32), and although no passage in these sermons as now available is exactly parallel, the teaching is similar.

73. The theme appears in the discussion of formal emanation in implicit fashion, e.g., *Comm. Jn.* nn. 25, 61–69 (pp. 129–30, 144–47).

NOTES

74. *Comm. Jn.* n. 342 (LW III, p. 291). The text as given by Koch reads *ebullitio* as the equivalent of the formal emanation (line 8), but since this goes against every other use as well as the tenor of Eckhart's thought, I suggest that it is a scribal error for *bullitio*. For other uses in the Latin works, see *Comm. Wis.* n. 283 (LW II, pp. 615–16), and *Sermons* XXV.1 and 2, and XLIX (LW IV, pp. 236, 239, 425–26).

75. *Comm. Ex.* n. 16 (LW II, pp. 21–22).

76. *Sermon* 35 (DW II, p. 180). See also *Sermons* 3 and 7 (DW I, pp. 54, 123).

77. E.g., *Comm. Jn.* nn. 4–13, 66, 75 (pp. 123–26, 145–46, 148–49). See also *Par. Gen.* n. 3 (p. 94). Among the vernacular works translated here, see, e.g., *Sermons* 22 and 52 (pp. 193, 200). The importance of the principial point of view has been stressed by C. F. Kelley, *Meister Eckhart on Divine Knowledge*; and in "Meister Eckhart's Doctrine of Divine Subjectivity," *Downside Review* 76 (1958): 65–103.

78. For an important discussion of the three types of production, see *Sermon* XLIX.3 (LW IV, pp. 424–26). Compare also with *Par. Gen.* n. 9 (p. 96).

79. *Comm. Jn.* n. 43 (p. 137), following *STh* Ia.41.5. See also *Comm. Jn.* n. 67 (p. 146).

80. *Sermon* 15 (p. 192). See also, e.g., *Par. Gen.* n. 12 (pp. 97–98).

81. E.g., *Comm. Jn.* nn. 513, 562 (LW III, pp. 444, 489), based on Augustine, *Christ. Doct.* 1.5.

82. E.g., *Comm. Jn.* n. 19; *Comm. Gen.* n. 20 (pp. 128, 89).

83. E.g., *Comm. Jn.* nn. 23–27 (pp. 129–30). See also, *Comm. Wis.* n. 283 (LW II, pp. 615–16), and *Sermon* 69 (DW III, pp. 168, 176–79).

84. E.g., *Comm. Jn.* nn. 25, 57 (pp. 129–30, 142–43).

85. E.g., *Comm. Jn.* nn. 35, 82 (pp. 132, 152–53). For a more extended analysis, see *Comm. Jn.* nn. 362–67 (LW III, pp. 307–12).

86. E.g., *Par. Gen.* nn. 9–15 (pp. 96–99).

87. E.g., *Comm. Gen.* n. 7, *Par. Gen.* n. 16, *Comm. Jn.* n. 73, and *Sermon* 53 (pp. 85, 99, 148, 205).

88. E.g., *Par. Gen.* nn. 10, 15 (pp. 96, 98–99).

89. *Comm. Gen.* n. 21, *Par. Gen.* nn. 9, 160 (pp. 89–90, 96, 119–20).

90. On acting with complete freedom without an intermediary, see *Comm. Gen.* nn. 10–11 (pp. 86–87); and on God as final cause see *Comm. Jn.* nn. 42–43 (pp. 136–37). For an extended analysis of the end of creation, see *Comm. Wis.* nn. 19–40 (LW II, pp. 339–61).

91. E.g., *Comm. Gen.* nn. 26–28; *Par. Gen.* nn. 11, 16, 19 (pp. 91; 97, 99, 100).

92. *Comm. Gen.* n. 4 (pp. 83–84).

93. See Ambrose, *Hexaemeron* 1.4; cf. Augustine, *Conf.* 12.20.

94. On the unity of Gn. 1:1 and Jn. 1:1, see *Comm. Gen.* n. 3 and *Comm. Jn.* n. 56 (pp. 83, 142).

95. The first interpretation of Jn. 1:1 centers on the relation of the Word to its Principle, the Father. There are three sections: (a) nn. 4–13 containing

fifteen general rules governing the relation of the Word to the Father; (b) nn. 14–22 on the relation of the just man to justice; and (c) nn. 23–27 on the Word as the Father's Image.

96. The second through sixth interpretations of Jn. 1:1 describe facets of the formal causality of the Word: (2) nn. 28–31—the Word as Principle; (3) n. 32—Idea as definition; (4) nn. 33–34—four properties of the Word; (5) n. 35—the four properties in relation to the Father; (6) nn. 36–37—the Word as Exemplar.

97. *Comm. Jn.* n. 38 (p. 135).

98. *Sermon* 53 (p. 205).

99. Things pre-exist in their ideas (see *Comm. Jn.* nn. 9, 12, 54; *Comm. Gen.* n. 25 on pp. 125, 126, 141; 91), and since they are in the Word they thus possess virtual existence as Word in the Father, the ultimate Principle (cf. *Comm. Jn.* nn. 44–45, and *Sermon* 52, on pp. 137, 200). The same teaching appears throughout the Latin works, e.g., *Comm. Gen.* nn. 77–78 (LW I, pp. 238–39), and *Comm. Ex.* n. 121 (LW II, p. 114).

100. E.g., *Par. Gen.* n. 62 (LW I, p. 529); *Comm. Ex.* n. 85 (LW II, p. 88); *Comm. Jn.* n. 323 (LW III, p. 271); and Defense (p. 75 below).

101. Eckhart cites passages from the eleventh book of the *Confessions* in his support, see *Comm. Jn.* nn. 217–18 (LW III, pp. 182–84). See also the text from the Defense (p. 75).

102. *Comm. Gen.* n. 7 (p. 85). This forms art. 3 of the Bull; art. 1 is taken from the passage immediately preceding. Art. 2 is from *Comm. Jn.* n. 216 (LW III, p. 187).

103. E.g., *Comm. Jn.* n. 18 (p. 127); *Sermon* XLV (LW IV, p. 380); *Bened.* 2 (pp. 238–39); and *Detach.* (p. 290).

104. Théry, p. 194. See also the appearance of the same argument in the general principles of the Defense translated here (p. 73). Eckhart also used the response at Avignon (Pelster, pp. 1109–110).

105. See Pelster, pp. 1110–111. The commission theologians give five reasons why the Meister's distinction cannot apply to creation.

106. *Sermon* XV.2 (LW IV, pp. 147–48).

107. Two of the most important of these are: (a) the distinction between two kinds of efficient causality, univocal and analogical, in, e.g., *Comm. Jn.* nn. 5, 31 (pp. 124, 131–32) and especially *Par. Gen.* nn. 116–27 (LW I, pp. 582–91); and (b) the discussion of the principles of created being, the *extrinsic*, i.e., active and passive, or heaven and earth (*Par. Gen.* nn. 21–26 on pp. 101–03) and the pairs of *intrinsic* principles, form and matter (*Par. Gen.* nn. 28–33 on pp. 103–05) and existence and essence (*Par. Gen.* n. 34 on pp. 105–06).

108. *Comm. Gen.* nn. 10–13 (pp. 86–87). See also the discussion in *Comm. Wis.* nn. 35–37 (LW II, pp. 355–59). For Eckhart the very etymology of *universum* said the same—*uni-versum*, or "toward the One."

NOTES

109. The three levels of creation are discussed in *Comm. Jn.* nn. 83 (4 grades counting angels) and 89 (pp. 153, 155–56); and *Par. Gen.* n. 151 (p. 115).

110. *Comm. Jn.* n. 63 (p. 144–45).

111. *Comm. Jn.* n. 64 (p. 145).

112. *Sermon* 15 (p. 192).

113. *Sermon* 2 (pp. 179–81). See also *Sermon* 5b and 52 (pp. 183, 200).

114. E.g., *Sermons* 22 and 48 (pp. 194, 198).

115. E.g., *Sermon* 2 (p. 181). For questions regarding such terminology a useful starting place is B. Schmoldt, *Die deutsche Begriffsprache Meister Eckharts* (Heidelberg: Quelle and Meyer, 1954).

116. E.g., *Sermons* 17 (DW I, p. 242), 77 (DW III, pp. 337–38), and LV.4 (LW IV, p. 458).

117. See B. McGinn, "The Negative Element in the Anthropology of John the Scot," in *John Scot Érigène et l'histoire de la Philosophie* (Paris: Editions du Centre National, 1977), pp. 315–25, for the history. For a contemporary version, see K. Rahner, "An Investigation of the Incomprehensibility of God in Thomas Aquinas," in *Theological Investigations,* Vol. XVI (New York: Seabury, 1979), pp. 244–54.

118. *Sermon* IV.1 (LW IV, p. 28).

119. *Sermon* 48 (p. 198). Such statements appear in other places in the vernacular sermons, e.g., *Sermon* 13 (DW I, p. 220).

120. "In agro dominico," appended art. 1, taken from *Sermon* 13 (see p. 80).

121. Théry, pp. 188, 191, 201, 211, 214–15; and Pelster, pp. 1111–112.

122. G. Théry, "Contribution à l'histoire du procès d'Eckhart. IV," *La vie spirituelle. Supplement* 13 (1926): 58–59, tried to find a psychological explanation in Eckhart's successive changes of mind.

123. The language of "piece" or "part" was apparently what disturbed Eckhart in the public statement he made in the Dominican Church at Cologne on Feb. 13, 1327; see M.-H. Laurent, "Autour du procès de Maître Eckhart. Les documents des Archives Vaticanes," *Divus Thomas* (Piacenza), Ser. III, 13 (1936): 345. See also the same theme at Avignon, in Pelster, pp. 1111–112. J. M. Clark in his *Meister Eckhart. An Introduction to the Study of His Works with an Anthology of his Sermons* (Edinburgh: Nelson, 1957), p. 89, also has a suggestion along these lines.

124. E.g., *Bened.* 2 (pp. 240–42); *Detach.* (pp. 290–91).

125. *Par. Gen.* nn. 135–65 (pp. 108–21), based on Augustine, *Trin.* 12.13.30, etc.

126. *Par. Gen.* nn. 139, 145–48 (pp. 109–10, 112–14).

127. *Sermon* 83 (p. 208).

128. *Sermon* 2 (pp. 179–80). In defense of this passage at Cologne Eckhart said: "God is taken by the intellect under the aspect of the true, by the will under the aspect of the good (these are powers in the soul); under the aspect of existence he penetrates the essence of the soul" (Théry, p. 204).

NOTES

129. On the Word as *imago Dei* see especially *Comm. Jn.* n. 23 (p. 129) and *Sermon* 69 (DW III, p. 168). For Eckhart's notion of image in general, see *Comm. Wis.* nn. 143, 283 (LW II, pp. 480–81, 615–16) and *Sermon* XLIX (LW II, pp. 421–28).

130. See my article "Meister Eckhart's Condemnation Reconsidered," *The Thomist* 44 (1980), p. 404, for further reflections on this.

131. For the soul as *imago Dei*, see *Comm. Jn.* nn. 84, 119–20 (pp. 153, 168–69); *Par. Gen.* nn. 139–40 (pp. 109–10); *Bened.* 2 (p. 243); *Detach.* (p. 285); and *Sermon* 83 (p. 206).

132. E.g., *Comm. Jn.* n. 123; *Par. Gen.* nn. 138, 143, 154; *Bened.* (pp. 170; 109, 112, 116–17; 243). K. Kertz, "Meister Eckhart's Teaching," pp. 344–46, stressed the importance of the *ad imaginem* texts.

133. S. Ueda, *Die Gottesgeburt*, pp. 62, 82–84, sees a dialectical transition from *ad imaginem Dei* to *imago Dei* in Eckhart's thought on deification. The frequent interchangeability of formulae is evident in the Meister's commentary on Gn. 1:26 ("Let us make man in our image and likeness") in *Comm. Gen.* nn. 115–20 (LW I, pp. 270–76). See also *Comm. Wis.* n. 274 (LW II, p. 609).

134. E.g., *Comm. Jn.* nn. 52, 55 (pp. 140, 141–42).

135. *Comm. Jn.* nn. 52, 91 (pp. 140, 156–57).

136. *Par. Gen.* n. 139 (p. 109).

137. E.g., *Comm. Jn.* n. 75 (pp. 149–50). See also *Par. Gen.* n. 89 (LW I, pp. 551–52), where sin in the broad sense of any evil is something alien or dissimilar to the form that should be present.

138. *Comm. Gen.* n. 21 (p. 90). See also *Comm. Gen.* n. 153 (LW I, pp. 303–04).

139. *Comm. Jn.* n. 494 (LW III, p. 426).

140. Art. 15 is close to a passage in *Couns.* 12 (pp. 261–62). The Avignon report, however, says that the error had been preached (*predicavit*—Pelster, p. 1123), so it may come from a lost sermon. Art. 14 is taken from *Bened.* 1 (pp. 216–17) and was also cited at Cologne (Théry, pp. 162, 189).

141. Pelster, pp. 1113–114.

142. Pelster, p. 1124.

143. Pelster, *ibid.*

144. *Par. Gen.* n. 144 (p. 112).

145. *Comm. Gen.* n. 115 (LW I, p. 272).

146. *Sermon* XVII (LW IV, p. 158).

147. H. Fischer, "Die theologische Arbeitsweise Meister Eckharts," pp. 58–59, n. 11, criticizes B. Weiss, *Die Heilsgeschichte bei Meister Eckhart* (Mainz: Grünewald, 1965) for not realizing that Eckhart's writings do not try to present a synthesis, or *summa*, of the whole of Christian belief, and therefore do not fully develop all elements of Christian belief.

148. For a study of the Incarnation in Eckhart's thought, see Ueda, *Die Gottesgeburt*, pp. 39–50.

149. *Sermon* XXV.1 (LW IV, pp. 237–38). On the theology of grace in Eckhart, see Clark, *Meister Eckhart*, pp. 54–57.

150. He does cite familiar Thomistic divisions in *Comm. Wis.* nn. 272–74 (LW II, pp. 602–04), and *Sermon* XXV.1 (LW IV, p. 235).

151. There is one interesting discussion of the relation of grace and freedom in *Detach.* (pp. 291–92) where it is said that God "finds or creates a willing cooperation." The example given, that of the loaves in the oven, may seem to give away too much to free will, but it is important to note that according to the same analogy it is the baker (i.e., God) who creates the various kinds of loaves.

152. See the summaries in *Sermon* II.2 (LW IV, pp. 16–20), and the *Sermon for the Feast of St. Augustine* n. 11 (LW V, pp. 97–98).

153. *Comm. Jn.* n. 89 (p. 156); *Sermon* IX (LW IV, pp. 93–94).

154. *Par. Gen.* n. 145 (pp. 112–13); *Sermons* IX, XVII.5 (LW IV, pp. 94, 168); *Comm. Wis.* n. 273 (LW II, p. 603); *Comm. Jn.* n. 521 (LW III, pp. 449–50).

155. *Comm. Jn.* n. 120 (p. 169); *Sermon* XXV.2 (LW IV, p. 240).

156. Théry, pp. 229–35.

157. Théry, pp. 230–31. On Christ assuming human nature, see also *Sermon* 5b (p. 182).

158. *Comm. Jn.* n. 102 (p. 161). Remember that Eckhart had spoken of the Incarnation as the mid-point between emanation and creation in the text cited on p. 27.

159. *Comm. Jn.* nn. 106, 117–20 (pp. 162, 167–69), and *Sermon* 22 (pp. 192–93). See also *Detach.* (p. 287).

160. Théry, p. 202.

161. Théry, pp. 233–34.

162. LW IV, pp. 380–87.

163. E.g., *Sermon* 22 (p. 196); *Bened.* 1 (pp. 230, 231–32); *Couns.*20 (p. 272).

164. On Church and sacraments in Eckhart, see Clark, *Meister Eckhart*, pp. 66–68.

165. Kertz, "Meister Eckhart's Teaching," pp. 347–51, 362–63, has argued that the Meister's understanding of the birth of the Son in the soul is based on the doctrine of the Church as the Mystical Body of Christ. See below, pp. 50–55.

166. *Sermons* V.1–3 for the Feast of Corpus Christi are heavily Thomistic (LW IV, pp. 33–49). *Sermons* 20a and b (DW I, pp. 326–52) make use of the Eucharist to initiate discussion of the internal appropriation of God in the soul.

167. *Couns.*20 on the Eucharist, and *Couns.*21 on zeal (pp. 270–77). On the latter, see also *Sermon* X (LW IV, pp. 102–03).

168. E.g., *Couns.*18 and 23 (pp. 268–69, 280–85).

169. E.g., *Sermon* 52 (p. 199). See the discussion on interior and exterior works below on pp. 58–59.

170. *Detach.* (p. 288).

171. Ibid. See also *Bened.*1; and *Couns.*7 (pp. 220–21; 254–55).

172. E.g., *Comm. Jn.* n. 100; *Par. Gen.* n. 31; *Bened.*1 (pp. 160; 104–05; 220).

173. *Comm. Jn.* n. 110; *Sermon* 15 (pp. 164; 191).

174. *Sermon* 5b (p. 183).

175. Arts. 7, 8, 9. Art. 7 is drawn from *Comm. Jn.* n. 611 (LW III, p. 534).

176. *Detach.* (p. 286).

177. *Sermon* 15 (p. 190). See also *Sermons* 48 (p. 197), 69 (DW III, p. 163), and VI.1 (LW IV, p. 54).

178. *Sermon* 6 (p. 187).

179. *Detach.* (pp. 285–87).

180. *Detach.* (p. 294).

181. On the importance of humility, see *Sermon*15 (p. 190); *Couns.* 23 (pp. 280–81); and *Comm. Jn.* n. 90 (p. 156).

182. *Detach.* (p. 292).

183. *Sermon* 83 (p. 208).

184. *Comm. Wis.* n. 282 (LW II, pp. 614–15).

185. *Sermon* 22 (p. 196). See also *Sermon* 53 on the kiss (p. 205); *Par. Gen.* nn. 146, 152 (pp. 113, 116); and *Comm. Jn.* nn. 292–93 commenting on the marriage at Cana (LW III, pp. 244–45).

186. *Bened.*1 (pp. 228–29). See also *Bened.*1 (pp. 221–22); and *Couns.*15 (pp. 264–65).

187. *Sermon* 2 (p. 178).

188. The importance of love for Eckhart the preacher is evident by listing the sermons that take *caritas* as their major theme—5a, 5b, 27, 28, 41, 48, 63, 65, 67, 75, and 82; and VI.1–4, XXX.1–2, XL.1–3, and XLVII.2–3.

189. The theme is not totally absent from the Latin works. See, e.g., *Comm. Jn.* nn. 119, 130–31 (pp. 168–69, 172–73); *Par. Gen.* n. 180 (LW I, p. 650); *Comm. Wis.* nn. 281, 283 (LW II, pp. 613, 615–16); and *Sermons* VI.2 and LV.2 (LW IV, pp. 57, 455–56).

190. See above pp. 7–9.

191. H. Rahner, "Die Gottesgeburt. Die Lehre der Kirchenväter von der Geburt Christi aus dem Herzen der Kirche und der Gläubigen," in *Symbole der Kirche* (Salzburg: Müller, 1964), pp. 13–87.

192. On Gregory and his follower Maximus the Confessor, see Rahner, "Die Gottesgeburt," pp. 48–56.

193. Rahner, "Die Gottesgeburt," pp. 71–79.

194. Rahner, "Die Gottesgeburt," pp. 82–86.

195. Important treatments are found in *Sermons* 2, 4, 5b, 6, 11, 14, 19, 22, 25, 28, 29, 30, 31, 38, 39, 40, 41, 42, 44, 46, 50, 59, and 75. It also appears in the treatises, especially in the *Bened.*1 and 2 (e.g., pp. 227, 243).

196. For a useful summary of texts, see Ueda, *Die Gottesgeburt*, especially pp. 81–97. Ueda stresses that the birth of the Son is the natural culmination

of the soul's character as image of God (p. 61). Among English works, the article of Kertz, "Meister Eckhart's Teaching," is of merit, but see also R. Schürmann, *Meister Eckhart. Mystic and Philosopher* (Bloomington: Indiana University Press, 1978), pp. 18–26, 74–80; and J. Caputo, *The Mystical Element in Heidegger's Thought* (Athens, Ohio: Ohio University Press, 1978), pp. 113–18.

197. Besides *Comm. Jn.* nn. 14–22 (pp. 126–29), see also *Comm. Gen.* n. 20; *Par. Gen.* nn. 147–49; and *Bened.* 1 (pp. 89; 113–14; 209–12).

198. *Sermon* 6 (p. 185). This statement was the source of art. 8 of the Bull. Eckhart's defense, both at Cologne (Théry, pp. 239–40) and at Avignon (Pelster, p. 1115) was to insist that God alone is the reward of the soul.

199. On the *in quantum* principle, see below, pp. 53–54.

200. This absolute equality is the source for the statement made toward the end of the sermon (p. 188) about not asking God for anything because this would presuppose the status of a servant. The passage became art. 9 of the Bull.

201. *Sermon* 6 (p. 187). Together with another sentence from this paragraph this forms art. 22 of the "In agro dominico."

202. *Sermon* 5b (p. 183). See also *Sermons* 2 and 53 (pp. 180–81, 205).

203. *Sermon* 6 (p. 187). The MHG text does not contain "as," added here to bring out the sense.

204. *Sermon* 22 (p. 194). Similar texts concerning the soul's identity with the Father in bearing the Son are found in *Sermons* 2 and 83 (pp. 179, 206), and in the Latin *Sermons* XL.3, LI and LV.2 (LW IV, pp. 345, 433, 455–56).

205. *Sermon* 6, ". . . there I spring out in the Holy Spirit" (p. 187). See also *Bened.* 1 (p. 227).

206. *Sermon* 52 (p. 202), and also the text on p. 203 where the soul is said to create all things.

207. Kertz, "Meister Eckhart's Teaching," pp. 329, 331–32, in reference to the text from *Sermon* 52 cited above.

208. Pelster, p. 1117. The phrase appears in both the Cologne lists as well (Théry, pp. 177, 242—see Eckhart's responses on pp. 199, 243–44).

209. Arts. 10, 11, 12, condemned as heretical, and arts. 20 and 21 as suspect of heresy. Art. 13, also judged as heretical, states: "Whatever is proper to the divine nature, all that is proper to the just and divine man. Because of that this man performs whatever God performs, and he created heaven and earth together with God, and is the begetter of the Eternal Word, and God would not know how to do anything without such a man." It is noteworthy that arts. 11, 13, and 20 in this group are not verbatim from Eckhart's surviving works, though 11 does relate to *Sermon* 5a (DW I, p. 77) and 20 to *Bened.* 1 (p. 229).

210. *Sermon* 6 (p. 188), and "In agro dominico," art. 10 (p. 78).

211. Théry, pp. 199 and 244. See also Pelster, p. 1118.

212. See Kertz, "Meister Eckhart's Teaching, pp. 358–62, a strained reading.

NOTES

213. In the course of the Cologne proceedings Eckhart admitted error and falsity twelve times and six times characterized articles as "evil-sounding," or the equivalents. All these cases refer to extracts from the vernacular sermons.

214. Pelster, p. 1117. For Eckhart's responses to attacks on his claims on the equality of God and man, see Théry, pp. 198–99, 201, 214–15, 220, 231–32, 243–44, 265, and 266.

215. E.g., *Comm. Jn.* nn. 106, 115, 117, and 123 (pp. 162, 167, 167–68, 170). See also *Bened.*1 (pp. 224–25).

216. See Kertz, "Meister Eckhart's Teaching," pp. 341–50. For the doctrine of the Body of Christ in Eckhart, the *locus classicus* is his commentary on Jn. 4:38 in *Comm. Jn.* nn. 381–404 (LW III, pp. 324–43).

217. Pelster, p. 1120.

218. Defense, pp. 72–73.

219. E.g., *Comm. Jn.* nn. 16 and 18 in the texts given here (pp. 127–28); and among later texts, nn. 362, 389, 426, and 438 (LW III, pp. 307, 324, 362, and 376).

220. *Comm. Jn.* n. 455 (LW III, p. 389). My italics.

221. Pelster, p. 1117 (my italics).

222. E.g., D. T. Suzuki, *Mysticism: Christian and Buddhist* (New York: Macmillan, 1957), pp. 13–20. More accurate treatments can be found in the works of Ueda, Schürmann, and Caputo.

223. *Sermon* 52 (p. 203).

224. *Sermon* 83 (p. 206).

225. *Sermon* 48 (p. 198).

226. *Par. Gen.* n. 165 (p. 121). See also *Sermon* 15 (p. 192).

227. The theme of the spiritual itinerary in Eckhart is stressed by Schürmann, *Meister Eckhart*, e.g., pp. 59sqq.

228. *Bened.*2 (p. 247). The desert metaphor occurs mostly in the vernacular works, e.g., *Sermons* 10, 12, 29, 60, 81, and 86. In the Latin works we find it in *Par. Gen.* n. 149 (p. 114).

229. E.g., *Sermons* 15 and 83 (pp. 191, 208); *Bened.*2 (p. 244); and *Par. Gen.* nn. 147–48 (pp. 113–14).

230. E.g., *Sermons* 6 and 83 (pp. 188, 208); *Bened.*1 (pp. 221–23); *Comm. Wis.* n. 282 (LW II, pp. 614–15); *Sermon* XLIV (LW IV, p. 367).

231. *Par. Gen.* n. 32 (p. 105).

232. *Sermon* XI (LW IV, p. 105). See also *Sermon* XXIV.2 (LW IV, p. 225).

233. E.g., *On Loving God* 10.28; and *Sermons on the Song of Songs* 71.7–10. The phrase *unus spiritus* is from 1 Co. 6:17.

234. *Sermon* XIX.1 (LW IV, p. 276).

235. *Sermon* XLIV (LW IV, p. 367). See also *Sermons* XI.2 and LV.4 (LW IV, pp. 111, 465).

236. *Par. Quest.* q. 3 (LW V, pp. 55–71). See also the reference to this in *Sermon* 9 (DW I, pp. 152–54).

237. E.g., *Comm. Jn.* nn. 673, 697 (LW III, pp. 587–88, 612); and *Sermon* XI.2 (LW IV, pp. 110–15).

238. *Sermon* 52 (p. 201). See also *Sermon* XI.2 (LW IV, p. 115).

239. *Couns.* 23 (p. 282).

240. *Sermon* 52 (p. 199).

241. *Couns.* 17 (pp. 266–68).

242. *Sermon* 5b (p. 183).

243. *Bened.* 1, *passim; Couns.* 18 (pp. 268–69); and *Detach* (p. 294). See also *Comm. Jn.* nn. 76–77 (pp. 150–51), and *Sermon* XLV (LW IV, pp. 380–87).

244. E.g., *Par. Gen.* nn. 37–40; and *Couns.* 20 (pp. 106–07, and 270–74). See also *Sermons* XXX.1–2 and XLI.1–2 (LW IV, pp. 271–81, 335–43). The metaphysical roots for the command are investigated in *Comm. Jn.* nn. 543–44 (LW III, pp. 474–75).

245. E.g., *Comm. Wis.* nn. 99, 109 (LW II, pp. 434–35, 445); *Comm. Jn.* nn. 389–91 (LW III, pp. 332–34); *Sermon* 30 (DW II, p. 103).

246. Art. 25 drawn from *Comm. Jn.* n. 728. On the equal love owed to all men, see, e.g., *Sermon* 5b (p. 182), and in the negative form, *Comm. Jn.* n. 112 (p. 165).

247. Art. 16 and 17 from *Par. Gen.* n. 165 (p. 121); art. 18 from *Comm. Jn.* n. 646 (LW III, p. 561); art. 19 from *Comm. Wis.* n. 226 (LW II, p. 561).

248. On the heresy of the "Free Spirit," first condemned at the Council of Vienne in 1312, see G. Leff, *Heresy in the Later Middle Ages*, 2 vols. (New York: Barnes and Noble, 1967), 1: 308–407, for the traditional picture. This view has been challenged by R. E. Lerner, *The Heresy of the Free Spirit in the Later Middle Ages* (Berkeley: University of California Press, 1972), who doubts that a "Free Spirit" movement ever really existed apart from the minds of Church leaders.

249. At Cologne (Théry, p. 195), he incorrectly cited *STh* IaIIae.20.4 in his defense.

250. *Par. Gen.* n. 165 (p. 121).

251. E.g., *Lectures and Sermons on Ecclesiasticus* n. 26 (LW II, p. 253); *Comm. Jn.* n. 307 (LW III, p. 255); *Bened.* 1 (pp. 225–27; *Couns.* 16 (pp. 265–66).

252. Pelster, p. 1114. *Couns.* 23 (p. 280).

253. *Detach.* (pp. 292–93).

254. See also *Couns.* 1 (p. 248) on true prayer.

255. On art. 7 see note 175 above.

256. Arts. 8 and 9 can be found on pp. 185 and 188 of *Sermon* 6.

257. Translated on pp. 72–73.

258. E.g., "In agro dominico," art. 13 (p. 79). See such expressions as those in *Sermon* 83 (p. 208) and *Comm. Jn.* n. 68 (pp. 146–47).

259. *Sermon* 5b (p. 184). See also *Sermons* 26, 39, and 41 (DW II, pp. 27, 253–54, 289, and 293). For a good study, see J. Caputo, *The Mystical Element*, Part

NOTES

III. "The Rose Is Without Why: Meister Eckhart's Mysticism"; and his article "Fundamental Themes in Eckhart's Mysticism," *The Thomist* 42 (1978): 197–225.

260. *Sermon* 28 (DW II, p. 5).

261. *Comm. Ex.* n. 247 (LW II, p. 201). See also *Sermon* IV.1 (LW IV, pp. 22–23). On God's having no "why," see *Comm. Jn.* n. 50 (p. 139).

262. DW III, pp. 481–92. On this sermon, see Caputo, *The Mystical Element*, pp. 137–39.

263. Eckhart follows the traditional interpretation in *Comm. Jn.* n. 130 (pp. 172–73).

264. DW III, pp. 491–92.

265. E.g., *Sermon* 75 (DW III, pp. 301–02); *Couns.* 10 (pp. 256–59).

266. *Sermon* 5b (p. 183).

267. *Couns.* 6 (p. 252). See also p. 255.

268. *Couns.* 4 (p. 250).

269. Schürmann, *Meister Eckhart*, p. 47.

270. E.g., *Sermon* 86 (DW III, p. 482). *Couns.* 10, 15, and 20 (pp. 258–59, 264, 271–72).

271. *Sermon* 16b (DW I, p. 272).

272. See the detailed study of these texts in R. Kieckhefer, "Meister Eckhart's Conception of Union with God," *Harvard Theological Review* 71 (1978): 221–24.

273. Kieckhefer (p. 224) sees him as a proponent of habitual or nonabstractive union. See also my paper "The God beyond God: Theology and Mysticism in the Thought of Meister Eckhart," pp. 17–19.

274. *Sermon* 66 (DW III, pp. 113–14).

INTRODUCTION: 3. A NOTE ON ECKHART'S WORKS

1. The most complete study of the history of Eckhart's reputation is to be found in I. Degenhardt, *Studien zum Wandel des Eckhartbildes* (Leiden: Brill, 1967). On the Romantic revival, see pp. 105–31.

2. H. Denifle, "Meister Eckharts lateinische Schriften und die Grundanschauung seiner Lehre," *Archiv für Literatur-und Kirchengeschichte des Mittelalters* 2 (1886): 417–615.

3. For the work of such scholars as Strauch, Spamer, Jostes, Pahncke, etc., see also T. Schaller, "Die Meister Eckhart-Forschung von der Jarhundertwende bis zur Gegenwart," *Freiburger Zeitschrift für Philosophie und Theologie* 15 (1968), especially pp. 262–84.

4. One interesting textual question concerns the two recensions of the "Prologues" to the *Three-Part Work*, the *Comm. Gen.* and the *Comm. Ex.*, one according to an Erfurt ms. (E) found in LW I, pp. 1–104, and the other, partially

translated here, according to mss. in Kues and Trier (CT), found in LW I, pp. 105–702.

5. LW I, pp. 149–51.

6. LW I, pp. 166–82, translated by A. Maurer, *Parisian Questions and Prologues* (Toronto: Pontifical Institute, 1974), pp. 93–104.

7. LW V, pp. 27–83. From Eckhart's Paris periods we also have a brief "collation," or introductory lecture to Peter Lombard's *Sentences* (LW V, pp. 17–26), as well as a university sermon delivered on the Feast of St. Augustine (LW V, pp. 89–99).

8. The *Par. Quest.* have been translated by A. Maurer in *Master Eckhart*, pp. 43–75.

9. See above, p. 28.

10. These have been edited in LW I, the *Comm. Gen.* on pp. 185–444, and the *Par. Gen.* on pp. 447–702.

11. *Comm. Ex.* in LW II, pp. 1–227; *Comm. Wis.* in LW II, pp. 301–634.

12. LW II, pp. 231–300.

13. LW II, pp. 636 sqq.

14. LW III, nearly complete in nine fascicules and 624 pp.

15. E.g., *Sermons* IV.1–2, VI.1–3, XI.1–2, XXIX, XL.1–3, XLV, XLIX.2–3, and LV.4.

16. LW V, pp. 109sqq.

17. Both of the authors of the Introduction have studied Eckhart's trial in greater detail, respectively in E. Colledge, "Studies on Eckhart's Life and Works," *The Thomist* 42 (1978): 240–58; and B. McGinn, "Meister Eckhart's Condemnation Reconsidered," *The Thomist* 44 (1980): 390–414.

18. M.-H. Laurent, "Autour du procès de Maître Eckhart. Les documents des Archives Vaticanes," *Divus Thomas* (Piacenza), Ser. III, 13 (1936): 331–48, 430–47.

19. F. Pelster, "Ein Gutachten aus dem Eckehart-Prozess in Avignon," *Aus der Geisteswelt des Mittelalters. Festgabe M. Grabmann* (*Beiträge* Supplement III. Münster, 1935), pp. 1099–124.

20. See below, p. 74.

21. One may note that only 33 of Pfeiffer's 111 sermons appear among Quint's 86.

22. DW V, pp. 185–311.

23. See "In agro dominico," arts. 14 and 15 and notes.

24. DW V, pp. 8–61.

25. DW V, pp. 109–19.

26. DW V, pp. 400–37.

NOTES

PART ONE: 1. DOCUMENTS RELATING TO ECKHART'S CONDEMNATION

A. SELECTIONS FROM ECKHART'S DEFENSE

NOTES. The critical edition of Eckhart's Defense has not yet appeared in volume V of the LW. This translation follows the order and text of the edition of G. Théry, "Édition critique des pièces relatives au procès d'Eckhart contenues dans le manuscrit 33b de la Bibliothèque de Soest," *Archives d'histoire doctrinale et littéraire du moyen âge* 1 (1926): 185–87, 195–97, 205–07. (Hereafter referred to as Théry.) In addition, I have compared Théry's text throughout with the earlier edition of A. Daniels, "Eine lateinische Rechtfertigungsschrift des Meister Eckhart," *Beiträge zur Geschichte der Philosophie des Mittelalters* 23.5 (1923): 1–4, 12–13, 34–35, 65–66. In several places noted I have preferred his readings.

1. Reiner, a canon of the Cologne Cathedral, was later replaced by a second Franciscan, Albert of Milan. A Custodian in the Franciscan order was a brother in charge of a *custodia*, or subdivision of a province. In this sentence I read *coram* with Daniels, rather than *contra* with Théry.

2. Eckhart's appeal to the exemption of the Dominican order from the local bishop was an important principle in the complex negotiations of late 1326 and early 1327.

3. Reading *nationis* with Daniels, rather than *rationis* with Théry.

4. Henry of Virneburg, the Archbishop of Cologne, was the chief instigator of the proceedings against Eckhart. This sentence also seems to refer to the activities of two renegade Dominicans, Hermann de Summo and William of Nideggen, in attacks on Eckhart.

5. This is a reference to the investigation leading to the condemnation of suspect propositions by Bishop Stephen Tempier in 1277.

6. A reference to the canonization of Saint Thomas in 1323 by John XXII.

7. The vernacular work here translated as the *Book 'Benedictus.'*

8. This response of Eckhart to attacks on the *Bened.* has not survived.

9. Letter 60.

10. That is, God insofar as he is (has existence) is not evil, although God insofar as he is understanding knows evil. This is true even though existence and understanding are the same in God. On the importance of the *in quantum* principle, see Introduction, pp. 53–54.

11. The "absolute," common, or essential acts of God are those performed by all three Persons in common. Eckhart's point is that even these are "appropriated," or metaphorically ascribed, to one or the other of the divine Persons according to their individual attributes or properties, e.g., sanctification to the

NOTES

Holy Spirit. For the use of the term "absolute" regarding predications of God, see Thomas Aquinas, *In I Sent.* 23.1.3.

12. *On Consideration* 5.5.

13. Compare this with the extended treatment of the identity of the just man and justice in the *Comm. Jn.* nn. 14–22 (pp. 126–29).

14. The analogical relation of goodness in God and in us is important to keep in mind in assessing Eckhart's desire to maintain necessary distinctions between God and the justified individual.

15. "Existence," literally, *id quo est.* See the distinction between *id quo est,* or existence, and *id quod est,* or essence, in *Par. Gen.* n. 34 (pp. 105–06).

16. *Phys.* 7.1 (241b24).

17. On this principle, see, e.g., *Comm. Jn.* n. 20 (p. 128).

18. On this, see *Comm. Jn.* nn. 41, 57 (pp. 136, 142–43).

19. See Thomas Aquinas, *STh* Ia.13.7, 14.8, and 28.1.

20. See, e.g., *Comm. Gen.* n. 24 (p. 90), and *Comm. Jn.* n. 107 (pp. 162–63).

21. *On the Trinity* 2.

22. Eckhart's refusal to admit to any accusation of heresy was the keystone of his Defense.

23. In responding to some ninety-two excerpts drawn from the vernacular sermons in both the List of Forty-nine and the List of Fifty-nine Articles (some single articles contain several excerpts), Eckhart admitted error or falsity in twelve cases and described six others as in some way "evil-sounding."

24. The text was originally from Augustine's *Gospel Questions* 2.40. Pseudo-Bede, *Exposition on Luke 5,* which served as a homily in the Dominican office, also used it.

25. Eckhart concludes by citing a text from Augustine's *Trin.* 1.3.6 where the bishop defends himself from misunderstandings of his views that have led some into error.

26. Augustine's teaching, e.g., Letter 43.1, was repeated by many later theologians and incorporated in Gratian's *Decretum,* II c.xxiv, q.3, cap.xxix.

27. See the fifth and sixth articles of the second group (Théry, pp. 169, 192).

28. See the response to the fourteenth article of the first group (Théry, p. 191).

29. Eckhart is incorrect in claiming that this was a common opinion of the Schoolmen, and in his response to this point (Théry, p. 195) he falsely cites Thomas Aquinas (*STh* IaIIae.20.4) as agreeing with him. The Meister's views about the relation of internal and external acts were condemned in articles 16–19 of the Bull "In agro dominico" (p. 79). See Introduction, pp. 57–59.

30. Both Théry and Daniels read *in alio nunc eternitatis,* but on the basis of Eckhart's constant usage, as reflected below in the repetition of this point on p. 76, the original reading must have been *in alio nunc quam in nunc eternitatis,* as translated here.

31. The implications that Eckhart drew from this teaching were condemned in articles 1–3 of "In agro dominico." See *Comm. Gen.* n. 7 (pp. 84–85).

32. *Conf.*1.6.3. A favorite Augustine quotation of Eckhart's, appearing, e.g., in *Comm. Jn.* nn. 580 and 638 (LW III, pp. 508, 554).

33. This position too was finally condemned in article 26 of "In agro dominico."

34. Eckhart is attempting to turn the tables on his opponents by claiming that their attacks on his teaching imply the following five errors, which, if obstinately defended, would be equivalent to heresy.

35. *Conf.*1.6.3.

B. THE BULL "In agro dominico"

NOTES. This translation is based on the text given by M.-H. Laurent, "Autour du procès de Maître Eckhart. Les documents des Archives Vaticanes," *Divus Thomas* (Piacenza), Ser. III, 13 (1936): 435–46, as compared with the partial text given in Denzinger-Schönmetzer, *Enchiridion Symbolorum* (Freiberg: Herder, 1976), nos. 950–80.

1. The text of the Bull reads *primo* (first), but the passage on which it is based and Eckhart's general use argue that *prius* (earlier) is correct.

2. Based on *Comm. Gen.* n. 7 (p. 85), but the second part is more a paraphrase and adaptation than a translation. On the first three articles, see Introduction, pp. 40–41.

3. From *Comm. Jn.* n. 216 (LW III, p. 187).

4. Also based on *Comm. Gen.* n. 7.

5. From *Comm. Jn.* n. 494 (LW III, p. 426). The next two articles are drawn from the same passage. For a discussion, see Introduction, pp. 44–45.

6. "Anything particular = *hoc aut hoc.* On this question, see Introduction, p. 48.

7. *Comm. Jn.* n. 611 (LW III, p. 534). On this article and the following two, see Introduction, p. 59.

8. From *Sermon* 6 (p. 185).

9. From *Sermon* 6 (p. 188).

10. From *Sermon* 6 (p. 188). See Introduction, pp. 52–53.

11. This is close to a passage in *Sermon* 5a (DW I, p. 77) that appears in abbreviated fashion in *Sermon* 5b (p. 182). On this article, see Introduction, pp. 17 and 52–53.

12. From *Sermon* 24 (DW I, pp. 421–22).

13. Not found verbatim in Eckhart's surviving works, though there is a distant parallel to a passage in *Bened.*1 (p. 228). For Eckhart's defense of this article, see Introduction, pp. 53–54.

14. Probably drawn from *Bened.*1 (pp. 216–17), though, as Introduction,

pp. 13–14, points out, the same teaching is found in *Couns.*11 (p. 261). For theological reflections on this, see Introduction, pp. 44–45.

15. Seems to depend on *Couns.*12 (pp. 261–62), though it is a paraphrase.

16. From *Par. Gen.* n. 165 (p. 121), which is also the source for the following article. On Eckhart's view of the relation of interior and exterior acts condemned in this and the following three articles, see Introduction, pp. 57–59.

17. From *Comm. Jn.* n. 646 (LW III, p. 561).

18. From *Comm. Wis.* n. 226 (LW II, p. 561).

19. This is related to a passage in *Bened.*1 (p. 229), but more by way of summary than by quotation.

20. From *Sermon* 14 (DW I, p. 239). See Introduction, p. 54 for Eckhart's response to this before the Avignon Commission.

21. From *Sermon* 6 (p. 187). See the discussion in Introduction, pp. 51–52.

22. The text of the Bull reads *nec ponit in unum cum aliquo*, but what Eckhart wrote was *nec ponit in numerum cum aliquo*, as translated here.

23. From *Comm. Ex.* nn. 58–60 (LW II, pp. 65–66). The first sentence is a quotation from Maimonides, *Guide* 1.51. See Introduction, pp. 36–37 for this and the next article.

24. From *Bened.*2 (p. 244).

25. From *Comm. Jn.* n. 728. What is under attack here is Eckhart's notion that in perfect love as it exists in the One, there can be no question of degrees. See Introduction, p. 58.

26. From *Sermon* 4 (DW I, pp. 69–70). See Introduction, p. 33.

27. Close to a passage in *Sermon* 13 (DW I, p. 220). See also *Sermon* 48 (p. 198), among other places. On the problems raised by this article and Eckhart's denials that he had made such statements, see Introduction, pp. 13 and 42.

28. From *Sermon* 9 (DW I, p. 148).

29. This apparently refers to a document signed by Eckhart on his deathbed, and not the similar public protestation he had made in Cologne on February 13, 1327.

30. See Introduction, pp. 14–15, for the importance of this phrase.

PART ONE: 2. COMMENTARIES ON GENESIS

1. Eckhart wrote two commentaries on Genesis: *Commentary on the Book of Genesis*, a more literal and basic interpretation (LW I, pp. 185–444); and the *Book of the Parables of Genesis*, a more allegorical and metaphysical treatment (LW I, pp. 447–702).

2. Eckhart briefly lays down the nature and purpose of the exegetical part of his *Three-Part Work* in two Prologues. This is the first, as translated from LW I, p. 183.

3. The first selection is the account of Gn. 1:1 found in *Comm. Gen.* (LW I, pp. 185–206).

NOTES

4. These are the major patristic sources for interpretation of the *hexaemeron*, or work of the six days of creation.

5. The influence of Maimonides on Eckhart has been studied by J. Koch, "Meister Eckhart und die jüdische Religionsphilosophie des Mittelalters," *Jahresbericht der Schlesischen Gesellschaft für vaterländische Kultur 1928* 101 (1928): 134–48.

6. The Latin *principium* can mean both "beginning" and "principle." Eckhart emphasizes now one and now the other of these aspects (as the translation tries to indicate), but both senses are always present.

7. The correlation of the Genesis account with Si. 18:1 was a traditional problem in Christian exegesis that had been discussed by Augustine.

8. Aristotle, *On Generation and Corruption* 2.10 (336a27).

9. These four preliminary points outline the first part of the exegesis of the verse. They are taken up respectively in nn. 3–7, 8–9, 10–13, and 14.

10. "Ideal reason" *(ratio idealis)*. Augustine, *Lit. Comm. Gen.* 6.9sqq. says that the first creation in which God makes all things at the same time is the *ratio creandi* and not the *actio creandi*.

11. The close relationship between the opening verses of Gn. 1 and the Johannine Prologue indicate that the two texts are meant to be mutually illuminating.

12. See the discussion in the *Comm. Jn.* n. 4 (p. 123).

13. This axiom is based on a conflation of two texts in *Republic* 6.19 (508E and 509B), and is cited elsewhere by the Meister (e.g., *Par. Gen.* n. 52 in LW I, p. 520). It was known and used by many of the Scholastics.

14. Averroes, *Commentary on the Metaphysics* 7.5 (on 1028b).

15. "What-it-is" *(quidditas)* is a term of scholastic coinage. The technical term translated here as "what" *(quod quid est)* and "why" *(propter quid est)* depend on Aristotle, e.g., *Met.* 1.8 (988b29) and *Post. Anal.* 2.2 (90a31–34). Eckhart took this basic vocabulary from Thomas Aquinas, on whose use see B. Lonergan, *Verbum: Word and Idea in Aquinas* (Notre Dame: University of Notre Dame Press, 1967), pp. 11–25.

16. *Post. Anal.* 1.8 (75b31).

17. Eckhart's point is that proof in metaphysics is always in the realm of formal causality.

18. *Consolation of Philosophy* 3, poem 9. This text on creation is also cited in *Comm. Jn.* nn. 41 and 60 (pp. 136, 143).

19. The identification of the Son with the "Principle" is found as early as Ambrose, *Hexaemeron* 1.4.15, and was repeated by many subsequent authors. See also *Comm. Jn.* nn. 13, 56 (pp. 126, 142).

20. A number of thirteenth-century authors (e.g., Thomas Aquinas, *On Truth* 3.1.1) ascribe such a text to Augustine's *City of God*, but it is not found there.

21. *On Free Choice* 3.5.13, a favorite text (see *Comm. Jn.* n. 55 on p. 142).

NOTES

22. *Book of Causes*, prop. 9, and its attendant commentary.

23. Eckhart joins Thomas Aquinas and the other Scholastics in attacking the necessitarianism of the Arab philosophers, e.g., Avicenna in his *Metaphysics* 9.4.

24. This paragraph, which seems to assert the eternity of creation, was attacked in the Cologne proceedings (Théry, pp. 174–75).

25. The preceding three sentences (with some additional material not found in Eckhart's surviving works) formed the first of the condemned propositions of "In agro dominico." On the problem of this aspect of the Meister's doctrine of creation, see the Introduction, pp. 40–41.

26. This sentence formed the third of the propositions of the papal Bull.

27. A popular text with Eckhart; see, e.g., *Comm. Jn.* n. 73 (p. 148), and Introduction, p. 39.

28. Aristotle, *On Interpretation* 2.10 (20b1).

29. *Top.*3.2 (117b10–17).

30. Averroes, *Commentary on the Physics* 4.43 (on 212a–b).

31. This part of the *Work of Questions* has not survived.

32. Aristotle, *On Heaven and Earth* 2.2 (284b28).

33. E.g., Augustine, *Lit. Comm. Gen.* 4.35; Bonaventure, *Breviloquium* 2.5; and Thomas Aquinas, *STh* Ia.74.2.ad 2, etc.

34. A key principle of the Thomistic doctrine of creation.

35. This slighting reference seems to be directed at Siger of Brabant, the radical Aristotelian, who holds such a position in his *Questions on the Metaphysics* 5.10. See Introduction, p. 6.

36. The identification of God's nature with intellect or understanding is one of the key elements in Eckhart's thought, especially evident in *Par. Quest.* 1–2. On this identification, see Introduction, pp. 32, 34–35.

37. Another important feature of the Meister's thought; see, e.g., *Comm. Jn.* n. 60 (p. 143), and *Comm. Wis.* n. 197 (LW II, p. 531).

38. Proclus, *Elements of Theology*, prop. 11.

39. *Conf.*1.6.10. Also used in the *Comm. Jn.* n. 52 (p. 140).

40. This treatise has not survived.

41. *General Prologue* nn. 15–21 (LW I, pp. 159–65).

42. A popular preacher's example found in Stephen of Bourbon's *Treatise on Various Materials for Preaching.*

43. An abbreviation of Horace, *Ep.*1.16.52.

44. *On True Religion* 38.20.39.

45. Cf. n. 5 (p. 84).

46. *Guide* 2.31. Eckhart made use of a Latin translation of the *Guide* that has not yet been critically edited but appears to differ in some details from the original.

47. Ibid.

48. *Comm. Wis.* nn. 19–22 (LW II, pp. 339–53).

49. *Conf.*4.12.18.

50. For a more detailed treatment of this central theme, see *Comm. Jn.* nn. 14–22, especially n. 19 (pp. 126–29).

51. Avicenna, *Metaphysics* 9.4. Eckhart attacks this view in other places, e.g., *Comm. Wis.* n. 36 (LW II, p. 356), and *Sermon* XXXVI (LW IV, p. 314).

52. See *Comm. Jn.* n. 125 (p. 173).

53. A position also held by Thomas Aquinas, e.g., *SCG* 3.71; *STh* Ia.22.2.ad 2, 48.1, 48.3, etc.

54. A common teaching based on Aristotle, *Phys.* 3.3 (202b10–14).

55. See note 13 above.

56. This part of the *Work of Propositions* has not survived.

57. Eckhart is probably referring to his famous *Sermon* XXIX on this text (LW IV, pp. 263–70).

58. Gabirol, *The Fountain of Life* 5.24. What Gabirol means is that the four fundamental questions (based on Aristotle, *Post. Anal.* 2.1–2) express the four essential levels of existence. See also *Comm. Jn.* n. 47 (p. 138).

59. The following three selections from *Par. Gen.* are translated from LW I, pp. 447–56, 479–507, and 601–36.

60. These three kinds of truths correspond to the three divisions of science found in medieval authors. Jerome had emphasized that all three truths were to be found in scripture, e.g., Letter 30.1. See Introduction, pp. 28–29.

61. Maimonides, *Guide*, Preface.

62. *Conf.*6.5.8.

63. *Guide*, Preface.

64. Augustine, *Enarration on Ps. 118.*

65. Cf. Lk. 6:1. The Augustine text referred to seems to be *Lit. Comm. Gen.*1.20, but the image was a popular one in medieval exegesis.

66. Eckhart here partially cites Thomas Aquinas, *STh* Ia.1.10, but without Thomas's distinction that the literal sense must be one because words intend one thing and that the further spiritual meanings come from the fact that the things signified by the words can themselves signify other things in God's intention. Thus Eckhart's position implying the multiplicity of literal senses is really closer to Augustine, e.g., *Conf.* 12.31.42.

67. *Conf.*12.27.37.

68. *Conf.*12.18.27.

69. Ibid.

70. Thomas Aquinas, *STh* Ia.1.10c.

71. *Christ. Doct.* 3.27.38.

72. A position based on Plato, e.g., *Meno* 15 (81C) and *Phaedo* 22 (76D–77A), and taught by Plato's followers in the Academy. See Aquinas, *On Truth* 11.1.

73. "By metaphors and allegories" *(sub metaphora fabulorum)*. On this important principle of teaching *in parabolis*, see the classic account in Macrobius, *Commentary on the Dream of Scipio* 1.2.17.

NOTES

74. *Art of Poetry*, lines 333 and 343.

75. Cf. Bede, *Allegorical Exposition on the Parables of Solomon.*

76. Ambrose, *Exposition on Luke* 6.93.

77. Terence, *Andria* 1.1.87.

78. In this lengthy question Thomas actually discusses both the literal and the mystical meanings of the various ceremonies of the Old Law.

79. *Comm. Jn.* nn. 661–62 (LW III, pp. 576–78).

80. Eckhart thinks of the virtues as the principles of ethical science, as in *Par. Gen.* n. 83 (LW I, pp. 549–51).

81. The same point is made more briefly in *Comm. Jn.* n. 3 (p. 123).

82. Eckhart agrees with Thomas that the parabolical or spiritual sense cannot be the basis for a theological demonstration; see *STh* Ia.1.10.ad 1.

83. *Guide*, Preface. The two kinds of parables also appear in *Comm. Jn.* n. 174 (LW III, p. 143).

84. Ibid.

85. The first example is drawn from Maimonides, the second is not.

86. The order of the commentary on Gn. 1:1 is as follows: (1) nn. 9–20. The differences between the divine and natural modes of producing; (2) nn. 21–27. The two external principles of the universe (the active and passive) and their properties, plus a moral application; (3) nn. 28–33. The composition of material things from matter and form; (4) nn. 34–36. Five other understandings of the meaning of "heaven" and "earth"; (5) nn. 37–40. Ten moral interpretations.

87. Aristotle, *Met.* 5.2 (1013a29–32), as interpreted by Thomas Aquinas, *Commentary on the Metaphysics* 5.2, lect. 2, 515a.

88. As J. Koch remarks in LW I, p. 480, Eckhart seems to mean that a horse is produced from the male seed that is not a horse itself.

89. An example also used by Thomas in his discussion of creation in *STh* Ia.45.1.

90. Augustine, *Trin.*7.3.4, citing the words of the Nicene Creed.

91. Cf. *Comm. Jn.* n. 60 (p. 143).

92. Aristotle, *Met.* 10.1 (1052b18–30).

93. Maimonides, *Guide* 1.59.

94. See *Comm. Jn.* nn. 14–22 (pp. 126–29).

95. Aristotle, *On Generation and Corruption* 2.10 (336a27). Aristotle's general principle regarding making is here used as a springboard for a discussion of God as the One and his relation to creation.

96. Eckhart here indulges in a wordplay *(adnominatio)* between *effectum* and *antefactum.*

97. A noted text from Augustine, *Christ. Doct.* 1.5.5, attributes unity to the Father. On the Father as the One in Eckhart, see Introduction, p. 35.

98. Thomas Aquinas, *STh* Ia.33.3.

99. A quotation from the Nicene Creed.

NOTES

100. Boethius, *Trinity* 2.

101. Thomas Aquinas, *In I Sent.* 29.1.1.

102. Cf. *Comm. Jn.* n. 5 (p. 124).

103. An expansion of Augustine's *Trin.*6.1.1 taken from Peter Lombard. Also cited in *Comm. Jn.* n. 31 (p. 132).

104. A theological axiom clearly formulated by Augustine (see his *Commentary on John* 95.1) and well known to medieval thinkers.

105. *Elements of Theology,* prop. 1.

106. *Commentary on the Dream of Scipio* 1.6.7–9.

107. An axiom found in the *Sentences from Aristotle,* a text falsely attributed to Bede.

108. For a treatment of the Selfsame *(id ipsum)* as a divine name, see *Comm. Ex.* n. 165 (LW II, pp. 145–46).

109. *Conf.*9.4.11.

110. As contrasted with spiritual beings, or angels, each of whom constitutes its own species.

111. *Metaphysics* 8.6.

112. Both Aristotle, *Met.* 10.1 (1053a30), and Aquinas, *STh* Ia.11.1. ad 1, teach that each number is composed of units or ones.

113. That is, number occurs only when something departs from the principle.

114. Albert the Great, *On Indivisible Lines* 5–6. This teaching on point and line is basic to Euclid's *Geometry,* a work that was available to the Middle Ages in Boethius's translation.

115. *Immortality of the Soul* 4.6.

116. Porphyry, *Isagoge* 2.

117. Aristotle, *Met.* 11.1 (1059b36); Porphyry, *Isagoge* 2.

118. Aristotle, *Soul* 3.5 (430a10–12).

119. Aristotle, *On Heaven and Earth* 1.22 (270a33–35).

120. Thomas Aquinas, *STh* Ia.66.2. ad 2.

121. In these six points Eckhart is speaking of efficient causes that are analogical, not of the univocal efficient causes (e.g., fire causing fire) that are discussed in twelve points commenting on Gn. 2:21–25 in nn. 116–27 (LW I, pp. 582–91). These two passages are central to the Meister's teaching on natural causality.

122. See, e.g., Aquinas, *Commentary on Aristotle's Physics,* 3.2, lect. 4.5.

123. See the more complete discussion of this in *Comm. Jn.* nn. 70–72 (pp. 147–48).

124. Aristotle, *Soul* 3.9 (432b21).

125. No such commentary on the parable of the sower survives from Eckhart's pen.

126. Cf. n. 122 of this exposition (LW I, pp. 587sqq.).

127. *Lectures and Sermons on Ecclesiasticus* nn. 42–61 (LW II, pp. 270–90). See also *Comm. Jn.* n. 182 (LW III, p. 150).

128. This commentary has not survived.

129. E.g., Ps. 113:1, Ba. 5:7, Heb. 5:4.

130. The same point is made in *Comm. Jn.* n. 70 (pp. 147–48).

131. The quotation is from the doxology at the end of the Canon, or Eucharistic prayer, of the liturgy (cf. Rm. 16:27).

132. After speaking of the extrinsic principles of created being in the last section, Eckhart now turns his attention to the intrinsic principles.

133. *Metaphysics* 2.4.

134. Thomas Aquinas, *In I Sent.*3.4.2.ad 4.

135. See nn. 124–27 (LW I, pp. 589–91).

136. Aristotle, *Soul* 2.1 (412b5–9).

137. Cf. *Comm. Jn.* n. 100 (p. 160).

138. *Trinity* 2. Eckhart means that a pure form cannot be the subject of accidents, but only a being composed of form and matter.

139. Aristotle, *Soul* 2.7 (418b26–28).

140. *Soul* 3.1 (425b25–26).

141. A text known from Aristotle, *Phys.* 8.5 (256b25) and *Soul* 3.4 (429a18–20). Eckhart cites it frequently.

142. *Soul* 3.4 (429b31).

143. Cf. *Comm. Jn.* n. 107 (pp. 162–63).

144. Eckhart seems to adhere to the Thomistic teaching of the real distinction of essence *(quod est)* and existence *(quo est)* in creatures and their identity in God, but B. Muller-Thym, *The Establishment of the University of Being in the Doctrine of Meister Eckhart* (New York: Sheed and Ward, 1939), pp. 78–79, points out the Avicennan cast of his understanding of the distinction.

145. *Metaphysics* 5.1.

146. Cf. *Comm. Jn.* n. 45 (p. 135).

147. J. Koch suggests that the phrase "by which they are directed to the will" should be added here to complete Eckhart's thought, as in other passages.

148. Eckhart appears to refer to the brief treatments in *Comm. Gen.* n. 77 and n. 68 (LW I, pp. 238, 232).

149. This passage has not survived, but see *Comm. Gen.* n. 21 above (p. 90).

150. *Comm. Gen.* n. 25 (p. 91), and *Par. Gen.* n. 217 (LW I, pp. 692–95).

151. *Enarration in Ps. 32.*

152. In a number of places the Meister identifies Sarah with the rational faculty in man and Hagar with the sensitive; see, e.g., *Comm. Gen.* nn. 229–33 (LW I, pp. 374–78).

153. Guibert of Nogent makes the same identification in his *Moral Commentary on Genesis* 1.1.

154. See nn. 135–37 (pp. 108–09).

155. This Augustinian theme was a popular one with Eckhart; see nn. 138–40 below (pp. 109–10) and *Sermon* XXI (LW IV, p. 189).

156. *Conf.*1.12.19.

157. Letter 87.24.

158. Augustine, *City of God* 14.28.

159. Eckhart does not treat cupidity explicitly in nn. 9–36.

160. *Comm. Gen.* nn. 15sqq. and nn. 22sqq. (pp. 88–91).

161. *Trin.* 12.13.20, etc.

162. The following position on parabolical or allegorical interpretation was attacked by the Cologne inquisitors. The Meister's response is worth quoting: "It must be said that this is true as it stands, but this is not to say that scripture is not true and is not to be explained in literal and historical fashion" (Théry, p. 193).

163. Peter Lombard, *Sentences* II. 24.4–11, popularized this Augustinian interpretation among medieval theologians.

164. The tropological sense can be taken either broadly as any symbolic or allegorical reading, or narrowly as a specifically moral allegory. Eckhart seems to intend the former.

165. Eckhart here agrees with Thomas Aquinas's principle that there are times when the figurative meaning is what the text literally intends. See *STh* Ia.1.10.ad 3, and 13.6.

166. Eckhart uses both "made to God's image" and "God's image," e.g., *Comm. Jn.* n. 31 (p. 132). *Sermon* XXV.1 (LW IV, pp. 234–35) seems to suggest that the former expression highlights the distinction between God and the soul, the latter the conformity. See Introduction, pp. 43–44.

167. Aristotle, *Soul* 3.4 (430a1).

168. Averroes, *Commentary on the Soul* 3.19 (on 430a).

169. Aristotle, *On Memory and Reminiscence* (449b31).

170. Aristotle, *Soul* 1.4 (408b11–25).

171. Aristotle, *Soul* 3.3 (439a1). I have translated *phantasia* as "imagination."

172. Cf. nn. 21 and 28 above (pp. 101, 103–04).

173. Avicenna, *The Soul* 1.5.

174. E.g., *Trin.* 12.30.20, etc. See also *Sermon* XXI (LW IV, p. 189).

175. The relation of the good to order was discussed by Augustine in *The Nature of the Good* 3sqq., and frequently by Thomas, e.g., *STh* IIaIIae.81.2.

176. This notion of the concatenation of all reality into the great chain of being by the joining of the highest point of the lower to the lowest point of what is higher is a general Neoplatonic principle. Eckhart's direct source appears to be the Pseudo-Augustinian *The Spirit and the Soul* 14, as is also suggested by the use of the term "height of the soul" *(supremum animae)* in n. 140 below.

177. Maimonides, *Guide* 3.53.

178. Ibid.

179. Augustine, *Enarration on Ps. 41:7.*

180. *Conf.* 10.26.37.

181. Brief fragments of Eckhart's *Commentary on the Song of Songs* have begun to appear in LW II, pp. 637sqq.

182. *Nichomachean Ethics* 1.13 (1102b25–31).

183. *Book of Causes,* prop. 3.

184. That is, the four elements and the heavenly bodies, which are composed of only form and matter. See *Comm. Ex.* n. 128 (LW II, p. 118).

185. Eckhart gives a fuller account of this in *Comm. Jn.* n. 265 (LW III, p. 220).

186. See his *Commentary on the Metaphysics* 12.8.lect.6.

187. That is, the "quintessence," or *aether*, which makes up the heavenly bodies in Aristotelian cosmology.

188. Aristotle, *On Heaven and Earth* 1.2 (269a30–32).

189. Thomas Aquinas, *STh* Ia.94.1.

190. *STh* Ia.94.2.

191. Based on Aristotle, *Met.* 11.1 (1059b30).

192. Aquinas, *STh* IaIIae.109.7, 113.1.

193. *Comm. Ex.* n. 219 (LW II, p. 185).

194. Cf. Thomas Aquinas, *STh* IIIa.69.3.ad 3.

195. This account of the threefold division differs slightly from that in n. 141 above (p. 111) where it is the sensitive faculty that is rational through participation.

196. On Eckhart's doctrine of loving union "without any medium" *(sine medio)*, see Introduction, p. 56.

197. Aquinas, *STh* Ia.54.4.

198. See *Comm. Jn.* n. 14 (p. 126).

199. "Concrete being" *(id quod est)*, "essence" *(quod quid est)*, and "what-it-is" *(quidditas)*. For a discussion of these terms, see *Sermon* XXV (LW IV, p. 230).

200. The Meister's exposition of this verse has not survived.

201. Averroes, *Commentary on the Soul* 3.5 (on 429a).

202. *Conf.*4.11.16.

203. *Conf.*9.10.24.

204. This passage is one of the rare appearances in the Latin works of the theme of the journey into the desert that is frequent in the vernacular works. The translation tries to convey something of Eckhart's wordplay of *solitudo* and *solus*. See also the use of Hos. 2:14 in *Bened.1* and 2 (pp. 230, 247).

205. Augustine's interpretation of Paul's blindness after the incident on the road to Damascus (Ac. 9:9), as found in his *Sermon* 279.1.1, et al.

206. *Soul* 2.8 (419b 25–27).

207. *Conf.*10.6.9–10, abbreviated and somewhat altered.

208. The same example is found in *Sermon* LV.2 (LW IV, p. 455).

209. These three classes of beings appear elsewhere in Eckhart's works, e.g., *Comm. Jn.* n. 63 (pp. 144–45). The source is in the Pseudo-Dionysius, *Divine Names* 5.2.

210. *Soul* 3.2 (425b25). Before the act of sight takes place, the power of sight and the visible object are only potentially seeing and seen. They are identical in the act of seeing.

211. See note 181 above.

212. Jerome, *Hebrew Names* 5.15.

213. See *Comm. Wis.* n. 91 (LW II, pp. 424–25).

214. *On Free Choice* 3.25.77.

215. Isidore of Seville, *Etymologies* 14.3.2.

216. Thomas Aquinas, *STh* Ia.94.1.

217. *Lit. Comm. Gen.* 11.33. Also cited by Aquinas in *STh* Ia.94.1.

218. Aristotle, *Soul* 2.9 (421a20–26).

219. This is based on *STh* Ia.98.2.ad 3.

220. *STh* Ia.91.3.ad 1.

221. Aristotle, *Soul* 2.9 (421a18–21).

222. This opinion and its refutation are taken from Albert the Great's *Commentary on the Soul* 2.3.23.

223. *STh* Ia.91.3.ad 1.

224. The teaching of this paragraph is drawn from a number of places in Thomas Aquinas.

225. E.g., n. 92 (LW I, pp. 556–58).

226. See nn. 111 and 93 (LW I, pp. 576, 559).

227. That is, a tendency whose external act is hindered or blocked, a standard Thomistic teaching, e.g., *STh* IaIIae.85.2, *SCG* 3.12.

228. Synderesis is the ineradicable tendency toward the good that belongs to man's rational nature. Cf. *Par. Gen.* n. 168 (LW I, p. 638). Eckhart follows Thomas, e.g., *On Truth* 16.

229. Pseudo-Dionysius, *Divine Names* 4.23.

230. This sentence forms the sixteenth of the propositions of "In agro dominico" (p. 79).

231. This sentence is the seventeenth of the propositions. Eckhart's response to the Avignon Commission on the question of the goodness of the external act is instructive. "He [Eckhart] proves these four articles because God commands the exterior act, but he does not command it properly. This is because the exterior act has no moral goodness without the goodness of the interior act, and hence God desires the good interior act more principally than the exterior one" (Pelster, p. 1114). See also the response given during the Cologne proceedings (Théry, p. 195). On this question, see Introduction, pp. 58–59.

232. Aristotle, *Nicomachean Ethics* 1.1 (1094a2).

NOTES

233. On this principle, see n. 86 (LW I, pp. 548–49).
234. *Trin.*8.3.4.
235. Aristotle, *Met.* 9.8 (1050a5–8).

PART ONE: 3. COMMENTARY ON JOHN

Translated from the critical edition of J. Koch in LW III, nn. 1–131, pp. 3–114. I have profited from a careful consultation of Koch's German version, as well as from a perusal of J. Clark's earlier translation of nn. 1–53 for some turns of phrase.

1. Albert the Great begins his commentary on John with the same citation. John was traditionally identified with the eagle figure of the four beasts of Ezk. 1:5–10 and Rv. 4:6–8.
2. This quotation and the following are taken from an anonymous prologue to Augustine's *Commentary on John.*
3. On Eckhart's manner of proceeding by natural arguments, see the Introduction, pp. 27–28; n. 3 below shows that the Meister believed that the complete conformity of reason and revelation could be demonstrated, a standard position of many Christian Platonists.
4. *Interlinear Gloss* on Rm. 1:20.
5. *Conf.* 7.9.13. Augustine actually said that much of John's Prologue could be read out of the books of the "Platonists," that is, Neoplatonic philosophers, especially Plotinus and Porphyry; but some medieval manuscripts of the *Confessions* contained the reading "books of Plato" rather than "books of the Platonists." See notes 151, 169, and 225 below.
6. *City of God* 10.29.
7. For the structure of argument in nn. 4–37, see Introduction, p. 40, notes 95–96.
8. "In its principle," i.e., *in principio.* The Latin *principium* means both "beginning" and "principle." Eckhart plays with this semantic ambiguity throughout his treatment of John and frequently in his other works too. Though both senses are always present to some degree, I have alternated between the two in this translation depending on which sense seems uppermost.
9. "Idea and likeness," i.e., *ratio et similitudo.* On the notion of *ratio*, see nn. 30 and 32 below.
10. A *suppositum* is an individual subsisting in a nature, the concrete subject of predication. See Thomas Aquinas, *STb* IIIa.2.2.
11. This emphasis on the substantive sense seems to be based on John the Scot, *Homily on John's Prologue* 6, as known through its use in Thomas Aquinas, *Exposition on John* 1:1.
12. Jordan of Quedlinburg, *Sermon* 68, makes a similar point.

327

NOTES

13. Aristotle, *Met.* 1.1 (980b27).
14. Aristotle, *Met.* 4.8 (1012a24).
15. Aristotle, *Post. Anal.* 1.8 (75b31).
16. In the discussion that follows Eckhart frequently moves back and forth between a discussion of the ideas of things to a discussion of their archetypal Idea, that is, the Word or Logos, in order to show the isomorphic relation between the two.
17. "What-it-is" = the technical scholastic *quidditas.*
18. *Book of Causes,* prop. 20.
19. *Trin.*6.10.11.
20. The just man's principial relation to justice is treated frequently in the Latin works and also appears in the vernacular *Book "Benedictus."* A remote source may be found in Augustine's discussion of the just man in *Trin.* 8.6, but the Meister's development of the theme is highly original. The important principle "insofar as" *(in quantum),* indicating that the discussion is based on a limited, formal and abstract point of view, was one of the key issues in Eckhart's defense of his thought during the process against him. See the Defense, pp. 72–73.
21. "The man that is taken up" *(homo assumptus)* is the sacred humanity of Christ. The text *(auctoritas)* cited here in a form found in many other scholastic authors is based on Isidore of Seville, *Questions in Exodus* 42.3.
22. Aristotle, *Cat.* 5 (3b19).
23. See n. 5 (p. 124). The equality of the just man with justice is one of the sources for Eckhart's many daring ascriptions of divine predicates to man. We must remember that he is speaking *in quantum.*
24. I.e., *justitia genita,* an important technical term for Eckhart.
25. The Father is called "Principle without principle" in Peter Lombard's *Sentences* I.29.1.
26. Literally, "because it exists along with fear of the other side [being true]." This is the teaching of Aquinas, e.g., *On Truth* 14.1.
27. For the doctrine of the image in Eckhart's thought, see especially *Sermon* XLIX.3 (LW IV, pp. 425–28).
28. *Emanatio formalis* is a key notion for the Meister. See, e.g., *Sermon* XLIX.3, and *Comm. Wis.* n. 283 (LW II, pp. 615–16).
29. Averroes, *Commentary on the Soul* 2.67 (on 418a). In scholastic terminology the visible species *(species visibilis)* is the form impressed on the faculty of sight by means of which we actually come to see.
30. For this theory of sight, see also Bonaventure, *In II Sent.* 13.2–3.
31. That is, like is known by like, a principle that Eckhart and other Scholastics received from Plato by way of Aristotle, e.g., *Soul* 2.3 (427a28).
32. *Book of Eighty-Three Questions* 63.
33. See Hugh of St. Victor, *Guide to the Arts (Didascalicon)* 1.11.

NOTES

34. See Thomas Aquinas, *STh* Ia.15.1.

35. The "principle by which" *(principium quo)* of any action is the form according to which the agent models its effects. The *principium quod* of an action is the supposit, or concrete acting subject.

36. *Trin.* 6.1.1, as expanded in Peter Lombard's *Sentences* I.9.2.

37. *Commentary on the Metaphysics* 7.5 (on 1028b).

38. See n. 8 (pp. 124–25).

39. Aquinas, *STh* Ia.28.1.ad 4.

40. *Christ. Doct.* 1.3 and 5. Two passages combined in Peter Lombard's *Sentences* I.1.2.

41. The Latin text of the *Book of Causes* contains a brief commentary on each of the propositions.

42. *Book of Causes*, prop. 4.

43. *Conf.* 10.27.38.

44. What follows is based on Albert the Great's commentary on Jn. 1:1.

45. *The Orthodox Faith* 1.7.

46. Letter 65.7.

47. *Commentary on the Metaphysics* 12.36 (on 1072a).

48. *Met.* 5.2 (1013b34–1014a6).

49. *Par. Gen.* n. 180 (LW I, p. 650).

50. Aristotle, *Soul* 3.4 (429b22–24).

51. *Consolation of Philosophy* 3, poem 9.

52. The "it" *(ipsum)* of "it comes" must refer to the exemplar as received by the artist and not as taken by itself.

53. *Met.* 12.7 (1072b3).

54. E.g., *Phys.* 2.3 (194b32), and *Met.* 2.2 (994b 9–11).

55. *Met.* 2.2 (994b13sqq.).

56. *Soul* 3.10 (433b14).

57. A lost part of the *Work of Propositions*.

58. On this disputed question among the Scholastics, Eckhart here follows Thomas Aquinas, *STh* Ia.41.5.

59. The difference between the simple existence *(esse simpliciter)* of God and the limited particular existence *(esse hoc et hoc)* of any created thing is fundamental to Eckhart's thought.

60. See nn. 52–53 (pp. 140–41).

61. Intellect or understanding *(intellectus)* is here taken as higher than existence *(esse)*, as in the *Par. Quest.* 1–2 (LW V, pp. 37–54).

62. *Par. Gen.* nn. 55, 58–72 (LW I, pp. 523–24, 526–37).

63. *Trin.* 8.6.9. Eckhart has rendered Augustine's argument obscure by abbreviating the passage, as J. Koch notes in LW III, p. 38, note 4.

64. Ibid.

65. *Post. Anal.* 2.1 (89b23).

NOTES

66. These four questions are not quite the same as those of Aristotle in *Post. Anal.* 2.1, but are closer to those of the Jewish philosopher Ibn Gabirol in *The Fountain of Life* 5.24. See *Comm. Gen.* n. 27 (p. 91).

67. E.g., Augustine, *Trin.* 8.6.9; Thomas Aquinas, *STh* IIaIIae.58.11.

68. The "land of unlikeness," a much used theme among Christian mystics, goes back to Plato *(Statesman* 273D), but was made popular for medieval authors by its appearance in *Conf.* 7.10.16.

69. "Drawn" *(afficitur)*. This paragraph and the next base their argument in part on the rich implications of the verb *afficio*, literally, "to exert an influence on something so that it is brought into a certain state or condition." I have rendered *afficio* and its compounds in various ways, including "affect," "draw," "change," and "transform," to bring out this richness.

70. *On the Epistle of John to the Parthians* 2.2, a key *auctoritas* that Eckhart frequently refers to in defense of his doctrine of divinization.

71. *Homilies on John* 26.5.

72. *Conf.* 10.23.34.

73. *Conf.* 10.40.65.

74. *Soliloquy of the Soul's Pledge.*

75. See n. 16 (p. 127).

76. The theme of living "without a why" *(sunder warumbe, sine quare)* is central to Eckhart's mysticism. In attaining to life "without a why" we approximate the divine existence, which is essentially "without a why." See Introduction, pp. 59–60.

77. *Divine Names* 4.32.

78. *Met.* 1.1 (980b27).

79. *On Free Choice* 1.6.15.

80. *Conf.* 1.6.10.

81. A Thomistic principle (e.g., *STh* IIIa.77.3. ad 3), based on Aristotle, *Met.* 7.7 (1032a 20sqq).

82. *Commentary on John* 1.13, a text incorporated into the *Ordinary Gloss.*

83. See the *Par. Quest.* 1.4 (LW V, p. 41).

84. *Ratio.* As J. Koch notes (LW III, p. 45, note 1), *ratio* is used in three senses in the following interpretations, as cause or ground, as idea, and as reason.

85. *Timaeus* 28A.

86. That is, everything that is in God (preexisting in him insofar as he is the First Cause) is in him eternally as an idea.

87. *Trin.* 3.4.9.

88. Augustine, *Lit. Comm. Gen.* 1.6.12.

89. Augustine, *Enarration on Ps. 38.*

90. Augustine, *On Free Choice* 3.5.13.

91. Augustine, *Lit. Comm. Gen.* 1.6.13 also sees the Holy Spirit indicated in this verse.

92. *Soul* 3.2 (425b26).
93. See note 47 above.
94. Aristotle, *On Generation and Corruption* 1.1 (314a15).
95. Averroes, *Commentary on the Physics* 4.124 (on 222a).
96. *Consolation of Philosophy* 3, poem 9.
97. *Book of Causes*, prop. 10.
98. *Soul* 2.2 (414a11).
99. Boethius, *Trinity* 4.
100. *Book of Causes*, prop. 12.
101. In the *Par. Quest.* 1 (LW V, pp. 42–43) Eckhart seems to reject this distinction, though we find it used in other contexts besides the one here, e.g., *Sermon* 82 (DW III, p. 262). On the relation of existence and understanding, see Introduction, pp. 32–35.
102. See Thomas Aquinas, *STh* Ia.79.2.
103. John Chrysostom, *Homilies on John* 5.
104. Origen, *Commentary on John* 2.20 (cited in the *Ordinary Gloss* on Jn. 1:9).
105. Porphyry, *Isagoge* 4.
106. *Book of Causes*, prop. 4.
107. Aristotle, *Met.* 5.2 (1013b36); *Phys.* 2.3 (195a32).
108. Aristotle, *Met.* 7.8 (1034a 5–8).
109. Aristotle, *Soul* 2.4 (415a 26–29).
110. Aristotle, *Met.* 5.15 (1021a11).
111. Thomas Aquinas, *STh* IIaIIae.95.5.
112. The notional acts are the distinguishing or personal realities in the Godhead, e.g., begetting as proper to the Father.
113. From the *Ordinary Gloss* on Jn. 1:4.
114. Letter 64.10.
115. *Art of Poetry*, v. 180.
116. Seneca, Letter 1.6.
117. See nn. 11–12 and 20–22 (pp. 125–26, 128–29).
118. For the metaphysical background to the Meister's theory of light, see *Par. Gen.* nn. 116–22 (LW I, pp. 582–88).
119. Literally, "not east before west, or west before east."
120. "In the manner of a reception" *(per modum passionis)*. *Passio* here is to be taken in the technical sense as that which is opposed to *actio* in the Aristotelian theory of movement.
121. See n. 12 (p. 126). A similar interpretation of the darkness is found in John the Scot's *Homily on the Prologue of John* 13.
122. See note 118.
123. Ps. 61:12, a favorite text of Eckhart's; see Introduction, p. 39.
124. Augustine, *Sermon* 279.1.
125. See the *Comm. Ex.* n. 237 (LW II, pp. 195–96).

NOTES

126. *Celestial Hierarchies* 1.2.

127. The Meister is speaking of the fire found in the highest sphere, or empyreum, of Aristotelian cosmology.

128. This is the interpretation of Maimonides, *Guide* 2.30. It is also noted by Thomas Aquinas, *STh* Ia.66.1.ad 2.

129. Aristotle, *Soul* 3.6 (430b21–23).

130. Pseudo-Bede, *Exposition on Luke* 5, following Augustine, *Gospel Questions* 2.40. See the appeal to the same text in the documents from the Defense, p. 74.

131. Gregory the Great, *Dialogues* 1.5.

132. Eadmer, *Anselm's Book of Resemblances* 95.

133. Aristotle, *Soul* 2.4 (415a16–22).

134. Augustine, *On Patience* 12.9.

135. Augustine, Letter 138.2.12.

136. Aquinas, *STh* Ia.21.4.ad 4.

137. Not in Chrysostom, but found in the ninth-century Christian of Stablo's *Commentary on Matthew*.

138. Pseudo-Chrysostom, *Incomplete Commentary on Matthew*, hom. 18.

139. Eckhart seems to be referring to a lost commentary on Romans.

140. *Conf.* 11.8.10.

141. *Book of Causes*, prop. 24.

142. *Conf.* 4.11.16.

143. *Conf.* 9.10.24. A condensation of the stages of the famous ascent to God in the vision of Ostia.

144. *Comm. Wis.* n. 280 (LW II, pp. 612–13).

145. Aristotle, *Sophistical Refutations* 1.15 (174b5–7).

146. Peter Lombard, *Sentences* IV.46.5.

147. Thomas Aquinas, *STh* IaIIae.29.2.

148. *Enarration on Ps. 98.12.*

149. The distinction of the two levels of reason is a familiar one in Eckhart; see especially *Par. Gen.* nn. 138–41 (pp. 109–11).

150. For a study of the history of this Augustinian theme, see R. Mulligan, "Ratio Superior and Ratio Inferior: The Historical Background," *The New Scholasticism* 29 (1955): 1–32.

151. *Conf.* 7.9.13.

152. *Lit. Comm. Gen.* 4.28.45.

153. *On Faith* 2.2.

154. Eckhart follows Thomas here, see *STh* Ia.13.3. For more detailed treatments of the Meister's teaching on the divine names, see the two extended treatments in the *Comm. Ex.* nn. 27–78 and 143–84 (LW II, pp. 32–82, 130–58).

155. Cf. n. 74 (p. 149).

156. Cf. n. 21 (pp. 128–29).

NOTES

157. *Continuous Gloss (Catena aurea)* on John 1:9.

158. *Book of Causes,* prop. 21.

159. *Per se* in the Latin. Eckhart is following Thomas Aquinas, who in his *Commentary on the Book of Causes* lecture 21, n. 372, says: "In any genus whatever, the first is that which exists through itself *(per seipsum).* What exists through itself *(per se)* is prior to that which exists through another *(per aliud).*"

160. Thomas Aquinas, *Commentary on the Posterior Analytics* 1.2, lect. 4.

161. Pseudo-Augustine (Ambrose Autpert), *Sermon* 208.10.

162. *On Consideration* 3.2.6.

163. Perhaps an allusion to *City of God* 5.19.

164. *Book of Causes,* prop. 1. The commentator is Thomas Aquinas, *Commentary on the Book of Causes,* lect. 1, n. 26.

165. God's equally immediate presence to all things, studied by Boethius in the fifth book of the *Consolation of Philosophy,* was strongly emphasized by Thomas, e.g., *STh* Ia.22.3; *SCG* 3.76.

166. *Soul* 3.5 (430a15).

167. This etymology is repeated in several sermons, e.g., *Sermon* XXII (LW IV, p. 199).

168. *Conf.* 11.8.10.

169. *Conf.* 7.9.13.

170. *Book of Causes,* prop. 21.

171. From a liturgical oration in the Gregorian Sacramentary.

172. *Commentary on John* 12.12.

173. *Conf.* 12.8.8., etc.

174. *Trin.* 15.15.25.

175. See n. 70 (pp. 147–48).

176. On the dialectic of distinction and indistinction, see Introduction, pp. 34–35.

177. *Conf.* 10.27.38.

178. *Soul* 2.2 (414a11).

179. *Soul* 2.7 (418b26).

180. *Soul* 2.5 (417a6).

181. Literally, "is nothing of all the things that are" *(nihil omnium est).* This doctrine, crucial to Eckhart's thought, is based on Aristotle, *Soul* 3.4 (429a24).

182. *Soul* 3.4 (429b25).

183. *Soul* 3.4 (429b31).

184. *Met.* 1.8 (989b6).

185. See n. 53 (p. 141).

186. *The Orthodox Faith* 3.6.

187. Peter Lombard, *Sentences* III.4.2.

188. Peter Lombard, *Sentences* III.3.4.

NOTES

189. Thomas Aquinas, *STh* IIIa.14.1; 15.1.

190. This theme was brought up against Eckhart in the Cologne proceedings, but did not figure in the final condemnation.

191. *STh* Ia.3.5.

192. Aristotle, *Met.* 3.3 (998b20–28).

193. This interpretation is based on Augustine, *Commentary on John* 2.12, and was repeated by many authors.

194. *Soul* 3.4 (430a3) and 3.2 (425b26). The words "is the intellective power the same as the intelligible object" are not in the text, but J. Koch rightly suggests that Eckhart left them out by mistake in his paraphrase of Aristotle (LW III, p. 91, note 4).

195. *Trin.* 9.12.18.

196. *Conf.* 6.4.7.

197. These positions were held by two Dominican contemporaries of Eckhart, Hervaeus Natalis and Durand of St. Pourçain. The Meister's attack on these views in the *Work of Questions* has not survived.

198. "Positive and negative appetites" *(appetitus concupiscibilis et irascibilis)*. These are the two inferior parts of the threefold classification of powers that goes back to Plato. See *Sermon* 83 (p. 207).

199. *Nicomachean Ethics* 1.11 (1102b28–31).

200. The Vulgate text, following the Greek, does use the plural *(non ex sanguinibus)*, and Eckhart here attempts to explain this grammatical anomaly. The passage from Augustine is found in the *Commentary on John* 2.14.

201. See n. 96 (pp. 158–59).

202. See n. 105 (p. 162).

203. *Book of Causes,* prop. 24.

204. See n. 97 (p. 159).

205. Jerome, *Little Book on the Psalms,* Ps. 26.

206. *On Order* 1.2.3.

207. *On True Religion* 34.64.

208. *On True Religion* 35.65.

209. *On True Religion* 36.66. Eckhart has slightly altered the text.

210. The interchangeability of the transcendentals was a key to Eckhart's thought, as it had been for Thomas Aquinas (e.g., *On Truth* 1.1). For more extended treatments later in the *Commentary* see nn. 513, 546–47, and 562 (LW III, pp. 444, 477, 489).

211. *Commentary on Ecclesiastes* 4.6.

212. *Par. Gen.* nn. 73–74 (LW I, pp. 538–40).

213. See n. 98 (p. 159).

214. Eckhart frequently uses this etymology of "son" *(filius)* from *philos.*

215. A story from Aesop well known to the preachers of the Middle Ages.

216. See n. 106 (p. 162).

217. Eckhart's wordplay here between *habitavit* and *habituavit* cannot be brought out in English.

218. This is the basis for one of the most controversial aspects of Eckhart's preaching, most boldly expressed in the vernacular works in such formulae as "The Father gives birth to the Son without ceasing and I say more: he gives me birth, me, his son and the same son" (*Sermon 6*, p. 187). Three excerpts relating to the birth of the Son in the soul were included in the Bull "In agro dominico." On these issues, see Introduction, pp. 50–52.

219. This theme (central to Eckhart), as well as the mirror analogy, go back to Augustine, *Enarration on Ps. 10.*

220. In this convoluted sentence the Meister is interested in stressing the agreement of 1 Jn. 3:1 and Rm. 8:29 in their use of the subjunctive to express the purpose of the Incarnation.

221. *Soul* 3.2 (425b26).

222. John Chrysostom, *Homilies on John* 12.

223. Aristotle (citing Plato) in *Soul* 1.2 (404b17).

224. Augustine, *Trin.* 7.6.12.

225. Augustine, *Conf.* 7.9.13.

226. "Share the modes of predication proper to each" *(communicant idiomata)*. This technical phrase, originating with John Damascene, generally used to describe how both divine and human things are predicated of Christ, is here used in a more extended sense.

227. *Soul* 1.1 (403a5–10).

228. This text has not been identified.

229. The following theme and the example of fire that illustrates it are frequent in Eckhart, e.g., *Comm. Ex.* n. 140 (LW II, pp. 127–28).

230. Eckhart here makes use of the traditional understanding of Martha as entailing a form of life inferior to that of Mary. For a daring reversal of this, see *Sermon* 86 (DW III, pp. 481–92).

231. *Conf.* 1.1.1.

232. See nn. 184–86 (LW III, pp. 153–56).

PART TWO: 1. SELECTED SERMONS
SERMON 2 (Translated from DW I, pp. 24–45.)

1. For a detailed exegesis of this sermon, see R. Schürmann, *Meister Eckhart. Mystic and Philosopher*, pp. 9–47.

2. "Received" the MHG: *enpfangen* also means "conceived," a wordplay that is basic to the sermon.

3. MHG: *enpfangen.*

4. Again *enpfangen* with the sense of "receive-conceive."

NOTES

5. *MHG: vruht* also has the sense of "offspring."

6. "Simple one" = MHG: *einic ein*, a favorite expression for God as Absolute Unity. See *Sermon* 15 (p. 192).

7. "Properties" = MHG: *eigenschaft*. This is another key word in this sermon, at the beginning indicating the selfish possessiveness of the soul, and here the distinction of Persons that stands between the soul and the simple unity of the divine ground. See Introduction, pp. 34–37, 42–44.

SERMON 5b (Translated from DW I, pp. 85–96.)

1. Quint considers this version of *Sermon* 5a to be only partially authentic. Although it is recorded in eight manuscripts, with fragments quoted in another nine, only one attributes it to Eckhart by name; and it is Quint's opinion that this is a later editor's attempt to render the original sermon, with its condemned passages, harmless. He thinks that the passage on the will is interpolated from another source, though he concedes that earlier scholars have shown that it was used by Tauler, though this in Quint's opinion does not necessarily imply that Tauler believed it to be by Eckhart.

2. Eckhart here appears to be citing himself. On the Incarnation's effect on the entire human race, see Introduction, p. 46.

3. Quint cites Thomas Aquinas, in *In II Sent.*, 32.2.3, making the specific equality of human beings compatible with substantial inequality in human souls.

4. "Everything good . . . in this human nature" is a close parallel to art. 11 from "In agro dominico": "Whatever God the Father gave his Only-Begotten Son in human nature, he gave all this to me. I except nothing, neither union nor sanctity; but he gave the whole to me, just as he did to him." The Latin has all of the authentic Eckhart ring, and it may well support Quint's theory that there was a more authentic German version that has not survived. Art. 11 was condemned as heretical. See Introduction, pp. 17, 50–52, for background.

5. Here Quint suspects a missing passage that should introduce the next theme, the birth of the Son.

6. MHG: *insweben*, "is suspended," or "hovers." The nature referred to in this difficult passage seems to be human nature in its principial existence.

7. Thomas Aquinas, *STh, Suppl.* 70.3.

8. This is difficult to translate, since MGH *niht* can be either adverb, "not," or noun, "nothing," but the context demands a noun.

9. On the importance of the identity of the soul's ground with God's ground, see Introduction, pp. 42–44.

10. Cf. Is. 45:15.

11. On living "without a why," see Introduction, pp. 59–60.

NOTES

SERMON 6 (Translated from DW I, pp. 99–115.)

1. For an important study of this sermon, see K. Kertz, "Meister Eckhart's Teaching on the Birth of the Divine Word in the Soul," *Traditio* 15 (1959): 336–39, 359–62.

2. Justinian, *Institutes* I, 1.

3. Cf. 1 Tim. 1:17.

4. "Who are not desiring possessions . . . these people pay honor to God": this is the material for art. 8 of "In agro dominico," which is condemned as heretical.

5. "Improvement and edification" is supplied, where the German manuscripts have a lacuna, from Quint's citation of a parallel passage in *Comm. Wis.* n. 59 (LW II, p. 386).

6. On the basis of one manuscript, Quint here supplies a phrase that could be translated something like: "that he is not indifferent to all things."

7. This is actually from Bernard of Clairvaux, *Of Precept and Dispensation*, 20.60; the Latin is making a play on *amat, animat.*

8. *Isticheit,* a term coined perhaps by Eckhart. This sentence appears in the Cologne proceedings (Théry, p. 240), where *isticheit* is rendered as *quidditas* ("what-it-is"), but it is not certain that this is what Eckhart had in mind, for his response here is totally in terms of *esse* or "existence."

9. *Bî gote;* Eckhart makes much play with *bî*'s two senses, "close beside" and "at the home of."

10. Art. 22 from "In agro dominico," deplored as suspect of heresy, is extracted from this.

11. This is Quint's interpretation of a difficult and doubtful phrase—MHG: *ein unglîch;* Latin: *unum, non simile.* For a slightly different rendering of the Latin translation as found in the Bull, see p. 78.

12. "We shall be completely transformed . . . There is no distinction": this is the material for art. 10 from "In agro dominico," beginning, "We are wholly transformed and changed into God," as if the notion were Eckhart's and not Paul's, and omitting the conceit about Eckhart's little finger. The article was condemned as heretical.

13. "Recently I thought . . . life everlasting": this is the material for art. 9 from "In agro dominico," very accurately translated and condemned as heretical.

SERMON 15 (Translated from DW I, pp. 244–53.)

1. The single manuscript, St. Gall 972a, in which this entire sermon is recorded is here extremely corrupt. Quint has with the help of corresponding passages elsewhere conjectually restored some of it but any translation would

be no more than a conjectural amplification of Quint's conjectures. The drift is clear: Goodness is a divine attribute, and the soul cannot be satisfied with attributes, only with essence.

2. That is, the Holy Spirit is flowing out with God's goodness, so that the soul, desiring only the attributes, obtains the essence.

3. Cf. Ps. 41:8. Quint interprets differently: "The sun corresponds to God; the highest part of God's unfathomable depths replies to what is most abased in the depths of humility." But the text as we have it shows that Eckhart is pursuing the theme of *Sermon* 14, of the "debased God."

4. On Eckhart's teaching that all created things are nothing in themselves, see Introduction, p. 33.

5. I.e., the *Metaphysics*. But Eckhart seems to have in mind the discussion in *Soul* 2:1 (412ab) in what follows.

6. This teaching is that of St. Thomas rather than of Aristotle, see, e.g., *STh* Ia.57.2.

7. Possibly a reference to *Soul* 3.8 (431b20–27).

8. *Consolation of Philosophy* 3, poem 9.

9. "Without a medium" = MHG: *sunder mittel*, or *âne mittel*. For this important theme, see Introduction, p. 56.

10. What Aristotle says about separated substances is found in *Met.* 12.8.

11. "Something" = MHG: *was*, Eckhart's simplification of the Scholastics' rendering of Aristotle's "that which was to be."

12. "The last end" is supplied by Quint.

SERMON 22 (Translated from DW I, pp. 375–89.)

1. This sermon has been discussed by H. Fischer, "Grundgedanken der deutschen Predigten," in *Meister Eckhart der Prediger* (Freiburg: Herder, 1960), pp. 45–50, 55.

2. A conflation of Lk. 1:35, Ws. 18:15 and Jm. 1:17.

3. As sources Quint quotes Leo the Great's *First Sermon on the Nativity:* "She conceived her divine and human child in the mind before she did in the body"; and Augustine's *Holy Virginity:* "When she said 'Behold the handmaid of the Lord,' she was conceiving Christ in her mind before she did in her womb."

4. That is, the idea represented by the word conceived.

5. See *Par. Gen.* n. 11 (p. 97) as a parallel.

6. On the notion of existence in the principle as found in this paragraph and frequently throughout Eckhart, see Introduction, pp. 39–40.

7. Eckhart tells the same story in *Comm. Jn.* n. 683 (LW III, p. 598).

8. See note 2.

NOTES

9. See Thomas Aquinas, *SCG* 3.21: "A created thing by what it does tends towards its divine likeness."

10. See *Comm. Wis.* n. 27 (LW II, p. 346).

11. The source of this has not been identified.

12. See *Comm. Gen.* n. 166 (LW II, p. 312): "God is at rest in every work, from every work, for he is not mixed in the things which are worked, as it says in the *Book of Causes.*"

13. The reference is to either *Sermon* 12 or 13, which Eckhart says were preached at the Benedictine convent of this name in Cologne (DW I, pp. 203, 209). Cross references to this sermon in *Sermon* 13 say that it was delivered at the Cistercian convent of Mariengarten in the same city, a fact that may account for the Bernardine themes at the end. These cross references and many similarities of themes led Quint (DW I, pp. 372–74) to argue that *Sermons* 10–15 and 22 were all delivered to groups of nuns at Cologne late in Eckhart's career.

14. Just as the "little town" of *Sermon* 2 (p. 181) is a "simple one" (MHG: *einic ein*), since it is identified with God who is the supreme "Simple One" (see *Sermon* 15, p. 192, and *Sermon* 83, p. 206).

15. This sentence is an anacoluthon, but the general sense is evident.

16. Quint considers that this must have been the Dominicans' institute of general studies at Cologne (DW I, p. 381).

17. That is, *insofar as* the soul is the "little spark," it is both eternally being born from the Father and eternally unborn as one with the Father. See Introduction, pp. 42–43.

18. The exact source for this has not been identified, but the idea is close to one found in Thomas Aquinas in *STh* Ia.47.1.

19. Presumably in the pulpit.

20. See *Sermon* 14 (DW I, p. 233) and elsewhere, for similar passages.

21. That is, the birth of the Son.

22. This rich paragraph combines the typically Eckhartian language of the hidden darkness of the divinity with both courtly imagery (the knight and lady in the pavilion) and Bernardine love mysticism (see the interpretation of Sg. 2:8–9 in Bernard's *Sermons on the Song of Songs* 53–55). See also Introduction, p. 49.

SERMON 48 (Translated from DW II, pp. 413–21.)

1. Of the possible sources indicated by Quint, the closest is Thomas Aquinas, *STh* IaIIae.29.1.

2. The "authority" seems to be Aristotle, *On Heaven and Earth, passim,* as used by Maimonides and others.

3. The parallel passages, e.g., *Sermon* XXXVIII (LW IV, pp. 327–28), seem to indicate that Eckhart is citing himself again as "the authorities."

4. Aristotle, *Soul* 2.7 (418b26). See, e.g., *Par. Gen.* n. 31, (p. 105) for a parallel use.

5. The Bull "In agro dominico" condemned as heretical the proposition that there is something in the soul that is uncreated and not capable of creation, although Eckhart denied making such statements. It seems clear from this passage and others (e.g., *Sermon* 13 in DW I, p. 220), however, that he did. On this problem, see Introduction, p. 42.

6. A conjectural rendering of a difficult and unclear phrase.

7. "Of the soul" is Quint's gloss, plainly justified.

8. "Divine essence" = MHG: *götlich wesen.*

SERMON 52 (Translated from DW II, pp. 486–506.)

1. Three different vernacular introductions to this sermon are extant in various manuscripts, and there is a Latin version in a Koblenz ms. edited by Quint in DW II, pp. 517–21.

2. Quint translates: "Be poor like this, to understand what I say." This seems unjustified, and the manuscript variants he quotes show that contemporary scribes did not so interpret it.

3. Albert the Great (c. 1200–1280), the famous Dominican theologian and teacher of Thomas Aquinas. The reference is to his *Commentary on Matthew* 5.3.

4. On this theme, see Introduction, pp. 46–47, 57.

5. *Ledic sîn,* "empty being" in the sense of free and absolute. On the principial existence discussed in this paragraph, see Introduction, pp. 39–40.

6. A reminiscence of Ex. 3:14.

7. On the debates concerning the concept of true beatitude and Eckhart's position, see Introduction, pp. 56–57.

8. "This or that," that is, particular beings.

9. Literally, "the saying." Quint translates to show that the "saying" is not Paul's, but what Eckhart has written. The Latin, however, does not support this.

10. On the soul as creator of itself, see Introduction, p. 52. "In agro dominico," art. 13 (p. 79) condemned the view that the divine man created heaven and earth together with God.

11. Some suggest that the "great authority" is Eckhart himself. For a similar instance, see *Sermon* 5b (p. 182). On this passage and the notion of the breakthrough, see Introduction, pp. 30, 55.

NOTES

SERMON 53 (Translated from DW II, pp. 528–38.)

1. Quint translates: ". . . so that he may come to God in a wonderful way," and cites a parallel from *Sermon* 24 (DW I, p. 415).

2. This seems to be a free rendition of *Christ. Doct.* 1.6.6: "Whatever has been spoken by me, if it were ineffable could not be spoken, and for this reason God is not to be said to be ineffable, because even when this is said something is said. A sort of verbal conflict ensues, because if that is ineffable which cannot be spoken, then that is not ineffable which can be spoken of as ineffable." The paradox of God's being both a Word and yet ineffable does not come across as clearly in Eckhart's rendition. Augustine discusses the ineffability of the Word of God in a number of places in the *Lit. Comm. Gen.*

3. The Son is "speech working" because all things are made through him (Jn. 1:3).

4. On the Son's remaining in the Father even when he is spoken, see *Sermon* 9 (DW I, p. 157).

5. See Seneca, *Natural Questions* 1.5.

6. Quint also finds this anecdote in a manuscript of Marquard of Lindau's *The Ten Commandments.* The observation echoes many passages in Eckhart's works, e.g., *Comm. Ex.* n. 174 (LW II, p. 150), quoting Maimonides.

7. Quint cites Thomas Aquinas, *STh* Ia.13.8 as a source.

8. See also *Bened.* 1 (pp. 225, 228).

9. On Eckhart's use of this text, see Introduction, p. 39.

10. For a parallel passage, see *Par. Gen.* n. 146 (p. 113).

SERMON 83 (Translated from DW III, pp. 437–48.)

1. *Mens* = mind.

2. Quint adduces Augustine's *Enarration on Ps.* 3.3, and also Albert the Great, *On Man* and *On the Good,* as sources.

3. *Book of Causes,* prop. 6.

4. A similar expression of apophatic theology was condemned by "In agro dominico" (p. 80).

5. In the *Counsels on Discernment* and the *Commentary on Exodus,* Eckhart attributes this (correctly) to pseudo-Dionysius, *Mystical Theology* 1.1.

6. Quint has several quotations, from Augustine, Albert the Great, and John Damascene, saying something like this, but none of them is the exact source.

7. The three lower powers of the soul are originally Platonic in origin. On the powers of the soul, see Introduction, pp. 43–44.

8. That is, if the work in question descends from the realm of eternity into

that of time (the "here" and "now"), the ideal cooperation between God and the soul becomes impossible.

9. "A nonGod, a nonspirit, etc." (MHG: *ein nit-got, ein nit-geist*) might also be translated as "One not-God, One not-spirit, etc."

10. The reading "out of something" (MHG: *ite*) is Quint's plausible conjecture to make sense of a difficult passage.

PART TWO: 2. TREATISES
A. THE BOOK "BENEDICTUS": THE BOOK OF DIVINE CONSOLATION (Translated from DW V, pp. 3–61.)

1. Compare with the exegesis of Jn. 1:12 in *Comm. Jn.* nn. 106–15 (pp. 162–67).

2. *Enarration on Ps.* 36.1.3.

3. MHG: *noch diz noch daz*, i.e., in any limited way.

4. "Love and holding dear" = MHG: *liebe und minne.*

5. *Conf.* 10.41.

6. *Sermon* 105.3.4.

7. *Sermon* 53.6.6.

8. Aristotle, *Nicomachean Ethics* 8.5.

9. See Aristotle, *Phys.* 4.1 (208a).

10. Augustine, *On the Greatness of the Soul* 6.9.

11. *Natural Questions* 3.12.

12. Seneca, Letter to Lucilius.

13. Thomas Aquinas, *STh* Ia.12.9.

14. Eckhart is here using a wordplay on MHG *rîche*, which can mean either "kingdom" or "riches."

15. The source of art. 14 of "In agro dominico." See. p. 79, and Introduction (pp. 13–14).

16. See *Trin.*8.3.4; "moving in its own bare and limitless orbit" seems to be Eckhart's own adornment.

17. Eckhart may have in mind the good thief of Lk. 23:41.

18. *Enarration on Ps.* 30.3.

19. Aristotle, *Soul* 2.7 (418b26).

20. See Thomas Aquinas, *STh* IaIIae.3.2.ad 4.

21. On God as the One or Absolute Unity, see Introduction, pp. 34–36.

22. On the identification of the One with the Father as the source of the Trinity of Persons, see Introduction, ibid.

23. E.g., 1 Co. 13:12, and 2 Co. 3:18.

24. For this common scholastic teaching on fire, see also *Comm. Ex.* n. 140 (LW II, pp. 127–28).

NOTES

25. ". . . this inner work" (Quint) as contrasted with the external work just described.

26. Cf. *Par. Gen.* n. 162 (p. 120).

27. ". . . and is born Son" = MHG: *und wirt sun geborn.* MHG capitalizes no nouns, modern German all nouns, and English usage allows the translator to proceed at his own risk. On the identity and difference between "son of God" and "Son of God," see Introduction, pp. 52–54.

28. The preceding five sentences form one long and obscure sentence in the MHG, for which this rendering is conjecturally advanced.

29. ". . . proper attribute" = MHG: *eigenschaft,* a central term in Eckhart's vocabulary. See *Sermon* 2, p. 181.

30. ". . . intellectual ambition" = MHG: *geist.* This creates a paradoxical wordplay with the "Spirit" in the second half of the sentence that the English does not bring out.

31. *Christ. Doct.* 3.27.38. Augustine teaches how profitable it can be to demonstrate the truth of one passage in scripture from others, since all scripture is the work of the Holy Spirit. But there is not Eckhart's reprehension of intellectual ambition.

32. From the *Glossa ordinaria* (Quint.).

33. "To understand it better . . . the divine nature." This is the closest source that has been found to art. 13, condemned as heretical, from "In agro dominico" (p. 79). The parallel is not close, though Eckhart elsewhere very often writes and speaks of the just man as co-creator and co-begetter of the Word. Even the last clause is not more audacious than some other statements of his.

34. See Peter Lombard, *Sentences* I.9.4.

35. For Eckhart's teaching on disinterested love, see Introduction, p. 49.

36. M.-H. Laurent adduced this as the source for art. 20 of the Bull, but the parallel is distant at best (see p. 79).

37. This indicates that Eckhart intended the sermon "Of the Nobleman" to be the complement of the *Book of Divine Consolation* and thus form the second part of the *Book "Benedictus."*

38. Eckhart is here writing of the sea's tidal motion up the shore.

39. See note 27 above.

40. Compare with *Par. Gen.* n. 149 (p. 114).

41. See *The Lives of the Fathers* 1.9.

42. Letter 138.3.12.

43. *Sermons* 105.3.4, and 53.6.6. See notes 6 and 7 above.

44. The source of this quotation has not been identified.

45. *Sermon* 17.4.

46. Literally "through God" = MHG: *durch got.*

47. See art. 23 of "In agro dominico," p. 79.

48. Quint observes how freely Eckhart has translated his source, Jerome's

Letter 120.10, and how far scribes have been led astray by mistaking Eckhart's *wahs* (wax), for *fasz*, Jerome's *vas* (vessel), which metaphor Eckhart chose to replace with his own.

49. *Lives of the Fathers* 3.

50. Quint suggests that this alludes to the Chalcidius version of Plato's *Timaeus*.

51. *Conf.* 1.6.10.

52. *Conf.* 10.23.34.

53. *Lit. Comm. Gen.* 12.14.19.

54. Letter 71.24.

B. THE BOOK "BENEDICTUS": OF THE NOBLEMAN (Translated from DW V, pp. 109–119)

1. Isaac Israeli, *The Book of Definitions.*

2. See Thomas Aquinas, *Commentary on 2 Corinthians* 4.1.5.

3. Cf. Ep. 4:22, Mt. 13:28, Lk. 19:13.

4. Cf. Rm. 6:6, 1 Co. 15:47, Jn. 15:15, Ps. 102:5.

5. *Commentary on Matthew* 3.18.10.

6. On Adam, Eve, the serpent and their conversation, see *Par Gen.* nn. 137sqq. (pp. 108sqq.).

7. By "the man in the soul," *vir in anima*, Eckhart commonly designates the "higher intellect."

8. "... anything particular" = MHG: *diz und daz.*

9. Cicero, *Tusculan Questions* 3.1.2; Seneca, Letter 73.16.

10. *Homilies on Genesis* 13.4.

11. Quint is probably correct in indicating *On True Religion* 26.49 as the source for this; but Eckhart's recollection of what Augustine wrote seems vague, and he may have confused it with other treatments of this very popular theme. Augustine says that in the first age of this new and inner and heavenly man he is nourished with examples from the breasts of profitable history, but the infant staggering about as it learns to walk is not there.

12. *Homilies on Genesis* 13.4.

13. The same example is found in the *Comm. Jn.* n. 575 (LW III, p. 503). It is drawn from the Pseudo-Dionysius, *Mystical Theology* 2.

14. *Trin.* 12.7.10.

15. This is Quint's interpretation, fully justified and documented, of this admittedly difficult passage.

16. A free rendition of elements of Ps. 4:2–7.

17. These two sentences form art. 24 of "In agro dominico," deplored as suspect of heresy (see p. 79).

18. "... being and essence" = MHG: *in wesene und in wesunge.*

NOTES

19. MHG: *ein mensche,* which could, and in modern German still can, mean "one man" or "a man."

20. On unity and distinction, see Introduction, pp. 34–36.

21. Macrobius, *Commentary on the Dream of Scipio* 1.6.7–10.

22. Eckhart here is indicating a derivation of "man" *(homo)* from "humble" *(humilis).*

23. This is Isidore of Seville's etymology of *humilis* from *humus* ("ground").

24. ". . . alone" = MHG: *blôz.* Eckhart often plays on the senses of this word—"alone," "merely," "directly," "barely," "nakedly," etc.; but in what follows there is no such play, and there seems to be no reason for translating it, as Quint does, *unverhüllt.*

25. Aristotle, *Met.* 1.1 (980a21).

26. Thomas Aquinas, *SCG* 1.71.

27. Augustine, *Lit. Comm. Gen.* 4.23.40.

28. *Blôz.* See note 24.

29. Close to a passage in *Detach.* (p. 292).

30. ". . . going out and return" = MHG: *ein ûszlac und ein widerslac.* On *exitus* and *reditus* as the basic structure of the natural (and supernatural) universe in Eckhart, see Introduction, pp. 30–31. Here the soul's contemplation of God is what reveals to it its true metaphysical essence as an example of this emanation and return.

31. That is, the ideal form, reason or principle is superior to what participates in it.

32. The justifications of this translation of an exceedingly difficult passage will be found in Quint's elucidatory notes, and his references to the controversies of the age between Thomists, who parted from Thomas over this, and Franciscans, who did not, about the nature of blessedness.

33. Quint points out, citing John of Pouilly, that Eckhart is here writing about the Scholastics' "particular sense" and "common sense."

34. Eckhart is attacking the view that beatitude consists in a reflexive act (knowing that we know God) rather than in direct, "medium-less" awareness. Reflexive knowledge is a necessary accompaniment, but is not the essence of beatitude.

35. J. Koch suggested, and Quint is prepared to accept, that the text as he gives it here and as it has now been translated may be corrupt (see DW V, p. 135, n. 56).

36. The play here is upon *adeler* = "eagle," and *edeler* = "noble."

37. ". . . desert" = MHG: *einoede,* continues the play on *ein,* the One.

NOTES

C. COUNSELS ON DISCERNMENT (Translated from DW V, pp. 185–309.)

1. Collation, i.e., the evening meal of the Dominican community.

2. "Hearing" could also mean "hearing confessions" or "listening to readings."

3. *Conf.* 10.26.37.

4. "Empty spirit" = MHG: *ledige gemüete.* One might also say "free heart, disposition or intention." *Gemüete,* meaning all man's capacities of thinking and feeling, is a frequent term in this treatise.

5. Probably Gregory the Great, *Homilies on the Gospels* 5.2.

6. On the relation between contemplation and action and Eckhart's lack of interest in ecstasy, see Introduction, pp. 60–61.

7. Literally, "love of the first kind."

8. This is the reading of one ms., which gives a better sense than the reading "knew" found in the others.

9. Quint conjectures: ". . . the less does God possess us."

10. Although for art. 14 from "In agro dominico" Laurent suggested as a source a passage from the *Book "Benedictus,"* he overlooked this Augustine citation. Quint provides the exact context in *On Free Will* 3.9: "Even our sins are necessary to the universal perfection which God has established." On this, see Introduction, pp. 13–14.

11. On Eckhart's teaching on not wishing not to have committed sins, see Introduction, pp. 44–45.

12. Quint's interpretation of this is: "Once the lover [God] knows that the beloved [the soul] loves him, he knows at once everything which is for his [the soul's] good." This is ingenious and plausible.

13. Eckhart is here referring to the opening of this chapter and observing that "private revelations" can often be deceptive and false.

14. Eckhart is actually thinking of 1 Jn. 14:18.

15. See *Bened.* 1 (p. 214, note 6).

16. Plainly, Eckhart has in mind Mt. 8:8 and Rv. 3:20.

17. Probably Eckart is referring to 1 Co. 12:4–11.

18. MHG: *wîse* = "manner of life" or "religious practice."

19. This is written for such religious as Dominicans who were assigned their clothing, including laundered habits, from a common store, following the Rule of Saint Augustine: "You should not call anything your own, but all things should be held by you in common; and let food and clothing be distributed to each one of you by your superior."

20. This seems to allude to the ostentatious piety of "enthusiasts."

21. That is, the attitude that one intends nothing or delights in nothing but God is a test of closeness to him.

22. The mixing of water and wine as an analogy for the union of God and the soul was traditional in Christian mysticism, used, for instance, by Saint

NOTES

Bernard in *On Loving God* 10.28. Eckhart employed it again in *Sermon* 82 (DW III, p. 430).

23. This epiclesis has been variously translated. Quint is undoubtedly right in his reading "lover," which he interprets as appositional to "teacher," and so too, one considers, is "life." Eckhart seems to have in mind "The way, the truth and the life" of Jn. 14:6.

24. Literally, "when God finds his will."

25. "Directly" = MHG: *âne mittel*. In later works this will have the technical meaning "without a medium."

26. Literally, "compulsion," that is, to perform good works.

27. *Mystical Theology* 1.1. See also *Sermon* 83 (p. 207).

28. "Poverty of spirit" is one of the eight beatitudes (Mt. 5:3).

29. This was Diogenes. Eckhart probably knew the story through Cicero, *Tusculan Questions* 5.92.

30. Literally, "an occasion and a hindrance," which Quint, after having emended from the corrupt mss. readings, still calls an "improvised formulation" of Eckhart's. This, in the context, seems to be what he may have meant.

31. Quint rightly describes the syntax of this as "loose and colloquial." This translation can only be approximate.

32. See *Bened.* 1, p. 219, note 17.

D. ON DETACHMENT (Translated from DW V, pp. 400–34.)

1. On the relation between love, humility and detachment, see Introduction, pp. 47–49.

2. Aristotle, *Phys.* 4.5(212b).

3. "Purity" = MHG: *lûterkeit*, where *lûter* has the same ambiguity as modern German *lauter*, that is, "pure" and also "mere" and "only." Unity and purity distinguish God's natural place because nothing else intrudes there; it is only "detachment." So Suso, borrowing from this work, writes in his German *Book of Eternal Truth*, "Keep yourself detached from all men," and in his Latin *Horologium*, "You must withdraw yourself . . . from all mortal men . . . for purity of heart exerts first claim." Later in the treatise, it will be seen that Eckhart equates the notions of "purity" and "emptiness."

4. Eckhart quotes Ps. 44:14 in Latin and then translates it into the vernacular. His translation is an interpretive one where the Latin *ab intus* ("from within") becomes MHG *von ir inwendicheit* ("from her inwardness").

5. MHG: *diz oder daz* = Latin: *hoc et hoc*, that is, "a particular thing."

6. Avicenna, *On the Soul* 4.4.

7. *Trin.* 5.16.17.

8. Actually *Trin.* 12.7.10. Eckhart quotes the Latin and provides his own translation.

9. *Sentences* 1.8.4.

10. The reference is to the famous conversion on the road to Damascus; see Ac. 9:1–18.

11. On the relation of this analogy to Eckhart's theology of grace, see Introduction, note 151.

12. An additional passage on prayer, first identified by K. Ruh, is printed by Quint in DW V, pp. 434–35, but its authenticity is questionable.

13. *Divine Names* 4.9 and 13.3.

14. This does not seem to be Augustine, and Quint is not satisfied with the "pseudo-Augustine" sources that have thus far been suggested.

15. Who this "teacher" may have been, or whether this is a scribal tampering with what was originally a reference to one of Eckhart's own sermons, has occasioned much controversy, and in Quint's opinion is still unresolved.

16. On the meaning of this passage, see Introduction, p. 46.

BIBLIOGRAPHY

There are several recent Eckhart bibliographies, notably that contained in *The Thomist* 42 (1978): 313–26. Hence, the following list need not pretend to any completeness, but can be selective and critical.

I. EDITIONS

The texts translated in this volume are primarily taken from *Meister Eckhart. Die deutschen und lateinischen Werke. Herausgegeben im Auftrage der Deutschen Forschungsgemeinschaft.* Stuttgart and Berlin: W. Kohlhammer, 1936–.
The following have also been used:

Laurent, M.-H., "Autour du procès de Maître Eckhart. Les documents des Archives Vaticanes." *Divus Thomas* (Piacenza). Ser. III 13 (1936): 331–48, 430–47.

Pelster, Franz. "Ein Gutachten aus dem Eckehart-Prozess in Avignon." *Aus der Geisteswelt des Mittelalters. Festgabe Martin Grabmann (Beiträge Supplement III).* Münster, 1935, pp. 1099–1124.

Théry, Gabriel. "Édition critique des pièces relatives au procès d'Eckhart contenues dans le manuscrit 33ᵇ de la Bibliothèque de Soest." *Archives d'histoire littéraire et doctrinal du moyen âge* 1 (1926): 129–268.

II. ENGLISH TRANSLATIONS

Blakney, Raymond B. *Meister Eckhart. A Modern Translation.* New York and London: Harper and Row, 1941 (with many reprints). Contains the German treatises, twenty-eight vernacular sermons (not all authentic) and the Defense. Filled with errors.

Clark, James M. *Meister Eckhart. An Introduction to the Study of His Works with an Anthology of His Sermons.* Edinburgh: Nelson, 1957. Twenty-five vernacular sermons along with some documents relating to the trial and condem-

BIBLIOGRAPHY

nation. Translations are of mixed value, but the lengthy Introduction is generally good.

Clark, James M., and Skinner, John V. *Treatises and Sermons of Meister Eckhart.* New York: Harper, 1958. Contains the German treatises, two vernacular sermons, eight Latin sermons, and selections from two of the Latin commentaries. Translations are generally good, and the Introduction is helpful.

Evans, C. de B. *Meister Eckhart by Franz Pfeiffer.* 2 vols. London: Watkins, 1924, 1931. An almost unreadable translation of Pfeiffer's edition.

Maurer, Armand. *Master Eckhart. Parisian Questions and Prologues.* Toronto: Pontifical Institute of Mediaeval Studies, 1974. Generally good translations of some of the important Latin works.

Schürmann, Reiner. *Meister Eckhart. Mystic and Philosopher.* Bloomington and London: Indiana University Press, 1978. Eight vernacular sermons well translated, along with an extensive major study of Eckhart's thought.

III. MONOGRAPHS AND COLLECTIONS

Albert, Karl. *Meister Eckharts These vom Sein. Untersuchungen zur Metaphysik des Opus tripartitum.* Saarbrücken: Universtäts-und Schulbuchverlag, 1976. Detailed study centering on the difference between *esse simpliciter* and *esse hoc et hoc.*

Altdeutsche und altniederländische Mystik. Ed. Kurt Ruh. Darmstadt: Wissenschaftliche Buchgesellschaft, 1964. An important selection of essays originally published in different contexts.

Ancelet-Hustache, Jeanne. *Master Eckhart and the Rhineland Mystics.* New York: Harper, 1957. A brief introduction, useful for the beginner.

Caputo, John. *The Mystical Element in Heidegger's Thought.* Athens, Ohio: Ohio University Press, 1978. A confrontation between Eckhart and Heidegger that manages to avoid many of the pitfalls of this genre and has some original insights into the Meister's thought.

Clark, James M. *The Great German Mystics: Eckhart, Tauler, and Suso.* Oxford: Blackwells, 1949. Introductory.

Degenhardt, Ingeborg. *Studien zum Wandel des Eckhartbildes.* Leiden: Brill, 1967. The history of Eckhart studies.

Haas, Alois M. *Sermo mysticus. Studien zu Theologie und Sprache der deutschen Mystik.* Freiburg, Switzerland: Universitätsverlag, 1979. Major new study containing a survey of Marxist interpretations of Eckhart.

Hof, Hans. *Scintilla animae. Eine Studie zu einem Grundbegriff in Meister Eckharts Philosophie.* Lund: Gleerup, 1952. Marred by tendentious interpretations.

Imbach, Ruedi. *Deus est Intelligere. Das Verhältnis von Sein und Denken in seiner Bedeutung für das Gottesverständnis bei Thomas von Aquin und in den Pariser*

BIBLIOGRAPHY

Quaestionen Meister Eckharts. Freiburg, Switzerland: Universitätsverlag, 1976. A useful, detailed treatment.

Kelley, C. F. *Meister Eckhart on Divine Knowledge.* New Haven and London: Yale University Press, 1977. An important study marred by unfortunate polemics and idiosyncratic use of text.

Le mystique rhénane. Colloque de Strasbourg 1961. Paris: Presses Universitaires de France, 1963. An important collection of papers, five dealing with Eckhart.

Lossky, Vladimir. *Théologie négative et connaissance de Dieu chez Maître Eckhart.* Paris: Vrin, 1960. A major book of central importance for Eckhart studies.

Meister Eckhart der Prediger. Festschrift zum Eckhart-Gedenkjahr. Edd. Udo Nix and Raphel Öchslin. Freiburg, Germany: Herder, 1960. A group of essays, including valuable ones by Fischer and Koch.

Muller-Thym, Bernard J. *The Establishment of the University of Being in the Doctrine of Meister Eckhart of Hochheim.* New York and London: Sheed and Ward, 1939. The only part published of a planned major study of Eckhart from the Gilsonian point of view.

Otto, Rudolf. *Mysticism East and West. A Comparative Analysis of the Nature of Mysticism.* New York: Macmillan, 1932. An interesting treatment of Eckhart and Shankara.

Schmoldt, Benno. *Die deutsche Begriffssprache Meister Eckharts.* Heidelberg: Quelle and Meyer, 1954. A useful tool for the study of Eckhart's technical vocabulary.

The Thomist. Vol. 42, No. 2. Meister Eckhart of Hochheim, 1227/28—1978. An uneven selection of essays.

Ueda, Shizuteru. *Die Gottesgeburt in der Seele und der Durchbruch zur Gottheit. Die mystische Anthropologie Meister Eckharts und ihre Konfrontation mit der Mystik des Zen-Buddhismus.* Gütersloh: Mohn, 1965. A summary of Eckhart's teaching on these key issues.

Welte, Bernard. *Meister Eckhart. Gedanken zu seinen Gedanken.* Freiburg, Germany: Herder, 1979. A major new interpretation.

Winkler, Eberhard. *Exegetische Methoden bei Meister Eckhart.* Tübingen: Mohr, 1965. Fullest treatment of Eckhart's exegesis.

IV. ARTICLES

Albert, Karl. "Der philosophische Grundgedanke Meister Eckharts." *Tijdschrift voor Filosofie* 27 (1965): 320–39. Summarizes Albert's thesis.

Brunner, Fernand. "L'analogie chez Maître Eckhart." *Freiburger Zeitschrift für Philosophie und Theologie* 16 (1969): 333–49. A useful study.

Caputo, John. "Fundamental Themes in Meister Eckhart's Mysticism." *The Thomist* 42 (1978): 197–225. A fine survey.

BIBLIOGRAPHY

———. "The Nothingness of the Intellect in Meister Eckhart's 'Parisian Questions.'" *The Thomist* 39 (1975): 85–115.

Colledge, Edmund. "Meister Eckhart: Studies in His Life and Works." *The Thomist* 42 (1978): 240–58.

Denifle, Heinrich. "Meister Eckharts lateinische Schriften und die Grundanschaung seiner Lehre." *Archiv für Literatur-und Kirchengeschichte des Mittelatters* 2 (1886): 417–615.

Fischer, Heribert. "Grundgedanken der deutschen Predigten." In *Meister Eckhart der Prediger*, pp. 25–72. A major summary article.

———. "Die theologische Arbeitsweise Meister Eckharts in den lateinischen Werken." In *Miscellanea Mediaevalia 7. Methoden in Wissenschaft und Kunst des Mittelalters*. Berlin: DeGruyter, 1970, pp. 50–75.

Gandillac, M. de. "La 'dialectique' de Maître Eckhart." In *La mystique rhénane*, pp. 59–94. An essential article.

Grundmann, Herbert. "Die geschichtlichen Grundlagen der deutschen Mystik." In *Altdeutsche und altniederländische Mystik*, pp. 72–99. The best study of the historical context of Eckhart's thought.

Kelley, Dom Placid (= C.F.). "Meister Eckhart's Doctrine of Divine Subjectivity." *Downside Review* 76 (1958): 65–103. A summary of the thesis later developed in the book.

Kertz, Karl G. "Meister Eckhart's Teaching on the Birth of the Divine Word in the Soul." *Traditio* 15 (1959): 327–63. One of the most important articles on this theme.

Kieckhefer, Richard. "Meister Eckhart's Conception of Union with God." *Harvard Theological Review* 71 (1978): 203–25.

Koch, Josef. "Kritische Studien zum Leben Meister Eckharts." *Archivum Fratrum Praedicatorum* 29 (1959): 1–51; 30 (1960): 1–52. Reprinted in his *Kleine Studien*. The most important work on Eckhart's life.

———. "Meister Eckhart und die jüdische Religionsphilosophie des Mittelalters." *Jahresbericht der Schlesischen Gesellschaft für vaterländische Kultur 1928* 101 (1929): 134–48. A key article.

———. "Meister Eckharts Weiterwirken im Deutsch-Niederländischen Raum im 14. und 15. Jahrhundert." In *La mystique rhénane*, pp. 133–56.

———. "Philosophische und theologische Irrtumslisten von 1270–1329." In *Mélanges Mandonnet*. Paris: Vrin, 1930. Vol. 2, pp. 305–29. Reprinted in his *Kleine Studien*.

———. "Sinn und Struktur der Schriftauslegung." In *Meister Eckhart der Prediger*, pp. 73–103. Valuable study of Eckhart's exegesis.

———. "Zur Analogielehre Meister Eckharts." In *Mélanges offerts à Etienne Gilson*. Paris: Vrin, 1959, pp. 327–50. The best study of Eckhart's view of analogy.

McGinn, Bernard. "Eckhart's Condemnation Reconsidered." *The Thomist* 44 (1980): 390–414.

BIBLIOGRAPHY

————. "The God beyond God. Theology and Mysticism in the Thought of Meister Eckhart." *Journal of Religion* 61 (1981): 1–19.

————. "Meister Eckhart on God as Absolute Unity." To appear in the Proceedings of the International Colloquium on Neoplatonism in the History of Christian Thought. Albany: SUNY Press, 1981.

————. "St. Bernard and Meister Eckhart." *Cîteaux* 31 (1980): 373–86.

Quint, Josef. "Einleitung." In *Meister Eckehart. Deutsche Predigten und Traktate.* Munich: Hanser, 1959, pp. 9–50. Perhaps the best short introduction to Eckhart's thought.

————. "Mystik und Sprache." In *Altdeutsche und altniederländische Mystik*, pp. 113–51. An important study.

Rahner, Hugo. "Die Gottesgeburt. Die Lehre der Kirchenväter von der Geburt Christi aus dem Herzen der Kirche und der Gläubigen." *Zeitschrift für katholische Theologie* 59 (1933): 333–418. Reprinted in *Symbole der Kirche* (Salzburg: Müller, 1964), pp. 13–87. Valuable for background to one of the Meister's favorite themes.

Schaller, Toni. "Die Meister-Eckhart Forschung von der Jahrhundertwende bis zur Gegenwart." *Freiburger Zeitschrift für Philosophie und Theologie* 15 (1968): 262–316, 403–26.

————. "Zur Eckhart-Deutung der letzten 30 Jahre." *Freiburger Zeitschrift* . . . 16 (1969): 22–39.

Schneider, Richard. "The Functional Christology of Meister Eckhart." *Recherches de théologie ancienne et médiévale* 35 (1968): 291–322.

Schürmann, Reiner. "The Loss of Origin in Soto Zen and Meister Eckhart." *The Thomist* 42 (1978): 281–312. A summary of the themes of Schürmann's book.

Théry, Gabriel. "Contribution à l'histoire du procès d'Eckhart." *La vie spirituelle. Supplement* 9 (1924): 93–119, 164–83; 12 (1925): 149–87; 13 (1926): 49–95; 14 (126): 45–65.

Tobin, Frank. "Eckhart's Mystical Use of Language: The Contexts of *eigenschaft.*" *Seminar* 8 (1972): 160–68.

Weiss, Karl. "Meister Eckharts Biblische Hermeneutik." In *La mystique rhénane*, pp. 95–108.

INDEX TO PREFACE,
INTRODUCTION AND NOTES

INDEX

INDEX

356

INDEX

INDEX

INDEX

INDEX TO TEXT

INDEX

INDEX

255; gifts of, 246; and good, 73; and
grace, 76; and love, 133, 189, 221, 222,
227; and man, 167, 187, 192, 193, 205,
246, 293, 294; and One, 97; procession
of, 76, 94, 97, 133, 152, 167; and
sanctification, 169; and Son, 76, 98,
167; and truth, 93, 94; withdrawal of,
92–93.

Horace, 93, 147.

Hosea, 2:14, 230; 12:10, 94.

Hugh of St. Victor, 139.

Ideas, and creation, 91, 101, 123, 126, 130,
131, 141; and definition, 125; and
existence, 83, 91; and God, 141; and
knowledge, 83, 91, 125; and Logos,
101, 126, 131, 132; and Son, 84.

Illumination, 117, 125, 128, 156, 158, 164.

Image, cf. also God, Son; derivative, 182;
and exemplar, 129, 130, 134, 143; and
Father, 193; free of, 177, 184, 211, 212,
239, 242, 274, 293; and memory, 206;
and Word, 130, 133.

Imagination, 74, 109, 274.

Incarnation, 152, 162, 167–170, 193.

Intellect, and abstraction, 131; agent-,
158; and creation, 141; as empty tablet,
105; and existence, 160; and God, 79,
86, 93, 141; and heresy, 72; and idea,
133, 137; and imagination, 74, 109;
knowing-, 137; and Logos, 132; and
nature, 84, 108, 137; object of, 105, 125,
162, 163; and phantasms, 109, 153; and
truth, 106, 116, 117; and Word, 133.

Isaiah, 7:14, 168; 9:6, 193; 11:6, 112; 12:6,
168; 45:6–7, 106; 45:7, 90; 45:15, 149,
192; 59:2, 112; 62:1, 222; 66:24, 121.

Isidore, 290.

Jacob, 95, 119.

James, 1:17, 154; 1:21, 132; 2:10, 166; 3:2,
166.

Jeremiah, 1:9, 203, 205; 1:10, 205; 23:24,
158; 32:19, 153.

Jerome, 72, 147, 165, 166–167, 235, 240.

Job, 5:6, 141; 7:20, 88; 22:14, 85; 33:14, 99,
148; 36:33, 113; 39:27–28, 122.

Joel, 2:28–29, 111.

John, 1:1, 187, 193; 1:3, 73; 1:5, 196, 219,
243; 1:12, 90, 210; 1:14, 193; 1:16, 169;
1:18, 127; 3:6, 164, 172; 3:13, 184; 3:21,
146; 3:31–34, 154; 4:14, 227, 242; 5:17,
89, 121, 210; 5:19, 73; 5:26, 210; 5:39,
94; 5:46, 94; 7:39, 227; 8:25, 89, 151;
8:35, 173; 8:44, 166; 10:10, 170; 10:29,

170; 10:30, 96, 98, 127, 129, 139; 12:26,
230; 13:3, 170; 13:13, 91; 14:6, 144, 146;
14:8, 223; 14:9, 130; 14:10, 210; 14:11,
96, 98, 129; 14:12, 76, 172; 15:4, 146;
15:11, 223; 15:14, 188; 15:15, 113; 16:7,
293; 16:13, 93, 94; 16:15, 113, 170; 16:20,
219; 16:21, 172, 233; 16:22, 168, 172,
173; 16:24, 172, 173; 16:28, 162; 16:33,
164; 17:3, 163, 164, 216, 246; 17:10, 116,
170, 210; 17:11, 222; 17:21, 75, 173, 229;
17:24, 137; 17:25, 137; 21:15 ff., 79.

1 John, 1:5, 128, 149, 155; 3:1, 168, 169;
3:2, 170, 173, 189; 3:9, 75; 4:9, 182; 4:16,
146, 229; 5:4, 164; 5:7, 96, 98; 5:20, 173.

John Damascene, 134, 161.

John the Baptist, 129, 154.

Joy, 179, 180, 185, 186, 195, 212, 217, 220,
221, 230, 233, 241, 242, 263, 281, 285.

Judas, 152.

Judges, 9:8, 108.

Justice, 107, 110, 120; exemplar in, 127;
and God, 97, 106, 152, 154, 186, 211,
218, 248, 284; participation in, 113,
126–130, 139, 146, 147, 154, 169, 186,
209, 211; striving for, 138, 186, 215,
219; Unbegotten, 113, 128.

Kingdom, of God, 88, 106; of heaven, 78,
168, 179, 185, 190, 199, 200, 214, 283.

Knowledge, and blessedness, 188, 201,
245; dependent, 85; free of, 201, 202;
and God, 73, 85, 110, 114 117, 127, 163,
164, 189, 198, 201, 216, 232, 245, 246,
247, 264, 272; and Holy Spirit, 228;
and ideas, 83, 91, 125–126, 132; and
justice, 120; of man, 85, 107, 128;
object of, 163; and phantasms, 128,
216; and principles, 128, 130; self-, 200,
210, 240, 271; and truth, 73.

Lamentations, 3:22, 224.

Life, 144–147, 164, 170, 182, 185, 186, 187,
188, 190, 210, 264–265, 267.

Light, cf. also God, Man; and darkness,
147–153, 155, 196, 219; and Father,
193; and knowledge, 245; of truth, 77,
117, 198, 218; uncreated, 198.

Logos, and causality, 141; and creation,
83, 89, 101, 123, 126, 130, 131, 132, 141;
and idea, 101, 126, 131, 132; and
reason, 83; and Word, 123, 133, 141.

Love, cf. also God, Good; and
blessedness, 201, 294; Concomitant-,
94; for enemies, 150; and Holy Spirit,
133, 189, 221, 222, 227; and justice, 120,

INDEX

Prayer, 78, 178, 184, 204, 205, 215, 216, 233, 236, 247–249, 288, 289, 292.

Prime Mover, 111.

Proclus, 87, 98.

Proverbs, 1:6, 94; 5:2–3, 95; 8:7, 74; 12:21, 211; 16:4, 228; 25:4, 243; 25:11, 92.

Psalms, 4:3, 166; 4:6–7, 140; 4:7, 110, 156; 8:5, 158; 8:8, 158; 16:2, 140; 16:3, 150; 18:2, 120; 18:2–4, 114; 18:4–5, 120; 18:7, 158; 24:11, 166; 26:4, 165; 32, 107; 32:6, 141; 32:9, 85, 119, 120; 33:19, 150, 232; 35:10, 110; 37:18, 72, 235; 38:5, 141; 41:4, 150, 215; 41:5, 110; 50:17, 121; 51:5, 166, 59:14, 146; 60:4, 156; 61:12, 85, 99, 205; 62:9, 110; 64:5, 127; 67:5, 204; 72:28, 110; 79:6, 150; 84:9, 114, 287; 90:15, 150, 233; 95:1, 225; 96:3, 234; 99:3, 120, 162; 101:26, 83; 101:27, 85; 101:27–28, 99, 141; 102:24, 84; 103:5, 86; 103:24, 141; 115:6, 138; 118:89, 121; 118:151, 138; 126:1, 112; 134:6, 225; 135:5, 84, 91, 106, 141; 138:8, 90; 148:6, 120, 121.

Reason, and action, 140; and creation, 88, 141, 142; faculty of, 108, 125; Ideal-, 84, 87; inferior, 107, 108, 109, 110, 111, 112, 113, 114, 116, 119, 153; and Logos, 83; and principles, 128; and senses, 110, 111, 112; and simplicity, 87; superior, 107, 108, 109, 110, 111, 112, 113, 114, 116, 119, 153; and Word, 140.

Repentance, 262–263.

Revelation, 1:8, 139; 2:17, 127, 154; 3:20, 151; 21:3, 168; 22:13, 244; 22:17, 110.

Romans, 3:2, 162; 3:20, 167; 4:17, 111, 151; 7:14, 92; 7:23, 241; 7:24, 241; 8:13, 107; 8:15, 107, 168; 8:17, 168; 8:18, 150; 8:28, 88, 261; 8:29, 168, 169; 8:32, 171; 9:3, 151, 216, 226, 259; 12:1, 140; 13:1, 109; 13:14, 293.

Salvation, 151, 267.

1 Samuel, 16:12, 147; 17:42, 147; 18:7, 147.

2 Samuel, 16:5 ff., 236.

Sarah, 107.

Saul, 147.

Scripture, and exegesis, 74, 82, 88, 93, 94, 95, 106, 108, 116, 123, 129, 162, 228; and God, 93; and Holy Spirit, 228; and parables, 92–121; and truth, 92, 95, 123.

Self, -knowledge, 200, 210, 240, 271; renunciation of, 249–251, 260–261, 265, 280, 282, 283; -will, 183, 186, 200, 201, 203, 230, 248–250, 259, 260, 276.

Seneca, 75, 107, 134, 147, 204, 215, 239, 241.

Senses, and Christ, 271; exterior, 118; faculty of, 105, 107, 108, 109, 110, 111, 112, 113, 115, 116, 117, 118, 119, 162–163; images of, 114, 290–291; object of, 105, 114, 163, 169; and reason, 110, 111, 112, 290–291.

Simon, (Peter), 79.

Sin, after-, 109, 112; before-, 109, 112; escape from, 108, 265; existence of, 140; fall into, 108, 261–262; and God, 75, 78, 79, 112, 217, 219, 261–263, 266, 274; inclination to, 256; and multiplicity, 166; and punishment, 88, 108, 119, 235, 236, 274; and repentance, 217; and sorrow, 261; under-, 109, 112; and will, 79, 216.

Sirach, 1:2, 166; 4:33, 146; 7:30, 161; 11:10, 165; 11:27, 213; 14:11, 293; 17:1–2, 112; 18:1, 83, 86; 24:5, 162; 24:12–13, 119; 24:29, 102; 24:30, 146; 24:41–42, 162; 26:19, 169; 27:6, 150.

Socrates, 146, 238.

Solomon, 94, 211, 213, 215, 221, 228, 243.

Son, cf. also Word; Only-Begotten, 94, 127, 129, 149, 170, 171, 172, 173, 181, 183, 188, 194–196, 211, 227, 228; birth of, 179, 181, 182, 183, 184, 187, 188, 194, 196, 205, 226, 227; and creation, 78, 84, 89, 90, 98, 142, 143; and Existence, 89, 96; and Father, 78, 79, 89, 94, 98, 119, 127, 130, 132, 134, 135, 136, 137, 143, 149, 167, 170, 171, 172, 173, 179, 181, 182, 184, 187, 188, 195, 204, 205, 210, 225, 227, 229, 231; generation of, 78, 85, 97, 119, 125, 127, 132, 133, 134, 135–136, 142, 148, 152, 167, 228–229; and good, 73; and Holy Spirit, 76, 98, 159, 167; as Image, 84, 170, 222, 243; image of, 168, 169, 221; Incarnation of, 152, 156, 168, 170; as power, 123; as Principle, 84; and world, 164, 181, 183.

Song of Songs, 1:1, 113, 168; 1:3, 110; 1:4–5, 243; 2:9, 196; 2:10, 116; 2:14, 110; 2:11, 168; 2:13, 168; 2:16, 116; 4:11, 168; 5:6, 110, 114; 5:16, 138; 7:10, 116.

Soul, activities of, 118; birth of Son in, 187, 194, 196, 205, 229, 243; as bride, 196; disordered, 107, 117; divine seed in, 75, 240–241, 243; emptying of, 220–223; and Father, 206, 208, 221;

365